WORD WITHOUT END

Word Without End

The Old Testament as Abiding Theological Witness

CHRISTOPHER SEITZ

WILLIAM B. EERDMANS PUBLISHING COMPANY
GRAND RAPIDS, MICHIGAN / CAMBRIDGE, U.K.

© 1998 Wm. B. Eerdmans Publishing Co.
255 Jefferson Ave. S.E., Grand Rapids, Michigan 49503 /
P.O. Box 163, Cambridge CB3 9PU U.K.

Printed in the United States of America

04 03 02 01 00 99 98   7 6 5 4 3 2 1

Library of Congress Cataloging-in-Publication Data

Seitz, Christopher R.
Word without end: the Old Testament as abiding theological witness /
Christopher Seitz.
p.   cm.
Includes bibliographical references and index.
ISBN 0-8028-4322-0 (pbk.: alk. paper)
1. Bible. O.T. — Theology.   2. Bible. O.T. — Criticism, interpretation, etc.
3. Bible. O.T. — Canonical Criticism.   4. Bible. O.T. — Use.   I. Title.
BS1192.5.S38   1998
230'.0411 — dc21   97-23187
                                                            CIP

Contents

BIBLICAL THEOLOGY

v

Contents

EXEGESIS

PRACTICE

Contents

Abbreviations

ATR	*Anglican Theological Review*
BETL	Bibliotheca ephemeridum theologicarum lovaniensium
CBQ	*Catholic Biblical Quarterly*
FS	Festschrift
HBT	*Horizons in Biblical Theology*
JR	*Journal of Religion*
JSOT	*Journal for the Study of the Old Testament*
LXX	Septuagint
MT	Masoretic Text
NRSV	New Revised Standard Version
OBT	Overtures to Biblical Theology
OTL	Old Testament Library
RSV	Revised Standard Version
SBS	Stuttgarter Bibelstudien
SBT	Studies in Biblical Theology
SJT	*Scottish Journal of Theology*
SLJT	*Saint Luke's Journal of Theology*
TS	*Theological Studies*
VT	*Vetus Testamentum*
ZAW	*Zeitschrift für die Alttestamentliche Wissenschaft*

Introduction

A canonical approach to reading Scripture begins with the recognition that biblical books have diverse origins and a complex history of development before their final shape is achieved. At the same time, and in distinction to most forms of redaction criticism, to speak of "canonical shape" is to imply a degree of intentionality stretching over an entire biblical book in its final literary scope. There are parts, but there is also a sum. That sum has its own integrity and rationale and is more than an adventitious stopping point before editors shifted their labors to another project.

The present volume, *Word Without End,* illustrates what is meant by canonical shaping, without intending to do so in the first instance. (Intentionality is there, but it resides at a different level.) Several of these chapters were delivered as public lectures, each for its own one audience and purpose. Others were composed for later periods, different audiences, and different purposes. Several essays were always intended to be read, not heard, and were not written in explicit conjunction with any others. At the same time, affiliation would not be surprising because of the persistence of single authorial voice, if not also a larger set of related concerns. In other words, there is an obvious diachronic dimension lying behind and manifested within the present collection of essays, pointing to diverse situations-in-life, genres, and sequences of composition.

At the same time, the book as it now stands does not seek to showcase this diachronic reality as an end unto itself, through the form of its final literary presentation. The close reader will be aware of it, just as she is when reading a biblical book from the perspective of the modern period.

Introduction

Yet the book has been shaped, by myself and by others, toward a set of concerns consistent with but also unintended by the individual essays as they were first conceived and delivered. Moreover, what a reader will make of my individual intentions will be taken up and altered by the simple fact of the literary presentation itself, where a chapter's position and arrangement among other chapters produces a certain effect on the reader, his apprehension, and the point to which he puts what he has read and digested.

The three headings under which the chapters are organized reflect a concern to move theory and hermeneutics in the direction of the church's actual practice. At the same time, the sections are not completely discrete, and the proportion given to biblical theology and hermeneutics means to underscore that vitality in the church's use of Scripture will not emerge without sustained theological reflection issuing from a fresh starting point.

The essays on Isaiah, which form the bulk of the section on Exegesis, were originally delivered as lectures at Luther Seminary and St. Olaf College, in the winter and summer of 1994. I wish to thank both schools and their faculties for the opportunity to read Isaiah with special attention to the context in which it now functions, the two-testament Christian Scripture and the life of the church. The opening two chapters were likewise first delivered as lectures, in response to the question, What is the place of the Old Testament in a theological curriculum? I benefited from the vigorous exchange with faculty colleagues, several of whom composed formal responses to these lectures, and from the discussions they engendered. In this regard, I wish to especially thank Nick Wolterstorff, David Bartlett, Lee Keck, Marilyn Adams, Ellen Davis, Kathryn Greene-McCreight, Ephraim Radner, and Brevard Childs. The context of other essays is indicated where necessary, but the final form of the book is meant to stand on its own. I hope its "canonical shape" is at least as perspicuous as is, say, Isaiah's.

As a written product with a publishable future, this volume has had a peculiar history, with different final forms, titles, and scope, which only the fine editors at Eerdmans Publishing know. I thank them for their patience and helpful counsel, most especially John Simpson. This book could not have been completed without support from the Henry Luce III Foundation, which freed me from teaching responsibilities and opened up the sort of sustained time necessary for writing, rewriting, and final editing. I wish to acknowledge their generous support here.

Introduction

Josephine Gammell has been a source of strength and inspiration throughout the project. I mention her name with gratitude and affection.

This book was written to the glory of God, who alone gives strength and wisdom, through a Word that has no end.

BIBLICAL THEOLOGY

The Old Testament as Abiding Theological Witness

Inscripting a Theological Curriculum

This essay and the one that follows were composed to answer the question, "What is the place of Old Testament studies within a divinity school curriculum?" The original context of these two chapters was a public forum at Yale Divinity School comprised of students and faculty. There is some general agreement, or intuition, that we now stand at a crossroads, as do other schools like our own, whose mission is less clear than it was when Protestantism, Liberal and Neo-Orthodox, was a cultural, moral, and intellectual force in American society. That is a facet of the problem over which we have only partial control.

Yet there is also an internal dimension. Part of the problem within institutions such as ours is increasing specialization and the lack of opportunity to engage one another across discrete disciplines. Our audience has become professional societies rather than colleagues or students within a reasonably affiliated enterprise. To talk about "pluralism" without the means to test and probe that in a sustained, intellectual manner could simply devolve into politics, with those in the majority graciously including others, but without serious effort at engagement. The purpose of addressing the place of Old Testament within the larger theological enterprise was to initiate a conversation in which over time each faculty colleague would have a similar responsibility, so that eventually we might learn who we are, as individuals and as a common faculty addressing a

---

This chapter appears in slightly different form in *Theology Today* 54 (1997) 216-23.

single student body. I have composed these essays for the context just described, but also as a lens through which to read the chapters that follow in this volume. For together they attempt to describe the abiding theological witness of the Old Testament as I have come to understand that from a vantage point on the far side of the historical-critical endeavor.

*   *   *

I will move through three areas of concern in this essay. 1. Why and how do Christians appropriate Israel's scriptures, called recently by Paul van Buren, "someone else's mail"?[1] 2. How is Christian reading of the Old Testament related to New Testament studies, as well as Systematic and Historical Theology? 3. I will conclude with three challenges for the discipline of Old Testament, as we approach the close of this millennium and the beginning of a new era in biblical studies.

What is the role of Old Testament studies within a theological curriculum? The question cannot be answered without first addressing a problem that frustrates all Christian appropriation of the Old Testament, especially within an academic environment.

Modern Christians are now almost entirely non-Jewish in background. This creates a strong tendency to see in Jesus' interaction with the Judaisms of his day a critique of the content of their scriptures rather than an argument over scripture's true governing center. This critical attitude of Jesus is then identified with the New Testament as such. This Second Testament becomes the developmental culmination of and correction of the Old Testament, its religion, its ethic, its God. In other words, what began as a struggle between differing sorts of Jews over what constitutes the governing heart of the only scriptures they know has become for a church now Gentile a warrant for reading two Testaments developmentally and independently.

But the most serious problem involves the Christian understanding of God himself. It is not just that the Old Testament has become someone else's religion en route to Christianity; rather, a criticism of Jewish appropriation of the scriptures, made by one within their own frame of reference, has become a criticism of God himself as depicted there, to be pitted against "the

---

1. "On Reading Someone Else's Mail: The Church and Israel's Scriptures," in *Die Hebräische Bibel und ihre zweifache Nachgeschichte* (FS R. Rendtorff; Neukirchen-Vluyn: Neukirchener, 1990) 595-606.

God revealed in Christ." The results are striking. We have a New Testament focused on Jesus but not God, a Jesus who reveals a new religion if not a new divinity, and an Old Testament with only historical, descriptive, or background — but not theological or normative or abiding — contours. Instead of being a correlative expression, "He is risen" replaces "the God of Israel raised him from the dead." Jesus relates not to the God of the scriptures, with an identity provided there, but to a private God, known somehow else. And so Christians struggle at present to give this God a name: Godself, Creator, Mother/Father, Mother. Ironically, what became an unutterable name in Israel out of reverence has become unutterable in the New Israel because the One who raised Jesus from the dead no longer seems to be riveted to the scriptures the church inherited as a gift.[2] The gift has proven awkward: a bad tie from a close relative at Christmas.

A further consequence of this Gentile confusion is that Israel becomes without further reflection "Jewish" (one can see the beginnings of this confusion in Calvin and Luther).[3] Having detached the God who raised Jesus from the dead from the God who gave the Law and the Promised Land to his people, Christians have in turn made Israel a past people and culture only, distinct from the church; or Israel has been conflated with those Jews under attack by a Jesus now distanced from his own people. To call Israel "the Jews" is thought to do honor to modern Jews. Yet the threat is that along with this alleged honorific will come a transfer of the first person of the trinity away from serious Christian reflection. The one whom Christians call Lord, however, is both one *of Israel,* and one *with the Father,* the Holy One of Israel who sent him.

Moreover, modern Jews must constantly reflect on the profound historical and theological distance of Israel from themselves, with a temple, priesthood, king, prophets, and ritual life no longer in existence. Their scripture is Tanak, Torah, read with a subsequent literature every bit as refracting as the New Testament.[4] The New Testament is not midrash on

---

2. On the centrality of the Christian name "Father" see chapter 17 below.

3. See Ephraim Radner's discussion ("The Cost of Communion: A Meditation on Israel and the Divided Church," in *Inhabiting Unity,* ed. E. Radner and R. R. Reno [Grand Rapids: Eerdmans, 1995] 134-51). Jacob Neusner puts it this way: "While the world at large treats Judaism as 'the religion of the Old Testament,' the fact is otherwise. Judaism inherits and makes the Hebrew Scriptures its own, just as does Christianity" (quoted in E. Frerichs, "The Torah Canon of Judaism and the Interpretation of Hebrew Scripture," *HBT* 9 [1987] 22). See chapter 6 below.

4. See chapter 6 below.

the Old, but a hard reading of a closed literature based upon a conviction as to its point, its goal, its messiah, and its word of address — not captive to historical description — in relation to the Word made flesh. All this means a form of appropriation quite different from midrash, halakah, aggada, even when points of similarity can be seen. That is because for Christians the words of the Old Testament are connected to the Word made flesh. The Christian problem is not how to update a text tied to the past, or to enlarge the imagination, or to provide bits of travelogue for the religiously inclined, but to show how the Word made flesh is "in accordance with the scriptures," in accordance with the God who called his elect people, Israel. And more than this: to show how Israel's past destiny is a typological foreshadowing of our own, before Christ returns in glory.

What the Jewish Christian Paul took as a rebuke to Gentile Christians — that they were aliens to the commonwealth of Israel, strangers to the covenants of promise, without hope and without God in the world — is now taken to be something of a relief, a disentangling from the God whose character is marked by holiness, demand, election, law, and final judgment. Instead, we whom Paul in Christ honored as fellow heirs, understand adoption to mean a privileged attitude toward a literature whose content, unfortunately, is so tied up with God's very character that it resists easy sorting out with some geiger counter set with a Jesus rheostat.

In some ways this description may sound too pessimistic. That is because of the promise held out by a historical approach that will avoid these pitfalls and release the abiding theological witness of the Old Testament. When I speak of this, I am not just questioning the legacy of historical-critical work in Old Testament studies alone. This approach has made the widest possible inroads and belongs to a consciousness at work in all fields, uniting the most unlikely of disputants, from a Bishop Spong to his most literalist opponent, both in different ways concerned "with what really happened."[5] A historical approach was once regarded as brac-

5. The problem is not only Spong's exegesis (rationalistic and historicist) but the theological confession supposedly driving it. This makes his published remarks sound in my ear "biblicist" in that the treatment is of isolated verses or passages, from a revisionist angle, with appeal to historical and cultural reconstructions. This sounds like reaction-formation against caricatured "fundamentalist" opponents, whose biblicism he rejects; yet both are in different ways concerned with historical reference. It is just that the latter are more optimistic that the plain sense really brokers historical reference, down to the smallest detail. What is unclear to me is the explicit theological framework that emerges from such exegesis and that then in turn informs and directs it.

ing, a deconstruction of something piously held. Now it belongs to the consciousness of an entire theological curriculum and of an entire generation of students, and so is no longer our problem in Old Testament alone.

We honor the distinctiveness of the Old Testament, it is held, by attending to its thought world, authorial intention, religious life and institutions, and sacred history without an intervening New Testament or Christian lens. We let it creep up on the New Testament and catch it unawares. We believe we have access to its religious point of view by disassembling its final form and ranging its texts in proper, that is, developmental, order. Theology becomes tradition history, partly because that makes the Bible look like us and like the way we do theology. Yet the very thing that makes us unlike the people within the Bible is the existence of the Bible itself, a full literary canon, *which we have in a form and scope no one there had*. Stable; cooked, not raw (that's preaching); no longer participated in by us, as prophets and apostles, but as the church, which depends upon their prior testimony for identity and for knowledge of God in the first place. This is what it means to speak of the Bible as a gift to the church and of the Holy Spirit as that which makes a written word living. When Jesus said, "I will no longer talk much with you" (John 14:30), it was not that there was nothing more to say or do that could then be researched and written up. It was, rather, that he had just spoken of the work of the Holy Spirit who would come and "teach all things and bring to your remembrance" all that was said (John 14:25). All historical inquiry must take this talk seriously, for it too is a piece of historical datum.

Moreover, what a historical approach usually gives us is theology in-the-making, with this moment better, that moment worse, according to some standard, differently conceived and forever slipping. Biblical theology is, however, also governed by intertextual reference and typology, capable of making sense without historical deconstruction. Categories like law, sin, election, atonement, and holiness are not open to endless ebbing and flowing because they are tied to God's own nature as God. It is law and narrative in their present inner-arrangement that had the power to disclose God himself in Jesus' day. In turn, this engendered disputes over who Jesus was and if the Holy One of Israel was the One who sent him.[6] That dispute was answered, Christians should remember, by claiming the closest possible identity between Jesus and the God of Israel short of conflation, Son and Father, now become "Our Father" too — which of

6. There is a Spirit who is Lord over both texts and readers, according to John 14:26.

course has nothing to do with "earthly fathers," but with the Father of Jesus Christ, the God of Israel and of all creation. In this confession consists both the gift and the work of the Spirit, whose identity is of equal glory to the Father and the Son.

Much of what I have said up to this point calls for a reattachment of the Old Testament to the New, self-consciously, and a return to older forms of typological reading, now taken up, post historical criticism. What a challenge it represents to stop reading things developmentally, with the conviction, run odd interference for by historical approaches, that Christians do not know where the lines of that old story intersect when in fact that is their confession and their only point of entry, because Jesus is "in accordance with scriptures" once not their own. Instead of asking how Israel thought about itself and God, how the New Testament then continued this, and then how we do that too, we should reverse the order of concern. How does the God we confess raised Jesus from the dead think about Israel and the world? The Old Testament does not present itself as Israel's reflection on God — that is a peculiarly Christian way of thinking, influenced by an assumption that Christians think about God from a rival perspective, that of Jesus.[7] Even with its extraordinary doctrine of election, the Old Testament presents itself from the very beginning from the perspective of God, who chose Israel in respect of larger plans for creation, whose final resolution Christians see in a Jesus who came and will come again. And, of course, Christians are only issued library cards to read in the first place by Jesus, else they would always remain outsiders to this privileged discourse between God and his people. This too counts as a "christological reading" of the Old Testament, though it does not entail tracking down types of Christ inside every burning bush or rock in the wilderness.

As George Lindbeck has recently urged, we need to reconsider a typological approach, post historical criticism. This would mean thinking about the church and Israel as types related to one another, *ante Christum* and *post Christum,* of the selfsame reality, and not allow Israel to be historicized and consigned to a past before Jesus.[8] The church should consider its present destiny in the light of Israel, and that includes cate-

7. See chapter 3 for a fuller discussion of the problematic of isolating "Israel's point of view" as the key to theological exegesis.

8. "The Story-Shaped Church: Critical Exegesis and Theological Interpretation," *Scriptural Authority and Narrative Interpretation,* ed. Garrett Green (Philadelphia: Fortress, 1987) 161-78.

gories like exile, rivenness, shortcoming, and even, as Ezekiel saw at one dark moment, a bride tragically become a whore — for all these are constitutive of God's people, there elected, here adopted, there awaiting the Messiah, here awaiting his return in glory, one destiny folded into the other, yet kept distinct in the sovereign purposes of God.[9]

What does this mean for theology as a larger discipline? For systematic theology, it means, as David Yeago has recently argued, that doctrine is at its essence exegesis.[10] There can be no specifically Christian systematizing that does not start with God's character as revealed in the oracles entrusted to the Jews, entrusted by bequest in Christ to the church. God is not a philosophical concept in search of content, but the Holy One, the living God who called Abraham and was called on by Jesus, who gave a holy and good law and sent the Son to obey it and take its curse that in exchange blessing might be had within a New Covenant. Talk about God must be talk about sacrifice, holiness, purity, Israel as type and as destiny, before any apologetic forays are attempted. Otherwise Christians will end up joining the Athenians at Mars Hill and mock when Jesus is brought into connection with a frame of reference suddenly quite strange, because attached to the God of Israel instead of "an unknown God." If "Godself" unambiguously names the Holy One of Israel, fine. Still, the decline in so-called "mainline Christianity" reflected in its Sunday morning attendance may not be busyness or spiritual sloth only, but general unclarity about who is being addressed, and therefore unclarity about Who is doing the addressing as well.

Also picking up from Yeago's concerns, historical theology is reminded that doctrine is not simply heresy's counterfactual. In the debate with Gnosticism, the assertion that the God of Israel was the Creator, of the same substance as the Son, was not made because of the negative implications for our view of creation's goodness, philosophically considered. The pressure was exerted from the side of scripture's plain sense, a departure from which meant a failure to acknowledge the One who inspired the text in the first place, who was at the same time under discussion. So, too, Augustine would surely have respected the suitability of historical criticism applied to his best and most inspired reflections, how or if they are relevant today, but it is doubtful he would have ever

---

9. See Radner's treatment cited in n. 3 above.
10. David S. Yeago, "The New Testament and Nicene Dogma: A Contribution to the Recovery of Theological Exegesis," *Pro Ecclesia* 3 (1994) 152-64.

anticipated such an attitude toward either Testament of the Christian canon. Just as the deuterocanonical books are frequently themselves the attestors to their own derivative character, even more so the relationship of Tradition to Scripture, despite the elevating eye that today sees all things past as equally past, in the name of the freedom to do the choosing. A typological reading of the Old Testament post historical criticism releases one particular slice of the past — God's ways with Israel — as forever contemporaneous, even to the extent of guiding and directing the church and figurally displaying her future. Even types that are passing away remain relevant, on just those terms, shadows whose contours are displayed in the presence of light.

In sum, the problem of hearing the abiding theological witness of the Old Testament is a problem we must confront from the perspective of the entire theological discipline, else though we are first, the Old Testament discipline will end up last. The very historical consciousness we believed would unlock the Old Testament's theological witness will actually serve to ensure that it is just one phase en route to something better, or just something else, to put it less dramatically. A baton with God's own identity and self engraved on it will be dropped, leaving us, if we are not careful, with carved-up fiefdoms of expertise, highly organized but also highly disconnected. Gerhard von Rad did not excite a generation of students because reading the Old Testament was suddenly an obvious good, or out of post-Holocaust guilt, or because all alone he developed the right new method. His colleagues in theology were vitally interested in scripture: not its form, not its ideological freight, not its potential to serve as a resource, but because of its witness to God in Israel and in Christ for a generation whose stopped ears had been opened.

My question is whether historical criticism, as practiced by von Rad or popularized here, was what made the Old Testament come alive; or whether it was the explicit conversation he was having with theology colleagues, themselves exegetes, that made the historical questions he posed relevant to them both. There was a heavy existential dimension that moved back and forth from theology to biblical studies in those days, but existence has become a very different matter today, before which the Bible has had to get out of the way, adjust, or be adjusted. My deeper question is whether that conversation was ever capable of further extension. Undaunted, historical questions began to take on a life of their own, and run today virtually on autopilot. The assumption is that theologians will put all this historical heavy lifting to use, but in the meantime they have rightly lost interest, while biblical scholars return to old chestnuts like the historical Jesus, or to the briar patch of hermeneutics.

I have called for a reconnection of Old Testament and New Testament studies, for that is where theological combustion occurs. Theological studies must also reconsider its role in specific exegetical relationship to the Bible, and to its substance, not just its form or its verses in isolation, in relation to a rule of faith. The central thrust of this rule is clear: the "emphatic coupling" of almighty God and his Son Jesus Christ, and an exegesis that flows toward and from this point of standing.[11] Adoption of this rule, post historical criticism, might open up the possibility of mutual enrichment in the wider curriculum, around the subject that is our true center, the triune God: Father, Son, Holy Spirit; Holy One of Israel, Holy One made flesh, Holy One the Counselor.

I will close with three challenges for Old Testament studies at Yale Divinity School and elsewhere.

First, the cultivation of a proper respect — reverence is not too strong a term — for what an honor it is to read this literature at all. When the Old Testament requires jacket blurbs, snazzy new translations every other week, and maybe even snazzy lectures to match, we need to stop and ask whether the problem is in or behind the text or in us. The basic challenge of the Old Testament is not historical distance, overcome by historical-critical tools, or existential disorientation, overcome by a hermeneutics of assent or suspicion.[12] The Old Testament tells a particular story about a particular people and their particular God, who in Christ we confess as our God, his Father and our own, the Holy One of Israel. We have been read into a will, a first will and testament, by Christ. If we do not approach the literature with this basic stance — of estrangement overcome, of an inclusion properly called "adoption" — historical-critical methods or a hermeneutics of assent will still stand outside and fail to grasp that God is reading us, not we him. "Second naivete" was fine as an antidote to liberalism's deconstructive acids; but at some point we are talking about a prior claim, made by the literature itself, within a rule of faith, by which God is believed to speak directly. I doubt that can be taught, and yet teaching cannot go on without it.

Second, the discovery of an intellectual horizon appropriate to the material itself. The challenge of the Old Testament is not essentially one of

11. The phrase is that of W. Countryman ("Tertullian and the Regula Fidei," *Second Century* 2 [1982] 209).

12. See chapter 4 below.

piety, but neither is it one of dedicated information gathering. Historical criticism offered for generations of readers of the Old Testament something to do: entire careers have been built fine-tuning the documentary hypothesis or wrestling with whether the early Israelites were donkey or camel nomads. Yet the question may not have been asked whether a universal point of view, based upon an authorial intent or a refined historical reconstruction, is the point of access the Old Testament itself assumes is to be ours. A fresh intellectual horizon for Old Testament studies is the rediscovery of the complex network of intertextuality that binds all texts together, not only in their canonical shape in the Old, but more especially as this intertextuality is taken up and filled to fullest capacity in the New. If I have said nothing else here, it is that special attention needs to be paid to reconnecting Old and New Testament studies. Cut apart, they are left to scrounge for comparative texts and social or historical contextualization, but may miss the most obvious context of all: the way the New has heard the Old — its own MS-DOS — and the way the Old, in the light of the New, renders God in Christ for those who were once without God in the world.

Third, and finally, a fresh challenge is to let the *sensus literalis* of the Old Testament become, not a historical sense or one connected to authorial intention alone — both contexts we have sought for several centuries now to lay bare.[13] Let the literal sense of the Old refer as well to a word that does not return empty, but in fact reaches out and creates of itself new scope and range of meaning, within the Old Testament and on into the New. The *per se* voice of the Old Testament it is the task of any Introduction to the Old Testament to teach. In so doing, let that voice not be so isolated within a past historical context that all we are left to do is worry about accuracy and proper updating, and yet we often cannot move from ancient word to modern situation, because the fullest choir of voices is never enthusiastically displayed or heard in one sitting. For this reason, there must be within the curriculum some course in Christian Scripture or Biblical Theology where a natural movement from Old Testament to New, and New to Old, is the focus of scholarly theological attention. If this were done, perhaps the next movement, from Bible to Theology, would take place much more naturally, as one sort of basic exegetical concern gives way to another, for both faculty colleagues and students.

13. See Kathryn Greene-McCreight, "Ad Litteram: Understandings of the Plain Sense of Scripture in the Exegesis of Augustine, Calvin and Barth on Genesis 1–3" (Yale Ph.D. dissertation; Ann Arbor: University Microfilms, 1994).

2

God as Other, God as Holy

Election and Disclosure in Christian Scripture

In the previous chapter, I focused on several specific problems. What does it mean for Gentile Christians to appropriate Israel's scriptures? Does this appropriation entail any specific exegetical constraints? If so, what are the consequences for New Testament studies and theological studies? Is there an external "rule of faith" that sets the parameters for exegesis, derived from scripture's own plain sense? This discussion, I hope, addresses certain felt problems within Old Testament studies. I am urging an alternative orientation that would reconnect Old and New Testament in a manner appropriate to their own intertextual relatedness.

The model of reading I am proposing is not a flight to the land of inner allusions or a sealed literary universe. That sonorous title *The Great Code* always seemed more appropriate to Northrop Frye's own book than to the Bible.[1] T. S. Eliot's 1935 remark remains just as forceful today: "Those who talk of the Bible as 'a monument of English prose' are merely admiring it as a monument over the grave of Christianity." The intertextuality I am assuming means to reconnect Old and New Testament so as to lay bare the deep theological forces at work across them: forces that created a second literary witness indebted to the Old while retaining the Old in the form it had been bequeathed to the church. That minor differences grew up between the Hebrew and Septuagintal traditions pales

1. Northrop Frye, *The Great Code: The Bible and Literature* (New York: Harcourt, 1982).

13

before their enormous conformity and their common resistance to Christian glossing. Both traditions, Greek and Hebrew, began as non-Christian productions, and as such they became the first part of a two-testament witness to God in Christ.[2] This two-testament witness renders not a great code, but God as he truly is, without remainder, save that blocked out by a darkened will and mind. Biblical language does not refract "the perfect God" imperfectly; but truly, fully, sufficiently, in Hebrew, Aramaic, Greek, and their various daughter translations.

As for the ongoing place of historical criticism, if there is a serious historical question to ask, it remains: just what sort of literature are we reading? This guards against the book of Joshua becoming an archaeologist's field report if that is not what it is. Alternatively, modern literary readings go awry when they fail to take seriously the literature's form and intention as aspects of the history of literature itself. Historical work at the formal, literary level is indispensable, or we will introduce anachronisms and false questions the text never wished to entertain. This includes questions of the "what really happened" variety (the adverb is ten months pregnant).

Historical-critical endeavor means developing a sensitivity to when a text means to broker facts and figures (which is fairly infrequently) and when it is doing something else. Seen in this way, the historical Jesus project may actually be wrong-headed on historical grounds, introducing a Jesus the texts do not intend to place before our eyes. Here the verb "intend" is linked not to an authorial mind but to the form of the Gospel genre *as historically given* and the readership such a form — by virtue of its form — has a right to expect. So too, one could use an English hymnal to reconstruct Methodist church history, but the danger is that one could forfeit the ability to sing hymns from it in the exchange. In sum, my concern over the past ten years has been to move beyond the consideration of individual forms to the canonical shape of books and larger collections and finally to a consideration of the form of Christian scripture itself, a two-testament witness to God in Christ.[3]

In this chapter, I will work at the set of problems I was addressing before, but from the reverse direction. "Reverse direction" is, I believe, what biblical studies must now consider, more generally. Having labored

2. See the recent discussion by B. S. Childs, "The Problem of the Christian Bible," in *Biblical Theology of the Old and New Testaments* (Minneapolis: Fortress, 1992) 55-69.
3. See chapter 9 below and the chapters in the section on "Exegesis."

for two centuries to free the Bible from dogmatic overlay, Protestant and Catholic critics alike should "concede victory." Now we must try to generate a theology — neither in the early reaction-formation mode, where "history" and "unchanging ideas" were the magic bullets, nor in what later came to be called in America "The Biblical Theology Movement," a mode now in full *rigor mortis* — but in something much more basic.

I will begin with the simple question: when we use the word "God," what do we mean? This will take me to a minefield marked "revelation," for which I prefer the term "disclosure." Behind that minefield is scorched terrain marked "election" and "the scandal of particularity." I wish to show how a proper understanding of these two matters is instrumental to our handling of scripture and to our understanding of who God is and how God makes himself known. Using this index — disclosure and election — I wish to show how God as Other and God as Holy are related, and how this is true not just modally, for the God of Israel disclosed in the Old Testament, but essentially, for the triune God, classically termed "Father, Son, and Holy Spirit." I will conclude with a look at Hebrews 10:26-31, as pointing toward a theological exegesis of the Old and New Testament within the rule of faith.

So as not to be misunderstood on a heated issue now before the church, it bears repeating that the term "Father" is intended to emphasize not a gendered deity but the Holy One of Israel, as addressed by the Son. Only from that son's perspective and access are we privileged to discover the appropriateness of other ways of referring to God given in Israel's scriptures (Holy One, Creator, Lord). To regard these as corrections or substitutions or improvements on "Father" would, of course, be modalism of a different sort and a departure from the rule of faith at its most basic generative assumption: that we know the Father by means of the Son and that together with the Holy Spirit, all three are worshiped in Christian confession as one and the same Lord.

I

I want to begin by simply considering three ways the word "God" might be used today, within and outside Christian churches.

1. First, as naming the God and Father of Jesus Christ, who is the Holy One of Israel. God is both the One addressed by Jesus in the Gospels

and the One who spoke to Abraham, Moses, and David. The church confesses this God, revealed in Israel's scriptures and in Jesus' relationship to the Father, to be one and the same.

The Nicene Creed does not assume this, but asserts it, at three points. First, before moving to "I believe in Jesus Christ, his Son our Lord," it begins with "I believe in one God, maker of heaven and earth." Though they are rightly named separately, the creed insists that they are in special relationship, unlike any other imaginable: only-begotten, before creation itself, of the same substance.

The second is more indirect. It appears in the assertion that Jesus rose again "according to the scriptures." This statement, taken from Paul (1 Cor 15:3), has behind it the concern for agency: the One who inspired Israel's scriptures is the One who raised Jesus from the dead. Jesus did not raise himself, without relationship to prior hopes or plans or agent. Jesus did not step into a void on Good Friday, but committed his spirit to God. The most dramatic moment of Christian belief occurred in relationship: Father and Son, Holy One of Israel and Jesus of Nazareth, the Christ.

Finally, and more indirect still, is the creed's statement concerning the Holy Spirit. The same Spirit "proceeds from the Father and the Son." The spirit that spoke through God's holy prophets of old, as individuals, by which God made creation itself and sanctified the Son, is the spirit given to believers in Christ at Pentecost: God the Father's singular and special gift of old, now poured out on all in Christ, bursting old bounds.

This understanding of God, by which the term points to the One who raised Jesus from the dead, also inhabits much Christian praying. Christians pray to God, through Christ, in the power of the Holy Spirit.

2. A second way for Christians to refer to God is as the one who consists of all three persons — Father, Son, and Holy Spirit — at once. By this is meant "the triune God." The Trisagion of Orthodoxy probably has this view of God in mind: "Holy God, Holy and Mighty, Holy Immortal One: have mercy upon us." Is this appeal to God restricted to the One who raised Jesus from the dead only? No, it has the entire Godhead in mind — or, in view, since the triune God is far more capable of worship than rational explanation (as a glance at the necessarily prolix *Quicunque Vult* shows).

Related to this understanding of the *unity* of the persons is also the use of the term to refer to each one individually: God the Father, God the Son, God the Holy Spirit.

In some sense, the warrant for this use of God is an act of the Holy

Spirit in the church, since the Bible itself lets the description fall more on the *relationship* of separate persons, together — Holy One of Israel, the Son sent by Him, the Holy Spirit proceeding from them both — than on the God they all three, separately, are. This has to do with the Bible's narrative form and purpose. The separateness of the persons of God belongs to the experience of God as the Bible narrates this: revealed to Israel, shared with adopted daughters and sons in Christ, in and by the power of the Holy Spirit. At the same time, key New Testament texts assert the closest identity between these persons, and it is from this assertion that the rule of faith takes its bearings and initial justification.

The point of the rule of faith in the early church was to insure that the separateness of the persons of God be seen as complementary with the confession that God is One. There was an exegetical dimension to this confession as well. The Bible was to be read within this rule. That is, the theological confession began with the Bible and then returned to it, with exegetical constraints or parameters. To my mind the same point was made subsequently in Reformed Anglicanism's Thirty-Nine Articles, where one reads, "the church does not have authority to expound one portion of scripture in such a way that it be repugnant to another."[4] The possibility of course exists, which is why it is explicitly proscribed. But the grounding of the proscription lies ultimately in the character of God himself: three separate persons, One God. Two testaments, one selfsame activity. We know there is difference, but theology by and for the church does not gain its capacity to teach by exposing and exploring difference for its own sake.

3. Yet it would be over-hasty to say that that was the end of the matter of God-talk, within Christianity and more broadly speaking. There is a third way in which Christians and others refer to God, and this should be considered as well before moving on. In some settings, it is a far more prevalent way to think about God than the first two I have reviewed.

This way of thinking about God proceeds from philosophical, or existential, or emotional starting points — and there is a good deal of overlap, and other starting points could be mentioned as well.

(a) "God" refers to that One beyond our capacity to think or imagine. "God" means the Ineffable, the Impassable — the Counterfactual to us as effable, passable, limited in thought and imagination. Or (b) "God" refers to that One who lies on the other side of our sense of finitude, or limit, or existence with end, or anxiety before death. "God" is the address to that

4. For a fuller discussion, see chapter 8 below.

existence, because the Only One not bound in the same sense — so Tillich's "Ground of Being." Or (c) "God" refers to that One who senses pain more deeply than our own expression of it, whose essence as Deity is an obligation to hear the cries of all victims, else their cry would be in vain.

Now there may well be points of contact with God as described earlier, but these are derivative or accidental, because the starting points are different. "O Love, how deep, how broad, how high, how passing thought and fantasy" could be the cry of the worshiper of God in the sense I am now describing, but the first two views of God *could not* come to such a conviction except by way of "that God the Son of God should take our mortal form for mortal sake."[5]

Because the starting point is different, this third view of what the word "God" means does not resonate with an understanding that human language could ever adequately name God as he is — or to put it in more accurate terms, "God as God is." Here is the nub of the matter: it belongs to the nature of the thing, in this case God as God, that God cannot be predicated. "God cannot make Godself known that way." Predications are provisional, at best.[6]

In the modern period, this understanding of God as beyond human, or biblical, language, has dovetailed with concerns to repair, it is hoped, the real damage wrought by patriarchy. The complaint that to call God "he" makes gods of men and demigods of women here joins up with the belief that God cannot be sufficiently described in human language and therefore lies beyond thought, existence, feeling — beyond language itself.

What is the proper response within Christian confession to this partly true, but also potentially misleading, view of what it means to name God? The position I am here arguing is that there has been a failure to comprehend what the Bible understands by *revelation* and *election,* as these work in tandem. In saying this I am grounding my starting point in scripture's own plain sense. As I understand it, the term "revelation" has, among systematic theologians, fallen into serious and perhaps deserved desuetude, in spite of recent efforts at resuscitation.[7] By emphasizing the aspect of

---

5. Incidentally, note the conflation of the first two views of God, brilliantly executed, because constrained by the rule of meter: "God" — "the Son of God."

6. I discuss this in more detail in chapter 17 below.

7. See Ronald Theimann, *Revelation and Theology: The Gospel as Narrated Promise* (Notre Dame: University of Notre Dame, 1985); Gabriel Fackre, *The Doctrine of Revelation: A Narrative Interpretation* (Grand Rapids: Eerdmans, 1977).

election, I hope to show why revelation — or disclosure — remains indispensable to our understanding God.

II

God, we learn in the Bible, makes himself known to women and men. We do not make our way to God, however much the apostle Paul acknowledges that even Athenians, and all humanity, at God's urging "seek God, in the hope that they might feel after him and find him" (the pronouns are Paul's and the Athenians'; Acts 17:27). To use the term "revelation" is to regard the agent and the event of revelation to be fully in God's own hands.

To say this, however, is to raise a question concerning particularity. To whom is God talking, revealing, acting — since presumably he, as initiator of the particular revelation of himself, has to start somewhere? Genesis 1–11 reveals that God had once revealed himself as broadly as possible (*'adam* is humanity as such), and yet with no encroachment on his own particular character. The particular nations emerge, however, first in blessing after God's gracious sparing (the descendents of Noah, Gen 9:1–10:32), but then also in disobedience (the Tower of Babel, 11:1-9). This spreading out and particularizing reveals that God did not repair the human condition of darkened mind and heart after the flood, but was prepared to live with these out of his own gracious compassion and forbearance (8:21).

The decision is made by God to relate particularly to a particular people, the children of Abraham, as a special act of forbearance, with a plan to bless all nations through his and Sarah's descendents (12:1-3). A further narrowing occurs in the events that follow, and Israel emerges as God's special possession (*segullah,* Deut 7:6), his law and prophets the means by which he makes himself and his word known to Israel. "Revelation" or "disclosure" is only comprehensible within the framework of election. It cannot be abstracted or universalized; it is a particular perspective to which one must be made privy, through adoption or ingrafting.

Now where is the rest of humanity during all this? God's spirit, Paul reports, makes all flesh "seek God, in the hope that they might feel after him and find him." Isaiah proclaims that those beyond Israel's boundary will come and find fellowship with God within the relationship established

19

with Israel: "They will make supplication to you, saying, 'God is with you only, and there is no other. . . .' O God of Israel, the Savior" (45:14, 15). The bringing near of those outside Israel will also serve as a rebuke to those within Israel who have not honored God. On Isaiah's final horizon lies the promise: "all flesh shall come and worship before me" (66:23). But the point is that those outside the original covenant relationship cannot know God fully, and those within know God by means of his particular relationship to particular individuals, the ignoring of which brings judgment. This makes election an unusually sharp two-edged sword. "You only have I chosen of all the families on earth" — God says to Israel through Amos — "therefore I will punish you." In Eph 2:11-22 Paul reminds (a) those outside the privilege of adoption and (b) those outside the revelation just what it is that they are being made heirs of in Christ: "Remember that you were at that time separated from Christ, alienated from the commonwealth of Israel, strangers to the covenants of promise, and without God in the world."

Paul is not bragging about his prior status in Ephesians, in order to show up those without it. So much of his discourse at other points goes in the opposite direction, to the point of counting everything manure in the light of knowing Jesus Christ, and being crucified with him. Paul's point has to do with revelation and election, which becomes adoption for those in Christ. "For through him *we* have access to the Father." The first person plural "we" signals the extent to which Paul in Christ has died to his former life. Then he switches back to the original second person address, "you," to underscore the character of differentiation that has existed and is being overcome. "So then you are no longer strangers and sojourners, but you are fellow citizens with the saints and members of the household of God" (v. 19). Yet in what does this household, and this house, actually consist? Its foundation, verse 21 concludes, is the apostles and prophets, and "the whole structure is joined together and grows into a holy temple in the Lord."

Here is a sorting out of the proper Christian understanding of God. For those outside the covenants of promise, access to God is through Jesus Christ. He gives new citizenship and reconciles all to God the Father. The foundation of the house to which Christians belong remains the witness of the prophets, joined by that of the apostles. "Prophets" is shorthand for the testimony of God to Israel, by which God's character was once known and is now to be shared with fellow citizens, for their illumination and instruction, now that they have been brought near by Christ.

Not working from the perspective of adoption, though assuming it, 2 Timothy makes more explicit the role of the Old Testament as bearing witness to God. He speaks of "the sacred writings which are able to instruct you for salvation through faith in Christ Jesus" (2 Tim 3:15). The profit for "teaching, reproof, correction, and training in righteousness" springs from inspiration by God himself (v. 16). When 2 Timothy speaks of "all scripture" he means of course the only scripture, "the oracles of God entrusted to the Jews" (Rom 3:2) — what outsiders brought into a New Covenant call, from that vantage point, "The Old Testament."

The perspective on God this understanding of scripture entails is the first one I described above: God is the Holy One of Israel, and his son gives us access to him. The witness to Jesus Christ in the New Testament is joined to the Old as Christ is joined to the Father.

Now what are the constraints under which this conjoining operates? First, outsiders read the Old Testament christologically. By this is not meant finding types of Christ in the Old in some rationalistic manner, but acknowledging that what we know of God there is related to what we know of God in Christ, who is our only point of access. This, it seems to me, rules out the search for any other independent access, including "God's mighty acts in history," the religious bearing of a prophet, or the worldview of the Yahwist. All these are possible areas for reconstruction and reflection. But unless they can first be justified theologically and then be brought into relationship with God in Christ at some point, the theological point of isolating them at all remains unclear. Venerable historical critics as distant from one another as Gerhard von Rad and G. E. Wright agreed on this much. The first, in my judgment, did not think sufficiently about the relationship between the Israel he was isolating *historically* and the typological exegesis he proposed for the church;[8] and the second, I believe, wanted to isolate God's acts from Israel's perception of them, because Wright knew Jesus was speaking and acting in relationship to some God, and he wanted to encounter that God straight on and without interference.[9] But whatever their failings, both were still aware they needed to justify their labors theologically, not just historically.

The larger point can be illustrated by means of contrast. It could make perfect sense for general readers to track down events in ancient

8. See my discussion in the following chapter.
9. Langdon Gilkey's critique retains its force still ("Cosmology, Ontology, and the Travail of Biblical Language," *JR* 41 [1965] 194-205).

culture, in religious psychology, in social and intellectual history, as matters worthy of serious independent research. But outsiders brought near to the Holy One of Israel through Christ are constrained by that same point of access to handle Israel's witness to God differently. This was the controversial point I spoke of at length in the preceding chapter. The rule of faith sets the parameters for the exegetical reflection, and in that rule the holiness of God is comprehended in reference to the holiness of his Son, to choose one example. Let it be emphasized that these parameters are Christian ones, based upon the New Testament's understanding of adoption. Jews have different parameters. The generally curious — anyone who can read and buy one of the many new translations — will have other parameters: historical knowledge, morality, the enjoyment of a good story, and so forth.

III

I want now to consider the theological locus, "God as Other," with this perspective in mind. "Other" in the most general terms means "outside," "beyond," or "different"; opposite predications would be "proximate," "present," or "similar." To call God "other" is to consider God apart, before considering how God is with us, and how that happens such that communication between God and humanity takes place.

From the biblical perspective I have just sketched, God's otherness is at least partly a function of election and its consequences. That is, those outside the covenant with Israel did not know God in the same way Israel did, to whom he had made himself known and continued to make himself known through prophet, priest, and sage, in blessing and in punishment, in promise and in memory. God is "other" for the nations in that he lies beyond their ken. They know other gods; or, in an irenic mood, Paul says they seek after God in the hope that they might find him. Like our own, there is a generic word for God, *'elohim*, that Israel shares with the nations, but which for Israel is comprehended by reference to *'ehyeh 'ašer 'ehyeh*, as revealed to Moses (Exod 3:14).

However, as soon as one reads the Old Testament narratives closely, the situation is much more complicated, both within and outside Israel. The opposite of knowing God (for those within Israel) and the opposite of not knowing the Holy One of Israel (for the nations) is, ironically, the same thing: knowing *other* gods. For Deuteronomy, general amnesia is almost never a neutral or semiconscious state: to forget God is to worship other gods, not to become an atheist (only the fool says in his heart "there is no god"). It is to become "like the nations," who do not know the Holy One of Israel and because of this are tempted to worship other gods, sometimes the more the better. The whole book of Isaiah is about Israel becoming like the nations and then forfeiting its capacity to hear, until a new generation emerges and is brought back into fellowship, now in the company of the very nations who had once been outside, agents of God's judgment without their knowledge of it, now to be brought near themselves.

Within Israel, the notion of God as Other has to be reconsidered, because otherness does not have to do with standing outside the elected relationship, as is true with the nations. To call God the Holy One *of Israel* implies presence, not absence, insiderness, not outsiderness — to use the adjectives just mentioned. Yet these misdescribe God's actual relationship to his own people because within Israel there are special individuals whose relationship to God points up the contrast with others within Israel (seventy elders beheld God, but not others; only Moses, not Aaron, approached the most holy place of exchange; the sons of Korah were not holy as were the sons of Aaron, and so forth). The word that describes God's relationship to Israel is "holy": sanctified, set apart. The holiness of God is not something generally numinous, but is conveyed by God's word, in command, in presence, in law, and in cult.

Here what those outside Israel may judge to be God's otherness due to simple exclusion, distance, or untimely birth — leaving them at best to "feel after him" — we learn in the Old Testament is not a matter of simple accident. God is holy. For this reason he guards his character, revealing it only to an elected people, and therefore that people is charged and held accountable for infringements against God's holiness in a direct sense, while the nations experience blessing and curse in some more indirect sense. In Jonah or the opening chapters of Amos the fate of the nations is still comprehended from a standpoint within Israel's own reflection on God — Jonah is not charged to address a felt dilemma in Nineveh, but to point one out on the basis of God's word to him. Strange as it may seem, Balaam's ass and Cyrus the Persian have more in common than either do with Israel. How God might deal with the nations within their own religious systems lies beyond the horizon of the Old Testament, precisely because of its understanding of the specificity of God's disclosure.

23

At the same time, the promise of ultimate bringing near emerges at the beginning, through Abraham's descendents, and this promise is not reneged on but reiterated up to the end.

The Christian reads of God's holiness in the Old Testament and is only in a position to understand its force because the promise to the nations has been made good on in Christ. God is no longer simply other, unknown, felt after. Rather, in Christ outsiders have been brought near and addressed as was Israel of old; they are thus made fully "response"-able. For all the energy the author of Hebrews expends describing how the Old Testament has become shadow in the light of the Gospel of Jesus Christ, it remains the case for exactly those brought near in Christ that we approach with boldness the sanctuary and the veil guarding God's holiness by means of the blood of Christ. God's holiness has not been relaxed in Christ, but brought near to those formerly outside.

Hebrews 10:26-31 offers an illustration of the sort of intertextual exegesis I have in mind.

> For if we willfully persist in sin after having received the knowledge of the truth, there no longer remains a sacrifice for sins, but a fearful prospect of judgment, and a fury of fire that will consume the adversaries. Anyone who has violated the law of Moses dies without mercy "on the testimony of two or three witnesses." How much worse punishment do you think will be deserved by those who have spurned the Son of God, profaned the blood of the covenant by which they were sanctified, and outraged the Spirit of grace? For we know the one who said, "Vengeance is mine, I will repay." And again, "The Lord will judge his people." It is a fearful thing to fall into the hands of the living God (NRSV).

To deny the Son is to incur the wrath of the Father. That is to say, in the New Testament witness to Christ, the Old's *per se* witness to God is retained with all its force. The "fury of fire" *(pyros zēlos)* of the Holy One of Israel is what awaits the apostate — the phrase is taken literally from Zeph 1:18. To break the Mosaic law through idolatry or blasphemy incurred death without compassion; the fate that awaits the one who profanes the blood of the new covenant is described in reference to it, *a fortiori*. The concluding warrant for this is grounded by "for we know the one who said" and the citation of Deut 32:35-36. In other words, at the point where it looked like the Old Testament and its understanding of God might become shadow only, the living God is not dismissed but invoked, into whose hands it is a fearful thing to fall (v. 31).

Attridge's comment on v. 30 ("we know the one who says") captures the point well:

> That the Christian proclamation brought *knowledge* of God was a commonplace, but Hebrews is not simply alluding to that knowledge which was a basic part of faith. Rather it suggests that Christians know the *character of the God who speaks in scripture* and who has acted in Christ and that an essential aspect of this God is a negative attitude toward sin.[10]

The Old Testament preserves the witness to the one with whom we have to do, to whom we have been brought near in Christ. The otherness of God for Gentile outsiders has not been erased — it has been disclosed as the holiness of God once known within Israel, now brought near in Christ. It is fully appropriate, therefore, for Christians to invoke before the moment of eucharistic unveiling what the seraphim exclaimed in Isaiah's temple vision: "Holy, Holy, Holy, Lord God of Hosts, Heaven and Earth are full of thy glory" (Isa 6:3). Is this confession made to Jesus, to the Father, or to the Holy Spirit? The rule of faith constrains us to acknowledge the holiness of God as the holiness of the son as the holiness of the Spirit, to know them as different, from different Testaments, but the same, in Christ, to whom both Testaments point.

IV

These two opening chapters have urged biblical studies to be more theological and theological studies more biblical. Otherwise the former will be prone toward historical reconstruction, then made relevant existentially; while the latter tends toward philosophical or political reflections geared to issues before the church, and their resolution, detached from serious exegetical engagement with the two-testament Christian canon.

A theological reading of Christian scripture, however, must take

---

10. *The Epistle to the Hebrews* (Hermeneia; Minneapolis: Fortress, 1989), ad loc., emphasis added.

seriously two opposing fronts. (1) The pressure from doctrinal theology to assert the unity of God, over against the persons of God, out of appropriate concern to guard against forms of modalism. God is — in Christian reflection — One. Yet the biblical presentation and exegetical reality is that God is known through his persons: Holy One of Israel, disclosed to adoptees in Christ, in and through the power of the Holy Spirit. How is the reality of the plain sense guarded, while we at the same time acknowledge the mature Christian confession of God as one? The danger with not wrestling with this question is that God's oneness may devolve into a sentimental "God revealed in Jesus," which then leads to a severance or domestication of the Old Testament within Christian confession, as truly rendering God. Yet the opposite danger is that God's character as One will become detached from the plain sense of scripture altogether and end up an abstraction not carnally related to Jesus or Israel or the church's own faith and life as that has preceded us in this place.

(2) The other front presents itself within biblical studies itself. This involves not just an emphasis on the persons of God, but their detachment from one another altogether, because of the success of the twin projects of historical contextualization and exegetical differentiation. Early patristic concern with varieties of modalism is here left fully in the shadows. We end up with the God of First Isaiah, the God of the Yahwist, the God of wisdom; Jesus of Luke and the Jesus of 1 John, Paul's Jesus; and we can track with ever greater precision the difference between these because of the energy expended in historical reconstruction. But what a far more rigorous task it is to see how these various aspects of difference in fact cohere, as the church has confessed this under a rule of faith. The interbiblical model of reading I urged in the previous chapter was but a first step aimed at exegetical reconnection of the Testaments, with obvious consequences for how we think about God.

In Hebrews we see the line being walked by which the *per se* witness to God's holiness in the Old Testament is not only affirmed, but experienced, within a new Christian framework. This occurs *precisely* in that book of Christian scripture most invested in describing the modes of God's relating, first in law to Israel, then to all humanity by the Son. Not only is the *per se* witness of the Old crucial to our understanding of the New's witness; so too our understanding of the holiness of the Son and the life he calls us to is derived by reference backward to what Israel knew of God in tent, temple, pillar of fire, and cloud. We who stood apart from the law now glimpse there, beyond the veil of our former outsiderness, the abiding theological witness of the Old Testament, a witness to the Holy God of Israel, with whom in Christ we have to do.

Let me close with a question about the professing future of Yale Divinity School. One of the intellectual virtues of this place also has its down side. We develop critical skills to such a high level that we see the implications — and problems — with our work better than others. It took outsiders to speak of a "Yale theology," and that is probably just as well. But we ought not seek incoherence when coherence is possible. Others spotted something they thought we were doing, and doing well. Whatever the problems with the Lindbeck, Frei, Childs heritage in this place, there was a shared concern for scripture and theology, and for the debates this engendered. I would prefer to stay with that legacy — to refine, correct, and redirect it — than to trade it away, like Esau. I hope and pray it will remain central to what we do, as we do it in our own day, faithful to the One who has called us here.

3

The Historical-Critical Endeavor as Theology

The Legacy of Gerhard von Rad

I

The Old Testament is one of the first subjects treated in a Christian theological curriculum. One can see the sense in this. Old comes before New, just as New comes before Theology, Church History, Ethics, and the Practical disciplines. Historically speaking, before there is Jesus, there is Israel.

This movement also captures a key existential dimension of the New Testament, not just in the Gospels but also especially in the person of Paul, "brought up at the feet of Gamaliel, educated according to the strict manner of the law" (Acts 22:3). In Jesus, as well as in Paul, the gospel confronts an Israel become Judaism, or Judaisms. The past existence of Israel is gathered up and presented in the New, in Jesus and in the Israel to whom he belongs and to whom he speaks. "Go nowhere among the Gentiles" is Matthew's extreme, but not misleading, way of underscoring this perspective (10:5). The legacy of the Old Testament — the law, the covenants, the forefathers and mothers — exists not just as a written testimony from the past, but also as a present existential reality, into which Jesus is born, out of which he makes his claims, in accordance with which others judge those claims to be valid or specious.

All Gentile confrontation with Jesus and the gospel of necessity takes place within the framework of existential realities whose point of origin is traceable to the Old Testament, or as the New Testament refers to it, "the

28

law and the prophets," "the scriptures," and "the oracles of God entrusted to the Jews" (Rom 3:2). To be sure, Jesus confronts Judaisms he considers departures or deviations from the scriptural legacy as he receives it (Matt 5:43-44), "thus making void the word of God through your tradition which you hand on" (Mark 7:13). The threat here is that the now predominantly non-Jewish Christian readership will miss this distinction and throw out the baby with the bathwater, seeing in Jesus' confrontation with "the Jews" an outsider's confrontation with the Old Testament, or with God himself, as those scriptures bear witness to him.[1]

In either case, the problem is that general human existence before God is manifested by Jesus in a context modern Christians do not bring with them to the New by way of the Old, however much they might seek to take that perspective in first. Paul is obliged, in some sense, to *theorize* about Gentiles who live apart from the law, since it is a perspective he does not share.[2] Existentially, Gentiles go to the first witness second, to the Old by way of the New, by way of God in Christ, because he is the means by which this first witness has been made available for those outside the covenants of promise and comprehensible for those inside and out (2 Cor 3:12-18; Luke 24:27). Or Gentiles go to the New by way of their own distinct categories of existence, only to find there a language and a frame of reference borrowed from a Testament virtually everybody there shares but them. Within the New Testament itself, the Canaanite woman does not pull up a chair at the table, but is fed — so strong is her faith — with food that comes by way of a feast already underway (Matt 15:21-28). When Paul tries to comprehend Gentiles without the law by recourse to a theory of conscience, he cannot help but project his own experience of accountability as derived from Torah's claim on him, or work with the perspective the Old Testament has bequeathed to him when it reflects on those before or beyond Sinai's reach.

This is not to say that Christians cannot hear the gospel, or that it cannot address the existential situation of non-Jews. Paul the Jew "educated according to the strict manner of the law" is the first to repudiate any notion of Gentiles coming to Christ through Judaism (Acts 15:1-21). But what this means for Old Testament studies is that Christians must con-

---

1. See the discussion above.

2. There is of course a history of such theorizing, in which Paul stands, that takes its point of departure from the Old Testament's own account of general human existence (e.g., Genesis 1–11) and divine activity with "the nations" (e.g., Jonah, Amos 1–2).

stantly labor over how then this testimony has indeed become a witness to non-Jews, arriving there as latecomers, as outsiders, who are at the same time not to become Israelites through an effort of imagination or Jews by actual incorporation. Yet the church has confessed this testimony to be indispensable and abiding, with which the death and resurrection of Jesus is in full accordance.

II

Historical-critical method is the most recent effort to retrieve the indispensable character of the Old Testament. It did this by seeking to plot the movement through history of Israel's reflection on God. That is almost a direct quote of Gerhard von Rad's stated purpose in his now dated, but — it gives one pause — unreplaced *magnum opus, Old Testament Theology* (in English, 1962).[3] "The subject-matter which concerns the theologian is, of course, not the spiritual and religious world of Israel . . . nor is it her world of faith . . . instead it is simply Israel's own explicit assertions about Jahweh" (I, 105). What von Rad and others like him wanted was to disassemble the literature as it was presented, not for its own sake, nor just because one could be trained to spot literary unevenness and historical disjunction in a text (here I disagree with John Barton's learned presentation).[4] Rather, the goal was to retrieve or lay bare its theology, which for von Rad and those of his day involved "the intention that the specific narrators had in mind" (106, n. 1). However much von Rad and others like him wanted to remain objective and hold their Christian point of standing at as much distance as was possible — and von Rad was brilliant in seeing how difficult and potentially artificial this was — he nevertheless wanted to get at the Old Testament first, not second. He wanted to see how Israel thought about God, to maximize the distinction recognized in the New Testament — by Jesus and by Paul — between Israel and Judaism, in order to come to the New afresh and

3. Gerhard von Rad, *Old Testament Theology* I (New York: Harper and Row, 1962).
4. *Reading the Old Testament: Method in Biblical Study* (Philadelphia: Westminster, 1984). Barton does a masterful job of analyzing literary method and describing its distinctive history within modern biblical studies, but fails, in my view, to assess adequately the theological concerns that lay behind the literary developments.

catch its force from the perspective of the Old. Yet in my judgment, however sensitively intended and even more brilliantly executed, this move by von Rad and others far less skilled was flawed in fundamental ways. In seizing on him to make this point, I trust I have chosen one of the best practitioners of historical criticism with a distinctly theological purpose. Still, I take the failure of his *Old Testament Theology* to be replaced, along similar historical-critical lines, as telling in a negative rather than a positive sense.

There was a far simpler way of dealing with the Old Testament, and von Rad's achievement, as well as that of the historical-critical method, should be seen over against this, namely, the simple detachment of the Old Testament from the New, or from the gospel, as an ongoing theological witness for Christians. Bultmann had his own very sophisticated version of this, and, like Marcion's before him, it cut with reductive force at the New Testament as well. This was due to his highly existential understanding of history as a medium of God's revelation. Such an understanding freed him to comment, with stunning force, that Socrates drinking the hemlock was as much a part of salvation history as God's deliverance of Israel from bondage in Egypt, seen from the standpoint of God's eschatological deed in Christ.[5] The inverse instinct to that of Bultmann can be seen in some recent efforts to honor the Old Testament — the term "Hebrew Scriptures" is preferred — by respecting it as "someone else's mail" (the phrase is Paul van Buren's).[6] The danger in this case is in conflating modern Judaism and Israel, in the wake of the Holocaust, and cutting away the ground that legitimately links Old and New as theological witnesses to God in Christ. Still, the failure of either of these approaches to appreciate the abiding theological witness *per se* of the Old Testament,

5. "The exodus from Egypt, the giving of the Law at Sinai, the building of Solomon's Temple, the work of the prophets, all redound to our benefit in so far as these are historical episodes which form a part of our Occidental history. In the same sense, however, it can be said that the Spartans fell at Thermopylae for us and that Socrates drank the hemlock for us" (31) — Rudolph Bultmann, "The Significance of the Old Testament for Christian Faith," in *The Old Testament and Christian Faith: A Theological Discussion,* ed. B. W. Anderson (New York: Harper and Row, 1963) 8-35. The heavy emphasis on human existence *(Daseinverständnis)* as a starting point means that whatever is particular in God's dealings with Israel must be coordinated into a universal experience, in the light of God's "eschatological deed" in Christ.

6. "On Reading Someone Else's Mail: The Church and Israel's Scriptures," in *Die Hebräische Bibel und ihre zweifache Nachgeschichte* (FS Rolf Rendtorff; Neukirchen-Vluyn: Neukirchener, 1990) 595-606.

addressed to Christian faith, sends us back to the theological agenda of historical criticism as typically practiced.

What did it, or does it, mean to speak of the theology of the Old Testament as consisting of Israel's reflection on God? First of all, it meant an extraction from the literary witness of the Old Testament of Israel herself and her reassignment to the realm of time and space. To say this is to realize at once that, strange as it may seem, the Old Testament does not present itself as Israel's reflection on God in some straightforward sense — else there would be no project called historical criticism, whose governing preoccupation is with retrieving and reconstructing "Israel." This is accomplished through highly sophisticated methods aimed at seeing the literature refracted through authors, editors, a long tradition history amid social and religious changes and chances, en route — though the way may seem obscure — to the New Testament and its authors, editors, tradition, social and religious history, in a Greco-Roman rather than ancient Near Eastern setting. What appeared to be a simple point of departure — "Israel's own explicit assertions about Jahweh" — turned out to involve fundamental matters of a historical nature, requiring a complex extraction from the literature of a point of view, "Israel's," to be ranged on a grid of evolving tradition history. That one could in time dispute the notion of authorial intention altogether meant that these two matters — author and intention — had been raised above the narrative itself as necessary for making sense of what was said by "Israel" at various points in time and from various points of view. The resulting concern for discrete and distinct intentions meant that over the course of time these intentions would take precedence over intertextuality or literary and theological coherence in a final, uneclipsed narrative form. Von Rad was concerned with setting his theological approach over against a history-of-religions agenda, or a "faith of Israel" approach. Yet in so doing he bypassed another possibility: that of taking seriously the literature's final form as itself a "theological assertion." More on this in the final section below.

It should be noted in passing that the very complexity of the project is what has given it such a long run. Even the onslaught of deconstruction, or concern with matters in front of the text instead of behind it, have not succeeded in terminating historical-critical reconstructions for theological or even antitheological purposes (e.g., "the Bible without theology"). Entire careers have been spent doing nothing but dating the Yahwist and refining and further refining our look at this author, whose reflections on God were the source of one of von Rad's most pentrating theological treatments.[7] That "the Yahwist" is now dated by some quite late in a tradition-historical evolution, rather than as von Rad preferred, in the late tribal period, leaves unaffected the basic notion that Christian interpreters could and should get to Israel and her thoughts about God first, at some point, either late or early in the tradition history, before that same history brought us into the New Testament itself, following a brief trek through the so-called intertestamental period, including now the Dead Sea literature.

As mentioned above, von Rad was fully aware that a quest for Israel utterly devoid of Christian presuppositions was naive. In fact one can see in his concern with typology as the means by which Israel's traditions will come to their final antitype resting place, in New Testament confession, a hint that von Rad had wanted both to eat and to have his cake at the same time. That is, "Israel's own explicit assertions about Jahweh" would need to be shown as leaning toward the New Testament's explicit assertions about Christ, or else von Rad's rejection of an indigenous history-of-religions investigation would extend to his own "theological" approach. Moreover, if isolating Israel first led so inexorably, if complicatedly, into the second witness's center, why was this self-evidence not more decisive in New Testament confession itself and in the encounters between Jesus and the Jews depicted therein? These are life-and-death debates, with more than superficial appeal to scripture being made on both sides. Critics early on saw the potential for a certain circularity in von Rad's otherwise brilliant effort at releasing the Old Testament's *per se* theological potential for serious Christian reflection.

But this is not the end of the story. If the theological point of von Rad's historical approach was viewed as flawed, concern with further historical reconstruction has nevertheless continued undiminished, as if now no longer bothered by the problem of theological integration or justification in the first place. For many, the critical, analytical work proceeds as if on autopilot, with a theological purpose that is unstated, unclear, or indeed repudiated — especially for a Christian biblical theology toward which the claims of the New Testament are likewise to be coordinated. The Jewish scholar Jon Levenson is one of the more recent to

---

7. "The Form-Critical Problem of the Hexateuch," in *The Problem of the Hexateuch and Other Essays* (Edinburgh and London: Oliver and Boyd, 1966). The original German essay appeared in 1938.

document this turn of events, in his own forceful way.[8] Christian substitution of a history of Israelite religion for a biblical theology of the sort practiced by von Rad has sidestepped rather than resolved the theological problem, especially for a two-Testament Christian theology. How a description of Israel's religious life even indirectly informs constructive Christian theology is by no means clear, and here the cautions of Bultmann seem well placed.[9] Not only are Israel's cult, priesthood, temple rounds, law, and ritual remote from a Christianity that regards these as transfigured in Christ in the church's own present liturgical life, for most modern Jews that religious history is equally remote and now functions prescriptively through some subsequent refracting lens.

III

Von Rad's sustained effort at locating his Old Testament theological approach within the context of the Christian canon can be found in the latter sections of *Old Testament Theology* (volume II) and in an essay entitled "Typological Interpretation of the Old Testament."[10] I will conclude this brief look at historical criticism as a theological endeavor by examining this important essay, and I hope in so doing to suggest an alternative approach.

As many have noted, von Rad is at pains in the first part of this essay to resuscitate "typology" from any possible confusion with "allegory" so that the former can be of use to a historical approach. This requires getting "typology," as he means it, to pass muster before Troeltsch's "almighty

8. "Historical Criticism and the Fate of the Enlightenment Project," in *The Hebrew Bible, the Old Testament, and Historical Criticism* (Louisville: Westminster/John Knox, 1993) 106-26. At one point he asks, "Will there be an 'Old Testament' or a 'Tanakh'? If the former, then why, if christological claims are not credited?" (125).

9. ". . . the relation of New Testament religion to Old Testament religion is not theologically relevant at all. It raises the question from the outside by viewing the two — Old Testament and New Testament religion — as historical phenomena and by determining their relationship from a higher vantage point" ("The Significance of the Old Testament," 12).

10. The article first appeared in *Evangelische Theologie* 12 (1952) and was translated by John Bright in *Essays on Old Testament Hermeneutics,* ed. C. Westermann (Atlanta: John Knox, 1963) 17-39.

analogy," by which all serious historical work was to take its bearings and theological justification.[11] Understood in this way, "theology" would entail drawing an existential or imaginative analogy between a moment critically reconstructed in the past — in von Rad's system, Israel's assertions about or experience of Yahweh — and the present moment of Christian faith and practice.[12] To bridge the chasm separating past and present in the case of the Old Testament as Christian scripture, however, would require a particularly deft exercise of Troeltsch's "almighty analogy." This is due to the fact that both radical discontinuity and radical continuity span the two Testaments from which Christian theology is constructed, and no "analogy," however mighty, can sidestep this or *come to terms with it from the perspective of historical criticism alone.* The New Testament's own plain-sense presentation of "fulfillment" and the rupture between Christianity and Judaism mean each in their own way that the past recorded in the Old Testament/Tanak will be analogized quite differently depending on subsequent literatures, histories, identities, and governing purposes. And yet the problem is not one that has been introduced *ab extra.* Its roots lie legitimately within the plain sense of the Old Testament's own witness. When this witness is brought into conjunction with a subsequent testimony or privileged interpreter (Matt 5:1–7:29; Luke 24:27) or ongoing religious existence, the problem is seen for what it is.

Von Rad believed, based upon his historical retrieval of Israel and her assertions about Yahweh, that this history and these assertions mean what they mean in their day, as historical criticism lays them bare. But it was his theological conviction, allegedly based upon that same historical work, that "the narrators are so captivated by the *doxa* of the event that once happened, they see and point out in the event the splendor of the divine gift in so exclusive a way, that they thereby *manifestly misdraw the historical picture.*"[13] He then shifts from the terminology of "narrator" —

---

11. "Historical method, once . . . applied to biblical study, is a leaven that transforms everything, and finally shatters the whole framework of theological method as this has existed hitherto" (quoted in von Rad's essay, p. 23). Whether one judges this a good thing is another matter, of course.

12. Troeltsch's own words are, "This almightiness of analogy, however, includes in principle the similarity of all historical events, which is, to be sure, not likeness . . . but presupposes in each instance a kernel of common similarity by virtue of which even the differences can be sympathetically grasped" (23-24). Compare the cautions of Bultmann, on the one side, and those of B. S. Childs, on another front (chapter 9 below).

13. "Typological Interpretation," 34 (emphasis added).

"since it is something that for the most part took place on a much broader basis" (34) — and adopts the term "tradition" (which he puts in scare-quotes). He concludes, "the 'tradition' is so zealous for God that the event is straightway broadened into the typical. It is precisely sober exegesis that must come across things of this sort and make the effort to understand what has taken place" (34).

Von Rad illustrates what he means by showing how the portrayal of the judges, or Israel's occupation, involves a more modest or "historical" reporting, which must in turn give rise to something larger and more unitary, as expressive of what God was up to. "Clearly a *credendum* has here been projected into history" (34). He concludes, therefore, that "interpretation must concern itself, perhaps more than heretofore, with what is intended by that later portrayal" (34).

My question is whether the shift from "narrator" to "tradition" is really an accurate statement of what von Rad had in mind as he struggled to come to terms with the way earlier traditions bore the marks of subsequent shaping. It was his training as a literary and historical critic that gave him the eye necessary to comprehend the depth dimension in texts; it was in turn his theological sensitivity that propelled him to take into account, theologically, what was going on as one earlier narrator's view matured into something else, in "later portrayal." Von Rad used the term "tradition" intentionally, I believe, in order to preserve the belief, grounded in historical criticism, that what was going on theologically within Israel's assertions about God could be isolated and described as simply some stage or two out beyond what one had sought by way of an "individual narrator." That is, such an inquiry into "tradition" was not different in kind, even as much as one needed to talk about "sober exegesis" when referring to it.

Von Rad's effort to keep the "later portrayal" he spotted within the realm of "tradition" entailed, in my judgment, a twofold concern. On the one hand, it meant that subsequent shaping was of the same essential character — however soberly one needed to approach it! — as what had happened in earlier stages, in Israel's assertions about God. By saying that one needed to take this subsequent shaping more seriously, he was indicating the degree to which historical criticism had previously not done this, and so in this sense what von Rad was proposing was quite radical. This is most clear when the degree of distortion he was prepared to spot was not viewed as at odds with the original historical task, for which an "almighty analogy" had stood ready at hand. But how does an "almighty analogy" properly cope with a historical picture "manifestly misdrawn" by later, theologically motivated "tradition"? I point out the problem of consistency not to chide von Rad so much as to reveal the extent to which his theological and literary sophistication was pushing him away from his own starting premises. In sum, the term "tradition" was used to keep the theological portrayal fluid and as consistent with the original goal of reconstructing "narrators" as possible — *even when that consistency was missing at the level of the basic content of what was being handed on.*

The second concern involved von Rad's hope that a true process — even with moments of discontinuity — could be exposed that linked the two testaments and their separate attestations about God. Employment of the term "tradition" could hold out hope that some stream of reflection surely if selectively was making its way from the Old Testament forward into the New. This would mean that Christian reading of the Old Testament was not a backward-looking matter only, undertaken by outsiders, but one that had a legitimate forward movement that would in time come to embrace Jesus Christ and the church that lives by his spirit.

This would explain why von Rad suddenly shifts his forward-moving discussion of "narration become tradition" to ask quite pointedly: "What part have I in the Old Testament as a Christian believer, and what part has the church, *if it cannot be that I identify myself, at least partly (it was never a question of more than that!) with the religion of ancient Israel?*"[14] He then notes, that for all his historical-critical labors at identifying with Israel's recital, he nevertheless stands outside: "God's gracious provisions, so lavishly bestowed on Israel, seem to pass me by, because I do not belong to the historical people Israel" (35). He worries that if a general religious connection is severed, however, even one that is wrong, "a great unease will once more make itself felt in many of our congregations" (36).

Here one must ask whether von Rad's own heartfelt posing of the problem was far more compelling than the typological solution he was able finally to provide. This may be not because the solution was wrong, but because it exposed how difficult it was to move from his historical-critical starting point, theologically considered, toward a typological reading capable of doing justice to the theology of Christian scripture as a whole. That is, the problem may not have been the typological retrospective with which he concludes, but whether that perspective was amenable to connection with the reconstruction of "Israel's own explicit assertions

14. Emphasis added. The parenthetical remark is quite pregnant. Is minimal participation being set over against something greater, or nothing at all?

about Jahweh" and the subsequent tradition-historical recasting of those assertions that he was at pains to describe with the tools of historical criticism.

Here it is necessary to establish that a true alternative existed to von Rad's otherwise accurate judgment regarding the character of "later portrayal" in developing biblical presentation. I have critiqued his adoption of the term "tradition" in order to describe how an individual narrator's perspective had been recast, for theological purposes, in later portrayal. What von Rad was trying to keep alive was some sense of identification of the theological intention of later editors, different only temporally and not materially, with earlier intentions. To keep this perspective alive meant that some forward-moving stream could be plotted with which Christian readers could identify, partially — "it was never a question of more than that." Yet for all that, at the end von Rad sensed some fundamental alienation, even from the highly theological reading of Israel's tradition history he had himself achieved.

A close reading of von Rad's final paragraphs reveals, I believe, an approach to the Old Testament fundamentally different from, if not opposed to, his own tradition-historical description *theologically grounded and defended.* While one could talk about forward-moving streams of tradition and describe them with historical tools, they suddenly flowed into a sort of oblivion. "Typological interpretation will thus in a fundamental way leave the historical self-understanding of the Old Testament texts behind, and go beyond it. It sees in the Old Testament facts something in preparation, something sketching itself out, *of which the Old Testament witness is not itself aware, because it lies quite beyond its purview*" (36, emphasis added). Now one could well have seen the seeds of this sort of understanding in von Rad's remarks concerning the fundamental disjunction between narrator and tradition, whereby the latter can "manifestly misdraw" what the former bequeathed. But surely this represents a kind of *via negativa* for tradition-historical understandings of the theological witness of the Old Testament, undertaken with an eye to coordination with subsequent New Testament proclamation.

My point here is to question whether there can be anything like a forward-moving tradition history, reconstructed by Christian interpreters on theological grounds, that self-consciously makes its way to the New Testament. The question centers on the very notion of "tradition history," as a theologically relevant redescription, capable of historical-critical and literary-critical isolation from the final form of the literature itself. Once von Rad finished his task of redescription, he was uncertain as to the theological relevance of what he had done, because of his fundamental isolation from Israel — an isolation that could not and cannot be overcome by an effort of theological imagination, however objectively and soberly undertaken. His intention and the intention of the "latest portrayal" were at perceptible odds. To hear then of a typological connection that knows itself to be unanticipated by the tradition-historical process, set alongside a "warning against a sharp separation of typological interpretation from the historical-critical exegetical process," sounds problematic. And if the point of sketching the tradition-historical process is to show its capacity for ingenious "misdrawing," then an explanation for the disjunction between typological reading and historical-critical exegesis is inadvertently discovered that should render illegitimate one or the other, or at least their ability to be conjoined in a positive theological sense.

An alternative would be to eschew any recovery of the "tradition history" lying behind the present form of the text. Instead, the "later portrayal" deemed by von Rad as relevant, over against earlier intentions, would be nothing more than the canonical shaping of individual biblical books and collections. The explicit assertions these books and collections make — about God and about Israel and about creation as a whole — would be the starting point for theological reflection from the standpoint of the wider Christian canon.[15] There would be a *prima facie* acknowledgment of alienation from the literature, at one key level, when read by outsiders brought near to God in Christ, and no effort to recover some forward trajectory — *historically reconstructed* — leading to the New Testament, apart from that *second* witness's own plain-sense claims to be the fulfillment of something spoken *earlier* to God's elect people Israel.

On the basis of the witness of the Second Testament, one could well read Israel's scriptures and see there "types of Christ." But ironically, when one uses a historical approach to get at the theological intentions of narrators, these types actually recede rather than come into prominence. Justin claimed that he was converted to Christianity solely on the basis of the Old Testament's predictive and typological character; but he was working backward as well as forward, already convicted by the truth claims of the gospel, and of course knew nothing of the sort of tradition-historical reading undertaken for theological purposes von Rad had in mind. There was, in short, no effort to read the Hebrew scriptures "first" except as a

15. See the chapters in the section on Exegesis below.

Testament seen to be both "Old" and true from the standpoint of a New Covenant and the work of God in Christ.[16]

The point of tradition history was to expose an existential dimension through highly sophisticated literary and historical tools. Yet that existence will remain remote or ethnic only unless the claims of Christ to be interpreter are acknowledged as indispensable to any Christian reading, and in fact the only true point of access, as von Rad in his own way concluded. On this score, much of what he had to say in closing about a typological approach was very illuminating. It was, however, unclear that he was actually building on what he had done tradition-historically, rather than simply trying to find his way backward with an altogether different torch than the one that had previously lighted his way.[17]

16. See the remarks of von Campenhausen on Justin (*The Formation of the Christian Bible* [Philadelphia: Fortress, 1972] 89ff.) and the especially fine analysis of T. F. Torrance in *Divine Meaning: Studies in Patristic Hermeneutics* (Edinburgh: Clark, 1995) 53-57, 94-101.

17. See now Francis Watson's contribution to this discussion in *Text and Truth: Redefining Biblical Theology* (Grand Rapids: Eerdmans, 1997).

4

"And without God in the World"

A Hermeneutic of Estrangement Overcome

This essay assumes that the terms presently employed in the field — hermeneutics of suspicion or assent — are based in part on the discussion by Stuhlmacher and those with whom he is in critical dialogue.[1] The topic will be addressed first by examination of a popular, modern treatment of the authority of scripture.[2] A criticism of this treatment and a contrasting view will be offered, based upon a very brief look at the use of the Old Testament in the early church. The highly theological way the early church understood its position over against the scriptures it inherited from Israel is seen to offer a clue as to how we might move beyond the positions of assent or suspicion today.

I

For the past two centuries, mainstream Old and New Testament scholarship has grounded its interpretive strategies in historical events, social and reli-

1. The former appears more frequently than the latter in scholarly usage. See, though, Peter Stuhlmacher's use of the term "the hermeneutics of consent" in *Historical Criticism and Theological Interpretation of Scripture: Toward a Hermeneutics of Consent,* tr. Roy Harrisville (Philadelphia: Fortress, 1977).

2. Edward Farley and Peter C. Hodgson, "Scripture and Tradition," in *Christian Theology* (Philadelphia: Fortress, 1985) 68.

gious description, authorial intention, or, more typically, in some combination of these. Recently, deconstruction has challenged the objectivism implicit in all three, though calls for a return to "precritical" hermeneutics remain rare. Instead, one is faced with a choice between a hermeneutics of suspicion or assent. This paper questions whether both are based on a notion of the "autonomous self" — here faced with a choice between one reader stance or another — that has in its own way been exposed by deconstruction.

This essay attempts to go beyond a hermeneutics of assent or suspicion by demonstrating that what has been achieved by God in Christ grounds theologically the relationship of Christians to the literature of the Old Testament, and by extension, the New. The New Testament texts that are important for our wider discussion are Ephesians 2:11-22 and Romans 3:1-20. In these, general hermeneutical theory — even grounded theologically in the manner of Stuhlmacher — must encounter the specific claims of election and estrangement, for Jew and Gentile respectively, and their reconfiguration in Christ. It is these claims that constitute the lens through which Christians comprehend their point of standing in respect of the Old and New Testaments.

Following on this perspective, the significance of atonement as a central Christian confession, for example, would involve two different aspects. First, not just as reconciling the godless to God, but also as tearing down the wall of division between Israel and the nations. To Israel has been entrusted the oracles of God (Rom 3:2). In Christ, those "without God in the world" (Eph 2:12) gain access to the life of Israel and the record of God's revelation of himself to the world through them. This, too, constitutes a benefit of Christ's atonement. For if by that is meant the reconciling of strangers to God, it is Israel's scriptures that reveal who that God is, now *for us Gentiles in Christ* and no longer far off or fundamentally estranged.

In order to place the New Testament's statements in a fresh context, I want first to widen the lens and examine several early patristic texts. Here the status of the Old Testament can be helpfully isolated through observing its use as the only true "scripture" of early Christianity. The argument advanced here is that this early use of Israel's scriptures by the church is eventually transferred to the wider canon of Christian scripture, including now a New Testament alongside that original single scripture. My larger point will remain the one just mentioned, namely, that Christian readers did not choose to assent or dissent from a scripture that preceded their existence. Rather, scripture was the means by which the only identity the church had, in Christ, came to form. The word once spoken to Israel would now address the church, displaying a host of figures by which the church would understand and configure its new life in Christ, through the power of the Holy Spirit. Scripture was not being chosen or rejected — it was choosing and creating and addressing and establishing its readership, in the estimate of those newly adopted in Christ. "I could cite many other prophecies too," Justin concludes, "but pause, thinking that these are sufficient to convince those who have ears to think and understand." Whatever else one makes of this remark, it is clear that a hermeneutics of assent or suspicion lie at a considerable remove. The fundamental question of the early church is not whether scripture will be heard or not, assented to or dissented from, but just who is being addressed by it.

II

It has been argued that an important difference exists between the status and function of scripture within Israel and Judaism, as against what evolved in the church. This is due, it is claimed, to the "person-event Jesus of Nazareth . . . the new focus of divine-human identity which *cannot be extended to any written representation, either primary or secondary*."[3] This view is grounded historically by appeal to the "first century and a half" of early Christianity, which, on the one hand, "inherited the Jewish scriptures and soon produced a collection of writings of its own," yet "did not necessarily have to adopt the scripture principle" (67). Such a "principle," it is argued, emerged for functional reasons within Israel, namely, "as a solution to a major crisis in Israel's history, the dispersion of the Jewish people following the Babylonian exile" (63).

This description of matters is problematic at several points. First, the authority accorded the written word in Israel was preceded by the authority of the spoken word, and the line separating these two is extraordinarily difficult to trace out. Secondly, the authority of the spoken word included its ongoing history as "a word accomplishing that which God purposes" (Isa 55:11), which "overtakes" the generations it once addressed to speak an

---

3. Farley and Hodgson, 68 (emphasis added). The collocations "person-event" and "divine-human identity" are, to be sure, the sort of dense abstractions that might well be difficult to represent literally. But there is the problem.

abiding word to later generations (Zech 1:6). The crisis of the exile may well have sharpened the sense of an authoritative and abiding word, but it did not create this. Whatever distinction existed between the written and spoken word in Israel is not capable of extension in the form of a contrast between the "divine-human" person over against a "scripture principle," said now to characterize the Christian community over against Judaism.

There is, moreover, scant evidence that the first century and a half of Christianity was in fact marked by a root tension between belief in the person of Jesus Christ (the "person-event Jesus of Nazareth") over against appeal to God's word written. If anything, as von Campenhausen has shown,[4] these early years were ones of particularly intense concern with scripture — not with a "New Testament," which was in a state of evolution, but with the only scriptures that existed, inherited from Judaism.

> An understanding of what it meant that Jesus was Messiah or Son of Man or the present and future Lord . . . could be arrived at only in the context of earlier prophetic and apocalyptic hopes, through the ever valid testimony of "the scripture." In the Christian faith from the very first both elements, Jesus and the Scripture, were mutually and inseparably related (21).

Functionalism would misrepresent the crucial issue, which was theological in the most basic sense: the sheer pressure of God's word, spoken once to Israel, in accordance with which the identity of Jesus had to be correlated. "From now on the ancient Scriptures are related to Christ, and it is on the basis of Scripture that Jesus Christ is understood as Lord" (1).

The sharp polarity between "person" and "scripture" is further problematic from the standpoint of emerging trinitarian convictions, themselves rooted in scripture. Jesus Christ is confessed to be in the closest possible relationship to the Holy One of Israel, revealed in Israel's scriptures. Rather than establishing a distinction between the risen Lord and the scriptures of Israel, faith in Jesus and in the God of Israel would demand that they be associated, and the New Testament is about demonstrating this association. "These things are written that you may come to believe" — not in a "person-event Jesus of Nazareth" — but "that Jesus is the Messiah, the Son of God" (John 20:31). "Messiah" and "God" gain

---

4. Hans von Campenhausen, *The Formation of the Christian Bible* (Philadelphia: Fortress, 1972).

the only content they have because of a "scripture principle" that the New Testament *never even defends,* because it is everywhere presupposed.

The larger point is that the Christian community is not related to a "person-event Jesus of Nazareth" apart from the claims of the triune God. This God is known in Israel's scriptures and in the second witness, the New Testament, whose purpose is to relate Jesus and his heavenly Father and the Holy Spirit as distinctively and as intimately as possible. This constitutes the gospel at its most basic expression, and it is this that the church lives by. The gospel not only *can* be extended to a written representation, it has no other possible point of origin or stable, abiding location.[5]

A collateral testimony to the strong "scripture principle" at work in the first century and a half of early Christianity can be seen in the primary sources themselves. Von Campenhausen introduces his treatment of the use of scripture by the *Epistle of Barnabas,* Clement, Ignatius, and Justin with a series of important statements, quoted here selectively.

> Christ is certainly vindicated to unbelievers out of the Scripture; but the converse necessity, to justify the Scriptures on the authority of Christ, is as yet nowhere even envisaged (64).

> . . . the concept of holy Scripture as a totality invested with authority is nevertheless already established. This is another point where there is no distinction between Jews and Christians (65).

The use of scripture in Clement and Justin is breathtaking in scope and variety.[6] Again and again Clement exhorts the community by means of explicit appeal to scripture. Nowhere is an alleged cleavage between the living

---

5. See Francis Watson, *Text and Truth: Redefining Biblical Theology* (Grand Rapids: Eerdmans, 1997) 1-2.

6. Wrede spotted more than seventy genuine quotations and at least twenty further allusions to the Old Testament in *1 Clement* (*Untersuchungen zum Ersten Klemensbriefe* [Göttingen, 1891]). His own comment on the function of scripture is worth citing (translated in von Campenhausen, *Formation,* 64, n. 9):

> Historically it would be a wholly unsatisfactory description of the case to say that the O.T. was *still* valid — either in whole or in part — for Christians, as though recognition of its validity had been a matter calling for some thought instead of what was the truth of the situation, namely that the possession of this miraculous and infallible book was in Christian eyes an advantage of the new religion which proved one of its greatest sources of enlightenment and strongest recommendation.

Christ and scripture shown to be more false than at *1 Clement* 22:1-2, where portions of Psalms 34 and 32 are cited with the words, "for this is how Christ addresses us through his Holy Spirit."[7] Clement's own argument, he asserts, is grounded in the Old Testament's own plain sense of itself:

> You have studied the Holy Scripture, which contains the truth and is inspired by the Holy Spirit. You realize there is nothing wrong or misleading written in it (45:2).

> You know the Holy Scriptures, dear friends — you know them well — and you have studied God's oracles. It is to remind you of them that we write the way we do (53:1).

For Justin, the surest demonstration of Christianity's truth lies in its congruence with what was spoken long ago in Israel's scriptures. Perhaps it might be argued that Jesus was a mere mortal and did mighty deeds as a magician. Justin counters charges such as these not even by appeal to the resurrection, or some other divine intervention attested in or by Christ, but by the record of scripture. It is as though the words of Luke 16:31 stood close at hand: "If they do not listen to Moses and the prophets, neither will they be convinced if someone should rise from the dead."

> We do not trust in mere hearsay, but are forced to believe those who prophesied [these things] before they happened, because we actually see things that have happened and are happening as was predicted. This will, as we think, be the greatest and surest demonstration for you too (*First Apology* 30).[8]

III

Up to this point we have displayed in the most general terms the role Israel's scriptures played in the early church, prior to the formation of a

---

7. *Early Christian Fathers,* ed. Cyril Richardson (New York: Macmillan, 1976) 54. English translations included here are from Richardson's volume.

8. The quotations from Clement and Justin follow the translation in C. C. Richardson, *Early Christian Fathers* (Philadelphia: Westminster, 1953).

collateral scriptural witness, the New Testament. This has enabled us to glimpse how the scriptures of Israel were being put to use within early Christianity. With the possibility of a second literary witness becoming a rival or replacement for the first still on the horizon, we can glimpse something of the way that the early church inherited a scripture belonging to the synagogue and used it both to "prove Christ" and guide the church's present life under the Holy Spirit.

An exclusively theological justification for the transfer of Israel's scriptures to the church was a volatile one, viewed with hindsight. In fact, it was *precisely* the theological character of the justification that made it so volatile, with an authority the New Testament sought to trace back to the person of Jesus himself (Luke 24:27). The point at issue is not to assess this volatile situation, but to make note of the particular starting point for the church's understanding of the way a written testimony, "scripture," would function in its ongoing life. Christianity did not invent a new mode of revelation and instruction. It inherited one and then adapted it according to its own theological convictions.

The most radical assertion of continuity can be found in *Barnabas*, the author of which sought to "wrest the Bible absolutely from the Jews, and to stamp it from the very first word as exclusively a Christian book."[9] What the position of *Barnabas* helps clarify is the degree to which Christianity knew nothing of a choice between "assent" or "suspicion" in respect to a scripture they had every right to sit loose to, in view of the dramatic work of God in Christ. Rather, the prior and more critical concern was how to hear a word everywhere acknowledged as God's own in the light of Christ and in ongoing address to the church. The choice was not assent or suspicion, but rather ongoing, fundamental estrangement or adoption into God's ways and word.

Once the church did establish a second literary witness alongside the scriptures it had inherited from Israel, the threat opened up that these two testaments would be seen as rivals or that the second would be used to correct, refine, or even reject the first altogether. A thesis suggests itself here. *It is the actual presence of two literary witnesses that has created the possibility of assent or suspicion as distinct reading stances in the Christian community.* Whatever critical principles might have been invoked in the reading of the Old Testament alone, by Jews or Christians, these have become far more highlighted, with far greater implications for the reading

9. Von Campenhausen, *Formation*, 70.

of Old and New, because of the emergence of a second literary testimony. Whenever the independence of the second is wrongly asserted, one is forced to defend on theological or more general existential grounds the preference of assent over suspicion, when the very terms themselves reflect the problem at hand. Both imply that a move external to the text unlocks the text's true potential to be the word of God. The argument of this chapter is that this gives away too much and ignores basic characteristics of the word of God revealed in Israel's scriptures, which the church takes over when it becomes, in Christ, related to these scriptures. Only then, by extension, are these same characteristics related to the New Testament as scripture.

Fortunately, it is the witness of the second testament that provides the best warrant against a *prima facie* critical posture, *made in the name of that second witness itself.* The New Testament contains continual reminders that God's adoption of outsiders into the household of Israel does not begin with the obligation to place their privileged scriptural witness under critical scrutiny, amounting to either suspicion or assent. In Ephesians 2:11-22 Paul reminds those without citizenship in Israel of the deepest estrangement possible — not just from the covenants of promise, but from hope and from God as such. To introduce terms like "suspicion" or "assent" as basic, entry-level, stances toward the Old or New Testament is to misconstrue the means by which we have any right to read or commune with God in the first instance. It is to shift the critical eye away from God as the One who has chosen some and adopted others, toward the bestowal on those newly ingrafted of the capacity to choose and discriminate about God and about those texts capable of letting God speak, as a sort of first-order, mandated, hermeneutical license.

Such a perspective does not rule out the need for hearing scripture theologically and making proper judgments about how texts are to be related to one another within a two-testament Christian canon. That has always been the case. But it does not seem to me that either a hermeneutics of assent or a hermeneutics of suspicion has come to sufficient terms with what the obligations of election or adoption entail. In Romans 3, Paul poses a rhetorical question about what the advantage of the Jew is. He answers rhetorically, "much in every way" — and then appears to give one example only: "they were entrusted with the oracles of God" (3:2). The *New Oxford Annotated Bible* glosses "oracles of God" with "i.e. the Scriptures, and particularly the promises they contain." This is because as the argument unfolds, Paul shifts the focus to a record of past unfaithfulness and its incapacity to nullify the faithfulness of God. Now the transition from being entrusted with God's oracles *as scripture,* to being faithful or unfaithful to God's oracles *as promises delivered in the past,* does seem on the face of it a bit rough. And yet the very roughness may expose the point.

To be entrusted with God's oracles in the form of scripture means more than being able to produce a library card. It is, in the most basic sense, to have a living relationship with God, to which reference can be made in the past and from which others — *by the very nature of the terms of relationship* — are excluded. Yet *within* this relationship and because of it, scripture stands ready to make a point in the present, to those formerly elected and those newly entrusted. This Paul does at Romans 3:4 and 3:10-18, where a variety of texts from the Psalms and Isaiah are cited as evidence of basic human unrighteousness. Because the words spoken from scripture are God's own oracles, in just this manner they show him *to be God,* fully "justified in his words" (3:4). In other words, to be entrusted with a scriptural legacy is to hear a word outside oneself as the only word capable of justifying and to know that word to be the very word of God. It is difficult to imagine a more theological grounding of scripture's authority. Basic to scripture's very existence is its attachment to a people God has addressed in a privileged way, for whom the choice between assent or suspicion is altogether to the side.

To be built upon the foundation of the prophets and apostles, brought into the household of God, is to stand in a similar, though derivative, relationship to scripture as the Israel-become-Judaism addressed by Paul in Romans 3. We do not justify ourselves before God's word, because God's word justifies God alone. It is the record of scripture, into which outsiders have been written, that shows that there is no ground on which human beings can take their stand before God's word. To be entrusted with God's oracles is to be shown a record in which the only thing that stands sure is God's grace, which of its very nature excludes individual human capacity for judging where and when that grace or that word can be heard, in assent or suspicion. Establishing the proper relationship in and among different texts, in Christ, through the Holy Spirit, remains the task of the Christian interpreter. But for this neither assent nor suspicion are relevant starting points, but rather "a hermeneutic of estrangement overcome," by which the oracles of God entrusted to the Jews, constituting God's promises and God's word, are transferred in Christ to the church, witnessed to in the Old and New Testaments of Christian scripture.

49

In sum, while I have great sympathy for Stuhlmacher's commending a "hermeneutic of assent" *(Einverständnis),* this will remain on too fragile a footing, even one grounded in deep Würtemburg piety, unless it penetrates to the mystery of Luke 16:31:

> If they do not listen to Moses and the prophets, neither will they be convinced even if someone rises from the dead.

Behind the decision of the early church to assent to Israel's scriptures lies no decision at all, but rather the awareness — coterminous with faith in Christ — that God's word to Israel is the first-order inheritance for those adopted in Christ, the fully sufficient and necessary broker of God's very self to Israel and the world. Whatever authority the New Testament will in time come to possess is no rival to such a view, but is based on it, without which its corollary claim to be scripture, alongside that first scripture, is groundless.

Little wonder it is now hard to hear 2 Timothy in a strictly historical sense, as speaking of inspired scriptures (3:16) *solely constituted* by what over the course of time would be called an "Old Testament." A natural confusion exists because the means by which we recognize and acknowledge the New Testament as "holy scripture inspired by God" is derived from our recognition and acknowledgment of the Old, once estrangement was overcome by Christ and "someone else's mail" became both theirs and ours together. To forget this critical transfer is to ask us to consider reading postures external to the text and its own claims about the means by which we are readers and hearers of God's word in the very first instance.

5

"In Accordance with the Scriptures"

Creed, Scripture, and "Historical Jesus"

I

In this chapter I will discuss three aspects of the phrase "in accordance with the scriptures," found in the Nicene Creed.

1. *Its biblical character.* "In accordance with the scriptures" is a phrase lifted bodily from 1 Corinthians 15. Therefore, any sharp separation between creed and scripture, between Bible and tradition, between exegesis and theology, misrepresents the situation. Popular formulations like "scripture, reason, tradition" are confused precisely at the moment that three individual authorities are posited as separate affairs.

2. *Its exegetical scope.* While the death and resurrection of Jesus are said by the creed to be in accordance with the scriptures, close reading of 1 Corinthians 15 demonstrates that much more is implied by the phrase than that something singular happened to Jesus, according to scripture. "In accordance with the scriptures" says as much about the present life of the risen Lord, and its relationship to us, as it does about dramatic Easter events once upon a time.

3. *Its theological significance* — especially in the light of modern historical Jesus research, and projects like the "Jesus Seminar." To say that Jesus Christ died and rose again in accordance with scripture means that his identity is tied up with Old Testament statements on the front end, and post-Easter convictions on the other. These accordances, preceding and following his earthly life, cannot now be, nor have they ever been,

51

impediments to understanding Jesus as a figure of time and space. "Historical Jesus," it will be argued, is an anachronism from the late modern period, retrojected artificially into the antique environment and then called "historical" after the fashion of our present intellectual concerns. "In accordance with the scriptures" is a shorthand for "in accordance with the reality for which God requires our conformity and our obedience." As Jesus was in accordance with scripture, so the church lives in accordance with the Jesus canonically presented and shared with believers through the work of the Holy Spirit.

II

Let me begin with a confession. The creed I recited growing up, from the Episcopal *Book of Common Prayer* (1928), was worded at this juncture, "and the third day he rose again according to the scriptures." I assumed what was meant by this was: a lot of people had different opinions about Jesus' death, at the time, but *according to the New Testament,* Jesus died and then rose again. In other words, a claim was being made by specifically Christian sources about the nature of Jesus' death, namely, that it was not the final word. Not, at least, "according to the scriptures."

But that is not what the creed means, and here the newer English rendering happens to point to the intended sense better. "In accordance with the scriptures" means: consistent with the plain-sense claims — not of the New Testament — but of the Old. Within the New Testament the Old Testament is not yet sufficiently old to be referred to with anything but the generic term "the scriptures." It is with this sense that the creed speaks of "scriptures" as that with which Jesus' death and resurrection are in accordance.

The fact that the creed does not say "and he rose again in accordance with the Old Testament," might call for comment, since the creed is late enough to presuppose a two-testament canon of scripture, carrying the names for these two different testaments with which we are now familiar. But it does not, and this is significant. Here, more than at other points, we see the *exegetical* character of the creed. The phrase, "on the third day he rose again in accordance with the scriptures," is derived from 1 Cor 15:3-4, where Paul says (NRSV):

For I handed on to you as of first importance what I in turn had received: that Christ died for our sins in accordance with the scriptures, and that he was buried, and that he was raised on the third day in accordance with the scriptures.

Other lines from the creed are based on the claims of scripture, of course, both New Testament and Old. But this one is especially so, in that it is a direct quotation from Paul's letter, and the actual content of the quotation reflects an assertion about the importance of Jesus' resurrection vis-à-vis the prior claims of scripture. In that sense, this line from the creed is unique. It quotes from New Testament scripture a confession grounded through Old Testament accordance.

What does "and he rose again in accordance with the scriptures" mean? In some ways I have begun to answer the question already, by clarifying that a claim is being made about Jesus' death, namely, it is consistent with the prior plain sense claims of the Old Testament. I want to explore that a bit more, but first a prior matter deserves comment.

The creed could have adopted a shorthand at this point and left the phrase out, moving directly from "on the third day he rose again" to "and ascended into heaven." The Apostles' Creed does just that. The pressure to be more explicit could be from the community's awareness of the plain sense of Paul's statements in 1 Corinthians 15. Notice that in 1 Corinthians the phrase appears twice in close quarters — first in relationship to Jesus' death for our sins, and second in relationship to his burial and raising. In other words, Paul is not just salting his assertions with a handy condiment. Precisely these critical episodes — death, burial, resurrection — he wants us to know were in "accordance with the scriptures." Because the Nicene Creed accepts as a given not just the memory of statements like these from Paul, or Jesus, but their status as scripture from a canonical New Testament, Paul's exact phrasing was not shortchanged at this critical point but carried over word by word.

One usual explanation for the phrase in conjunction with these episodes (both in Paul and in the creed following him) is that they were the ones most demanding careful defense as congruent with or provable by the Old Testament. Christian faith was obliged to make an assertion about Jesus' death and resurrection as in accordance with scripture precisely to counter the claims of faithful Jews, to whom these scriptures were entrusted (Rom 3:2), that it was otherwise. In other words, the plain-sense claims of the Old Testament could only with difficulty be squared with a dying and risen Messiah. Along these same lines it has been argued that one of the earliest levels of New Testament tradition consisted of a collection of Old Testament proof texts, whose point was to prove that Jesus was indeed the promised Christ of the scriptures of Israel.[1] The more general view of the matter understands, as von Campenhausen once put it, that the problem facing the early church was not what to do with the Old Testament. Rather, in the face of a scriptural legacy everywhere seen to be God's very word, what was one to do with Jesus?[2] In this sort of climate, the creed asserts that the stickiest moments in the life and ministry of Jesus — his death and resurrection — were fully congruent with the Old Testament and its presentation of the Christ to come. Isaiah 53:5-12 had spoken of an expiatory death; Hosea 6:2 and Psalm 16:10 are likewise pressed into service as proof texts from the Old Testament, demonstrations that Jesus' death and raising were "in accordance with the scriptures." The annotations in modern versions of the New Testament list these texts as standing behind the claims of Paul in 1 Corinthians.

For our purposes here, I do not want to dispute this way of understanding the character of scriptural accordance. But I believe it is exegetically too narrow and theologically too functional a view of the matter. One should note in this regard that if the case rested on just a scattering of proof texts to establish congruence between Jesus' resurrection and the plain sense of scripture, the case might well prove unconvincing. The problem with this way of understanding the issue is that it has picked up the wrong end of the stick. It has failed to understand what is at stake in Paul's larger argument in 1 Corinthians 15, where the phrases appear.

So what does it mean when Paul asserts that what he received of first importance was that Christ had died and been raised in accordance with the scriptures? We have to get the sense of direction right. It was not so much that a straight line pushed forward from the Old Testament to Jesus' death and resurrection and could compel faith on those terms — which it failed to do in the instance of Judaism, instead birthing an entire collateral faith and community and bringing much anguish to Paul (Romans 9–11). Rather, in the light of Jesus' death and resurrection, the inherited scriptures were seen from a different angle. They did not predict

1. R. Harris, *Testimonies: Part One* (Cambridge: Cambridge University, 1916) and *Testimonies: Part Two* (Cambridge: Cambridge University, 1922).
2. Hans von Campenhausen, *The Formation of the Christian Bible* (Philadelphia: Fortress, 1972).

his death and resurrection in some straightforward manner — the creed does not say that. Rather, his death and resurrection accord with, are congruent with, scripture. This accordance is not about scattered proof texts, but about a much broader skein of convictions. In a word, these involve God: the agency of God, the relationship of God to Jesus, and the present life of Jesus in relationship to the Father until the Second Coming. "In accordance with the scriptures" means: related to claims about God and God's promises as presented in the Old Testament scriptures — not to individual proof texts about the details of Jesus' death, burial, and resurrection. To speak of God raising Jesus is to ask how such raising fits into a larger scriptural depiction of God's plans with the world.

This becomes clear when one follows Paul's larger argument in 1 Corinthians 15. There we see that Christ's resurrection is precisely *not* significant because it is a singular event, focused on one moment for him alone. To say that Christ rose again on the third day is not to make a statement about him only, as though he had been elevated to heroic status and now was worthy of homage. It should be remembered that Herod was convinced that John the Baptist had been raised from the dead and that his powers were at work in Jesus' miracles and ministry. Others were persuaded that Elijah had been raised, or would be. Lazarus is raised by Jesus in John's account of things. By contrast, to say that Jesus rose "in accordance with the scriptures" stipulates how we are to understand his specific raising. That singular event was also extraordinarily social and involved the entire creation, at once the most singular and most unsingular event that ever occurred, without analogy to Lazarus's actual raising or Elijah's and John's theoretical raisings.

In verses 12-28 Paul focuses on the fact of Jesus' resurrection — not as a fact unto itself — but as a fact inextricably related to the general resurrection of those united to his death and rising in baptism. To say that Jesus' resurrection accords with scripture, which is where Paul begins his argument, means that the scriptures are where the answer can be found about what God is presently doing in Jesus and in those baptized into his death. Apparently there were those in the Corinthian community who were ready to say that Christ had been raised. What they did not believe was that his resurrection had anything to do with them and their life and death. But for Paul, to say that Jesus died and rose "in accordance with the scriptures" was to forbid such an understanding. If, "according to the scriptures" all died in Adam, then the reverse would equally be true and in accord with scripture: that Jesus Christ was the new Adam in whom all would be made alive. Christ's rising was not an isolated harvest, but the firstfruits of a much broader harvest, to which those in him would belong. Furthermore, Jesus' death and resurrection "in accordance with the scriptures" means that those in Christ are presently living between two times: the time of Christ as firstfruits, and the final time, when those who belong to Christ will be united with him at his coming again. That God had not brought the curtain down on time and space was not a fact out of accordance with scripture, but was consistent with God's delay action in bringing in the Gentiles. Jesus' death and resurrection were in accord with scripture, in accord with God's own statements about how he intended the Christ to rule.

What actually happens during this meantime? Again, scripture provides the "accorded" response. The meantime is a time when God puts all things in subjection to Christ. Then at the end Christ will hand the kingdom over to God the Father, "after he has destroyed every authority and power" (v. 24). This scenario, with its bundle of related convictions, spells out what is meant by God raising Jesus on the third day *in accordance with the scriptures*. Paul means here — and the creed follows him — that Christ's death and resurrection have implications whose lineaments can be seen in scripture. This is nowhere clearer, for example, than in the motif of God's subjecting all things to Christ — all things, that is, with the exception of God himself. Here Paul explicitly takes his bearings from scripture (v. 27, NRSV):

> But when it says [citing Psalm 8:6] "All things are put in subjection," it is plain that this does not include the one who put all things in subjection under him.

In order to understand what Jesus' resurrection entails, Paul searches scripture for clues. To begin his argument with the assertion that Jesus died for our sins and rose "in accordance with the scriptures" is to designate the scriptures as the place where the meantime scenario can be found. Paul then explains the final significance of Christ's raising (v. 28, NRSV):

> When all things are subjected to him, then the Son himself will also be subjected to the one who put all things in subjection under him, so that God may be all in all.

To say that Christ rose again in "accordance with the scriptures" is at its heart a statement about God's long-range plans, with Christ, on our behalf, as this has been set forth in scripture. It is not that a straight line moves from the Old Testament to Christ in some mechanical fashion. Rather, we comprehend what God is doing in Christ right now and to eternity by returning to the Old Testament and seeking to find within its manifold testimony accordance with what we are coming to know about God in Christ. Once again we are brought up against the reality that the Old Testament, as Christian scripture, is not just before Jesus, but after him as well. It is both B.C. and A.D., because Jesus lives in relationship to the Father, to Israel, and to the world; and the Father has set forth his broader plans for the world in his word to Israel, plans at whose center stands Christ. For an understanding of Christ's present rule and relationship to God, from the moment of God's raising him from the dead to that final point when God is all in all, it was necessary to search a first testament to learn about last things.

The problem with the "Jesus Seminar" is twofold. It resists the force of the scriptures, as Paul and the creed mean that, on our understanding of Jesus, and consequently, it does not take seriously Jesus' relationship to God as imprinted by scripture's prior word and guided by that word's according potential. In order to understand the one who came to do the Father's will, we should assume that he took significant bearings from the scriptures of Israel, in exactly the public form we can now read them. To ignore this dimension in the name of massive historical sifting and reconstruction is to make a category mistake of the first order.

Here the Jesus Seminar is not a benighted peculiarity, but the logical outcome of years of preoccupation with questions of origins and evidences behind the text as that which is truly revelatory. One has every right to observe the root system of a tree. To do so, however, involves uprooting the tree itself. If, furthermore, one begins to insist that the tree is not as it should be, given the underground investigation, that the mature growth is a misunderstanding in need of correction by experts, or, more enticingly, that the underground tree *is the tree itself,* is the "historical tree," is that which should occupy our attention, that we have had things upside-down — then it seems to me that we are beginning to approach the logic of the Jesus Seminar and the intellectual thrall it has been able to exercise on culture. And note carefully that once this concern for origins and evidences is validated, it can preoccupy the right wing of Christianity as theologically necessary in the same way that it occupies the left as historically necessary.

We should, however, stop and consider the hold "historical Jesus" has at present in culture. Why the thrall of Borg, Crossan, and other uncoverers of "historical Jesus"? Why? — because if "Jesus" is something to be un-covered, then the necessary conditions have been met to require that Jesus be a source of fascination and devoted, even painstaking, interest. The Jesus Seminar is nothing if not hard work, by any standard of measurement, even if it is shown to be toil in an unproductive vineyard. The element of Jesus as requiring unveiling and discovery is not wrong, but has been translated and domesticated by the Jesus Seminar and much historical-critical endeavor. It is not that Jesus is hidden behind the words about him, which must be sifted and probed to get at "historical Jesus." It is, rather, that the words that tell about him simultaneously convey their inadequacy, in formal terms, because of the subject matter that they are trying to reach. The very fourfoldness of the gospel record is a witness to the majestic difficulty of the endeavor of presenting Jesus as a character of time and space, fully man, fully God. But this is not an inadequacy that can be remedied through historical-critical heavy lifting, because it inheres with the subject matter itself, which is God in Christ — who exposes our inadequacy in trying to speak of him, and yet simultaneously remedies this through the work of the Holy Spirit in the church, allowing the frail testimony of human minds to be the lens on the glory of God, a touching of the ark of the covenant.

When in John 14 Jesus announces, "I will no longer talk much with you," he does not mean that he has run out of things to say. What he has said will be sufficient to convey the truth about him. John 14's discussion of the Holy Spirit makes it clear that sufficiency will be insured by God himself, through the canonical witness to Jesus and the work of the Advocate, who "will teach you everything and remind you of all that I have said." The precedent witness of the Old Testament will have its antecedent counterpart in the construction of New Testament witness.

To assume that the church is responsible for any overlay from the Old Testament on a reconstructed "historical Jesus" (as has been the case almost by definition since the dawn of historical Jesus projects) is to set up a problem of enormous proportions. For if the church came to formulate its under-standing of the implications of Christ's death and resurrection on the basis of their accord with scripture — and yet no such correlation is believed to be at work in Jesus' own case, as a historical figure — then the entire faith of the church is inconsistent with the orientation of Jesus and of those who sought to provide the record of his life for a specific posterity, the church.

Some are prepared to accept this diagnosis and offer up an alternative Jesus, "the historical Jesus." The problem is not only that this "historical Jesus" resides somewhere behind and is not fully congruent with the total witness of the New Testament, in the form we have it; but that in addition this Jesus stands apart from the witness of the Old Testament scriptures and their claims about what God was and is and will be doing, in and through Jesus. One could argue that the entire enterprise of historical Jesus searches began when one decided that it was both possible and necessary to extract a Jesus from the welter of beliefs preceding him in scripture and following him in the church, in effect marooning him in time and space so as to give him the label "historical" Jesus. Interestingly, once this was done in the name of freeing him from subsequent theological interpretation, but now we see the most recent project demanding fresh theological interpretation to replace what was there from the start. A new tree for a freshly replaced root system. A "historical Jesus church" for uncoverers of "historical Jesus." The thesis itself suggests that here we have a postmodern version of premodern Gnosticism. Again we see the emphasis on special truth, the hidden unveiled, and initiation into expert findings and the "real truth" about things. A certain piety and concern for the church's life — less critical to earlier "quests" — serve to complete the picture.

Though it should seem obvious, we should remember that a "historical" Jesus has never been the object of the church's faith, but rather the triune God, revealed in Old and New Testaments and presently alive in the body of Christ through the presence of the Holy Spirit. Consequently, to search for "historical" Jesus apart from the witness of Israel's scriptures is to drive a wedge between the One raised and the One doing the raising. It is this avenue that Paul shuts off, as do the creeds, when they say that Jesus rose again "in accordance with the scriptures."

III

I will conclude with three final remarks.

1. The creeds are not just churchly efforts to identify heresy and then construct a series of statements to serve as a firewall against it. They are natural extensions of the earlier rule of faith, which presented a précis of core Christian belief intended to guide scriptural exposition in the church. Consistent with that intention, the Nicene Creed seeks to summarize and comprehend the scope of scriptural authority, as inherited and passed on. That is particularly evident in this case, where the creed merely replicates what can be found in longer form in scripture, in Paul's first letter to the Corinthians.

It would therefore be wrong to draw a sharp line between scripture and tradition, as is sometimes done. Rightly understood, the latter should flow organically from the former, as is so well modeled at this juncture in the creed. Whenever one begins to talk about fresh insights, even given by the Holy Spirit, a serious question should be raised about the life of the church and its connective tissue in relationship to scripture, which is the legacy of the prophets and apostles, upon which we are built. The Holy Spirit does not provide fresh insights. The Holy Spirit is not an ongoing *source* of revelation. The Holy Spirit equips us to hear God's word in our day in accordance with what has been revealed. We are not Mormons or Swedenborgians.

2. To say that Jesus died and rose again in accordance with the scriptures reminds the church of its status as adopted into the promises of God begun with Israel. Far from being a problematic, outdated, or downright misguided witness to God — filled with what Jack Spong calls "examples of pre-modern ignorance" — the Old Testament is God's shared gift to the church, meant to guide its present life in Christ.[3] Paul and the church understood this when they declared Jesus' death and resurrection to be "in accordance with the scriptures," the Old Testament. Jesus understood this when he declared that he would give his life as a ransom for many. Such a death is only comprehensible against a background of Old Testament accordance.

3. To say that Jesus rose again in accordance with the scriptures is as much a statement about God as about Jesus — that God did a thing that he said he would, and that he will continue to stand in relationship with the risen and ascended Lord until all things are subjected to God and the kingdom is handed over to him. Those of us once "without God in the world" have, in Christ Jesus, been brought near and grafted into plans that reach to eternity. In Christ, we are given eternal life with the Living God, the God of Abraham, Moses, Isaiah, the apostles, and the faithful who have preceded us in this place. Jesus did not arise from the tomb like the dying and rising phoenix. God raised him from the dead, and our rising in Christ is not to some spiritual state, but to fellowship with the Living God, the God of Israel, the God of all creation, Father, Son, and Holy Spirit.

3. John S. Spong, *Living in Sin? A Bishop Rethinks Human Sexuality* (San Francisco: Harper and Row, 1988) 146.

$\approx$ 6 $\approx$

Old Testament or Hebrew Bible?

Some Theological Considerations

Something like a subspecialty has emerged on the question of terms for the first part of the Christian canon. Prominent biblical scholars Jon Levenson (Harvard, Jewish) and John Collins (Notre Dame, Roman Catholic) have recently titled whole books nearly as I have titled this essay.[1] After serious reflection a popular journal, *Biblical Theology Bulletin*, adopted for editorial purposes altogether different terms than the ones in question, "First Testament" and "Second Testament." There is also the common Jewish practice of referring to this material not as Hebrew Bible but as *Torah* or *Tanak* or *Mikra'*.

I do not want to enter the topic from what is now becoming (as a result of this recent discussion) familiar territory, that is, as involving modern sensibilities and other considerations. Several examples will give indication of what I mean. Does the term "Old Testament" imply a senile or overshadowed precursor to the robust and virile New Testament, thus making the term problematic? Or, from the ecumenical angle, do Jews find the term "Old Testament" unhelpful or offensive, such that Christians

---

1. Jon Levenson, *The Hebrew Bible, the Old Testament, and Historical Criticism* (Louisville: Westminster/John Knox, 1993). John J. Collins and Roger Brooks, eds., *Hebrew Bible or Old Testament? Studying the Bible in Judaism and Christianity* (Notre Dame: University of Notre Dame, 1990).

This chapter originally appeared in *Pro Ecclesia* 5 (1996) 292-303. See now my further comments in *Pro Ecclesia* 6 (1997) 136-40.

would be wise to abandon it? Or from the learned angle, since there is Aramaic as well as Hebrew in the Old Testament, "Hebrew Bible" is strictly speaking inaccurate.[2] Or consider the standpoint of the Bible itself. The New Testament never refers to an "Old Testament" but instead speaks of "the Law and the Prophets," "Moses and the Prophets," or simply "the scriptures." Parenthetically, something *is* to be learned from recognizing that when reference is made to "all scripture" being "inspired by God" (2 Tim 3:16), the author is not including his own contribution to what would later be called the New Testament, but instead means only what we have come to call the "Old Testament." Yet so far as I know there have been no proposals to refer to the "Old Testament" more accurately as "The Scriptures" in Christian circles, with the "New Testament" then referring to a nonscriptural sort of addendum to this main corpus.[3] That would be an interesting proposal. That it has not been proposed ought to be considered in more detail, since we are apparently under pressure for revision.

There is also an important historical dimension to this discussion that I want to leave partly to the side. For instance, it has long been a practice to refer to the Old Testament, on occasion or for variety's sake, as the Hebrew Scriptures, the Scriptures of Israel, or the Hebrew Bible. But not in the sense that I mean it or the modern discussion means it, namely as offering a more acceptable replacement for "Old Testament." And then, finally, there is the matter of structure and symmetry, which is by no means devoid of theological significance. The necessary consequence of pairing "Hebrew Scriptures" with "New Testament," for Christians, is that two different genres (scripture and testament) are being introduced in one pairing, now no longer linked by the familiar, if problematic, adjectives "old" and "new." Where is the continuity at a formal level, one might ask, between "Hebrew Scriptures" and "New Testament"? We are describing four different genre possibilities: language (Hebrew), a form of writing (scriptures), relative age (new), and theological concept (testament). What held the other pair together was the common term "testament," and jettisoning this may be far more complicated than the revisors

2. Could the Septuagint be referred to as the "Greek Hebrew Bible"?

3. Paul van Buren seems to flirt with this understanding, but never uses the specific terminology. He appears to prefer "Apostolic Writings" for the New Testament and "Israel's Scriptures" for the Old Testament. See "On Reading Someone Else's Mail: The Church and Israel's Scriptures," *Die Hebräische Bibel und ihre zweifache Nachgeschichte* (FS R. Rendtorff; Neukirchen-Vluyn: Neukirchener, 1990) 595-606.

have as yet considered, for a proper Christian understanding of *either* collection, Old or New.

None of the considerations I have here canvassed is theologically neutral — not even (especially not) those that profess to be so.[4] It has never been entirely clear what it might mean to talk about the Bible neutrally, or about any other piece of literature neutrally for that matter. That some terminological options claim neutrality or objectivity does not make them so, except in a relative sense, which we will examine below. Still, there may be a way to investigate these terms in a self-consciously theological manner as yet untried.

I have already mentioned that the terms Old and New Testament are not, ironically, biblical terms. They belong to a period of self-consciousness that the Bible is only en route to, for the New Testament is not in a position to regard itself as scripture, on strict analogy to the Old Testament. Only concerning the scriptures of Israel is Paul prepared to apply the honorific "oracles of God" (Rom 3:2). The writings of the New Testament, from the beginning and as they began to form an analogous collection, are about showing that Jesus is the Messiah of Israel and the fulfillment of the one scriptures' hopes and originating rationale — not about setting themselves up as a rival or overshadowing witness to the Old as scripture.[5]

So the terms Old and New Testament were not coined to establish parity between two witnesses, which were otherwise from the beginning vying for ascendancy. The absolute authority of the one (the "Old") was a given, even while the other (the "New") was taking shape. Each witness has a different scope and a different purpose, which even the common term "testament" was not chosen to eradicate. Though in the Christian understanding that would evolve, based on the arguments found in the New, the purpose of Israel's scriptures was to witness to Christ, each witness doing this in a very different way.[6] That difference amounts to much more

---

4. John Collins has recently defended a principle of autonomy in reading that sounds like an effort at theological neutrality. "Neither church nor state can prescribe for the scholar which conclusions should be reached" ("Is a Critical Biblical Theology Possible?" in *The Hebrew Bible and Its Interpreters,* ed. W. Propp (Winona Lake: Eisenbrauns, 1990] 2). This is fine so far as it goes, but what would it mean to be able to eliminate "prior commitments" in the manner suggested by Collins?

5. See the fine discussion by Hans von Campenhausen in *The Formation of the Christian Bible* (Philadelphia: Fortress, 1972).

6. See the thorough discussion by B. S. Childs in *Biblical Theology of the Old and New Testaments* (Minneapolis: Fortress, 1992).

than a matter of something old having to be correlated with something new, old being better than new or new being better than old as rival literary witnesses. To see it that way in the modern period is therefore to impose a foreign sensibility that formed no part of the decision to adopt the terms "old," "new," and "testament" to begin with.

The key word in all this is shared by both witnesses: "testament." Testament, like reconciliation, redemption, and salvation, is a religious word and as such is always threatening to fall into a bin of abstraction or pious disregard. Does it mean anything in any immediate sense, apart from its usage related to parts of the Christian Bible? Could part of the sensitivity to old versus new or Hebrew versus Christian (whatever that means exactly) be traced to the fact that "testament" lacks sufficient force, is too theological a predication, or is simply not a term of meaningful currency in the most general sense? Moreover, to adopt a new term, "Hebrew Bible," for "Old Testament," has a ripple effect on what Christians mean by "New Testament," though one has had the impression that repair work on the term "Old Testament" can be carried out with the "New Testament" entirely unaffected.

One thing that should be clear is that the Christian terms "Old Testament" and "New Testament" arose as distinct impositions on the literatures in question. As we have seen, the New Testament as a literary corpus carried no name as a correlate of its origin and development. Neither were the writings of Israel's scriptures supplied with one unequivocal and wholly agreed on title — this would be to imply a homogeneity for a literary witness that is equally lacking for the people to which this literature was fundamentally and inextricably attached.[7] The New Testament's uncontroversial variety of terms for the Old is no Christian invention, just as describing the New Testament as "Christian" in the first place would be misleading and anachronistic.

Here we begin to touch on a striking fact that is distinctly unmodern. All scriptural writings, as individual witnesses found in discrete books, in larger divisions, and in fullest form, derive their "titles" from a combination of internal and external factors. Individual Old Testament books would, in time, come to be called by the words with which they began ("In the beginning" for Genesis, "Now these are the names" for Exodus, "And he

7. Consider the variety of "Judaisms" represented by Qumran, the Pharisees, the Sadducees, and the Samaritans, each with a different scriptural emphasis and scope of preferred writings.

[the LORD] called" for Leviticus), by the "authors" or main figures with which they were associated (Jeremiah, Esther, Qoheleth), or by some other quite general terms (Song of Songs, Proverbs of Solomon). This could be extended to larger divisions (the five-fifths of Moses). Larger and later divisions could take on new and at times confusing nomenclature (e.g., Former Prophets).[8]

Divisions were not always entirely fixed (see the LXX and many early listings).[9] Some have argued that the general category "Prophets" meant only non-Mosaic books, inclusive of the "Writings," while others have argued that it was limited to the prophets per se.[10] Does Luke's "Moses and the prophets and psalms" (Luke 24:44) mean the first five books, then all the prophets, and then the Psalter only, or is "psalms" *pars pro toto* shorthand for the "Writings" as a third division? Or can we say anything quite definitive in answer to such a question when the variety of terms found in the New Testament is itself a testimony to the flexibility with which individual books or larger divisions asserted their own specific claims to titles? That is to say, "titling" is always a matter of the literature's own adumbrated or general sense of itself and a specific community's claim regarding what is being read or heard. The false assertion that variety of terminology for and citation of Old Testament books in the New is a sign of an "open canon" or complete fluidity in the scope, number, and authority of these writings — to be closed and finalized by Christians or by Jewish synods — should not lead to an equally false conclusion, namely, that these sacred writings had one unambiguous and historically given title that a rejection of the Christian term "Old Testament" in favor of "Hebrew Bible" successfully restores.[11]

Though it lies somewhat to the side, a rough analogy can be drawn for purposes of illustration. I refer to decisions to vocalize the divine name in modern versions. For Christians (or Jews) to present "Yahweh" as the proper name for God in the name of historical accuracy may be to nail down for the name a sort of meaningless specificity. Even if this were to restore to the name an accuracy of pronunciation (about which there can

---

8. See the subdivisions referred to in Babylonian Talmud *Baba Bathra* 14b.

9. E. Earle Ellis, *The Old Testament in the Early Church* (Tübingen: Mohr, 1991).

10. For a full discussion see John Barton's *Oracles of God* (London: Darton, Longman, and Todd, 1986); T. N. Swanson, *The Closing of the Collection of Holy Scripture: A Study of the Canonization of the Old Testament* (Diss. Vanderbilt, 1970); B. S. Childs, *Biblical Theology*, 55-69.

11. See Childs's discussion in *Biblical Theology*, 54-69.

only be conjecture!) no non-Hebrew speaker in the modern period — not even one scientifically trained to read and understand biblical Hebrew — will pick up any of the nuance we are told the name was supposed to convey (Exod 3:14). Plus it is to impose on the modern reader a sense of the actual widespread and fixed use of the name within Israel for which we lack a complete picture — this all to the side of the problem that the name is now no longer vocalized by those to whom it was first revealed.

Here the analogy with proper titling for the "Old Testament" breaks down somewhat. "Hebrew Scripture" could in time have served as a title for what Christians would refer to as "Old Testament." At the same time, the term is not used in the New Testament, which reflects the practices of the day, whereby "the scriptures," "the law and the prophets," "Moses said," and simply "it is written" are the means by which "the oracles of God entrusted to the Jews" (Rom 3:2) are referred to. Morever, substitution of the term "Hebrew Bible" in the modern period may be an effort to secure greater generality, not greater specificity of a sort that in Christian circles is implied by the name "Old Testament."

II

Thus far I have been circling around my thesis. My point has been to contest adoption of the term "Hebrew Bible" if this is being done in the name of historical accuracy. It has also been my assertion that all titling has always taken the form of imposition.[12] This has occurred in such a way as to honor both the literature's own claims about itself and the larger theological purpose into which these claims are to be fitted. One sees this immediately in the fact that, in what Christians refer to as the Old Testament and Jews call the Torah, neither title is a simple replication of the literature's own claims. Both terms are derived from a selective understanding of the literature's wider meaning and purpose.[13] On this view,

12. See the fine treatment by Ernest Frerichs in "The Torah Canon of Judaism and the Interpretation of Hebrew Scripture," *HBT* 9 (1987) 13-25. Frerichs includes a quotation from Jacob Neusner to bolster his own argument: "While the world at large treats Judaism as 'the religion of the Old Testament,' the fact is otherwise. Judaism inherits and makes the Hebrew Scriptures its own, just as does Christianity" (22).

13. Frerichs goes yet further and insists that "Torah is not confined to the Hebrew Bible" (21). For this reason he cautions, "It can be the case that Christians wish to posit

"Hebrew Bible" is no more an inherently Jewish term than a Christian term. It might be better to refer to it as a minimal term, since it imposes very little (and some of what it imposes, as we have seen, is inaccurate).

I have also raised a more general question. If a term of scientific neutrality could be found, what would this actually mean? What would this form of imposition claim as its purpose?

The notion of a "minimal claim" needs to be pursued further at this point. To call the Old Testament "the Hebrew Bible" may imply several things. The fact that these several things are not entirely clear, or do not line up one after another, itself underscores this minimalism. Perhaps a claim is being made about the language employed in the texts (Hebrew). At the same time a claim could simultaneously be made about the antiquity of the material (biblical Hebrew is no longer spoken). A claim may also be hovering nearby that the literature is the literature of "the Hebrews." If one is interested in antiquity, this is fine: Hebrews are the people of Israel "from olden times." The term also has something of a "travelogue" character about it, since "Hebrew" is the term used by those outside Israel to refer to Israel (see the stories of Joseph or Moses in Egypt).[14] Whether or not a claim for ecumenicity is being made would turn on whether "Hebrew" is an appropriate term for modern Jews. What Christians may wish to give away in this regard may not actually be received, or it may be received for reasons other than those intended. It frequently comes as a surprise to Christians that an immediate identification of Judaism with the Israelites of the Old Testament may be as strained as an identification of the church with Israel.[15]

This being said, it seems to me uncontroversial that whatever else Christians may sense about the Old Testament, they recognize the fundamental connection of the literature to God's people Israel. Paul almost makes this connection and the literature to which it points the cause and not just a symptom of Israel's election and special purposes in God's plans for creation (Rom 3:2). A term like "Hebrew Bible" may seek to honor

---

their dialogue with Jews on the basis of a seeming common ground — the Hebrew Scriptures, the Jewish Scriptures, and not in the traditional controversial form of Old Testament. But to do so is to ask the Jewish tradition of Torah to emasculate itself in unacceptable ways" (20).

14. It would be ironic to see the same tendency at work in the modern period.

15. Matitiahu Tsevat speaks of "sparse and uncertain paths [that] lead from the Old Testament to the Talmud" and can conclude at one point, "Thus the Talmud judaizes the Old Testament" ("Theology of the Old Testament — A Jewish View," *HBT* 8 [1986] 46).

this connection, though as just stated there are legitimate questions whether in fact it succeeds. When modern Jews refer to the Old Testament as Torah or Tanak, non-Jews should recognize immediately the claim to a special connection. "Torah" gives centrality to the prescriptive character of the literature, while "Tanak" speaks to an order specifically preserved within Judaism *(torah, nebi'im, ketubim)*. The very fact that these are Hebrew terms, or adaptations thereof, makes non-Jews immediately aware of the special connection between this literature and modern Judaism.

On this understanding, for Jews to refer to the Old Testament as "Hebrew Bible" might even be to assert a connection that is unnecessary to assert, or one that might be better asserted with the term "Jewish Scriptures." But why would those who already hold "copyright" need to make this explicit; would not the assertion itself actually raise a question? Ironically, and as one more instance of flawed revision, some Christians have recently paired "Jewish Scriptures" with "Christian Scriptures" as an alternative to Old and New Testament. But this immediately reveals that Marcionism is the latent dark side of any effort, from the standpoint of the Christian canon, to move in this direction, precisely in the name of "honoring" Judaism.[16] Also, Christian Scripture is not the New Testament, but Old and New together. An effort to honor the connection through the use of a term like "Jewish Scriptures" creates more problems than it solves and ultimately raises the question: if these are in fact "Jewish Scriptures" why are Christians reading them?[17]

16. Although he does not want to follow Marcion (or Harnack) explicitly, van Buren regards Marcion as "historically *and* theologically correct" (602). "He seems to have been the only Christian leader of his day, indeed the only one from his day until Harnack, to have recognized that the Scriptures were Israel's, unquestionably the Bible of the Jews" (602). The alternative to this understanding is "forced reinterpretation" in order to make Israel's Scriptures directly address the Gentile church. Marcion, of course, was not content merely to reject the Old Testament but also a vast majority of the New. Marcion's truncation was not just bad politics or ecumenical insensitivity, but an assault on the Jesus of the church's memory.

17. Jon Levenson is frequently worried about Christian supersessionism in the way that the Old Testament is used, and yet ironically many Christian efforts to honor the distinctive character of Judaism and the Scriptures of Israel ultimately founder. Van Buren's praise for Marcion and Harnack is a good example. Those who have been brought within a new covenant by Israel's Messiah — a confession made in the first instance by Jews — must retain the Old Testament to clarify how the New Testament is to be heard. All would be much easier on this score if Jesus were not Israel's Messiah and instead were a cosmic deliverer with no connection to any specific human family or hopes. Efforts to leave the

The same question applies to the term "Hebrew Bible." I have been speaking as though only two distinct groups read the Old Testament/Hebrew Bible, even as I have tried to show that a good deal of confusion reigns over the question of proper terminology for those who would readily identify with one group as against another. To speak of Jewish and Christian readers is to imply that religious identity plays a major and important role in the matter of what we call this literature. This is by no means uncontested. Many who wish to argue for the propriety of the term "Hebrew Bible" either seek to minimize such distinctive identity or its importance, or they regard a term like "Hebrew Bible" most helpful precisely because it sets this consideration fully to the side. Being a term not fully at home in either Jewish or Christian circles is its very appeal.

It is at this juncture that one sees most clearly what is at stake. Christians have always recognized that the literature has a special attachment to Israel. "Hebrew Bible" does not make this clear except in imprecise ways. The very term "Old Testament" has in the first instance to do with asserting this literature's connective status. These writings all emerge from the context of Israel's covenant relationship with God, what from a Christian perspective can be called an "old testament" (*testamentum* is the Latin equivalent of *berit*, covenant). For this very reason Jews have never condemned use of the term as such by Christians and have on occasion themselves adopted it.[18] But the far more obvious means by which Jews emphasize the "connective status" of these writings is through their ongoing place in Jewish religious life, as torah, tanak, miqra (scripture).

For Christians to describe the Old Testament as "Hebrew Bible" or "Jewish Scriptures" could conceivably leave this connection intact, though in a less than satisfactory manner. But what is then left unclear for Christians is *what their own point of connection might be.* How is "Hebrew Bible" related to "New Testament" — or, should we say, "Greek Bible"? The term fails, on the one hand, to properly describe modern Judaism's relationship to the literature, while on the other it makes problematic the use of the material by the Christian community in the first place.

But what of those who seek to minimize or eliminate specific religious identity as crucial to the question of proper terminology? As we have

---

Old Testament as Jewish scripture, as someone else's mail, no longer properly comprehend who Jesus was, on his own terms and on the terms that the New Testament writers — is there a Gentile among them? — understand him.

18. See the article by Tsevat (n. 15 above), where the term is used throughout.

seen, "Hebrew Bible" may here find its greatest cachet. But it seems to me that here too lies the greatest problem. As a proposed term "Hebrew Bible" has its most decided effect in blurring the question of who is doing the reading. The Old Testament/Tanak becomes a book like any other book in one very specific sense: like any other book it can be purchased and read by anyone who chooses, without first clarifying *whose* book it is, apart from a vague claim involving something "Hebrew," which as we have seen involves a skein of various possibilities.

We have emphasized that for both traditional Jewish and Christian titles, a measure of imposition has taken place. At the same time we have argued that this imposition takes its cue from the literature itself. As titles, "Tanak" and "Torah" are interpretations of the larger sense of scripture, one based upon a distinctive Jewish order and one that emphasizes the books of Moses (Pentateuch) as a central lens through which to interpret the whole. Can the term "Hebrew Bible" lay claim to the same continuity between title and content? Yes, but not nearly to the same degree and, as we have shown, with a considerable tolerance for vagueness or confusion about just what "Hebrew" means.

Far more problematic are the implications for specifically Christian readers of a rejection of the term "Old Testament." "Hebrew Bible" may be a minimal term in the manner we have described it, one that seeks to keep at arm's length the question of specific readerships. As such it is well suited for the most general of audiences. But what does it mean for a specifically Christian reader to adopt this term instead of "Old Testament"? What is at stake in this decision? It may be wrong to think one can just add new titles without any effect at all, finitude not having as yet been eliminated.

It would seem consistent that Christian readers who adopt the term "Hebrew Bible" over "Old Testament" would likewise be obliged to find a better term for "New Testament" as well. And, indeed, some have begun to do this, though usually in a less direct way, by raising questions about the limits of the canonical New Testament writings or by preferring to speak of Early Christian Literature (is even this too narrow?) as distinct from patristic literature or a "New Testament" per se. The important point is this: the term "New Testament" is not on strict analogy to "Hebrew Bible" and for Christians this should call into immediate question any pairing of "Hebrew Bible" with "New Testament." Unlike "Hebrew Bible" the term "New Testament" makes a very direct theological statement, one that does not leave to the side the question of intended readerships (cf.

"Greek Bible"). Moreover, "New Testament" as a title is specifically based upon Old Testament texts (Jer 31:31-34; Ezek 34:25-31), as well as New Testament texts in conscious relationship to them (Heb 9:15-22; 1 Cor 11:25).

The upshot of this is clear. To continue to speak of a "New Testament" is to make unavoidable ongoing reference to an "Old Testament," for the two terms both point in the same direction and involve parallel commitments. These two terms are alone capable of making clear why it is that Christians, as against the simply curious, read the Old Testament to begin with — something that "Hebrew Bible" cannot do. The term "New Testament" makes it clear that Israel's covenant with God is the sole rationale for the existence of sacred texts to begin with, whatever we might call them. God covenanted with Israel, and not just with humanity in general. The only means by which others have access to that relationship is by the blood of Christ, which is itself described as a covenant "poured out for many for the forgiveness of sins" (Matt 26:28). The first covenant was ratified by blood, as the New Testament understands it, based upon the Old (Exod 24:6-8), and in like manner so too the second (Heb 9:15-22). In this way, those far off — "without God in the world" (Eph 2:13) — were brought near. In this process the "oracles of God" (Rom 3:2) received a new title that explained how what had been entrusted to the Jews was now a scriptural witness with wider significance and wider readership. Because of the new covenant made by God in Christ, the "scriptures," the "law and the prophets" and "Moses and the prophets and psalms" became for new readers, members of the new covenant, the Old Testament. New library cards were issued, and copyright squabbles ensued, as a glance at the patristic literature demonstrates. This exclusively theological decision was not made to render something old or outmoded that had theretofore been more neutrally "Hebrew Bible." It was instead to clarify how and on what terms these scriptures of Israel remained scriptures for the church, and by what manner of inclusion they could be read in the first place.

It remains a pressing and I believe fully legitimate question whether the Bible — Old Testament, New Testament, Tanak — can surrender its specific attachment to particular communities of faith with a specific stake in what this literature is to be called. If the term "Hebrew Bible" is being adopted to cloud or sever this attachment and this specificity, then to my mind the consequences are not neutral on some more-is-better logic. It may look possible to range "Hebrew Bible" on a grid of possible names

71

together with Old Testament, Tanak, Torah; but inclusivity on this score may also amount to exclusion of important theological connections that the traditional terms sought to maintain. And whether "Hebrew Bible" adequately captures the governing principles and central rationale of the literature itself is a matter for debate. I think not.

Seen along these lines, what does the awkward neologism "Old Testament/Hebrew Bible," now in widespread use and not just in academic circles, actually mean? It is not clear if "Hebrew Bible" is a parallel or a displacing term. The new convention might be parsed this way: "Old Testament" is a term that arose within Christian (religious) circles and therefore points to that context of reading, while "Hebrew Bible" is a more neutral term and could be used by readers without specific religious convictions of any sort. Not by accident, therefore, was the convention "Old Testament/Torah" not to find its way into recent parlance, since it would cover different territory than "Old Testament/Hebrew Bible."

If this is an accurate parsing, why in specifically Christian contexts would "Old Testament" be replaced by "Hebrew Bible"? Who if anyone is being served by such a modification? Christians, but also Jews, would simply be thrust back on a critical theological consideration the term "Old Testament" was chosen to clarify: what is the Christian relationship to Israel's scriptures? Answer: Israel's scriptures are constitutive of God's covenant with Israel, to which the church is related because of the covenant made in Christ. There is thus an Old Testament and a New Testament record of this series of decisive and non-substitutable theological moments. Abandoning the term "Old Testament" would be to abandon a statement of the relationship of Christians to the literature of Israel and to modern Judaism. It would be to place Christians in the same category as the simply curious, before whom this literature offers profound, or banal, glimpses at antiquity, things "Hebrew."

In the light of these theological considerations, the term "Old Testament" ought not be simply replaced or even glossed by "Hebrew Bible." Too much is lost in the exchange, and one cannot forever count on the memory of what was being glossed or modified remaining in consciousness. With all its generality and ecumenical possibility, the term "Hebrew Bible" helps clarify what has traditionally been at stake in the matter of titling, by showing what would be lost. "A rose by any other name would smell as sweet" is an adage precisely not true of the scriptures of Israel, which together with the writings that bear witness to Jesus Christ, are constitutive of Christian Scripture, Old Testament and New Testament.

Finally, for those who identify with one of these two groups with specific religious commitments, it will need to be shown why a term for the Old Testament should be found that makes the question of readership and access less acute. A demurrer can also be lodged from the standpoint of the scriptures themselves, which make claims like, "He declares his word to Jacob, his statutes and ordinances to Israel. He has not dealt thus with any other nation" (Ps 147:19-20). That the Old Testament can be bought and read like any other book ought not blind one to the very specific connection it asserts *in the substance of its discourse and as the correlate of its very existence* to be the record of God's discourse with one particular people. It is "someone else's mail," as one recent interpreter has phrased it, even as it is much more than that as well.[19]

The term "Old Testament" honors the specific connection of the literature to Israel as God's covenanted people. In conjunction with the New Testament and the gospel to which it bears witness, the term also holds the potential to disclose how it is that God's work begun with Israel could finally become a blessing for all peoples, through the confession that Christ had made those "without God in the world" members of a new covenant with the One who raised him from the dead, the same One who called Abraham and spoke to Israel on Mount Sinai. As a consequence of that New Covenant, the scriptures of Israel were shown, through faith, to be someone else's mail but also mail addressed to those who had once walked in darkness, and it is precisely that mysterious and dialectical movement that is best preserved by the terms "Old Testament" and "New Testament." One could not even know the extent of the darkness without glimpsing the richness of the Old Testament's plain sense testimony.

It remains dubious whether before this literature there can be an objective and neutral reader for whom a term that matches that objectivity can be found and have permanent cogency. The literature's own claims to be privileged speech forbid it. As terms which work in conjunction with one another, "Old Testament" and "New Testament" present a theological argument for how someone else's mail is not "Hebrew Bible" or "Jewish Scripture" but the permanent, accessible witness to the One with whom we have to do, who has been fully revealed in Jesus of Nazareth. Without this core theological confession, the literature remains fully someone else's mail — not just for the Christian, but for the simply curious as well. And, as the metaphor implies, it would in fact be wrong to read mail that is

19. Van Buren, "On Reading Someone Else's Mail."

73

not one's own. It would also be wrong to declare real mail not mail at all, in order to justify reading it for some other more general purpose (historiographic, sociological, reader-response, or for "imaginative construal"). The terms "Old Testament" and "Torah" both safeguard this dimension, even as they do so in the name of different theological decisions and in conjunction with different interpretive literatures and governing convictions.

For the Christian community such convictions take their bearings from the person of Jesus Christ himself. As Luther once put it, using the same metaphor of mail:

> For the New Testament is nothing more than a revelation of the Old, just as if somebody at first had a sealed letter and then opened it. So the Old Testament is a testamental letter of Christ, which he caused to be opened after his death and read and proclaimed everywhere through the Gospel.[20]

What was self-evident for Paul and the apostles, namely the use of Israel's scriptures to "preach Christ," becomes a deliberate and self-conscious decision in the church's retention of "Old Testament." Each of these theological decisions is grounded christologically, as extensions of Christ's own act, the unsealing of the scriptures, as Christ's own testamental letter, to be read now everywhere. As a term for Christians, "Hebrew Bible" fails to comprehend this christological center, and for the simply curious it fails to explain how Israel's mail has become a word of address for all creation.

20. From Luther's sermon on John 1:1-14, here quoted from Kornelis H. Miskotte, *When the Gods Are Silent* (London: Collins, 1967) 109.

7

The Changing Face of Old Testament Studies

A scholar trained in current critical theories, Theo knew that any objectives of that human creature, the writer, were entirely beside the point; that the text's intentions were irrelevant and the author was absolutely a goner — as dead to the modern world as God — with no more authority than a rose has over its scent. Still, deep in Theo's bones tradition pulled; he hankered for meaning and purpose. He was troubled by Plato's notion of the artist-as-divine-moron; he was annoyed by that recent play in which Mozart came across as a lewd, giggling, imbecilic conduit for the divine harmonies of the universe. Was it really plausible that Shakespeare could have been as dumb as Shaw thought him? Was it conceivable that Michelangelo didn't have a clue as to what the David was going to end up looking like? Could anyone ever seriously believe that Jane Austen might be stupid?

Michael Malone, *Foolscap*[1]

Reading Gabe Fackre's essay "What Theology Professors Are Teaching" in these pages[2] last year evoked in me a great deal of envy. In a day of diversity

---

1. Michael Malone, *Foolscap: A Novel* (Boston: Little, Brown, 1991).
2. G. Fackre, "What Theology Professors Are Teaching: Reorientation and Retrieval in Systematic Theology," *The Christian Century,* June 26, 1991, 653-56.

This chapter originally appeared in *The Christian Century,* October 21, 1992, 932-35.

and hypercontextualization, he was able to spot areas of common concern in the teaching of systematic theology. And he supported his claim with empirical fact: a survey of 115 syllabi.

I have no access to anything like empirical fact, but I hazard the guess that the teaching of Old Testament is not so unified. To begin with, the term "Old Testament" itself is suspect in some quarters in a way that even "systematic theology" is not. Terms like "Hebrew Scriptures," "Hebrew Bible," "Tanak," "First Testament," and even "Older" or "Former Testament" have been proposed. I was confronted by a prominent ethicist the other day who wasted no time in asking "Is the Old Testament Christian scripture or not?" with something of the same gravity associated with old doctrinal inquiry. Terminology matters. What one calls the field says a lot about what one believes about it.

Proper terminology is not just a matter of Jewish versus Christian sensibilities. It has to do with the wide variety of institutional contexts in which biblical study takes place. The contrast with systematic theology is striking. The fact that the Old Testament may be an object of investigation in (1) church seminaries and divinity schools, (2) undergraduate departments of religion, (3) Near Eastern language and civilization programs, (4) archaeological institutes, (5) comparative literature studies, (6) English classes, or (7) anthropology departments makes for a considerably diverse angle of vision on the subject. A specific discipline for the theological study of the Old Testament is asked to meet the special challenge of defining itself and the terms under which it operates — challenged, ironically, by the very disciplines it has spawned.

The ability to narrow the field of inquiry is, in my view, an enviable thing, given the very wide range of service into which an introductory course in Old Testament is now being pressed. A comparison with the European setting — where so much of Old Testament method was developed — is revealing. In German universities the "introduction" is but one limited segment of Old Testament study. It is distinguished by being (frequently) the most tedious and least interesting course, but also the most indispensable for studying other areas such as "the history of Israel," "the theology of the Old Testament," and "the history of interpretation." In our system "Introduction to Old Testament/Hebrew Scriptures" is generally expected to cover all these things: literary introduction, exegesis, history, theology, and history of interpretation.

There are other constraints on adequately "introducing" the Old Testament, constraints that cannot be remedied by being sure other electives will be offered later. The two-semester basic course can no longer do all it is asked to do because students simply do not have the sort of general familiarity with the content of the Bible they once had. This leads to a further complication. Most critical method was predicated on students' possessing a working knowledge of — if not a confessional commitment to — the Bible in its present form, a form that was then deconstructed by means of historical tools. The goal was to recast the Bible's narrative into new and different bins involving hypothetical authors, editors, and communities. This made for a challenging, sometimes threatening, always critically imaginative two-semester journey through the Old Testament, beginning with the rudimentary antecedents of the Yahwist and continuing through to portions of Daniel and the last chapters of Zechariah.

But if one takes away a working knowledge of the present form of the text, a different effect is achieved. One gets all the critical conclusions, but the genuine push-pull of movement from confessed text to historical reconstruction is differently transmitted and received. If one tries to move from the present text to a historical-critical reconstruction and then to "postmodern" or "second naive" reading, the results may be even more mixed. Why are we doing this at all? Students lack a command of the general content of the Bible, and yet at the same time they are restless with gaining familiarity with this basic content for its own sake. They are also restless with critical method or with newer literary alternatives — unless, of course, they are accessible and directly relevant to modern issues. Fackre spoke of the commendable concern to link systematics to modern issues; my sense of biblical studies is that the greatest danger is the opposite: not appreciating the simple foreignness of the Bible and its world. I mean not its historical distance or its cultural distinctiveness only, but its theological edge — what Barth meant when he once referred to the "strange world" of the Bible.

Older critical method, for all its deficiencies, raised the stakes in proper biblical interpretation in ways that were threatening and immediately felt by most students. I am not sure that that is true any more. For many the Old Testament is simply old, and therefore "out of touch." Older critical attempts to illustrate the relevance of the past by means of historical analogy require too much recasting of the narrative and simple speculation, and may presume too great a curiosity about these matters to begin with. One senses that today readers are confronting the world of the Old Testament (that is, the world presented by the text in its present form) for the first time and not being altogether sure that they like what they see;

or, if they like what they see, not being sure what all the historical-critical commotion is about to begin with. In short, today's readership is very different from the one teachers confronted at mid-century. Looking back at Brevard Childs's 1970 essay on biblical theology, *Biblical Theology in Crisis*, one finds it hard to comprehend how powerful the Biblical Theology Movement was in the 1940s and 50s — and how one could have spoken of a crisis of truly momentous importance, one that concentrated so much energy and debate. What we now have is a more mundane affair: a crisis in approach and method of the most basic sort. Its effects are more immediate in terms of curriculum, institutional context, and the teaching of Old Testament.

In a recent essay Phyllis Trible suggested that Childs's end point in his survey of the Biblical Theology Movement (a date she pinpoints as 1963) was not fortuitous. "The timing is uncanny," she says. "That same year Betty Friedan wrote *The Feminine Mystique*."[3] It is undoubtedly true that cultural factors led to the demise of the Biblical Theology Movement and, more generally, to challenges to a certain historical-critical way of reading the Old Testament. One thinks not just of feminism but also of the Vietnam War, changes in sexual values, and the decline of mainstream Protestantism and the strong pulpit associated with it. Childs had already mentioned many of these culture factors and the role they played in what he called the "cracking of the walls" of the Biblical Theology Movement in the U.S. Childs, of course, described both the movement and its decline in order to pave the way for his own proposal: a biblical theology tied to canon.

One of the chief problems with Childs's approach — not usually discussed by scholars — is pedagogical and has to do with the present climate of Old Testament teaching. Childs's 1979 *Introduction to the Old Testament* demands that the student participate fully in the older historical-critical discussion. Ideally, the student should move from a basic grasp of the contents and narrative of the Bible, into a critical mode informed by source, form and redaction criticism, and then come to see the limitations of this movement so as finally to appreciate the insights of Childs's canonical approach. The movement is from precritical to critical to a canonical reading that is neither of these forebears, but demands a sensitivity to them both. And yet what is lacking among most students is any

3. "Five Loaves and Two Fishes: Feminist Hermeneutics and Biblical Theology," *TS* 50 (1989) 284.

deep-seated, long-nurtured, instinctive, prerational commitment to the Old Testament in its present form. What happened to Sunday School, Bible reading at home, or knowing a thing by heart? Episodes of "Beverly Hills 90210" or "The X-Files" are much better known — and loved — in their synchronic order than is the Old Testament. Without a thorough knowledge of the biblical text, Old Testament introductions threaten to become, as James Barr once said in another context, Old Testament conclusions.

In the waning years of the Biblical Theology Movement, the walls with the most stress cracks were those involving historical inquiry. The stated end point of Childs's survey of that movement was associated with the work of Langdon Gilkey (not Betty Friedan) and specifically with essays written by Gilkey in 1965 and 1966. Gilkey's famous 1961 savaging of revelation in history delivered one of the more damaging tremors ("Cosmology, Ontology, and the Travail of Biblical Language").[4] The Biblical Theology Movement had sought to retrieve, in stripped-down form, a dimension of the old cohesion between natural world and biblical world by positing points of contact between the crafted narrative and the real world of cause and effect: the Mighty Acts of God. Gilkey rightly saw both that these Mighty Acts of God were in fact not so mighty (a strong east wind parting the Red Sea) and that if they were, a dilemma was created for modern men and women who were left to wonder how God was acting in their lives in a way at all comparable to the way God was active in the Old Testament — where people witnessed hills of foreskins, the sun standing still, meals with angels, the parting of the Red Sea and the like. Not so mighty and not so able to produce the wanted cohesion, the acts upon which the Biblical Theology Movement were built vanished, taking with them the Biblical Theology Movement itself.

I wonder if Old Testament study ever fully recovered from Gilkey's essay. If one is not searching for the core historical events that triggered the growth of tradition, then why should one engage in the source/form/redaction criticism meant to uncover these matters? Childs used critical approaches in order to gain a purchase on the final form of the text and the theological complexity it represents as the consummation of all previous interpretive efforts. His canonical approach was not simply a new form of redaction criticism. It now appears clear, however, that the distance that separates Childs from his historical-critical forebears is not so great as that

---

4. *JR* 41 (1961) 194-205.

which separates him from more recent readings of the Old Testament, whether literary, neo-midrashic, formalist, artifactual, New Critical, or deconstructionist. This is because Childs never abandoned one matter close to the heart of historical-critical inquiry: the intentionality of the text, the notion that this is a deliberately crafted narrative.

It is the lack of a clear and persuasive understanding of the role of "the author" and of intentionality in texts that most troubles Old Testament study at present. The notion of authorial intention was not abandoned with the rise of historical-critical method. Rather, the concept was enriched, multiplied, and extended as a host of anonymous authors and editors, ranging far and wide in terms of circumstance, setting, and purpose, began to populate the biblical landscape. The difficulty was with overcoming authorial diversity and a complex picture of historical change. Childs has sought to make a claim for the stability of the final form of the text that respects the critical insight into authorial diversity, yet presses beyond this toward an appreciation of the normative claims of the text in its received form. In his subtle formulation, there is an intentionality that derives from critically reconstructed authors, editors, and prior receivers of revelation. This intentionality as reflected in the final text also has its own special integrity as it participates in but also brings to consummation earlier levels of intentionality.

Whatever else might be said about Childs's approach, he clearly has an enlarged and sophisticated notion of authorial intention. He depends upon a view of revelation in history that begins with events and their immediate interpretation, but also looks to the divine word as received by the community of faith, reheard and reshaped, continuing to call forth new theological insight, obedience, and a life of faith congruent with the divine will.

But we can now list alternatives to Childs's subtle version of authorial intention: (1) The text has an intentionality that transcends and is not strictly derivative of any authorial intention; such intentionality is supple and pluriform (New Criticism). (2) The various intentionalities revealed by critical method must not be correlated in such a way as to give undue priority to the final form of the text, which is only one of many, either enriching or distorting, points of view (redaction criticism). (3) The search for intentionality is a deception — readers alone supply intentionality, not texts (deconstruction). (4) What intentionality we can discover in the Old Testament is culturally bound and must be run through a critical sieve to determine its political usefulness; to do otherwise would be to distort the

Bible's essential political and materialist handling of God and reality (various forms of materialist demythologizing).

We have come full circle. The reason for such wide diversity in Old Testament studies has to do with basic disagreements over the genre of the material in the first place and the divided convictions of interpretive communities. An older generation believed that if it simply described the genre of the Old Testament — more in its parts than as a whole — readers would conform themselves to the genres discovered. Interpretation would be "actualization," "re-presentation." To a degree, this is what took place. What was true and could be discovered about the Bible as a historical document would also be true of an interpretive community seeking to model itself after the Bible and its world. But with the widespread failure of the field to come to any agreement about the Bible's own categories of discourse, its special modes of literary expression and intentionality, and especially those social and religious factors that handed the Old Testament over to us, we have simply been thrown back on ourselves and the deeply felt convictions with which we began the process of interpretation. The focus has shifted from the text and its background to the reader and the community that interprets.

Yet even on these terms it should remain possible for an interpretive community to make a conscious decision to hear the Bible as scripture, to believe in the coercive and constraining force of the Bible's own unique literary construction, and to regard itself as trying to live out the demands of a word and a God that stand over it, in continuity with communities of faith within the Bible and in the church's ongoing history of interpretation. Such a community can also argue that in so doing it is seeking to hear a word truly external to itself, is straining to hear intended acts of communication, and is involved in a process of faithful reception — one in which accurate and inaccurate hearings both happen and matter theologically. Let the debate rage over whether a particular reception is right or appropriately critical. But let there be no delusion about the willful decisions of all interpreters and the prior commitments they bring to the reading process.

Yet a final question remains: Does one willful decision to read the Bible better conform to the intentions of the literature than another? That is, what of the genre of the Bible as a whole, and of the Old Testament within it? No matter how much the golfer with a sand wedge and cleated shoes wants to play squash, the squash court expects something else: rubber-soled shoes, a squash racket, and a player who has come to play squash. Does the Bible also expect a certain sort of reader? Is the Old Testament both an open book for all to read and in some sense a closed book with a distinct readership in mind? Does the Old Testament conform to a genre that has been externally imposed by coercive readers and hard misreadings, or is its genre a reflection of the will of communities that produced it, assented to its ongoing word of address and handed it over to new communities of faith, of which we are one? One answer that has been given makes a strong case for the genre "canon" or "scripture." Do we need more precision here? Are other alternatives more convincing? It is to this sort of form-critical question that the field must now turn if it is to understand both its curricular obligations and the constraints that shape and define its various institutional situations.

What is a theological handling of the Old Testament? In what sort of context — curricular and institutional — will it exist and thrive? Is the proper legacy of the historical-critical method a continued concern for intentionality in biblical texts, not so much in precanonical but rather in final scriptural form? These three questions have been my concern here. In the passage from Michael Malone's *Foolscap* quoted at the beginning of this chapter, Theo is right to worry that a text's intentions may be regarded as irrelevant and the concept of an author "absolutely a goner." More troubling perhaps is his association of these two matters with the death of God in the modern world. But that is a topic for another day.[5]

---

5. One could, of course, applaud the loss of "the author" in modern biblical studies, and yet not conflate this loss with the loss of concern for intended communication. Even figural reading works with some nuanced understanding of intentionality (on this see chs. 1-4 above). By broadening what is meant by "author," a shift toward the text itself is possible, away from the independent "mind" of the imagined writer/speaker (on this see ch. 10 below).

8

Biblical Authority in the Late Twentieth Century

The Baltimore Declaration, Scripture-Reason-Tradition, and the Canonical Approach

In this essay I wish to look at the use of scripture in Anglicanism in the modern period, using as a point of departure the "Baltimore Declaration" of 1991. I am interested both in what the Declaration has attempted on its own terms, but also in the wider discussions about the Bible's use at present, intertwined as these are with debates over authority in the church, which have given rise to the Declaration and to which its positive proposals are directed. In the course of this brief analysis I want to emphasize the very limited usefulness of the so-called "scripture, reason, and tradition" paradigm now popularized in modern Anglicanism (as well as in its several adaptations) and question whether it was ever the sort of historic and comprehensive principle its advocates now maintain. I will conclude with a very modest proposal about an alternative model for comprehending the authority of scripture in the modern church.

The limitation of the essay will be seen in its emphasis on pointing out problems both with the Baltimore Declaration and with the so-called three-legged stool, with only suggestions of a comprehensive alternative for reading scripture. As such, this analysis should be properly regarded as

This chapter originally appeared in *Anglican Theological Review* 75 (1993) 471-86. The Baltimore Declaration can be seen in *Reclaiming Faith: Essays on Orthodoxy in the Episcopal Church and the Baltimore Declaration,* ed. E. Radner and G. Sumner (Grand Rapids: Eerdmans, 1993) 276-83.

preliminary and reactionary (if the term can be used in a positive sense!). The reader is directed throughout the essay to a much broader discussion regarding modern use of scripture associated with the work of Brevard Childs and will find at the conclusion a brief summary of my own efforts to bring a canonical approach to bear on the exegesis and exposition of scripture. It is that sort of approach I would posit as an alternative to either propositional uses of scripture or the overloaded and inherently diffuse "triadic" conception presently in vogue.

PROPOSITIONAL ARGUMENTS FROM SCRIPTURE

The "Baltimore Declaration" is not so successful in solving a problem as in pointing one out. The problem involves the Bible. More specifically, it involves confident modern use of the Bible. The problem with confident use of the Bible is one acutely felt in the Anglican tradition in the modern period, but it is by no means a problem for Anglicans alone.

The form in which the Declaration is presented exposes the problem. Each article begins with one or more statements from scripture, highlighted with special italicized print. There then follows a short prose account in defense of some theological confession thought to be under attack by modernity but in reality consistent with scripture's own plain-sense declaration. A negative repudiation clause in bold print recapitulates the argument and presents a forceful summary.

The implication of the form adopted is that scripture is authoritative, that its authority *can be stated propositionally* through the citing of individual verses, and that argumentation involving matters of Christian faith should begin and end with scripture. In addition to this formally structured assertion, a similar statement is made within the body of the final article (VII). In language reminiscent of the Thirty-Nine Articles, the Holy Scriptures are said, according to this article, to "contain all things necessary to salvation." Then, in addition, several further statements are made in an effort to describe the nature of the Bible's authority, the character of inspiration infusing "God's Word written," the appropriate place of tradition and context in modern interpretation, as well as a cautious endorsement of "responsible biblical criticism." The Declaration's language ("writers, redactors, and editors") similarly reveals an irenic acquaintance with modern biblical criticism, where such terms are the stock-in-trade of seminary textbooks, commentaries for scholar and churchman, and even more popular aids for Bible study. To bring things to conclusion, the repudiation clause reasserts that over and above the content of Holy Scripture nothing can rightly be claimed as authoritative. The final sentence states that the "Old and New Testaments [do not] stand hermeneutically, materially, and formally independent of each other."

The content of this final article, both because of its detail and because of its effort to square a certain responsible modern use of biblical criticism with more traditional views of inspiration and the role of "tradition" as such, represents a special matter of concern that must be looked at on its own. It is the formal structure of the Declaration, and particularly its propositional use of scripture verses to introduce and buttress an argument, that points up the chief problem with the document.[1] By using the term "problem" I mean the "problem" with the document as a vehicle of change in the modern Episcopal Church. It could of course be argued that the document does not have this purpose, but is self-consciously non-apologetic. But this seems doubtful. The tone of the final article suggests that an effort is being made to articulate a doctrine of scripture that the authors both endorse and wish to commend to a wider body of faithful Christians.

The problem, then (if I am entitled to use the term based upon my understanding of at least a partial intention of the document), is that precisely such a propositional use of scripture as the document adopts is what has come under assault in the modern period. Even more pious and "responsible" forms of biblical criticism would not take a turn toward propositionalism of the sort adopted in the form of Declaration, even if many of the central theological convictions were of shared concern (the Trinity, doubts about "inclusive" language, etc.). Even were we to wish it otherwise, this form of "argument from scripture" will only persuade the insider, the one already disposed to read scripture in this fashion, the one already doubtful about modernity's legacy and ongoing contribution to the church and the world. (Over and above this, it is another question altogether whether such a person is interested in the nuanced use of biblical criticism hinted at in the final article.) This returns us again to the question of intention and the degree to which the document truly seeks to bring

1. For a discussion of various models for interpreting the Bible and assessing its authority, see David Kelsey, *The Uses of Scripture in Recent Theology* (Philadelphia: Fortress, 1975).

about change through argument and persuasion. If it does not, then one could conclude from the general noninterest the document has generated in the Episcopal Church that the authors' purpose was ironically achieved: they felt a need to commend the faith and did so, whether anyone was interested or not. No one felt a need to adopt their view of the character of biblical authority, and so did not.

But I want to look at the document as proposing a way of reading scripture that the authors both believe in and wish to commend to the church at large. And under this set of circumstances it is the final article and the form of the argument from scripture adopted in all the articles that present the greatest problem for the modern church — and that includes a church that may otherwise share the authors' concerns about the assaults of modernity and inclusivity.

Propositional use of scripture has been rendered problematic by the modern world with its rival descriptions of natural, social, and historical science. For a host of reasons far too numerous to explore here, the Bible has since the eighteenth century been dethroned as a document of propositional authority.[2] The authors themselves seem aware of this in the final article, which is not a defense of propositional scriptural warrants but rather a fairly modern-sounding attempt to square biblical criticism with more traditional statements regarding the sufficiency of scriptural authority or the continuity of God's revelation across Old and New Testaments, matters of special concern to early (sixteenth-century) Anglicanism in its struggle for identity over against Puritanism and Roman Catholicism.

Precisely in their wanting to have it both ways, the authors expose a tension particularly acute in the Anglican tradition, with its twin and sometimes paradoxical commitments to traditionalism in worship and prayerful assembly, on the one hand, and optimism about the use of reason and natural law, on the other. Obviously the authors of the Baltimore Declaration would more readily admit an allegiance to the first commitment than to the second. And yet the final article appears to flirt with the same familiar Anglican "trinity" (scripture, reason, tradition) that, in my view, produced the very climate of biblical and theological reflection the authors are at pains to expose and repudiate.

2. See Hans Frei, *The Eclipse of Biblical Narrative* (New Haven: Yale University, 1974).

SCRIPTURE, REASON, TRADITION:
THE SO-CALLED "THREE-LEGGED STOOL"

It is quickly becoming something of a commonplace in modern Anglican thought to justify liberal application of historical criticism to the Bible on the grounds that this jibes with a "traditional Anglican principle" of scripture, reason, and tradition, referred to as a "three-legged stool" of authority or a "threefold cord" not otherwise quickly broken.[3] Historical criticism is to be fully endorsed because of this (unique) understanding of dispersed authority generally and a more specific commitment to reason as an authoritative "leg" of even length and durability as other "legs" on this sturdy stool.

To be sure, Anglicans are also quick to place riders on this already rather imprecise conception of authority and the special role of reason. Is the order correct? Are all the legs of equal length? Instead of a stool with three legs, should we adopt instead the (not entirely inappropriate) metaphor of a couch, with four or more legs, including most often "experience," if not also, as in one recent formulation, "episcopacy" and "vocation"?[4] More complicated, what is the exact relationship of one pole

---

3. This sort of notion appears both explicitly and implicitly in two recent handbooks, *Anglicanism and the Bible*, ed. F. Borsch (Wilton: Morehouse Barlow, 1984), and *The Study of Anglicanism*, ed. S. Sykes and J. Booty (Philadelphia: Fortress, 1988).

4. See T. Wright, "What Is the Anglican Communion?" *Virginia Seminary Journal* 44 (1992) 31-39. Wright says, "I would like to see a fifth element added, and placed, if anywhere, before Tradition and Reason: Scripture, Vocation, Tradition, Reason, and Episcopacy" (36). John Booty proposes his own modification: "Scripture and the Tradition aligned to it possess priority over reason and experience. . . . We must, however, acknowledge another priority, the priority of perception. We are first of all reasoning, experiencing people. . . . Human development, too, holds a priority. . . . Tradition, understood in terms of the Church's authority, comes first, conveying the Scripture to us, convincing us of its nature until by experience we affirm its truth . . ." (*What Makes Us Episcopalians?* [Wilton: Morehouse Barlow, 1982] 32). At another place he recognizes that the Anglican divines "on the whole regard Scripture interpreted through tradition and reason as authoritative" ("Standard Divines," *The Study of Anglicanism*, 164). Borsch states: "In the dialogue of our experience and reason with tradition and Scripture it would be a mistake to grant one an absolute primacy" ("All Things Necessary to Salvation," *Anglicanism and the Bible*, 219). But then he seems to back off: "There are, however, reasons why the Bible may be said to have certain forms of primacy" (219). In David Scott's view, "scripture, tradition, and reason/experience work together with each other, informing each other like good marriage partners," becoming as it were a "gyrocompass for the flight of faith" ("Liberalism and the Episcopal Church," *Good News* [magazine of the Diocese of Connecticut] 1986). This is

of authority to another?[5] And more complicated still, when and where do we see an actual application of this "traditional Anglican principle" to help address a real modern issue before the church, such as the ordination of women, abortion, or homosexuality? The general impression left by this, on the face of it, extraordinarily synthetic principle is that it is impossible to use synthetically and only serves a negative or restrictive function in modern discussions, that is, to argue for the inadequacy of one or two legs (usually scripture and tradition) over against a third leg (usually reason or experience). It may be that as a synthetic principle the triad functions unconsciously in modern discussion. But then what is the point in elevating it to the status of a principle to begin with, as well as claiming that it is somehow a unique "Anglican" way of reading the Bible that avoids the charges of fundamentalism on the one hand (to be avoided as leprosy once was) and yet allows Episcopalians to be "enlightened traditionalists" on the other?[6]

Problematic for a different set of reasons is the notion that the authority of scripture, reason, and tradition is a true, uniquely indigenous Anglican "principle" in the first place. In addition there is the notion that this "principle" belongs both to the classic period (associated with the thought and writings of Richard Hooker) and subsequent centuries of Anglicanism, thus establishing a sort of thread of continuity — like apostolic succession? — spanning five centuries of biblical interpretation, if not more. That Hooker mentions authorities alongside scripture is not to be denied, and surely among them are tradition and reason. But several

---

all very confusing. How helpful (or transparent) is the "Anglican triad" when it requires so much further modification and clarification?

5. See (and note the order) *Scripture, Tradition and Reason: A Study in the Criteria of Christian Doctrine,* ed. R. Bauckham, B. Drewery (Edinburgh: Clark, 1988), where "(w)hat is at stake throughout the volume is *the one problem of the relationship between the three*" (vii).

6. See Reginald Fuller's caricature of John Burgon in "Historical Criticism and the Bible," *Anglicanism and the Bible,* 147; repeated in "Scripture" in *The Study of Anglicanism,* 79. Recently P. Cuthbertson has seized on Burgon for another lampooning in "The Authority of Scripture in the Episcopal Church," *SLJT* 34 (1991), with his own repeat performance in "Known, Knower, and Knowing: The Authority of Scripture in the Episcopal Church," *ATR* 74 (1992), in both places citing a still earlier essay and critique of Burgon by A. Richardson (1944). It is odd to see Dean Burgon repeatedly dusted off from a very different climate of debate to serve as a foil for more enlightened historical criticism, simply because he regarded the Bible as the Word of God, a very real danger to be avoided!

matters plague easy identification of the "three-legged stool" as a principle of great antiquity, much less as one that has also characterized Anglican biblical interpretation through the intervening centuries, and that can now be used with equal force and commendation in the modern period.

First, to speak of scripture, reason, and tradition as a sort of principle or even hermeneutical lens in the writings of Hooker is misleading. The very few explicit references to the triad in Hooker's writings establish the general rule.[7] Second, Hooker's understanding of all three is extraordinarily different from ours in the late twentieth century. Hooker defended a use of reason and tradition over against Puritanism in order to give room for the authority of the church in matters where the scriptures *were silent* (church vestments, architecture, etc.). Then, over against the claims of Roman Catholicism to possess the sole authoritative tradition of biblical interpretation, Hooker sided with the continental reformers in elevating scripture above the church and in making a fairly clean distinction between canon (i.e., "canonical scriptures") and tradition. The question for those who seek to retrieve the "three-legged stool" of Hooker for our century is whether anything like the same context of argument and church controversy as existed in the sixteenth century exists now to provide a warrant for using the triad and for claiming that in so doing Episcopalians are being true to the mind of historic Anglicanism. Vigorous defenders of historical criticism as applied to the Bible should exercise the same critical faculties with respect to church history, lest a loose "principle" that functioned in one historical context is dragged kicking and screaming into a very different climate of intellectual, ecclesial, and cultural debate.

Third, and related to this concern, it is outrageous to think that one could conflate Hooker's sixteenth-century understanding of reason (corporate, Thomist-Aristotelian, tied to natural law before the cleavage between natural and revealed truth) with reason as understood in the seventeenth, eighteenth, and nineteenth centuries (consider Spinoza, Locke, or Schleiermacher),[8] much less reason as understood in our cen-

7. "What Scripture doth plainly deliver, to that the first place both of credit and obedience is due; the next whereunto, is what any man can necessarily conclude by force of Reason; after these, the voice of the church succeedeth" (*Laws of Ecclesiastical Polity* V [London, 1597] 8.2).

8. Or Kant. Winfree Smith rightly notes, "Richard Hooker meant by reason what Thomas Aquinas meant. He did not mean what Immanuel Kant meant when he wrote his little book *Religion Within the Limits of Reason Alone*" ("Dominical Authority in Time and the Roles of Scripture, Tradition, Reason," *SLJT* 34 [Special Issue, 1991] 47).

tury (individualistic, experiential, capable of distinctions between revealed and natural truth), and much less still with the application by
"unaided reason" of the historicalcritical method of interpreting the
Bible.[9] Hooker would have been shocked and confused by the notion
that reason is the faculty given to humankind to establish which New
Testament Epistles were truly authored by Paul and which were not,
which sayings of Jesus can be trusted as "authentic" and which not, what
really happened at the Reed Sea (sic), the social background of deutero-
Isaiah, and the like. To defend critical approaches in the modern period
on the grounds that biblical folk also exercised authority over the divine
word[10] would have puzzled a Hooker for whom the distinction between
canon and tradition, prophets and apostles within the biblical record and
interpreters outside it, was simply assumed.[11] Fourth, where can it be

9. A view explicitly articulated by A. S. McGrade in "Reason," *The Study of Anglicanism,* 106. "Hooker held that the Church could reasonably prescribe contrary to a biblical
precept, if the purpose of the precept *in its historical context* could be understood to be
irrelevant in current circumstances" (106, emphasis added). McGrade then compares
Hooker to Locke on this score. But to suggest that Hooker was a proto-historical-critic
because of his understanding of reason is to confuse a hermeneutical problem with a
problem of historical criticism. I do not know what biblical texts McGrade has in mind
(none are cited). When in the Thirty-Nine Articles the ceremonial law of Moses ("as
touching Ceremonies and Rites") is said not to be binding on Christians, this is not due
to an insight from biblical criticism or reason, but because of an inner-biblical theological
discussion about the law (see Paul). To call such a move an exercise of historical-critical
reason confuses a hermeneutical and theological problem with a modern historical problem.

10. Compare especially Cuthbertson's analyses in the works cited above.

11. On the role of the canon as establishing a distinction between modern interpreters and figures within the Bible itself, see the remarks of Brevard Childs (*Biblical
Theology in Crisis* [Philadelphia: Westminster, 1970], especially chapter 6; and most recently, *Biblical Theology of the Old and New Testaments* [Minneapolis: Fortress, 1992]).
Precisely what gives the church its identity and its unique standing is that it orders its life
according to a canon of biblical writings; to state it crudely, characters in the Bible had no
Bible in the same sense. To say, as Childs does, that "we are not prophets or apostles" is
neither to denigrate the church as "latecomer" nor to encourage a nostalgia for a sort of
"pure revelation" vouchsafed to the original biblical men and women, somehow indirectly
analogous to our own experience of God (on this, see John 20:29-31). Rather it is to
recognize that a fundamental feature of the canonical process is its capacity to transform
a tradition-historical process into a final stabilized text, a lively "charter document" against
which the church can measure its common life and, under the prudence of the Holy Spirit,
continue to confront its mission and hope, based upon the foundational legacy of the
apostles and prophets, whose experience of God is different in kind, but not in substance,
from that of all succeeding generations.

shown that "scripture, reason, tradition" functioned as a hermeneutical principle especially Anglican in the centuries that separate Hooker's from our own? (More on this in a moment.)

Finally, what does it mean that historical criticism took its initial bearings by severely questioning all corporate, ecclesial interpretations of scripture prior to the Enlightenment? That move can be seen in as late and as irenic a figure as Gerhard von Rad, for whom allegory and even some forms of typology were threatening ahistorical tendencies to be avoided and eschewed. The point is this: historical criticism established the very ground on which it stood by arguing for a sharp disjunction between "tradition" and "the plain sense of scripture" interpreted according to the emerging historical and literary-critical canons. How then are we to embrace historical criticism as defensible on the grounds of an alleged Anglican principle of "scripture, reason, and tradition" when it was exactly this same post-Enlightenment "reason" that insisted on a sharp polarity between scripture historically interpreted and the tradition of the church, thus by definition ruling out any clean notion of complementarity? And yet in Hooker's formulation, the complementarity of all three was assumed as indispensable, allowing the church to interpret reasonably where scripture was silent ("reason"), with one eye trained on past, corporate, catholic interpretations ("tradition"). Historical criticism is not and never was content to pick up its shovel only where scripture is silent.

But to return to the fourth point. Where did the modern notion of a three-legged stool of authority, rooted in Hooker and a unique legacy of subsequent Anglicanism, come from? In my view, it is nothing more than a twentieth-century invention,[12] smuggled in so as to accommodate an older, traditional understanding of the Bible's authority with a new and sometimes hostile worldview, now fully in place. This worldview is one for which the basic biblical narrative has long since been eclipsed (both by modernity and by the critical method set up to cope with it).[13] It forces us to speak of categories like fundamentalism, literalism, or liberalism, where Hooker and his contemporaries would

---

12. It is anticipated in the nineteenth century by the final acceptance of historical criticism by the Anglo-catholic Charles Gore, now a sort of vanguard figure for Anglicans of otherwise different churchmanship and stripe. See "The Holy Spirit and Inspiration," in *Lux Mundi*, ed. C. Gore (London: Murray, 1889) 315-62.

13. See Hans Frei, *Eclipse*.

have contemplated very different lines of division for altogether different cultural and intellectual reasons.

In the modern church "scripture" remains a historic given, but its authority is difficult to perceive and articulate in anything but a personal sense because of our awareness of the distance of its historical and social context from our own. No century has felt this distance more acutely than our own.[14] "Tradition" points to a reality Hooker would probably have considered under the rubric of "reason," namely, our belief in the trustworthiness of natural law in a corporate, nonindividualistic sense. And "Reason" has come to mean the exercise of individual human emotion and rationality as applied to authoritative texts, church decisions, and all manner of ethical discourse and general decision-making. The triad "scripture, reason, tradition" may speak volumes about where we are as a modern church, but in my judgment it says very little about either the century of Hooker or subsequent centuries of so-called classical Anglicanism. And much less still does it offer a possibility for biblical interpretation in the modern period that will move beyond the conservative versus liberal impasse. Nor does the triad present us with a truly corporate reading of scripture prepared to deal with the historical distance, literary complexity, social and ethical sharpness, and sheer theological force of the biblical text within the context and challenge of late twentieth-century Christianity. Before discussing in more detail the possibility of such an option, it is necessary to return to the Baltimore Declaration and reexamine its understanding of scripture in the light of these remarks concerning the inadequacy of the so-called "three-legged stool" model for modern biblical interpretation.

14. Here I would disagree with the opening sentence of the Declaration: at no point in time has the church faced such a massive encroachment on its texts, its authority, its ability to speak with a clear voice to itself and to society as it must at present, by a worldview poised to rival both scripture and tradition without trying very hard.

ARTICLE VII AND THE
"SCRIPTURE, REASON, TRADITION" APPROACH

It should be clear from the previous two sections that the propositional argument from scripture approach used in the Declaration is in effect a throwback to the climate of confessional and scholastic arguments from scripture popular in the sixteenth and seventeenth centuries. This is in some sense consistent with the intention of the Declaration to model itself on confessional formularies, though to be sure more recent ones. But the question was raised in the opening section whether or not the same could be said of the content of the final article (VII), where the most substantive statements are made concerning the character of scripture and the nature of biblical authority. We must also consider the possibility that by articulating one view of scripture in some detail in article VII, and by modeling another approach to scripture in the actual form and structure of the document, the Declaration is in fact at cross-purposes with itself and as such reflects precisely the sorts of tensions regarding use of the Bible in the modern period also revealed in our discussion of the "scripture, reason, tradition" model.

As noted above, the opening statement of the final article is nothing more than a quotation from Article VI of the Thirty-Nine Articles, though lacking the stipulation clauses of the latter ("so that whatsoever is not read therein, nor may be proved thereby, is not to be required of any man, that it should be believed as an article of Faith, or thought to be requisite or necessary to salvation"). Both the original article and its abbreviation in the Declaration are concerned to circumscribe the proper realm of the Bible's authority as involving matters of our salvation — not, for example, descriptions of the origin of the universe, inerrant geographical and historical reckonings from antiquity, nor a concern with "authentically" or "inauthentically" ascribed authorship and other such matters dear to the heart of historical-critical method. The second line (and a similar sentence in the repudiation clause) makes even more explicit that with respect to inspiration there can be no external critical criterion that would render one portion of scripture more or less inspired than another. Here we see a full recognition of the social, historical, and literary complexity of the biblical text in its final form, and at the same time a steady refusal to use this sort of critical recognition as the means by which to set up a grid of priority, with higher value placed on some one critically reconstructed portion of text than another.

It is in the third sentence that we confront the endorsement, such as it is, of modern biblical criticism. To be sure, biblical criticism is to be used responsibly, it is to be used "under the guidance and lordship of the Spirit," and it is to be used within a specific context: "the tradition and community of the Christian Church." But who is to determine when these various criteria are met? What may well be one person's "responsible" use of biblical criticism is almost certainly another person's irresponsible use. And what eventual heretic did not claim to be working under the "lordship of the Spirit"? Here we have biblical criticism, a highly rationalistic method, according to its own canons ineluctably "objective," now to be hedged in by these various subjective criteria that the document enjoins ("responsible," "spiritual," "Christian"). As to "tradition," it again strikes me as naive to assume for even the best of reasons any easy rapprochement between "scripture" and "tradition" in the same breath as one endorses a biblical criticism whose entire originating purpose was to call into question "tradition" as an adequate category of biblical interpretation.

In this third sentence we see a classic Anglican tendency, namely, the attempt to justify a critical endeavor by placing its practitioners under various subjective constraints. But why go down this road to begin with? The real question to be raised is: what positive value do the authors of the Declaration truly place on biblical criticism? If it is such an unqualified good, why the need to place it under the very constraints it originally sought to be free of? The phrases that follow return to notions of the Bible's authority virtually foreign to the climate and ethos of biblical criticism (the scriptures in their entirety have to do with Jesus Christ; they are the decisive moral and confessional authority; the Holy Scriptures confront us daily, devotionally, with God's Word). And if there is any conviction dear to the heart of biblical criticism, it is that the Old and New Testaments are "hermeneutically, materially, and formally independent" of one another. Yet precisely the opposite is held to be true by the Declaration.

THE WORD VERSUS THE WORD

A somewhat different approach to the question of authority in Anglicanism from that represented by the Baltimore Declaration would seek to establish a distinction between the Word of God as the (incarnate or risen) Lord, the second person of the trinity, and the Word of God written, that is, the Holy Scriptures of the Old and New Testaments. On this logic, the church does not stand under the authority of God's Word written (the Bible) so much as under the authority of the Word of God, Jesus Christ. Theologians otherwise as divergent as Karl Barth and Paul Tillich are claimed as twentieth-century proponents of just such a distinction. Modern Anglicans otherwise as divergent as David Scott, Philip Cuthbertson, Jack Spong, and Frederick Borsch — and, for other reasons, James Barr and John Barton — also make reference positively to such a distinction and commend it to their respective audiences.[15] Such a distinction plays nicely into one agenda of early biblical criticism: namely, the isolation of

15. Cuthbertson commends Tillich (*SLJT* 36); Barton commends Barth (*People of the Book?* [Louisville: Westminster/John Knox, 1988] 81). Presumably here was a place where the two theological combatants agreed! Scott (with C. Hancock) is the most subtle on this matter: "The unity of the scriptures, likewise, does not reside ultimately in the words on the page as much as in the one in whom 'we live and move and have our being'. . . . Classical Anglicanism believes that God's Word of truth is found in the pages of the Bible, but it is not contained (without remainder) in the pages of the Bible" (unpublished essay read to the Conference of Anglican Theologians, 1992). What does it mean that "God's word of truth" is not contained "without remainder" in the pages of the Bible? Cuthbertson and others are far less subtle: "The Bible as the word of God is not to be confused with Christ as the Word of God, for the Christian's fullest revelation is in our loving relationship with the Person of Christ" (*SLJT* 36; *ATR* 173). Spong contrasts the "literal Bible," "quoting the scripture," "the Bible I read" which "justifies slavery," "treats women as male chattel," "justifies a tribal mentality" with "the grace of God, made known in Jesus Christ," "the call of Christ out of limiting prejudices," and "the inclusive love of God" (*Virginia Seminary Journal,* 52-53). Further examples could be multiplied. He says that the "clear teaching against homosexuality" comprises "the only two verses in Leviticus that anybody's ever heard of" (53). Ironically, it was the interpretation of Leviticus by Henry VIII (against that of the Roman Church, regarding marriage laws) that brought the debate over authority to a head and eventually led to the establishment of an independent Church of England, from which Spong's baptism, ordination, and episcopacy ultimately derive. But this is only one of the more outstanding examples of the failure of the bishop's historical consciousness ever to reach much beyond the twentieth century, or one suspects, the limits of his own life experience. If what "one has heard about Leviticus" or any other biblical book is to be the measure by which the authority of the Bible is established in this age of biblical illiteracy, we are in trouble. Borsch states, "Indeed, to imagine and worship a God that could somehow be defined by human words would be a form of idolatry" ("All Things Necessary," 222). I wonder how Wycliff, Tyndale, Coverdale, Cranmer, Luther, and other Bible translators would have responded to this sort of distinction? See also James Barr, *Holy Scripture: Canon, Authority, Criticism* (Philadelphia: Westminster, 1984), especially chapter 1, and John Barton, *People of the Book?,* who states without further ado: "it is not the Bible that is the Word of God, but Jesus Christ" (81).

eternal ideas and abiding theological truths apart from the dross of historical contingency, with the Bible in its entirety representing historical contingency, and Jesus Christ the eternal Word of God. With respect to the Word of God distinction argued for, presumably only those portions of scripture that truly inculcate Christ, the Word of God, are to be regarded as the Word of God, else a charge of "biblicism" might be lodged. (To be sure, exponents of this view rarely make a distinction in such crude form, Spong being the least subtle.)

While this approach bears a superficial resemblance to the *Sachkritik* logic of Martin Luther as applied to the whole of scripture (truly authoritative is "what inculcates Christ"), it could only with difficulty be attached to the sort of reformed Catholicism of sixteenth-century Anglicanism, which on this score tended to move more instinctively in the direction of Calvin than Luther.[16] It is for this reason that Article VII of the Thirty-Nine Articles refuses to set the Old Testament over against the New ("for in both everlasting life is offered to Mankind by Christ"), and similarly resists any easy demotion of portions of scripture not explicit in manifesting a concern with the Word of God, Jesus Christ ("wherefore they are not to be heard; which feign that the old Fathers did look only for transitory promises"). Similar concern to avoid such simple distinctions can be seen in the commendation of the Old Testament law, from which "no Christian man whatsoever is free from the obedience of the commandments which are called moral." And when Cranmer wrote his famous collect regarding the authority of scripture, there is no whiff whatsoever of concern with a distinction between the Word of God written and the Word made flesh: "Almighty God who hath caused all Holy Scripture to be written for our learning. . . ."

On this score the Baltimore Declaration is a distinct improvement over most modern formulations. It speaks of the Word of God, Jesus Christ, and the Word of God written with no suggestion of an implicit tension between the two, and in fact with a degree of complementarity truly reminiscent of sixteenth-century Anglicanism. In my judgment this has to do with its more positive assessment of the third person of the trinity, the Holy Spirit, which is both the author of scripture and the insurer of its proper reception and obedient response. "Through the Holy Scriptures the Church hears anew every day . . . that divine Word who

16. Note Hooker's appreciative commendation of Calvin in the introduction to his *Laws of Ecclesiastical Polity.*

renews and inspires, teaches and corrects, judges and saves." One recent essayist concerned to guard this complementarity in the name of a positive assessment of scripture's material function in the church was the late Winfree Smith.[17] In a minority-voice article he was likewise concerned to retain a positive role for scripture and was particularly cautious about the abiding value of most of biblical criticism for the church.

REPUGNANCE, BIBLICAL CRITICISM, AND MODERN USE OF SCRIPTURE

It is time to return to the question posed earlier: what positive value can be placed on biblical criticism? This, it seems to me, is the question raised by the Baltimore Declaration, by "scripture, reason, tradition" proponents, and by the church and the world in the late twentieth century. For nearly two centuries diverse forms of biblical criticism have dominated the intellectual life of theological institutions abroad and, to a lesser degree, in this country. For at least the entirety of this century, Episcopal clergy have been trained in biblical studies fully under the domination of historical-critical methodology. While the influence on laity and larger ecclesial decision-making may be more "trickle-down" in character, nevertheless there has been no clear rival to the methods, approach, and general ethos of historical-critical interpretation of scripture.

In my view, historical criticism plays no positive theological role whatsoever. Its only proper role is negative. It establishes the genre, form, possible setting, and historical and intellectual background of the individual biblical text. It shows how the Bible is not like other books: history books, novels, encyclopedias, comic strips, and medieval liturgical tracts. Its force is explanatory. Its entire rationale is to explain the origins, development, and final stabilization of biblical texts. It does this in order to address a modern dilemma, one that has its roots in the Renaissance and its maturer form in the Enlightenment and the centuries that followed and that now must contend with widespread secularity, post-modern intellectual trends, and a church in confusion and disarray.

This dilemma was brilliantly chronicled by the late (Anglican) Hans Frei in his book *The Eclipse of Biblical Narrative*. Prior to the eighteenth

17. See the *SLJT* essay cited above.

century, the Bible was thought to cohere with the world it described, directly and without "authorial" (in the historical-critical sense) imagination or interference. The distance from God to world to text to reader was potentially (when available in the vernacular and without clerical overlay) quite narrow. One needs only to read a sample of the accounts of sixteenth-century Bible translators (Erasmus, Tyndale, Cranmer, Luther) to get a clear sense of this cohesion. This cohesion was splintered with the rise of the modern historical, social, literary, and natural sciences.

Now this is an absurdly brief summary of Frei's and others' observation. What historical-critical method was designed to do was explain the cleavage between the biblical text and the world it described by recourse to theories of authorship, editorial shaping, and historical and social settings. Or, to use the language of the Thirty-Nine Articles, conceived for a very different purpose, the first task of biblical criticism was to spot repugnance in the literature, that is, evidence of narrative disjuncture, literary seams, and logical breaks and inconsistencies. Portions of the text so dissected were then assigned to various "human writers, redactors, and editors" (Baltimore Declaration, Article VII) argued to occupy various points of standing on a reconstructed historical and social map. A distinct chronology, worldview, and intellectual, social, religious, and theological history was then imaginatively reconstructed that very soon overshadowed the world of the biblical text in its own form and literary configuration.

Prior to this "eclipse" of the biblical narrative, the "tradition" of biblical interpretation had been concerned with other matters, but chief among them was the identification of organizing patterns and types that would provide literary unity and theological cohesion across a very complex two-testament story. And, of course, major concern was devoted to proper hearing and obedient response to these narratives, which were thought to give the church life in this world and access to the divine life. In no small measure (look only at the history of art), it was the biblical world that informed our world, and not the reverse. But the reverse is precisely what the modern world — with its rival descriptions of cosmology, psychology, natural science, anthropology, and now theology! — has bequeathed to us.

In my judgment, the patterns of inclusivity and modernity that the Baltimore Declaration is at pains to repudiate are nothing more than attempts to address a world very far removed from the climate of the confessional statements that the document imitates and to a certain extent participates in. Much of the inclusivity agenda is carried out with an awareness of, and indeed enthusiasm about, the conclusions of biblical criticism as a critical discipline that has the (positive) capacity to render the biblical world interpretable, but which in so doing domesticates the Bible and leaves it impotent truly to change our church, our world, and our life before God. The Baltimore Declaration correctly spots this threat. My only caveat is that in its even mild endorsement of biblical criticism as a positive good, the Declaration confuses the true role biblical criticism can and must have, if the church is to gain life from its scriptures again.

What then is the proper role of biblical criticism? First, it is to exercise its explanatory function in helping us to appreciate the letter of the biblical text in all its foreignness and complexity. It is to teach us to be close readers, straining to hear something other than our own voices. Second, it is not to confuse its explanatory function with matters of exposition, ethical and theological application, or simple rhetorical persuasion. Explanation is not the same thing as *kerygma,* exposition, synthesis. Third, it is to restrict itself to the task of spotting repugnance, of showing how it is that the Bible is not a simple, single-authored document, free of seams and tensions, literary, theological, and logical.

In all these ways, then, biblical criticism has only a preparatory function. It is not to be used as an end unto itself. The true goal of biblical interpretation for the church is not ignoring or denying, but moving beyond "repugnance." Here the method of biblical interpretation associated with the work of Brevard Childs comes as a welcome complement to prior critical proclivities.[18] Childs is concerned with the biblical text in its final, stabilized form, the form as it is (generally) presented to the church in liturgical settings, devotional reading, and some forms of biblical study. Canon has implications for the text itself, and the seeking of synthesis and patterns of figuration, but it likewise self-consciously identifies the context in which it works as ecclesial. The Bible expects a certain type of readership: it is not an inert positive, even as it retains this potential eternally, but requires also the assistance of the Holy Spirit.

In making important distinctions about the character of the biblical text and the proper context for interpretation, a canonical approach can

18. *Biblical Theology in Crisis* (Philadelphia: Westminster, 1970); *Introduction to the Old Testament as Scripture* (Philadelphia: Fortress, 1979); *The New Testament as Canon: An Introduction* (Philadelphia: Fortress, 1984); *Old Testament Theology in a Canonical Context* (Philadelphia: Fortress, 1985). Childs's most recent work, a study on biblical theology, appeared in 1993 (see note 11 above).

positively harness the negative function of biblical criticism in such a way as to bridge the chasm presently separating the biblical text from the modern world. It fully recognizes the eclipse identified by Frei, and stands in the same general tradition as that which gave rise to biblical criticism as a positive tool. But it now seeks to move beyond the limited descriptive role of biblical criticism as historical or social analysis toward a recovery of the abiding theological value of the biblical text in its final form.[19] Here the tension between "scripture" and "tradition" is not overcome by reducing the Bible to a "tradition process" just like our own (so Cuthbertson), but rather by refusing to set "objective biblical criticism" over against so-called precritical exegesis by the church, identifying the former with "scripture's plain sense" and the latter with crude, primitive, fanciful exegesis from an unenlightened age.

Article XX of the Thirty-Nine Articles captures nicely one concern of Childs's canonical approach when it states: "the Church may not expound one place of Scripture, that it be repugnant to another." Critical method is trained to spot repugnance as part of its responsibility as a literary science. But the church has a charge to move beyond this spotting of "repugnance" toward an assessment of larger theological purpose, something most preachers instinctively understand. It was precisely here that their critical biblical training has seemed most unhelpful. Because the canonical approach works with the negative findings of biblical criticism and then pushes beyond these toward a reading "non-repugnant," it offers the preacher, teacher, pastor, and devotional reader an alternative to either biblical criticism or a fundamentalism concerned with riveting the biblical text to a worldview with which it never should have been expected to cohere.

There is much about the Baltimore Declaration that should give the church hope. It represents a courageous effort to say something of positive theological value to a church in disarray. But it is time for the church to move beyond both propositional arguments from scripture and a biblical criticism whose chief purpose must now be shifted into a new arena, if it is to have any abiding afterlife. Anglicans are notorious seekers of the *via media*. Here is an opportunity to seek what is positive about the concerns of both fundamentalism and biblical criticism (understood as a negative, preparatory discipline), but then to move beyond both toward the recovery of a method for interpreting scripture not antagonistic to "traditional"

19. This abiding theological value cannot be reduced to propositional statements.

readings from an earlier age, a method capable of reasonably assessing literary "repugnance," but finally concerned to find larger unitary purpose and theological synthesis in a book on whose proper interpretation the life of the church depends.[20]

20. There is not space in an essay such as this for further illustration of the sort of approach to biblical interpretation I am advocating. For further study, see above all Childs's 1979 *Introduction to the Old Testament as Scripture,* where fresh readings of individual biblical books are set forth on the basis of a canonical approach. From the perspective of a systematic theologian, see also George Lindbeck's essay, "The Story-Shaped Church: Critical Exegesis and Theological Interpretation," in *Scriptural Authority and Narrative Interpretation,* ed. Garrett Green (Philadelphia: Fortress, 1987) 161-78. I have presented a series of exegetical proposals in several essays, among them: "Isaiah 1–66: Making Sense of the Whole," *Reading and Preaching the Book of Isaiah* (Philadelphia: Fortress, 1988) 105-26; "Job: Full Structure, Movement, and Interpretation," *Interpretation* 43 (1989) 5-15; "The Prophet Moses and the Canonical Shape of Jeremiah," *Zeitschrift für die alttestamentlich Wissenschaft* 101 (1989) 3-27; "The Divine Council: Temporal Transition and New Prophecy in the Book of Isaiah," *Journal of Biblical Literature* 109 (1990) 226-46. In two recent books I have attempted to move beyond the older historical-critical reading of Isaiah toward a fresh canonical interpretation: *Zion's Final Destiny: The Development of the Book of Isaiah* (Minneapolis: Fortress, 1991) and *Isaiah 1–39* (Interpretation: A Bible Commentary for Teaching and Preaching; Louisville: Westminster/John Knox, 1993). Other chapters in this section on Biblical Theology give examples of my governing concerns.

≈ 9 ≈

"We Are Not Prophets or Apostles"

The *Biblical Theology* of B. S. Childs

I

My first encounter with Brevard Childs was in the pages of his 1974 Exodus commentary. His total command of the secondary literature and mastery of critical method were everywhere apparent, and these have been consistent hallmarks of each of Childs's publications. But there was something else going on in that commentary. It had partly to do with the distance he kept from the very critical methods whose successful negotiation was pivotal for the commentary to work. But it was not distance for its own sake. Clearly Childs felt the methods were not wrong, but were being put to wrong use. On the other hand, what the right use was to which they should have been put — constituting the "something else" at the heart of the commentary — was then elusive to me, or was overshadowed by his engagement with critical method, which at that time was the "something" else I was most interested in.

The "something else" I sensed in the Exodus commentary came into much clearer play in Childs's 1979 *Introduction to the Old Testament as Scripture,* a book with arguably the greatest impact on Old Testament scholarship in this century. This is not to say that all followed Childs as a result of his labors, but that the impact of that work, with its criticism of older historical-critical methods and its emphasis on canonical shaping, was

This chapter originally appeared in *Dialog* 33 (1994) 89-93.

widespread and lasting. Surprising, then, was how little impact his New Testament introduction, which set forth a similar approach for this part of the Christian canon, had on the field. Perhaps the wake created by the 1979 *Introduction* was still too strong. It was, however, the inability of this stimulating work to have any sustained impact that makes me skeptical about the reception and positive implementation of his recent contribution, *Biblical Theology of the Old and New Testaments*.[1] I say this as one who thinks this is unfortunate, as I regard the sheer scope and force of argument the logical culmination of a courageous proposal for biblical theology, with roots reaching back to that 1974 Exodus commentary and earlier.

Childs's manifest concern is to bring biblical studies and theological reflection into renewed connection, to tear down the "iron curtain" (xvi) separating the two disciplines. He speaks of "the pressing need for the next generation to build strong links between the Bible and theology" (xvi). He also opines that doing biblical theology "is far more than simply joining together the critical study of the Old Testament with that of the New" (xvi). At the same time, it seems to me that the true strength of the volume is not that it moves from Bible to theological reflection; after all, earlier neo-orthodox efforts all did this, and one would need only turn to the works of a modern interpreter like Walter Brueggemann to demonstrate that the movement from biblical text to theological exposition is both alive and enormously popular. This would not come as news to Childs, of course. What he means by closing the gap between Bible and theology would be, as the title aptly puts it, a biblical theology of the Old and New Testaments. For how one does biblical theology is not by effectively moving from biblical text — whether a passage from Old Testament or New — to theological exposition in a modern context. Rather, biblical theology is for Childs coming to terms with the unique character of Christian scripture, which always involves a reflection on both Old and New Testament witnesses, and on their relationship one to another.

For this reason, Childs spends much time establishing how unique a thing the shaping process that gave us a two-testament canon was and is. Options not taken are pointed out. The New is not the final chapter or simple climax of a continuous story beginning in the Old; something came to an end before something new began (compare most tradition-historical approaches). At the same time, the New cannot be detached from the Old on account of its bold and *sui generis* independence (compare

---

1. Minneapolis: Fortress, 1992.

Marcion); nor is its continued attachment due to simple historical or literary expedience. The voice of the Old continues as a *per se* witness and cannot be subsumed under the New's construal of it. Yet a proper hearing of the Old will include reflection on its subject matter, Jesus Christ. At the same time, the Old was not internally glossed so as to Christianize it, identifying its "true" subject matter by changing the semantic level of the Old's plain sense (e.g., "Behold my servant [Jesus Christ] will prosper, he will be high and lifted up," Isa 52:13), thereby making even the formation of a New Testament unnecessary. Having set these parameters, the interpreter's task is to explore the witness of the Old and New with reference to its subject matter, Jesus Christ.

What lies at the very heart of Childs's proposal as its most controversial thesis is his insistence on the interdependence of reflection on the Old and the New as that which constitutes biblical theology. This returns me to the matter of the reception of Childs's *New Testament as Canon.* The problem is not just that biblical studies and theological reflection have come apart, though one might well ask about the vigor of theological exegesis at present or the theological justification for much that goes by the name of biblical interpretation, especially in religious studies or Society of Biblical Literature settings. The problem is that Old Testament and New Testament studies are with rare exception virtually separate disciplines, even when — or precisely when — they make reference to one another as phenomena worthy of consideration. This is what makes Childs's earlier New Testament contribution an anomaly and — for the most superficial of reasons — something akin to Albright's Matthew commentary for the Anchor Bible.

My own view is that what has prevented a serious rejuvenation of biblical theology is not the failure of theologians/dogmaticians to talk to biblical scholars, and the reverse. This is but a symptom of a form of specialization whose more damaging strain persists at the level of biblical studies itself, namely, the relative isolation of Old Testament from New Testament interpretation, at the level of instruction, publication, and serious theological reflection — a gap that Childs's new work seeks to fill, but will surely meet with resistance. It is not just that Old Testament scholars can make no lasting contribution to New Testament study, and vice versa. This is but a formal matter. To seriously connect these separate disciplines would be to raise theological issues that the biblical field has lost confidence in addressing, especially in this country, where in a great many places Bible is taught from avowedly nontheological perspectives, or from perspectives in which theology is at most "accidents" derived from a more central "substance" (reading for reading's own sake, meaning engendered by text-reader encounter). As Jon Levenson has pointed out in another setting, a similiar "problem" arises when Tanak is read in the light of Talmud: suddenly the particularity of religious communities and the theological issues that give them life come to the fore in a way which the study of one apart from the other will never fully expose.

To study the Old in light of the New, or the New in light of the Old, is likewise to make explicit the theological context in which such connections were first made and which, over the centuries, has continued to provide the arena for yet further theological discussion and dispute. For the Christian community to read this literature not as Old Testament but as discrete "Hebrew Scriptures" is to read it in ways unfamiliar to traditional Jewish or Christian interpretation: either it treats the Old as profound religious reflection or history-of-religion, in ways incompatible with the New's witness to it and in a manner curious to many Jews; or it assumes the literature to be particular religious literature so linked to the life of a past historical people that it cannot, except with great artificiality, be tied to Jesus of Nazareth and the literature that argues that he is Israel's Christ, that is, the New Testament. The strength of Childs's proposal for theological reflection on Christian scripture is his refusal to separate the reflective, theological task from an assessment of the unique *form* of the witness, as well as its unique subject matter. It is precisely here — reading the Old in light of the New and the New in light of the Old — that combustion takes place and fresh theological hearing, in a modern context under the influence of the Holy Spirit, occurs.

Setting the parameters for Christian reflection on the canon does not mean generating timeless theological truths. Those who come to this biblical theology looking for a standardized outline of overarching themes and loci, ready-made for modern consumption and application, will be disappointed. Childs does make his own proposals here, but the very structure of the book works against believing that this is its main burden. Once Childs has set the context for theological reflection and modeled it exegetically and even doctrinally, the reader has a sense more of invitation than proscription (though modern positions Childs rejects are clearly pointed out). To my mind, this is the true strength of Childs's *Biblical Theology*. He sets the context for Christian theological reflection through a fresh analysis of the form of Christian scripture, and models his own approach and his own categories as a consequence of this. But this is less an end in itself than an indication of the starting point and goal of biblical theology.

II

Biblical Theology contains a breadth of coverage and engagement with secondary literature so vast that to offer a review is to be driven toward absurd reduction and selection. Every new publication of Childs gives one the opportunity not just to hear his own proposals, but also to hear his response to the widest variety of recent literature, in this instance from ethics, hermeneutics, theology, and of course biblical studies itself. Childs sets further distance between himself and an alleged Yale School by shifting attention from narrative to the narrative's subject matter; efforts to ground theological exegesis in ecclesiology or the stance of the reader/community are likewise rejected. At the same time, Childs fully recognizes the emergence of two differing principles for rendering scripture in the early church, one that was concerned with preserving the truth of the biblical witness as received from Israel and the apostles, the other that appealed to catholicity, in terms of the actual use by Christian communities of these writings (see pp. 64-68).

Having acknowledged these two principles, it seems to me that Childs's clearest allegiances begin with the former and move only derivatively to the latter. The best illustration of this comes in the reiteration in this volume of a principle that Childs articulated early in his writing: "we are not prophets or apostles." It seems to me that if one can comprehend Childs's concern here and come to an understanding of how this caution has positive as well as restrictive consequences, one will have penetrated to the heart of his biblical theology, as this developed in work on both Old and New Testaments and now comes to fruition in this volume. Let my "absurd reduction," then, focus on this one feature of Childs's work.

To say that we are neither prophets or apostles means several cautionary things. The modern reader of the Old cannot break through the final form of the witness to earlier levels of revelation and inspiration through critical reconstruction; to do this would be to ignore the very process by which ancient testimony became scripture in the first place. The point of canonical shaping is to distinguish between original recipients of revelation ("prophets") and those who come to this revelation through a textualized witness ("Israel"). Where the debate will continue to rage over this conception is whether canonical shaping has in fact accomplished what Childs claims it has, and whether such a thing even exists to begin with.

If Childs is correct, it seems to me that an added burden is placed upon the specifically Christian reader of the Old. All too often it has been appeal to "freedom of the gospel" that has provided the warrant for Christian critical endeavor in respect of the Old, focused in the modern period on retrieving a more authentic or earlier or less biased (more "neutral" or "objective") witness to God's revelation, detached from the witness of the final form, which is either a meaningless assemblage of tradition or a politically motivated "hard reading." Stress cracks were of course noted around this retrieval process when it rested too heavily on a theory of "revelation in events"; but to my mind, no satisfactory alternative theological justification has been set forth, and at times the field appears to use traditional critical methods as if on theological autopilot. Childs has offered an alternative that relies heavily on the notion that the final form is a perspicuous and meaningful statement. I would add that Christian readers come to the material, not only not as "prophets," but also outside the circle of Israel; we only receive as Old Testament these Hebrew Scriptures because of beneficial inclusion in God's plans for his own people, witnessed to in their scriptures, in a *particular given form.* Let the form be shown to be an empty theological lens before one runs too quickly to either a historical orientation or one focused on the reader's quest for meaning, a now-popular alternative to older historical-critical approaches.

The second half of the principle, "we are not apostles," also cuts with particular force. On the one hand, to say that we are not apostles means that we cannot approach the Old Testament as did Jesus and the apostles, as though their reading can be naively our own — if even for the most pious and theological of reasons, or perhaps precisely because of these. Childs calls this sort of move "biblicist" because it likewise ignores the intruding witness of the New Testament and an accurate assessment of its role as canon: which is to serve as a testimony to Jesus Christ and not a guidesheet for Christian exegesis of the Old Testament.[2] To say that we are not apostles is to recognize that with the formation of the New Testament as canon, a distinction was made between original recipients of revelation and the church, on rough analogy with that established between "prophets" (here read more generally, Old Testament scripture) and later generations of faithful Israelites. The Christian exegete is not an unfortunate "latecomer" to a purer form of revelation, vouchsafed once

2. Compare the recent reflections of Francis Watson, who is trying to deploy a late modern version of christological exegesis, especially in "Old Testament Theology as a Christian Theological Enterprise," in *Text and Truth: Redefining Biblical Theology* (Grand Rapids: Eerdmans, 1997) 179-224.

to prophets and apostles, or even apostles reading the prophets; the same God is revealed, but through a different form of witness, whose form must be respected as constitutive for what it means to be a church that gains its identity and life from the scriptural legacy of the prophets and apostles. The task of the church is to hear the Old in light of the New, and the New in light of the Old; to undo either side of this equation is to renounce what it means for the church to take seriously its specific point of standing under a particularly formed scriptural witness. Having said this, what biblical theology might look like one cannot say exactly. The parameters are set for beginning the task of interpreting Old and New when one understands the unique point of standing of the church vis-à-vis this scriptural legacy; but exegesis and exposition involves hearing the two-testament witness under the power of the Holy Spirit and within the life of the church, always respecting its particular form and content.

This brings me to my final concern. One can see how Childs's initial interest in the form and character of the witness eventually leads him to recognize the unique position of Christian exegesis: that of neither prophet nor apostle, but of the church in the modern world. This means, presumably, that with Barth one can remain confident in the face of churchly dissolution or a rapidly changing modern world that the Bible will retain its effectiveness as the unique, indispensable witness to God in Christ. My question concerns how much modern liberal Christianity still feels confident that the scriptures of the Old and New Testaments, in their final form and in reciprocal relationship with one another, have the power to witness to divine reality — without a heavy dose of human rationality, on the one hand, or experiential identification with the prophets and apostles on the other — directly, individually, and without interference of church or any corporate claim whatsoever. I appreciate Childs's efforts here and earlier and agree wholeheartedly with both his approach and concerns. Yet I remain skeptical that liberal Christianity, which is in a position to understand his concerns and his approach, will accept what he has to say, on a variety of grounds; while those churches that might be receptive will misread Childs as rejecting critical reading altogether in favor of a more appropriate appeal to piety and general theological conservativism. The fact is that Childs is trying to set forth an approach to Christian scripture that will disappoint both ends of a spectrum. The question is: is there an alternative either to rationalism on the right or left or to an experientialism of the pious, but also modern consumerist, sort? Childs's *Biblical Theology* may prove to be a book in search of an audience, and for that reason it will be judged by the widest variety of readers as learned but unsatisfactory and by an even smaller audience as the most brilliant proposal for theological exegesis offered in recent memory, but one unlikely to gain the sort of foothold necessary to transform the church in its use of scripture.

I put myself in the second group. It is time to ask very basic questions about where we are teaching and to what end. Childs presumes to work from a distinct perspective, though I doubt very much whether it is shared by many at work today in modern seminaries, divinity schools, or departments of religious studies. It is a time of great transition, when basic questions are taking new form, and new answers for them are being provided, by a new generation of students and teachers. Childs has raised timely questions about how we approach our scriptural legacy, and he has again set forth his own proposal. Is such a proposal now outmoded, or have we simply shifted our questions so radically that the answers he gives seem too learned, too churchly, or too irrelevant for the modern individual reader? I am more optimistic about Childs's approach than I am about its reception. For that reason I think it is important to keep his voice at the center of the discussion, even when, or precisely when, he begins to sound like a participant in an older discussion no longer deemed relevant. We are moving quite fast these days in terms of publication and intellectual trends within church and society. To remind the church to pay attention to the shape of its Christian scriptures, Old and New, New and Old, would seem like a remedial note to sound. But perhaps now is precisely the time to sound it.

EXEGESIS

≈   **10**   ≈

Isaiah and the Search for a New Paradigm

Authorship and Inspiration

I. Introduction

This chapter poses a basic question. How and why did interest develop in the man Isaiah as a biographical figure and, alongside him, the prophets Second and Third Isaiah? This will involve a brief survey of historical, literary, and theological factors. Because one cannot fully understand the search for a new paradigm unless one recalls what motivated the older one, such a survey should help put things in perspective.

One of the arguments I wish to put forward is that *theological,* and not just literary or historical, questions were what stimulated a search for the person of Isaiah and his counterparts — a fact at times forgotten in the present period of biblical studies. These theological questions revolved most fundamentally around the doctrine of inspiration. The prophet Isaiah and other anonymous individuals, under divine compulsion, at various historical moments in the book's development, were inspired to write or speak what God had spoken to them. Yet the book of Isaiah did not come to us in a form that made the connection between these inspired individuals and their inspired speech clear. So historical criticism received its mandate: to uncover the connection and thus show us how theology had been generated, inspiration lying at the heart of the process.

Now, with an interest in unitary readings or canonical approaches, questions of a theological character have once again resurfaced. But we should stop and ask: why a focus on the book as a unitary whole? For

113

theological reasons, or for aesthetic reasons? Because older fragmentation has tired us out? Or because meaning is regarded as the imposition of a reader's concerns on a text, and we now have readers interested in unity? This is clearly problematical. If readers are the ones finding unity, how would this shift be any more theological than what obtained in an older model? Questions such as these point to a considerable degree of confusion among Isaiah interpreters at present.

To anticipate, my larger thesis will be that while theological meaning was once sought by clarifying the *subjects* of inspiration in the book — Isaiah and other anonymous authors — the emphasis has now shifted to the book itself and to readers. One might call this a shift from subject to *object*, from Isaiah as inspired subject, to the book as an objective, inspired record addressing particular objects: readers outside the book's frame of reference, instead of the historical contemporaries of the originally inspired subjects within the book. This shift has been taking place slowly over the last 100 years (and in some respects it marks a return to pre-nineteenth-century readings, in a different guise). The remaining question, in my view, is just what sort of reader is ideally being addressed? My very broad answer will be: a specific reader within the religious life and hope of Israel, addressed by Isaiah and other explicitly ordered religious literature.[1] For this reason, in the next two chapters I will read Isaiah over against Lamentations and the Psalter. Isaiah does not exist in isolation as an ancient unitary witness, brilliantly constructed and hermetically sealed. Rather, Isaiah belongs within the specific hopes of a specific people with a specific interpreting literature. All of these together form what could be called a "canonical context."

Let me digress for a minute because one of the ways in which changes are occurring in the reading of Isaiah or any other book is to stress the literary or classical character of these books as literature. Yet to speak of specific readers intended by the book of Isaiah is actually to imply that this book is the furthest thing from a "classic" — a work that from the beginning has no one restricted audience in view and that over the course of time reaches out for the widest possible readership because of the eternal relevance of its discourse as such.[2] By contrast, what makes the Old Testament literature what it most essentially is is the claim of a restricted

---

1. See ch. 14 below.

2. See David Tracy's discussion in *The Analogical Imagination: Christian Theology and the Culture of Pluralism* (London: SCM, 1981).

election, encompassing its authors and audience. This means that no matter how lofty or how timeless its themes, these find their inner logic and most essential purpose always through the constraints of that election. Seen from this perspective — which the literature itself asserts — the Old Testament is not a classic (Ps 147:19-20). The material did not take shape and become scripture because of profound themes or an inherent capacity to transcend time and space with a message for all. The characteristic mark of this literature is the claim made within it to God's special election and inspiration, and its proprietary attachment to God's people Israel.[3]

That over time Isaiah became a book with very wide readership is in some measure an accident, even when new readers wish to confess a beneficial divine intent. For Christian readers — who were first among the outsiders — the importance of Isaiah had to do with the promise made within the book that God's ways with Israel would also involve those outside the commonwealth of Israel, and that the promise of a Messiah from Isaiah had been filled full in Jesus of Nazareth. And Isaiah remained scripture for the church because it spoke of promises from God still straining toward their final fulfillment, most especially, the return of Christ when at last the wolf lies down with the lamb (Isa 11:6) and the dwelling of God is with all humanity (Rev 21:3).[4]

By focusing on this question of intended readers I want to redirect the older question about the particular historical circumstances that gave rise to the book toward a concern with the book's final form and its reception by a particular community of faith. By this I do not mean determining when the book reached its final form and what sort of readers first encountered it in this form, under what historical or sociological conditions they lived and so forth. This would amount to nothing more than shifting the place of historical interest to a later moment on the timeline of the book's development (something many believe a canonical approach is up to, and then criticize it for giving undue emphasis to what is only the last of many stages of growth).

Instead I want to keep the focus on *a theology of reception:* what does it mean that Isaiah was intended for a particular readership (Israel) but that its message had non-Israelite implications (for "the nations") and that any modern reader who approaches the book also begins not as some

---

3. Compare the discussion above in ch. 2 and below in ch. 18, where election is discussed, especially in respect to hermeneutics.

4. See the discussion in chs. 12 and 15 below.

disinterested individual (the "ideal reader"), but as a member of some specific religious (or even non-religious) community with specific conditioning and expectations? For the Christian reader in the broadest sense, this means being clear how it is that this book of Israelite prophetic witness has become part of our Old Testament and even a witness to Christ, in past incarnation; but also as witness to Christ in future eschatological hope. To speak of general readers encountering a unitary and aesthetically challenging "classic" is to misunderstand what the Old Testament is at its most basic level. Questions of genre apply not just, as the older theory held, to small units, but also to these scriptures in their fullest scope. That Israel's religious literature eventually circulates beyond her circle has firstly to do with theological factors: the emergence of a community who confessed, in faith and worship, insight into Isaiah's fullest frame of reference and larger purpose now filled to fullness in Christ. It bears remembering that the notions of "classic" texts or even freely accessible literature are relatively modern ones. There were no "bestsellers" in the sense we mean it today prior to the eighteenth century.

At this particular phase of Isaiah interpretation, it is important to bear in mind that saving the book from historical or literary fragmentation will not occur by granting it the honorific "unified literature." Rather, it will occur as we come to appreciate what, in the very basic sense of the term, this book means to be, as one book within the sacred books of Israel's canon, intended for a certain specific sort of readership, and then to develop more dexterity in interpreting books with attention to scope and context.

I want now to a look at the older paradigm as a way of reexamining the early theological concerns in what is now a very different climate.

II. A LOOK AT THE OLD PARADIGM

It is a time of fervent change in Isaiah studies. An older emphasis on the historical figure of the prophet — at least three in the case of Isaiah — has shifted toward an assessment of the book's unity. But how is that unity to be conceived?

In order to get the proper perspective we need to ask some prior questions. Why was there an interest in the historical figures of Isaiah — and his counterparts Second and Third Isaiah — to begin with? How and why are such figures instrumental to interpreting the book? I ask these questions because an interest in Isaiah's unity need not be viewed as the latest scholarly fad. It might well be a return to modes of reading quite time-honored and uncontroversial, obliging us to view the concern with "historical figures" as itself the oddity in Isaiah's history of interpretation.

So why an interest in Isaiah as an individual, biographical figure, and the author[5] of the book associated with him — or at least parts of it?

The first reason usually given is *historical*. The prophet Isaiah lived during the reigns of Ahaz and Hezekiah, in the eighth century. Yet images and figures from a later period appear in chapters 40–66 of the book: Cyrus the Persian, a destroyed temple, Babylonian exile.

The only way to hold the man Isaiah and the presentation of the book together was by recourse to a theory of prediction or supernatural prophetic foresight. The prophet saw in advance and announced to his people events that lay far in the future. So to the oddly "traditional-but-becoming-critical" mind of the eighteenth century, chapters 40–66 must have been composed "in the latter part of the reign of Hezekiah," the last king mentioned in the book's superscription and therefore the last occasion for the man Isaiah to write what followed.[6] But mention of Cyrus, a destroyed temple, and Babylonian exile do not appear in the book as predictions, strictly speaking, made by Isaiah to his contemporaries. Rather, they are what critics have held them to be: references from a later period without relevance for Isaiah's contemporaries.

Moreover, when distant predictions do appear in the Old Testament, which is relatively rare, these are usually vague or sufficiently general in tone ("now it shall come to pass in the latter days that the mountain of the house of the LORD shall become the highest of the mountains . . ."). Precise predictions of future events occur in the book of Daniel — but they confuse the wise Daniel (Dan 7:15, 28) and even make him sick (8:27). That is because, as God tells him, they are not for him or for his contemporaries but for others (8:17). This complicated mode of discourse is nowhere employed in Isaiah (Isa 21:1-10 may be an intriguing exception).

5. For the purposes of this chapter, by "author" I mean either speaker or writer. I am not trying to make subtle distinctions between oral speech, tradition, *Überlieferung*, rhetorical forms, and the like. I simply mean by "author" the prophet (and his colleagues in the book) as individual composer of the material associated with him, now in written form.

6. J. G. Eichhorn, *Einleitung in das Alte Testament* III (3rd ed., Leipzig, 1803).

In sum, the references to later events unrelated to the life and times of Isaiah gave rise to a picture of the prophet as an *author* separable from the material associated with him. Questions of a historical nature drove a wedge between the book itself with its presentation of the prophet and the biographical figure of Isaiah now to be understood as author. It is another question altogether whether this account of the book's origins is the proper way to understand either the book of Isaiah or the prophetic office; it bears consideration that early rabbinic sources attributed actual authorship of Isaiah to "the men of Hezekiah," whoever they were (Babylonian Talmud *Baba Bathra* 14b). This forces us to ask just what we mean by "authorship" in the first place. We are used to a modern concept: the spine of a book carries both the title and the author's name. Does the book of Isaiah mean to make this claim about Isaiah, a claim that simultaneously brought with it debates about how much of the book Isaiah, as author, actually wrote or spoke, and which parts belonged to others?

A second reason for a shift toward interest in Isaiah and other authorial voices in the book was the book's problematic *literary character.* Isaiah, more than any other prophetic book, is a difficult read. Luther spoke of the prophets as moving strangely from topic to topic, so that one could not make head or tail of them or see what they were getting at. Literary problems, simple problems of reading, are therefore not just modern. At the same time, they were handled differently in an earlier age. It was not that Isaiah's haphazardness led Luther to posit numerous authors alongside him — Isaiah simply had a "queer way of talking," as he put it, that made it difficult to tell what he was getting at.[7] One even has the sense — and this is often overlooked — that precisely this haphazardness, this curious mode of presentation, belonged to what it meant to be a prophet in the first place. In their peculiar manner of presentation, the prophets showed themselves to be God's special people, and not of like nature with ourselves.

However, when joined with the historical problems just mentioned, this literary haphazardness was seen to be, not the hallmark of prophecy, but rather a matter for critical resolution. So it was that the original Isaiah was joined by other anonymous authors, responsible for other sections of the book, whose aggregation to the original had, unfortunately, created literary chaos. Reasons for the additions in the first place were never satisfactorily adduced.

7. Compare the discussion of Luther below in ch. 14.

What looked like an effort at resolving literary complexity became a monster of yet greater and even more complex making. It reminds one of the verb at the end of a long German sentence: the speaker was determined to keep the verbal resolution forestalled until all sufficient predication had taken place, with the result that the listeners became exhausted and began to forget what the point of beginning had been. Isaiah was joined by two others. Their literary contributions were the subject of yet further analysis. These were sifted and recast, on the lookout for yet further authorial and editorial intrusion, in an effort to find literary coherence somewhere in the text's dark prehistory. The original Isaiah, trimmed back to the first thirty-nine chapters, thoroughly resisted efforts at unitary reading and turned out to contain other-authored sections that in fact postdated even the hybrid contributions of Second and Third Isaiah. The quest for literary coherence was on. But its target kept being pushed further and further back into the text's prehistory, requiring an explanation for the present form of the book so abstruse as to numb the senses. That this is no exaggeration demands only a quick look at the work of Vermeylen or Steck, each in his own way marking the outer limit of what is possible for Isaiah as a literary product in terms of editorial complexity — now en route to unity![8]

Up to this point my remarks could be fairly taken as negative in tone and substance. But when we move to the third reason for an interest in Isaiah as prophetic individual, *bios* and author, we begin to touch on matters for which I have considerable sympathy. Indeed, this third factor — it could be called theological — could be regarded as the engine driving both the historical and the literary analyses in the first instance. The fact that we could talk about literary or historical matters in isolation from theological matters — something Barton attempts in a recent survey of Old Testament method — is itself revealing of the present state of biblical studies, where theology must define itself against historical analysis, but not the reverse.[9]

That Isaiah and his counterparts became authors and individualized speakers set within specific time frames was not only the consequence of

---

8. Odil H. Steck, *Bereitete Heimkehr. Jesaja 35 als redaktionelle Brücke zwischen dem Ersten und den Zweiten Jesaja* (Stuttgart: Katholisches Bibelwerk, 1985); Studien zu Tritojesaja (Berlin/New York: de Gruyter, 1991); Jacques Vermeylen, *Du prophète Isaïe à l'apocalyptic* (Paris: Gabalda, 1977-78).

9. John Barton, *Reading the Old Testament* (Philadelphia: Westminster, 1984).

literary incoherence or a fascination with history for its own sake, even when this may at first blush appear to be the case. The first true critical commentator on Isaiah, J. G. Eichhorn, regarded chapter 21 as late because the single reference to "riders on camels" in v. 7 was suggestive for him of Persian warfare techniques, known through Xenophon's reports, and therefore clearly later than Isaiah's own time.[10] What at one time looked like shrewd historiography now appears somewhat remedial, and isolated from larger interpretive issues. Yet set against even this backdrop the isolation of Isaiah and other anonymous "authors" did have a theological purpose. So long as theological coherence turned on the capacity to regard the entire book as unified by a single authorial point of view, when Isaiah's individual authorship was called into question on literary and historical grounds, the theological task simply became more complicated. It did not go away.

The search for the historical Isaiah and his anonymous counterparts was fueled by the desire to understand what they said as individuals within their respective time and space. Understanding what they said meant coming to terms with the character and substance of their inspiration, as men speaking under divine compulsion. A more theological purpose is hard to conceive of. But this came at the cost of separating these inspired speakers from the literary work of Isaiah itself, which had in the meantime become a set of clues from which to reconstruct inspired speech residing somewhere behind the book in its present form.

In sum, Isaiah interpretation in the modern period has labored under three assumptions, none of which may be true. The first is that theological coherence involves a single point of view, which is understood to go back to an author, in this case Isaiah. The second is that inspiration is what is vouchsafed to individuals as individuals, in time and space: Isaiah, Second Isaiah, Third Isaiah, and a myriad of redactors, traditionists, editors, and glossators, all to be ranged on a complex grid of primary and secondary inspiration. The third is that the present literary presentation of Isaiah is incoherent, if for no other reason than that too many authors and editors with too many different inspired messages were responsible for expanding the book of Isaiah into its curious shape and scope.

The most important of these three assumptions is the first, from which the other two are in large measured derived, namely, that overarching point of view in a book demands a single inspired author. Under a

10. Eichhorn, *Einleitung,* 101-4.

postmodern guise, it seems to me that this is what more recent interpreters, anxious to move beyond fragmentation and literary complexity, mean by the "unity" of the book of Isaiah. The problem has been that what one reader sees as "unity" in Isaiah is not the same as what another sees, and this is more than a matter of "reader incompetence" or not having worked hard enough at it.

Still, variety in unitary readings is not itself sufficient to call the whole thing off and retreat to the glories of "disunity." The very fact that an older method would not have been content with the label "disunity" should put us on guard that what we are concerned with is its theoretical opposite.[11] What does the term "unity" actually mean? Does it have a constructive sense, or is it more a term of opposition or correction, over against something else? Beyond this, a more telling objection is the theological one, even if this objection is not frequently voiced. For all its complexity, the beauty of the older multiple author and editor model was that it understood its theological justification. To know the mind of an author or redactor was to be privy to a distinct point of view, though the more of these one accumulated and detected in the first place on the basis of inconsistency or tension, the less theological and the more ideological or tendentious they began to appear. Perhaps one's definition of theology was what was uncovered as inconsistent or less than perspicuous when the model was free to run its logical course.

That being said, the older model believed that by uncovering authorial point of view, even through inordinately complex reconstruction, one still had some handle on theology, however removed from "Isaiah wrote it under divine inspiration" such an understanding was. The question now is: how is one to understand *from a theological point of view* a conception of the book of Isaiah as "unified" and at the same time as divorced from the older authorial or editorial understanding of inspiration? Does such a conception proceed from the general weariness of readers, tired of endless reconstruction, or is there something more to it? If theology knew its place in a model that stressed multiple inspired voices behind the literature, what place does theology have in a climate anxious to read the book on its own terms and in its own present shape, where the buzzword "unity" may well obscure more than it illumines?

---

11. David Carr, "Reaching for Unity in Isaiah," *JSOT* 51 (1993) 61-80.

III. What Is Theological in the New Paradigm?

In much of what I have said thus far I am treading on parts of the same terrain covered by Brevard Childs under the rubric of "a canonical approach." Canonical readings are not interested in a reconstructed, earlier level of intentionality on which to build theological reflection; this rules out concern for a life and times of Isaiah retrieved for its own sake. It also means that the final form of the material has priority over earlier stages of development. And it follows from this that the final literary form of a book, however haphazard (to return to our earlier phrase), nevertheless forms the starting point for theological reflection and application. In all three of these ways Childs has moved away from the traditional concerns of critical method.

But has the approach met with wide acceptance? Not entirely. Objections are varied and numerous. Why should the final form of the material be something different than any other earlier phase in the book's development; and if not, then why should one privilege it theologically? How does a view of individual inspiration shift when the book, not figures responsible for it, takes center stage? Is not a concern with literary *shape,* as a formal discipline, just a strictly literary preoccupation, owing much to New Criticism and general trends in departments of literature, but certainly lacking the capacity to make any theological claim?

John Barton and Walter Brueggemann have, each in his own way, asked this last question.[12] So it seems that we are back to our fundamental concern. What is theological about the new paradigm or a shift away from interest in authors, editors, tradition history, and the like, toward a concern with the literature itself in its present form and shape? As Brueggemann himself puts it, "It is not yet clear how one moves from literary shape to theological claim."[13] And where does a concept like "unity" fit into theological inquiry and application?

12. Barton, *Reading the Old Testament,* 100: "we may take up the suggestion . . . that canon criticism may be best seen as a *literary* rather than as a theological approach to reading the Old Testament." Walter Brueggemann, "Bounded by Obedience and Praise: The Psalms and Canon," *JSOT* 50 (1991) 63-93.

13. The full quotation reads: "While Childs has indeed changed the discussion, it is not clear what outcomes will result from his work. It is not yet clear how one moves from literary shape to theological claim, and that connection is the crucial one for canonical study. If that connection is not made, canonical study becomes, as John Barton has seen, merely literary analysis" ("Bounded," 64).

In an essay on Maimonides and Mosaic authorship of the Pentateuch, Jon Levenson has, I believe, pointed to a set of concerns that might help us answer these questions.[14] The concern to defend Mosaic authorship of the Torah, which Levenson seeks to understand in this essay, may offer us an angle of vision on questions of inspiration and unity useful for the book of Isaiah as well.

Levenson points out that premodern readers were well aware that passages appeared in the Pentateuch that could not have been authored by Moses, for they betrayed a narrative perspective from a later period. Gen 12:6 was the parade example: "Now at that time the Canaanite was in the land." By saying, quite in passing, that "at that time," during the period of Abraham, the Canaanite was in the land, the author of the verse reveals that "at his time" the Canaanite was no longer in the land, and the distance from the time period of the narrative itself is made explicit. (Wellhausen saw the honesty of this narrator, whom he regarded as the Yahwist, as evidence of his good will and trustworthiness, to be contrasted with the deceit of the Priestly writer who was always trying to dupe his readers into believing he was writing at the time of Moses, when he was not.)[15] An older explanation for this apparent problem appeared in the comments of the fourteenth-century rabbi Joseph Bonfils:

> It stands to reason that the word *'az* was written in a time when the Canaanite was not in the land, and we know that the Canaanite did not leave until after Moses' death, when Joshua conquered it. Accordingly, it appears Moses did not write this word here; rather, Joshua or another of the prophets wrote it.[16]

Examples such as this could be compounded, and Levenson and other interpreters have catalogued many of them.

An interesting problem not discussed by Levenson is the bulk of the Pentateuchal material *earlier* than Moses, including the verse under present

14. Levenson, "The Eighth Principle of Judaism and the Literary Simultaneity of Scripture," *The Hebrew Bible, the Old Testament, and Historical Criticism* (Louisville: Westminster/John Knox, 1993) 62-81.

15. ". . . the Priestly Code . . . tries hard to imitate the costume of the Mosaic period, and, with whatever success, to disguise its own," while, as for the Yahwist, "the distance between the present and the past spoken of is not concealed in the very least" (*Prolegomena to the History of Ancient Israel* [New York: Meridian, 1957] 9).

16. Quoted in Levenson, *Hebrew Bible*, 67.

discussion as well as all the stories of Genesis. To say that Moses collected traditions passed down to him is an explanation of similar standing and alike in its logic to arguing Joshua inserted the verse at Gen 12:6, but it still leaves open the question of both inspiration and unity in the Pentateuch. Who was inspired to write the stories of the patriarchs, or pass them on, such that they might become available to Moses at a later time? Is the Pentateuch still a unity if Moses wrote down the bulk of it firsthand, based upon his own experience with God's people before and after Sinai, while the first-fifth (Genesis) he merely redictated or committed to writing as a prelude to his own contribution?

Of course, to ask questions such as these is to begin to see how flat a concept like authorship could become if pressed to its limit. For this reason Levenson is at pains to show that Mosaic authorship served another sort of purpose in the interpretation of Torah. "What is essential is not the authorship of the Torah but its divinity and unity," he claims.[17] At another point he suggests that what is crucial in Mosaic authorship is the decision of the Jewish community to accept that what is found in Torah comes from God, not humans; ironically, then, as he points out, an overemphasis on Mosaic authorship could lead in a wrong direction, away from the necessary community acceptance of "Torah from heaven" over and above — so to speak — "Torah from Sinai" alone.

At least three factors surface in Levenson's discussion of the significance of a claim for Mosaic authorship: (1) the claim to divine authority, (2) the decisions of the community in acknowledging that authority, and (3) unity within the Torah. Yet he stresses the first two because he is seeking to understand Maimonides' so-called eighth principle, which involves the divine origins of Torah. This means that his discussion tends to give emphasis to the community's assent to the divine authority implied by Mosaic authorship, because for Maimonides in twelfth-century Spain other distinct options for interpretation were available and unacceptable: the Christian tendency to see Torah as provisional in character and especially the tendency of Islam to view the Torah possessed by Judaism as a forgery and thus not truly from heaven. Yet before turning to decisions made by the community concerning authority, there is another way to examine the divine origin of Torah associated with the figure of Moses not highlighted in Levenson's thought-provoking analysis. This involves looking at two key texts in the book of Exodus where the *singular* role of Moses is set forth.

17. Levenson, *Hebrew Bible*, 212.

Because Moses is the central figure of the Pentateuch, and more than that, the essential source of Israel's knowledge of God, without whom such knowledge would have been unavailable, it stood to reason that a claim to authorship, now more broadly understood, arose. Note how even the terms authority and authorship are ultimately related. Texts of the Pentateuch make clear that it was Moses who communicated what God revealed of his will, and that otherwise Israel would have known nothing. Even in illustrating to Moses how Aaron will work with him and speak to the people, we see the underlying principle of God's singular speech to Moses revealed:

> And you shall speak to him and put the words in his mouth; and I will be with your mouth and with his mouth, and will teach you what you shall do. He shall speak for you to the people; and he shall be a mouth for you, and you shall be to him as God (Exod 4:15-16, RSV).

"In the specific way in which *you* know what *I* have said," God tells Moses, "*Aaron* will know what *you* have said, and in no other way but that." In a later scene the possibility of some other more democratic or direct form of communication is vetoed by the people themselves:

> You speak to us, and we will hear; but let not God speak to us, lest we die. . . . And the people stood afar off, while Moses drew near to the thick darkness where God was (Exod 20:19, 21, RSV).

This story is clearly intended to highlight the singularity of God's speech to Moses when that does occur, on Mount Sinai, in the next verse.

The point I am trying to make here is that a concept of inspiration and revelation was what led to a claim for authorship, and not the other way around. But equally important is that this concept of inspiration was flexible enough to be extended beyond its strictly logical scope to cover texts unrelated to the revelation of God to Moses at Sinai. Now Levenson's larger point is something like this: the overriding concern of a claim for Mosaic authorship was to establish the divine origin of the material in question, here, the central authoritative texts of Judaism, the Torah. That is good so far as it goes, but we need to know just how it did that. The answer is that authorship was so closely associated with a claim to divine inspiration that the two concepts were simply collapsed into one, Moses becoming the author of Genesis as well as those books more obviously associated with his own life, *because he was the only means by which Israel knew anything about God to begin with,* as those later books would make clear. A confession of singular inspiration involved divine authority involved Mosaic authorship — roughly in that order. Mosaic authorship — like Isaianic authorship — as a fact unto itself leads only in absurd, rationalist directions.

Only at this juncture do we see what role a concept like *unity* in Torah means — a notion Levenson defends but fails to explain fully. We are in a position to understand what unity in Isaiah might mean as well. At some points in discussing Torah's unity, Levenson prefers the terms totality, simultaneity, or synchronicity. Clearly he does not mean that all events are happening at the same time in Torah. Rather, when all is said and done, "simultaneity" implies something about constraining a reader's interpretive decisions, and here we again bump into the broader claims involving Mosaic authorship. The material, coming as it does from one singular, individual perspective, is open only to the sorts of contradictions and tensions *understandable on direct human analogy.* To say that the Torah is authored in its entirety by one inspired figure is to place the reader under the obligation of seeking *the same comprehensive and synthetic sense of the whole that one seeks when encountering, over time, any individual person.* One may hear many different things, but if understanding is desired and the person speaking is healthy and trustworthy, insuring the trustworthiness and coherence of what is communicated, one will seek to make connections and efforts at synthesis rather than render a preemptive judgment of self-contradiction or schizophrenia. And Moses is of course not just trustworthy, but is the one singularly loved by God, the one who has, unlike any other, seen God face to face.

Simultaneity, therefore, has less to do with the synchronic referent in time of what is said across the length and breadth of Torah, from Genesis to Deuteronomy, from creation to the death of Moses, and more with the expectation of intelligibility and coherence from a single perspective, even a very complex one.[18] To call the sixty-six-chapter prophetic book "the vision of Isaiah" is to expect a coherent and unitary perspective, even one spanning centuries or more. It is also to insist that the divine authority breathed through the historical prophet has left its mark on the work associated with

---

18. Compare John Barton's remarks on the notion of simultaneity in scriptural interpretation in his most recent work (*The Spirit and the Letter: Studies in the Biblical Canon* [London: SPCK, 1997]).

him in such a way as to oblige the reader to seek the same intelligibility through respectful attention to detail and final purpose, matters of scope and context, that one was obliged to seek in the face of the prophet himself, the man of God before whose words kings and nations shook.

IV. Conclusions: The Unity of Isaiah

What we have seen is that three factors lie at the heart of a text's authority prior to the sort of community assent to authority emphasized in Levenson's reading. These factors are so intimately related it would be a mistake to isolate them too cleanly or set them in strict chronological order. The singular revelation from God, the act of communication beginning in speech and ending in written form, and the assent to that agent and that speech as divinely inspired — all three of these factors, the text insists, were there from the beginning. All three turn on distinct but at times overlapping orbits and all three conspire to create authority culminating in written texts with a given form and scope, regarded as authored by the original agent of revelation. What lies at the heart of the process — Moses, Aaron, God's word, the community's assent in fear — will eventually be seen to persist to the end: God's word, inspiring Moses, whose authority and authorship extend over the Pentateuch in its entirety, Moses being the singular means by which God's word was made known to Israel in the first place.

What is theological about an appeal to unity in Isaiah is in the first instance negative: a rejection of a theory of inspiration too narrowly tied to an historical search for the original inspired subject, his speech, and that of his successors. More positively, concern with the book of Isaiah *in its entirety* involves the expectation that a single perspective — that of God or that of Isaiah as God's spokesman — pervades all sixty-six chapters. This does not mean that everything that appears in the book must be constrained to fit one uniform temporal perspective, traceable to an Isaiah mechanically predicting from his eighth-century vantage point events into the distant future.[19] Neither was Moses' authoring the Pentateuch meant to imply an extension back retrospectively of his vision to include the book of Genesis, in some clever or more contrived manner.

19. See ch. 13 below.

Rather, single authorship is linked to an expectation of larger coherence despite a complex and varied range of texts and perspectives. What is theological about an emphasis on Isaiah's unity is this expectation of larger coherence, which will be differently evaluated by interpreters, as it has always been.[20] Along with this comes a refusal to grant primary and secondary status to levels of a text through recourse to literary analysis, ultimately derived from a theory of original inspiration, and instead to seek to see inspiration across the length and breadth of a work because it has been authored — in this more general sense — by the inspired agent Isaiah. This even rules out a more-or-less congenial emphasis on variety or multiple perspectives in the book, perspectives popularized as the point of entry to a modern interpretation of Isaiah under the rubrics First Isaiah, Second Isaiah, and Third Isaiah. That this insistence on single authorship should not be viewed too narrowly is underscored by the fact that some later readers attributed the book not to Isaiah but to "the men of Hezekiah," whoever they were. But this was not a foreshadowing of modern critical thinking, any more than premodern awareness of the lateness of material in chapters 40 and following signaled stress cracks in a bulletproof conception of Isaianic authorship.[21] In both cases the same expectation of coherence and the possibility of larger synthesis remained.

It seems to me that two mistakes have followed from an emphasis on reading the book of Isaiah as a unity. The first is that a unified book must mean a single reading and just one as the goal of modern interpretation. The second is that unity is only something imposed by readers. As we have seen, "unity" is not a literary claim for single, tightly constructed uniformity of perspective. Rather, it is a concept meant to constrain emphasis on multiplicity of perspectives in a single work. This constraining has not been artificially imposed by later readers armed with a theory of Isaiah's authorship. Rather, it flowed from the historical process that stretched back through time, ultimately to bump into the prophet Isaiah himself, regarded by the community as coherent and trustworthy and above all as God's man — even when what he had to say was fearsome and condemnatory. The book grew and developed only with loose attention to that original perspective in a strictly literary sense, and was content to break out into fresh historical and theological territory under the freedom of God's word of address.

---

20. Against Carr's objections, made for other purposes (see n. 11 above).
21. See the discussion below at the end of section I of ch. 13.

Nevertheless, the book did not jettison its original form but worked with reference to it, making the final sixty-six chapters more than just the sum of discrete parts. In the next two chapters I will examine the place of chapters 40–66 within the whole by comparing its message to that of Lamentations and will then look at the messianic hope within Isaiah, which figures more prominently in the first part of the book than in later chapters. Does that mean that messianic hopes associated with Isaiah of Jerusalem were surrendered or transformed as the book grew? Or does precisely such a way of considering the matter betray a reading that overemphasizes multiple perspectives in the book? Here we can see clearly how a concern with unity in Isaiah is not some reader-imposed or strictly literary preoccupation but rather lies at the very heart of what it means to try to interpret this book of prophecy in a consistent and faithful way, attentive to those forces which made it scripture in the first place, the inspired "vision of Isaiah" (Isa 1:1).

II

Isaiah and Lamentations

The Suffering and Afflicted Zion

Isaiah and Lamentations: the pairing may sound unusual, making the decision to read them together either contrived, or perhaps a sign of the times. A survey of recent book titles would show that "reading" this or that book is a popular tack to take. If reading one is good, why not read two? Even arbitrarily.

A more traditional — and familiar — pairing is Lamentations with the prophet Jeremiah. The circulation of Jeremiah with Lamentations has a very long history, even though that history is reflected today only in Christian orderings of the Old Testament; the location of Lamentations in the Writings — not the Prophets — as one of the five festival scrolls remains the Jewish practice. Still, even this different ordering would not necessarily sever a close association of Lamentations with Jeremiah. A connection between the two presumably goes back to 2 Chron 35:25, which speaks of the prophet Jeremiah as responsible for raising laments over King Josiah at his death: "Jeremiah also uttered a lament for Josiah, and all the singing men and singing women have spoken of Josiah in their laments to this day."

The notion of association is therefore not an external churchly one — let every book be given an author; Jeremiah is known for his laments — but belongs within the ancient sources themselves, whatever ordering eventually emerged (incidentally, these pre-codex orders are preserved in lists, in early rabbinic and patristic sources, and they are by no means uniform on this or many other matters of order). It remains to be seen whether an association of Lamentations with Jeremiah was made even earlier on, not on historical grounds but for hermeneutical or liturgical purposes. This would make the association earlier than the Chronicler's incidental reference regarding Josiah's death and Jeremiah's skill as a lamenter.

I do not want to go too far down this road yet, but by way of anticipation, let me ask a simple question. Did the book of Jeremiah attract early supplemental additions, with the independent and sustained character of the book of Lamentations, in the same manner as the emerging book of Isaiah attracted the sustained and independent poetic response in chapters 40–55(66), the so-called Second Isaiah? Sections of a supplemental character have been critically identified in Isaiah and Ezekiel — if not also in Daniel — and these now circulate as concluding sections within these large prophetic collections (Isaiah 40–66, Ezekiel 40–48, Daniel 7–12). Whether then, over the course of time, an ordering emerged that then severed a more immediate literary connection between the two need not be of such great moment. Jeremiah, and the singing women with him, are remembered in Chronicles as offering great laments over the death of King Josiah. Lamentations became one of five cultic scrolls whose purpose, not surprisingly, was to commemorate the destruction of the temple in 586 B.C.E. These are clearly complementary conceptions of lamentation and prophetic agency. The singular purpose of Lamentations in mourning the destruction of the temple in Israel's religious life perhaps overrode a need to maintain the two works in close editorial and hermeneutical connection. Overridden as well was the fiction of Jeremiah's authorship, if such a concept ever played the major role in their association to begin with. We have already seen how flexible a concept like "authorship" was. To say this is not, therefore, to say that Jeremiah was originally the first-person voice in Lamentations (which is doubtful) and then ceased to be so when the book no longer circulated in proximity to that prophetic collection. More will be said on the question of who is speaking in Lamentations shortly.

I jump the gun here somewhat intentionally in order to move the question of Lamentations' association with Jeremiah or Isaiah into another context of discussion. We may not be talking about strict either-or, Jeremiah or Isaiah, but about processes of growth within major prophetic books, taking place at about the same period of time, that are roughly analogous. The far more familiar association of Isaiah with the Psalter, which will be the focus of the following chapter, is of a different sort than this more literary or editorial association. The piece of critical information generally beyond dispute is the dating of Lamentations and the Second Isaiah material to roughly the same period. This means that it is highly likely they might hold similar views, use similar language, discuss similar topics, and so forth, even if this similarity were to turn out to be nothing so spectacular as their respective authors having been thinking at the same period of Israel's history about similar sorts of matters. But, in my view, the association is yet more intimate and deliberate than that, and this chapter is devoted to showing just how that is so.

But there is one major stumbling block to this that should be put on the table immediately. While a general consensus may exist about the dating of Lamentations and Second Isaiah — even when one is quibbling about distinctions like exilic and postexilic and the question of later expansions and unity within either collection, not to mention the problem of Third Isaiah — the two works are thought not to have any point of contact because "exilic" means in the case of Second Isaiah, composed in and for exiles in Babylon, while for Lamentations "exilic" means relating to the destruction of the temple and exiling of Judah's citizenry, from the perspective of Jerusalem itself. So, for example, Norman Gottwald, who in a very perceptive work on Lamentations[1] is prepared to see a close connection with Second Isaiah, nevertheless must account for the connection in this way: "If the assumption that Deutero-Isaiah wrote in Babylon is correct, then Lamentations must have circulated in the exile as well as in Palestine proper." Perhaps the assumption of Babylonian provenance is not correct. But the positive side of the argument is where Gottwald's emphasis falls. He is at great pains to show how the affinities between Lamentations and Second Isaiah are not just at the level of shared vocabulary but "often strike deeper than mere verbal parallelism."[2] They involve "stylistic features and forms of expression" of such a compelling nature that Gottwald must not only entertain the curious notion of the book of Lamentations traveling to Babylon, but also assert it as a great likelihood. The obverse of this in less travelogue form is the argument that the prophet Second Isaiah wrote in Babylon to exiles from Judah but still thought from

1. Gottwald, *Studies in the Book of Lamentations* (SBT 14; Chicago: Allenson, 1954) 45.

2. Gottwald provides (*Studies,* 44f.) an exhaustive listing of vocabulary and forms of expression held in common by Isaiah 40–66 and Lamentations, dependent in part on M. Lohr, "Der Sprachgebrauch des Buches der Klagelieder," *ZAW* 14 (1894) 41-49.

the perspective of one living in Jerusalem — the sort of argument C. C. Torrey enjoyed attacking.[3]

More important than Gottwald's very perceptive conclusions about literary relationships between Lamentations and Second Isaiah are their significant shared theological and religious affinities. The author of Lamentations and the author of Second Isaiah not only wrestle with similar problems, chief among them the suffering and sin-bearing future of Zion, they wrestle with these problems using similar religious conceptions (guilt, cultic purity, expiation and its possibility, the relationship between the individual and the group as regards sin and expiation). On literary grounds, the two authors use very similar genres to explore this relationship. Anonymous or metaphorical voices exchange reflections on sin and suffering, the very alternation of which produces both confusion and comprehensiveness as the "I," "we," "they," "he," and "she" of these books seek to penetrate to the heart of suffering and sin and the possibility of their being put away — not just by divine fiat — but through some concrete, earthly manifestation of sin-offering every bit as fleshly and real as a goat driven out into the wilderness (Lev 16:20-22).

A sample inventory illustrates the shared concerns, language, and varied perspectives of Lamentations and Isaiah 40–55.

I am the man who has seen affliction (Lam 3:1).
I hid not my face from shame and spitting (Isa 50:6).

He sits alone and is silent (Lam 3:28).
He opened not his mouth (Isa 53:7).

He gives his cheek to the *smiter* (Lam 3:30).
I gave my back to the *smiter*,
   my cheeks to those who pull out the beard (Isa 50:6).

We have sinned and rebelled;
   thou hast not forgiven (Lam 3:42).
All *we* like sheep have gone astray;
   the LORD laid on him the iniquity of us all (Isa 53:6).

---

3. "There is not a word in II Isaiah which could be said to point plainly to Babylonia as the place of its composition" (C. C. Torrey, *The Second Isaiah: A New Interpretation* [New York: Scribner, 1928] 20).

133

My sins are bound together as a yoke . . .
    they ascend upon my neck (Lam 1:14).

Zion stretches forth her hands; she has no *comforters* (Lam 1:17).
Listen when I groan, there is none to *comfort* me (Lam 1:21).
Comfort, comfort my people, says your God (Isa 40:1).
For the LORD will *comfort* Zion,
    he will *comfort* all her waste places
    and make her wilderness like Eden (Isa 51:3).

It may be that we can spot slightly different handlings of these issues by Isaiah and by Lamentations, particularly concerning Zion's guilt or innocence, but the differences are far outweighed by the similarities and by the fact that the *issues* under debate are in large measure the same ones.

The brief quotation from Gottwald shows there are two ways of approaching the question of the relationship between Lamentations and Second Isaiah. One could argue negatively that Second Isaiah was not composed in Babylon, thus increasing the likelihood that similarities in diction, genre, and subject matter were the consequence of similar background; one could then be offering a rather direct literary response to the other ("where is my comforter?" Lamentations asks repeatedly, with Second Isaiah responding to that plea). More positively, one could simply seek to show the intimate nature of the literary features held in common by both works and argue that the association is so strong the material in Second Isaiah must have been composed in greater proximity and in essentially the same religious circumstances than could be better accounted for by a "travelogue" theory. To state this matter another way: is the travelogue notion mentioned by Gottwald only necessitated because of the widespread consensus regarding Second Isaiah's composition in Babylon? Without it, nothing would stand in the way of the natural conclusion that the affinity between Second Isaiah and Lamentations is to be explained as due to similarity of religious circumstances, date, and actual setting, that is, life in Jerusalem following the destruction of Jerusalem. Lamentations had opined that Zion's "prophets received no vision from the LORD" (2:9); Second Isaiah is just such a comforting and God-sent vision.

Instead of choosing between one or the other theory, I want to offer a brief challenge to the Second Isaiah in Babylon notion, and then use the literary evidence from Lamentations to bolster that argument. But there is one other matter to consider that is a holdover from concerns about the unity of Isaiah raised in the previous chapter. Clearly I am not arguing for a close association between Lamentations and Isaiah 40–55 in the first instance to assert unity of authorship in the book of Isaiah as a whole; that could only be a derivative conclusion. Yet it should be borne in mind that one of the chief reasons for reading the book of Isaiah in three major sections — instead of one complex and slow-to-develop unity — is the sharp break that is thought to exist at chapter 40. Many premodern interpreters, Luther and Ibn Ezra among them, were prepared to see much of the material in chapters 40 and following as composed at considerable temporal distance from material associated with Isaiah of Jerusalem. But they still stood far at the outskirts of a theory that chapters 40–55 were written in the Babylonian exile by a "Great Prophet of the Exile," as he would come to be called — and then depicted through contrast with the prophet who in the meantime had received his own critical title "Isaiah *of Jerusalem.*" This geographical criterion was immediately outfitted with a very powerful existential backdrop for the prophecies of Second Isaiah: the anonymous prophet confronting despondent refugees on foreign soil, with melancholy tunes from the lyres of Psalm 137 filling the air, the destroyed temple but a memory, and hopes for return to Zion dashed. That this highlighting of Babylonian exiles traded uncritically on a picture of Israel moving wholesale out of the land, that it might enjoy its sabbaths, never suffered serious doubts (C. C. Torrey notwithstanding).[4]

It took only further reading of the composite biblical record to show that the picture of wholesale deportation into a strange and hostile land, forming the backdrop to Second Isaiah's preaching, was frustrated at two points: first, the incidental but illuminating glimpses at life in Judah during this period, which according to Jeremiah, Zechariah, and Ezekiel suggested efforts at ongoing life, economic stability, civil order, and even special religious observances, including fasts and mourning rituals, carried out during this period; and, second, the observation that what was problematic about life in exile was not necessarily its hardship, but its capacity for

---

4. In a similar instance of selective critical thinking, 2 Kings 22–23 were thought to provide a reliable picture because the origins of the book of Deuteronomy were at stake, while all other accounts in the Deuteronomistic History were viewed as historically suspect since their critical yield in other respects was too low. There needed to be at least one snapshot in sufficiently clear focus (the finding of the book of the law) so as to bring all the others into proper critical perspective. To regard the finding of the book of the law as only a literary fiction demanded by its having been "lost" during Manasseh's reign would mean the forfeiture of the key historical-critical pivot.

general accommodation and also religious and social thriving, of a sort that threatened, not encouraged, enthusiastic overtures for the population to return to Zion. Not despondency nor ennui, but the possibility of a good life in a foreign land without cult or temple began to emerge as a live option.

A dark and empty land in Judah and a pained but nevertheless special existence in exile proved to be a picture far overstated and at odds with much of the biblical record. Chief among witnesses — though usually unrelated to Second Isaiah — was the book of Lamentations, which both depicted life in the land during the exile and also provided the sort of grim and comfortless picture of Israel's existence presupposed by Second Isaiah chapters. If one wishes to find a destroyed Zion, unparalleled despondency, the fruitful land become a wilderness, no comforter, cries of uncleanness and longing for the return of the LORD to Zion, one need look no further than the five poems comprising the book of Lamentations.

To focus on Lamentations, then, instead of the reconstructed picture of Babylonian exile, as the proper literary and religious context for Isaiah 40ff. is also to bring into play an even closer context pertinent to so-called Second Isaiah, shut out when these chapters were exiled to foreign soil. That is the book of Isaiah itself. Here the issue of Isaiah's unity is clearly relevant. For the one thing both Isaiah as a whole and the book of Lamentations have in common, in the most general sense, is a concern with Zion. I have argued elsewhere that Isaiah chapters in 40ff. were composed with one eye trained exegetically on the emerging First Isaiah material — what Second Isaiah refers to as the "former things."[5] That is, Second Isaiah never had an independent life apart from these "former things"; rather, these chapters represent an effort to respond to and extend the Word of God spoken to Isaiah into a new context, for that Word would not return to God empty but would accomplish what God had first purposed (55:11).[6]

Much of the concern of First Isaiah involves the future of God's holy place Zion within his plans both for Israel and for the nations, as the mount to which the nations will stream, with Israel, to learn Torah and

5. See *Zion's Final Destiny: The Development of the Book of Isaiah* (Minneapolis: Fortress, 1991) and other works; this view trades on arguments mounted by B. S. Childs and others, especially Ronald Clements, Peter Ackroyd, and Rolf Rendtorff. See chapter 13 below for a complete bibliography.

6. See also chapter 13 below.

to be instructed by the God of Israel (2:1-4). Yet the destruction of the temple by the Babylonians, the rod of God's own righteous fury, replacement for the haughty Assyrians, had raised questions about God's plans for Zion and his people. Second Isaiah chapters respond to these "former things" by returning to the divine council and hearing a fresh word of comfort and an announcement that a full payment for sin had been accomplished by Zion (40:2). Latter things had overtaken former things, and these were now about to give way to new things, "hidden things, which you have not known, created now, not long ago" (48:6, 7) concerning a yet more glorious manifestation of God and restoration of Zion. One eye is trained exegetically on the "former things" while the other is trained on the circumstances facing the prophet and his community. But to comprehend this we need no imaginative reconstruction of life in Babylon for exiles awaiting return to Judah and the rebuilding of the temple, quickened by the word of the Great Prophet of the Exile. Rather, the book of Lamentations itself provides direct literary testimony to life for captive Judah to which, like the former things of Isaiah, Second Isaiah is a response.

I will focus on only one of the main features of Isaiah 40ff. that has led scholars to place the material in the Babylonian exile, or in some other region of deportation and captivity (Egypt or Syria). Perhaps the best known of these features is the so-called second exodus motif, whereby the vast territory separating the Babylonian golah from Judah is reckoned to be a second wilderness, like the one separating God's people in Egypt from the promised land. The notion of a second exodus is not to be rejected altogether, but requires modification. These chapters clearly look forward to God returning his people from regions of dispersion and captivity.

> Lo, these shall come from afar, and lo,
>> these from the north and from the west,
>> and these from the land of Syene (49:12).

> Fear not, for I am with you;
>> I will bring your offspring from the east,
>> and from the west I will gather you;
>> I will say to the north,
>> Give up, and to the south, Do not withhold;
> Bring my sons and daughters
>> from the end of the earth (43:5-6).

Promise of return of the dispersed of Israel belongs within the promises of Isaiah of Jerusalem and forms part of the witness of the former things spoken of old by God to his prophet Isaiah and to his prophets in general. One can see from these two quotations, and from a host of others like them, that the question is not whether the prophet Second Isaiah promised return of those exiled, but whether he did so from the Babylonian exile itself and whether a focus on the situation of exile there has distracted the reader from seeing God's plan for return as directed to all corners of the universe.[7] Furthermore, the prophet is not just speaking in general terms, but in line with prophecies of old that expressed God's intentions in this precise manner (see Isa 11:11, 15-16; 19:23-25; 27:12-13; 35:1-10). As such, the prophet's promises of return are not "new things" but "former things" now about to be fulfilled. The promises are of course important in themselves. But equally important is the prophet's ability to show that what he knows in this regard had been revealed to Israel long ago, and as such that the veracity of Israel's God and his sovereignty over all other claimants to be god is fully upheld (see 41:21-29; 43:8-13; 45:20-21). The nations are constantly being told to present evidence of their foreknowledge of God's plan, which they cannot; yet God had revealed these things of old through Isaiah to Israel and has thereby established his claim to be God, and God alone.

As for the wilderness motif, rightly seen as widespread in chapters 40ff., here too a modification is in order along something of the same lines. For the second exodus notion on which the motif is thought to trade would again be less rooted in the prior literary testimony of Isaiah — where as von Rad noted, exodus is not a prominent tradition stream, but rather Zion and royal traditions — and instead would represent an application of an old, non-Isaianic notion, presumably part of the fresh inspiration vouchsafed to the "Great Prophet of the Exile." But on closer inspection the wilderness motif in Second Isaiah is something other than a direct borrowing of the concept from the story of Israel's sojourn after release from bondage in Egypt, with the wilderness representing a sort of *terra intermedia* of testing and trials leading to failure or loyalty as from bride to bridegroom (so Hosea's exegesis). Note rather that wilderness or desert frequently describe Zion's *own actual state as such,* which God is about to reverse, to fructify in preparation for — or at the very moment of — his

7. See Hans Barstad's *A Way in the Wilderness* (*Journal of Semitic Studies* Monograph Series 12; Manchester: University of Manchester, 1989) for a comparable treatment. Also his "Lebte Deuterojesaja in Judäa?" *Norsk Teologisk Tidsskrift* 83 (1982) 77-87.

own appearing. God's own personal return to Zion is far more prominent in Second Isaiah than any other sort of mundane return by God's people. Addressing Zion the prophet says:

> Surely *your* waste and *your* desolate places and *your* devastated land — surely now you will be too narrow for your inhabitants (49:19).

> For the LORD will comfort Zion;
>   he will comfort all *her* waste places;
> And will make *her* wilderness like Eden,
>   *her* desert like the garden of the LORD (51:3).

> Break forth into singing, you waste places *of Jerusalem* (52:9).

Or, with a focus on the return — not of exiles — but of God to Zion, recall the opening verses:

> In the wilderness prepare the way of the LORD, make straight in the desert the highway *of our God* . . . for the glory of the LORD shall be revealed and all flesh shall see it together (40:3, 5).

> For eye to eye they see
>   the *return of the LORD* to Zion (52:8).

The notion of wilderness and desolation is not derived from the first exodus only or primarily, even while there are obvious points of contact; rather, the theme of chaos and desolation familiar from the Psalms (e.g., Book IV) and especially the Priestly writer is the form deployed by Second Isaiah. The poet is talking about a form of primordial chaos to which Zion, Judah, and even the whole cosmos itself threatens to return. In a passage where the restoration of Zion is promised, it should not be surprising to hear the poet refer to these central texts not from Exodus, but from the opening chapters of Genesis.

> For this is like the days of Noah to me:
>   as I swore that the waters of Noah
>   should no more go over the earth,
> So I have sworn that I will not be angry with you
>   and will not rebuke you.

139

> For the mountains may depart
>   and the hills be removed,
> But not my steadfast love (54:9, 10).

And when the redemption of Israel from Egyptian bondage *is* explicitly referred to, the yet older motif employed even there — the drying up of the sea — is what comes to the fore in Second Isaiah as well.

> Was it not thou that didst cut Rahab in pieces,
>   that didst pierce the dragon?
> Was it not thou that didst dry up the sea,
>   the waters of the great deep;
> Thou didst make the depths of the sea a way
>   for the redeemed to pass over (51:9-10)?

Yet again, this motif of a Zion returned to chaos and wilderness is familiar — not from a reconstructed Babylonian setting — but from First Isaiah, as a description of the great judgment God will wreak on his own people and on their destroyers as well (see Isaiah 24–27). Yet now in Second Isaiah God is about to return to Zion and redeem her, turning her wilderness into a way of majestic growth, transforming her into a new and glorious vineyard.

The same notion of Zion herself being exiled and desolate, rather than the wilderness territory between Babylon and Zion or the Israelites as themselves exiled, can be detected in Lamentations:

> The punishment of your iniquity,
>   O daughter Zion, is accomplished,
> He will keep you in exile no longer (4:22).

> Mount Zion lies desolate;
>   jackals prowl over it (5:18).

> The chastisement of the daughter
>   of my people has become greater
> than the punishment of Sodom, which was
>   overthrown in a moment (4:6).

But for Lamentations the far more prominent motif is that of uncleanness and cultic impurity. Examples could be multiplied greatly.

Jerusalem sinned grievously,
    therefore she became filthy (1:8).

Her uncleanness was in her skirts
    she took no thought of her doom (1:9).

Jerusalem has become a filthy thing among them (1:17).

Should priest and prophet be slain
    in the sanctuary of the LORD (2:20)?

One passage in particular appears almost verbatim in Second Isaiah, although the context seems much clearer in Lamentations. Again it is one of uncleanness and cultic defilement, caused by the shedding of blood.

[Prophets and priests] shed in the midst of her
    the blood of the righteous.
They wandered blind through the streets,
    so defiled with blood none could touch their garments.
Away! Unclean! men cried at them;
    Away! Away! Touch not!
So they became fugitives and wanderers;
    Men said among the nations,
    "They shall stay no longer with us" (4:13-15).

Isaiah 52:11 has exactly the same phrase, "Away! Away! Unclean! Touch not!" But with it is the charge for the priests "who bear the vessels of the LORD" to "go forth from the midst of her" and "purify" themselves. The verse has long been the subject of disputed readings, with many modern interpreters opting for Babylonian exile as the place of uncleanness from which the priests are to depart. But this has by no means been an uncontroverted reading in the history of interpretation; "from her" has frequently been taken to mean "from Jerusalem," that is, a place full of cultic uncleanness, as in Lamentations. Whereas in Lamentations priests tainted with blood were not to be touched, not even by the nations, now priests are charged to go forth from uncleanness and purify themselves.

It may be simply adventitious that the verse held in common by both Lamentations and Isaiah, obscure as it is in the latter context, takes us directly to the passage much honored in the history of interpretation but equally obscure, the so-called fourth "servant song" (52:13–53:12). The going forth of the priests, not in haste and with God as a rear guard, serves to introduce this poem concerning the affliction and exaltation of God's servant. Unlike the first two "songs" this poem belongs in the section of the book most concerned with Zion (49:14–55:13); and unlike the servant poem at 50:4-11, which resembles a first-person commissioning, this poem describes the fate of the obscure servant in the third person.

As mentioned above, the alternation of first-person lament and third-person description is part and parcel of the larger form of Lamentations. This alternation helps provide flow and comprehensiveness across what might otherwise become a monotonous series of highly structured lamentations. The difficulty of interpreting the speaker intended by the first-person voice in chapter 3 is similar to the obscurity surrounding the third-person voice in Isaiah 52–53. Where in other places the first-person voice is clearly that of Zion (1:12-22), the poem in Lamentations 3, introduced with the plainly intoned "I am the man who has seen affliction," appears to admit of two interpretations.

In strict form-critical terms, which would take the poem as a unit unto itself, we open with a psalm of individual distress, perhaps inviting "everyman" to participate in the suffering of Zion described in chapters 1 and 2. A different interpretation might well accept this form-critical conclusion but still keep the attention focused on the Zion *figura*, who plays the signal role in the drama of Lamentations in all the surrounding chapters. A psalm of individual lament, introduced with stock language, "I am the man," would then be here taken up and employed by the specific figure, the afflicted daughter Zion. That the masculine term *geber* ought not stand in the way of Zion being the speaker is argued by many commentators; it either reflects a usage typical of the form adopted here, or it is simply more irrelevant than modern readers — especially ones now sensitive to gender issues — are prepared for.

This interpretation would allow the voice that reflects in vv. 25-48 on the suffering expressed by the individual in vv. 1-24 to be cleanly differentiated. The "everyman" voice is not that of the individual sufferer but of the respondent in vv. 25-48. In other words, the specific suffering of Zion articulated in the first-person speech is the grounds for general reflection on the ways of God, leading even to a call to examination and general confession of guilt (vv. 40-48). The poem ends with a return to the specific suffering of the individual spoken forth in the first person as in the opening verses (49-66), now to conclude with a statement of confidence in the justice of God in redeeming his servant.

In other words, the correct interpretation of Lamentations 3 may turn on understanding what specific role surrounding *context* is to play, where the individual first-person voice is consistently that of Zion. That context would appear to play an important role is suggested by the extraordinarily complex, baroque structure of the book as a whole. Each individual poem is tightly organized according to some form of acrostic, in order to represent an examination of suffering "from a to z," the acrostic differently presented from poem to poem. At the same time, a sense of larger unity is enforced by the use of not just any random number of poems in whatever order, but a fivefold pattern with this key poem as the centerpiece. So just as there are five-fifths of the law of Moses and five-fifths of the Psalms of David, so there are five-fifths of the laments of the afflicted city Zion.

When we turn to the interpretation of Isaiah's suffering servant, the same question of context must be faced, though here the tight structure of Lamentations is sadly not available for help. We have only a few guidelines to the overall structure of chapters 40–55. Recent interpretation of Second Isaiah differentiates between a first section concerned with Cyrus, the bolstering of servant Israel by appeal to the former things, and God's self-defense before his people and before the gods of the nations, comprising chapters 40 through 48. In the second main section, running up to chapter 55(56), these themes recede before a concern with Zion, first and foremost.

To be sure, there are exceptions to this focus on Zion, and it is usually maintained — almost without argument — that the fourth servant song is one of them. The very designation of a cycle of four servant "songs" has itself worked against a notion of a recognizable section in Second Isaiah concerned with Zion, on the one hand, or themes of "former/latter things," Cyrus, and servant Israel, on the other.[8] For such a cycle would run through both sections and would urge a relatively uniform conception of the servant as such — hence some early efforts to describe the servant songs as even

8. For a classic expression, see K. Baltzer's "Zur formgeschichtlichen Bestimmung der Texte vom Gottes-Knecht im Deutero-Jesaja-Buch" in *Probleme biblischer Theologie* (FS G. von Rad; Munich: Kaiser, 1971), where the four poems comprise a "biography" of the servant. Most recently, compare "Jes 52,13: Die 'Erhöhung' des Gottes-Knechtes," in *Religious Propaganda and Missionary Competition in the New Testament World*, ed. Lukas Bormann et al. (FS D. Georgi; Leiden: Brill, 1994) 45-56.

comprising a "biography" of God's servant, not to mention the search for the identity of who this famous servant might be.

Striking, then, is the fact that the context surrounding the servant poem is wholly about Zion. Zion is addressed at the beginning of chapter 52 and told to dress herself in beautiful garments; those who will now enter her will not be unclean; watchmen posted announce the return of God to Zion; all flesh will see the manifestation of God's salvation (52:1-10).[9] On the other side of the servant poem, Zion is once again addressed (54:1-17). The children who will now populate her will be more numerous than before her term of punishment; the afflicted, storm-tossed one will no longer be oppressed and terrorized, and just as once God judged his own creation in the days of Noah, so also his steadfast love toward Zion will be as unbreakable as the covenant God struck with Noah after the punishment (54:1-10). It is clear, then, that the material surrounding the servant poem concerns the fate of Zion, as God's return is announced before, while after Zion's exaltation and protection is promised.

So also in the book of Lamentations Zion is the personified figure addressed, depicted, and herself lamenting in chapters 1 and 2 and 4 and 5. And even while in chapter 3 the images of besieging, walling about, and hindering with chains and blocked paths are all quite sensible for a personified city, nevertheless features of the old formal lament still press for a reading that at times seems better suited to any individual, the "everyman" of suffering. What seems reasonably clear in Lamentations 3 is that the opening psalm of distress in vv. 1-24 gives rise both to a righteous response in vv. 25-39 and a corporate confession of transgression and rebellion (vv. 40-48). This in turn places before us a final first-person psalm in verses 49-66, but now one that appears to offer a positive response, picking up where the first psalm ended and going well beyond it. This individual speaker is confident that God will judge the cause of his afflicted one, even one whose punishment is merited so far as God is concerned, yet whose sentence is executed by assailants who misunderstand their own role and circumscribed mission as that of Israel's own God. The last word will therefore be God's judgment over them.

The point to be made is that while the identity of the speaker seems unclear, the movement of the chapter is not: the afflicted one laments

---

9. The passage has been rightly identified as an *inclusio* keyed to 40:1-9. See J. van Oorschot, *Von Babel zum Zion* (Beihefte zum *ZAW* 206; Berlin: de Gruyter, 1993) 106-27; O. H. Steck, *Gottesknecht und Zion* (Tübingen: Mohr, 1992) 52-59.

before God her or his situation; a response to this lament both commends the justice of God as neither whimsical or arbitrary and then confesses rebellion and its consequences; and finally the first-person voice again makes her or his complaint known, but this time with confidence that God's judgment is not simply equivalent to the taunts of human assailants, arbitrary and devious, but is itself the hope of the one judged. Here is a difficult if not powerful theology of suffering. The very strong likelihood is that Zion speaks the lament at beginning and at end and is herself the figure of suffering and affliction who gives rise to the response that intervenes. But the book of Lamentations is content to let language of lament, response, and final psalm speak for itself without nailing down the speakers in some airtight manner that will admit of only one interpretation.

The situation in the servant poem is somewhat different in that we do not have a formalized description of distress (for all the specificity that does emerge in Lamentations 3) but instead an almost narrative account concerning the afflicted one: whose appearance is marred (Isa 52:14); who had an ignominious origin (53:2); who was afflicted not just for his own sake, but for others (53:5); who was executed, or so it would seem, as a sin offering (53:10); and who will nevertheless be vindicated and rewarded (53:11-12), as the poem promised at the beginning (52:13). It is especially difficult to account for the minor details (grave with the wicked, like a root out of dry ground). But more difficult is the existence of such detail to begin with, asking us to view what might otherwise be familiar phrases known from psalms of individual lament (kings will shut their mouths, wounded for our transgression, sheep dumb before shearers, cut off from the land of the living — see for example Psalm 22) in a somewhat different, more particularized, light.

We have already mentioned a point of contact with Lamentations, and that is the oddly intrusive two-verse unit that sits between the poem telling of the return of God to Zion and the servant poem itself. The phrases of Lam 4:15 appear here in virtually the same form, making the slight changes significant. Lamentations spoke of unclean priests, not to be touched, even shooed away, becoming then fugitives and wanderers. Among the nations, men say about them, that their stay will not be long (4:15). The voice that continues to speak in 4:17ff. sounds also like one driven away: "they chased us on the mountains . . . the LORD's anointed was taken in their pits, he of whom we said, under his shadow we shall live among the nations." This may be the point of departure for 2 Chronicles' attachment of Josiah to Jeremiah's lamenting.

Both Lamentations and Second Isaiah make reference to ritual un-cleanness in the context of the verse in question (Lamentations quite explicitly). Even the priests themselves, those responsible for maintaining purity, are unclean, and so are driven away. The sanctuary is likewise defiled by blood and by the presence of those who do not belong, chiefly ritually unclean and uncircumcised foreigners. Isaiah 52:1, which introduces the theme of Zion's restoration and the return of God himself to the sanctuary, states that the unclean and uncircumcised will no longer come into Zion. Captive daughter Zion is to arise from the dust, where she sat so defiled and ignominious in Lamentations. Yet a priestly question remains: how is the cultic impurity bewailed in Lamentations and referred to in Second Isaiah to be removed? And what if the priests, themselves defiled, are not in a position to render an unclean cult site, God's own abode Zion, clean?

The problem of an unclean cult site, defiled by blood and the presence of foreign invaders, whose chief concern is, after all, to make Israel's sanctuary useless, is known in other sources for the period (Haggai, Zechariah, Ezra). Ezekiel and Lamentations are explicit that a further problem is the defilement of the priests themselves, who are the agents of God's cleansing and expiatory actions. The elaborate ritual described in Leviticus 16 for the Day of Atonement clarifies how the sin offering of a live goat sent out into the wilderness, dispatched by Aaron, shall bear the iniquities of all the people to a solitary land (16:20). Preliminary to this is a sacrifice of a goat as a sin offering to make atonement for the holy place itself and for Aaron "himself and for his house and for all the assembly of Israel" (v. 17). Then blood is sprinkled on the altar to "cleanse it and hallow it from the uncleannesses of the people of Israel" (v. 19). Only then does the ritual of the scapegoat sent alive into the wilderness come into play.

This ritual is to be carried out yearly, so it is a regularization of atoning for priesthood, cult, and people quite independent of the sort of egregious case of defilement made manifest when Zion was invaded by foreign soldiers bent precisely on rendering unfit Israel's sanctuary. How is such a situation of defilement to be addressed, before the prophet in Second Isaiah can even hope for a time when neither uncircumcised nor unclean would again enter Zion's holy precincts? Clearly a special sin offering, over and above the sort of cleansing ritual described for the Day of Atonement, though perhaps on rough analogy to the additional scape-goat ordeal that took place following this elaborate ceremony, was in order. In verses 11-12 of Isaiah 52 the priesthood is to prepare itself by purification. No haste is necessary. Unclean things were touched at the first exodus — namely, the jewelry of the Egyptians. Nothing is to be touched this time. The goal of that first exodus was not liberation alone, but the giving of the law and the establishment of a sanctuary for true worship of God. So too here Zion is to be bedecked ("I will lay your foundations with sapphires . . . your pinnacles with agate . . . all your wall of precious stone," 54:11-12). But not as at the first exodus and the first sanctuary construction.

Now it would appear that nowhere in the servant poem itself is reference made to cleansing the sanctuary. It looks as though God can by his very words to Zion — to rise from the dust, to put on beautiful garments, to sing and enlarge the place of her tent for children more numerous than before, to forget the time of her shame and grief and divorce, to wear jewelry of a new bride, words that ring on either side of the servant poem — effect for Zion a new beginning. Yet it is also striking to note what is said in the intervening servant poem: chiefly, that atonement is being made, affliction leading to death, which nevertheless serves as a sin offering for Israel, accounted righteous because the Israelites' iniquities have been borne up. A similar, though less dramatic, movement was noted in Lamentations 3, where the suffering and affliction of an individual effects a change for a wider constituency, culminating in God's vindication of the now trusting individual.

It would be tempting to identify the individual in both cases as Zion, an identification that is quite frequently made by interpreters of Lamentations 3 but is virtually never asserted for the famous suffering servant poem. Is Zion the servant who will be high and lifted up, language used of her in Isaiah 2? Is Zion the figure recollected by Ezekiel as having ignominious origins: unwashed, not pitied, abhorred, yet told by God to grow up as a plant of the field, and who upon reaching full flower is bedecked with jewels, renowned for beauty and splendor among the nations (15:1-14) — images strikingly similar to those used by Second Isaiah? Is this servant the same afflicted, grieving, rejected, smitten-by-God figure whom Lamentations understands to be none other than Zion herself? And yet how can Zion offer intercession or make her grave with the wicked, and why would the feminine imagery used for her give way here to masculine forms — a move perhaps at work in Lamentations, too, but far less sharply there?

But perhaps the most difficult question is why such obscurity surrounds this figure to begin with, giving rise to an unending search for the servant's proper identity? To say that the identity of the servant was probably known by the prophet and those he first addressed, but this has not been clearly transmitted to eventual, unintended readers of the text in its present form, may only be an answer of convenience, however circumscribing. What we do know is that the present form of the text has placed greater emphasis on the fact of atonement than the exact agent of atonement. There is obscurity about the servant, not about what the servant has accomplished, nor about what the consequences for Zion mean: full restitution and the accomplishment of a sentence of judgment for iniquity once rendered.

So much for the obscurity, whether intentional or unintentional, surrounding the servant's identity. This much is clear, and it comes as a consequence of reading chapters 40–55 with greater attention to the book of Lamentations. These chapters of Isaiah are concerned with Zion: her defilement, debasement, vindication and restoration — themes introduced in First Isaiah and continued on into the final eleven chapters of Isaiah, where restoration raises questions about proper membership within Israel and also within those same nations who were once oppressors. Exiling Second Isaiah to Babylon has diverted attention from Zion, which must be kept to the fore if the language of cult, priesthood, sin offering, guilt, and atonement — the lexicon of Lamentations and Isaiah 40–55 — is to be properly understood and appreciated. When the classic interpreter Claus Westermann can say about the unit at 52:11-12 "it is not the case that here, in his final words, Deutero-Isaiah displays an interest in cultic practices and vessels which he has never shown before" we learn far more about his innate Protestant hesitancies than we do about chapters 40–55 of Isaiah, especially as these are concerned with Zion's cultic purity.[10] A reading of this material in closer proximity to Lamentations, which in my view is appropriate to its own language and religious circumstances, keeps before us the clear significance both works place on God's special place of habitation, defiled and punished for sin but also the place that remains the light to Israel and the nations.

To conclude, the book of Acts records an episode not unlike the one we have been engaged with in this essay. The Ethiopian eunuch asks a question of exegesis: about whom is the prophet Isaiah speaking in this poem about a suffering individual? (Acts 8:27-40). Even granting the conventional character of the scene, it is striking that a question of the

10. *Isaiah 40–66: A Commentary* (Old Testament Library; Philadelphia: Westminster, 1977) 253.

servant's identity persisted up into the period of the church's birth. The identity of the obscure servant remained obscure enough that the inquiry could be reasonably made. What was known was what the servant had accomplished — atonement for others, himself innocent and bearing sins and punishment more fitting for others, who knew themselves to be guilty and meriting just punishment, like the thief on the cross.

It is the task of Christian exegesis to respect silence and obscurity in the Old Testament when it seems to defer to, or stand in service of, something more clearly known and forthrightly proclaimed — here, the *fact* of atoning sacrifice, over and above the *agent*. For the church to see more, to penetrate to a different level of understanding, is as much a move of worship and doxology as of one-referent-only exegesis. This level of understanding flows from but also moves beyond what was known to the author of Isaiah 52:13–53:11, namely, that Christ's death on a cross was a sacrifice intended to cover the sins of the entire world.

This form of "fulfillment" is in many respects far more profound than strict promise-and-fulfillment, if by that is meant predictions made long ago that find their target in events associated with Jesus of Nazareth, that being their sole originating purpose and rationale. Rather, they are something far less mechanical than that: the filling to fullness and overflowing of what had only been adumbrated, sketched, hinted at, longed for, pointed toward, forming types of what would later become explicit. This would entail specific Christian confession being poured into a mold for which it had been prepared in advance, through what has traditionally been called an act of the Holy Spirit, at work in both Israel and the church, requiring new eyes of faith and a capacity to perceive in the plain sense of scripture the vehicle through which fulfillments gain their gravity and eternal purpose.

Only by honoring this silence and learning to listen for what *is* being said can our hearts be prepared to hear, in all its fullness, what the silence portends: that the act of atoning sacrifice accomplished by Zion and this obscure servant trained the eyes of Israel, and through them the world, to see in the crucifixion of Jesus not a ghastly, singular execution, but the plans of God being accomplished, filled to fullness, in those events and that man. This took place on behalf of Israel and on our behalf, who were at that time strangers both to the commonwealth of Israel (Eph 2:12) and to the oracles of God (Rom 3:1). To be brought within this commonwealth is to share a scriptural heritage that both describes our predicament and God's addressing of it, as seen by the prophet Isaiah and brought to fulfillment on Calvary, for the sake of the whole world.

12

Royal Promises in the Canonical Books of Isaiah and the Psalms

I

One of the more obviously controversial aspects of the Dead Sea Scrolls has involved the interpretation of messianic texts and messianism. The topic is of obvious importance for Jews and Christians and for our understanding of both groups as they emerged around the time of the scrolls through a process of what linguists would call "dissimilation." Subject of most recent discussion has been 4Q285, a text that suffers badly from broken and fragmentary readings. At the center of the controversy is whether or not the fragments refer to a slain messiah or — less controversially — to a messiah who slays. Unclear, then, are the subject and object of the slaying. (Hebrew is unpointed at Qumran and usually lacks direct object markers in poetic texts.)[1]

Uncontroversial is the exegetical character of the text in question. That is, 4Q285 is, like many non-biblical texts at Qumran, "virtual biblical" — that is, it contains a wealth of biblical citation, allusion, and verbatim quotation. In fact, one could argue that interpretation of this difficult Qumran text turns on understanding just *how*, in detail, it has utilized biblical texts — texts that are not now fragmentary, or unpointed, or even in most cases all that unclear. Here would appear to lie a way out

1. For a full discussion, see most recently, Martin G. Abegg, "Messianic Hope and 4Q285: A Reassessment," *JBL* 113 (1994) 81-91.

of the impasse, because this parabiblical fragment is so thoroughgoingly biblical and exegetical.[2]

Not surprising, given the eschatological climate of Qumran texts in general and this text in particular, is the frequent reference to the book of Isaiah. Of the three great prophets, Isaiah, Jeremiah, and Ezekiel, New Testament and parabiblical texts agree in seeing the prophet Isaiah as a voice directed to the future — to their own day and their own concerns. The importance of great truths spoken long ago is only now being fully revealed, and Isaiah is the bearer of these great mysteries. Another way to put this is that while many early Christian and Jewish readers of this period see the scriptures as directed to their own day, Isaiah needs very little coaxing to serve this purpose because its own plain sense is frequently eschatological. "Now in the latter days the mountain of the house of the LORD will be the highest of all mountains" is typical of its rhetoric (Isa 2:2).

To return to our Qumran fragment, it has been argued that the Isaiah citation which offers help in clearing up the question of a slain or slaying messiah is Isa 11:4:

> He will judge with righteousness the poor,
>> decide with just measure for the afflicted of the earth;
> strike the earth with the rod of his mouth,
>> and with the breath of his lips slay the wicked.

Alternatively, in Isa 65:15 reference to *God himself* slaying the wicked — this time *within* Israel — has also been thought to lie close at hand. Both texts of Isaiah use the same causative form of the verb "to die" employed in the Qumran fragment (*yamit* or *hemiteka*) and both may well have influenced the Qumran text. What is interesting in comparing these two Isaiah texts is the clear presence in 11:4 of a Davidic figure who is responsible for the slaying, while in 65:15 God is himself at work to slay the wicked without need of messianic agency. Or to adopt a modern critical perspective: there is a royal messiah figure in "First Isaiah," but no such figure in "Second" or "Third Isaiah." This is true even though both passages speak of slaying — divine or royal — as dramatic future events

---

2. The term "parabiblical" is proposed by Joseph Fitzmyer in place of "intertestamental" to designate "a body of Jewish literature that grew up alongside of the Hebrew Bible" (*Responses to 101 Questions on the Dead Sea Scrolls* [New York/Mahwah: Paulist, 1992] 13).

associated with God's eschatological purposes. Another classic critical distinction — extramural judgment of the nations in First Isaiah, greater focus on intramural judgment of the impious within Israel in Third Isaiah — also comes into potential play here. Yet striking — and here I come at last to my point — is that just such a distinction between rival perspectives in Isaiah frequently falls to the side at Qumran, permitting a modern interpreter to see both Isa 11:4 and Isa 65:15 as influencing 4Q285.

The reason I begin with this point is to make an important discrimination from the outset. It could be inferred that Qumran texts know no such distinction because they view the entire book of Isaiah as operating, not from three or more distinctive, but from one essentially self-same perspective, that of Isaiah of Jerusalem. Or, more generally, Qumran readers, like most of their contemporaries, ignored all critical distinctions regarding author, setting, literary context, and the like and read scripture — ransacked it, the modern would say — without regard for internal critical constraints, or even constraints of a basic book-by-book character that would keep quite separate interpretation of Isaiah from, say, interpretation of Jeremiah, Hosea, or the Song of Songs. On such a view, *all* of scripture is equally and even-handedly "prophetic" and revelatory of the events of the day. John Barton moves close to this view in his stimulating book, *Oracles of God.*[3]

Barton's depiction is to my mind too sweeping, but my main point involves something else. We are now working in a climate in which many are interested in reading Isaiah as a unity. Yet no unitary reading I am aware of would merge sections of the book in such a way as to imitate the perspective of Qumran, where sharp distinctions within the book fall to the side concerning God's appointed messiah. Instead, even interpreters interested in the unity of Isaiah maintain a fundamental distinction between the lively royal hopes of First Isaiah chapters and the modification of these in the second main section (40–66).

The situation is made yet more complicated by the fact that some royal passages in First Isaiah chapters are considered postexilic additions. Frequently mentioned are Isaiah 11, 32, and sometimes even 9. The complication involved is clear. The exilic and postexilic perspectives of Second and Third Isaiah are said to reflect a modification, an adaptation, a recalibration, or even a rejection of the messianism of First Isaiah; while

3. *Oracles of God: Perceptions of Ancient Prophecy in Israel after the Exile* (London: DLT, 1986).

at the very same time a lively array of messianic texts are being outfitted to the original perspective of Isaiah of Jerusalem now found in chapters 1–39. It would serve no good purpose to point out here how very complicated and assorted are the explanations given for how these various postexilic perspectives on Davidic kingship both originated and then found their path editorially into the present book of Isaiah.[4]

It would be helpful to illustrate just two ways in which the royal hopes associated with First Isaiah are thought to have been modified — not in First Isaiah itself — but in Second and Third Isaiah. This is a bit easier to describe since it does not require an elaborate defense of what is primary and secondary within chapters 1–39.

Explanation number one is older than unitary readings, but it persists in some form among those interested in unity nonetheless. Cyrus is God's messiah. Isa 45:1 makes this explicit, and a number of other Second Isaiah texts suggest similar things: "Thus says the LORD to his anointed, to Cyrus, whose right hand I have grasped." So it is argued that the Davidic line and hopes were doused or brought into total reconfiguration with the exile to Babylon, the blinding of Zedekiah, and the eventual failure of efforts at resuscitation in the period of Ezra-Nehemiah. More positively, Second Isaiah proclaimed that God had himself shifted an older indigenous model over to Cyrus the Persian, an adaptation required because of the loss of statehood in the postexilic period. The end of the books of Chronicles would also reflect such a perspective: God stirs up the spirit of Cyrus, to whom he has given all the kingdoms of the earth (36:23), to build a house for him as once David and Solomon proposed and carried out. A new king for a new and changed dispensation.[5]

Problems with such a view have persisted up to and include the Waco debacle involving David Koresh and the Branch Davidians. The picture of Cyrus found in Isaiah is not an altogether positive one, and would certainly represent a strange transformation to a strange form of kingship. Cyrus is called by God to deliver his people, but the text makes it clear that Cyrus does not know him whom the prophet addresses as "the LORD,

---

4. Representative are the views of O. Kaiser in his rewritten commentary (*Isaiah 1–12* [2nd ed., Philadelphia: Westminster, 1983). See also, more recently, A. Laato's *Who Is Immanuel? The Rise and Foundering of Isaiah's Messianic Expectations* (Åbo: Åbo Akademis, 1988); *idem, The Servant of YHWH and Cyrus: A Reinterpretation of the Exilic Messianic Programme in Isaiah 40–55* (Stockholm: Almqvist & Wiksell, 1992).

5. See now R. G. Kratz, *Kyrus im Deuterojesaja-Buch* (Tubingen: Mohr, 1991).

there is no other, and besides me there is no God" (45:3). Seen within the context of the book of Isaiah itself, it is difficult to see this as much of a transformation of the negative language about the rulers of the nations found elsewhere in Isaiah ("Ah, Assyria, rod of my anger . . . against a godless nation I send him . . . but he does not so intend and his mind does not so think," 10:5, 7). Isaiah of Jerusalem may state clearly that Assyria is the rod of God's fury, but when the Rabshakeh wishes to make more of this than God intends on behalf of King Sennacherib — "is it without the LORD that I have come up against this place?" — this turns out to be blasphemy of the highest order and deserving of death, a sentence that is carried out within the year (in fulfillment of 10:16). Second Isaiah's views regarding the claims of the nations made on their own behalf are on occasion yet more denunciatory than anything found in First Isaiah:

> They will come in chains and bow down to you.
> They will make supplication to you, saying,
> "God is with you only, and there is no other" (45:14).

Would the author of these verses have considered Cyrus or the Persians exempt from these themes, inaugurated in First Isaiah, regarding the obeisance and honoring of YHWH by the nations? Moreover, that there is no afterlife to this sort of Cyrus messianism should itself be a clear sign of the very specific, very circumscribed character of Cyrus' mission: he is to let God's people go free, defeat hostile kings as promised of old by Isaiah, and even build God's fallen city. But not for price or reward, as Isaiah puts it (45:13) and certainly not in some sustained or sustainable manner to be carried on beyond this task as such. It should also be remembered that alongside positive depictions of the task of Cyrus stand equally strong depictions of the wealth of the nations streaming into Zion and the reassertion of old messianic hopes associated with the Davidic house (see Haggai 2:20-23).[6]

The second possibility likewise predates unitary approaches to Isaiah, emerging from a close reading of Second Isaiah on its own terms. This possibility, too, has been picked up and asserted with fresh currency by unitary approaches. Isa 55:3 is held to assert that royal promises have been

---

6. Given the prevalence of second exodus themes, one might regard Cyrus as a transformed Pharaoh, befitting a transformed exodus, wilderness, and final destination (Zion). But of course that still leaves him at some distance from a messianic depiction.

transferred away from David to the people as a whole. Addressing the widest assembly — "Ho, everyone who thirsts" (55:1) — the prophet states:

> Incline your ear and come to me;
>> hear, that your soul may live;
> and I will make with you
>> an everlasting covenant,
> my steadfast sure love for David (55:3).

Failure to refer to messianic promises in Second Isaiah is explained by the fact of their having been transferred to the people at large. David Meade stands in a long line of interpreters who adopt this position, including among others Otto Eissfeldt, Paul Volz, Christopher North, Gerhard von Rad, Claus Westermann, and others. Meade states: "Though political realities would not allow him to simply repeat Isaiah's promises to the Davidic monarchy, he skillfully actualizes this tradition by 'democratizing' it, and applying the Davidic promises to the entire nation."[7] Twenty-five years earlier, Claus Westermann (following North and von Rad) put the matter this way:

> [Lamentations and Psalm 89] called everything into question. [They] gave rise to two entirely different hopes or proclamations. The first was that a new and entirely different king would come into being from the house of David (the "shoot," the messiah). The second was this trans- formation of the old prophecy in Deutero-Isaiah. . . . And what he does say is extremely bold. Unlike the messianic predictions, he does not take as the way of comforting his people telling them of some supernatural king who is to come at some time in the future and effect their salvation. Instead, he is daring enough to proclaim that, with the imminent divine act of release, the tokens of grace vouchsafed to David are transferred to Israel.[8]

I quote at some length to show how forcefully Westermann puts it, implying precisely the sort of distinction between Second Isaiah and the

7. David Meade, *Pseudonymity and Canon* (Tubingen: Mohr, 1986) 34.
8. C. Westermann, *Isaiah 40–66: A Commentary* (Philadelphia: Westminster, 1969) 283-84.

statements of First Isaiah or Psalm 89 lost on the Qumran text with which we began. Meade I mention because he stands among interpreters interested in unitary readings, and yet his position remains essentially that of Westermann. So too Edgar Conrad.[9] Striking in Sweeney's unitary reading is the lack of mention of the Davidic theme at all — central, peripheral, or otherwise.[10] So on this score at least, efforts to break down sharp lines between First, Second, and Third Isaiah have produced no fresh integrative reading, but merely a restatement of developmental or transformative interpretations.

When we read on in Isaiah 55, the statement of the prophet does not end with this bold finale, the making of an everlasting covenant with those addressed, but continues on with a bold if curious encomium to David for two verses. David was a witness and leader and commander "for the peoples," the prophet states, in a somewhat unusual image. The image is also attested in the Psalms, where David's rule was not just for Israel, but for the nations:

> Thou didst make me the head of the nations;
> people whom I had not known served me (Ps 18:44).

In the key introductory Psalm 2, kings and rulers of the earth are warned not to set themselves against God's anointed or the place of his abode, but rather to serve the LORD with fear and with trembling kiss his feet. Have the promises once made to David been taken from him and given to the people as a whole — a "democratization of kingship," as Meade and others have put it? Or does the role of David vis-à-vis the nations now have implications also for the people, who shall call nations they once knew not, as did David according to the Psalter? In other words, the question may involve a distinction between transfer, on the one hand, or paradigmatic illustration, on the other. The sort of covenant made to David is made to the people so that "nations that you knew not shall run to you" (55:5).

9. *Reading Isaiah* (OBT; Minneapolis: Fortress, 1991) 136: "It is as royalty that the community will bear witness in the world of nations — a role that was formerly performed by Davidic kings." Also: "The implied death of Hezekiah in the Book of Isaiah suggests the death of Davidic kingship itself. . . . The vocation of Davidic kingship . . . has become the vocation of the community, Jacob-Israel" (144-45).

10. *Isaiah 1–4 and the Post-Exilic Understanding of the Isaianic Tradition* (Beihefte zum *ZAW* 171; Berlin: de Gruyter, 1988).

What is also clear is that the Psalter has taken up the matter of kingship and its possible dissolution at several key points. Westermann makes much of Psalm 89, where the eternal covenant with David is referred to, just as in Isaiah 55, but where the renunciation of that seemingly unbreakable covenant is made by God himself.

> Thou hast renounced the covenant with thy servant;
> Thou hast defiled his crown in the dust (89:39).

Unlike Isaiah 55, however, the psalm does not end with a surprising or happy transfer to new objects of divine-royal covenanting, the people themselves, but instead ends with a bitter lament reminiscent of Lamentations.

> How long, O LORD? Wilt thou hide thyself forever?
> How long will thy wrath burn like fire (89:46)?

> Where is thy steadfast love of old,
>   which by thy faithfulness thou didst swear to David? (89:49).

Westermann believes that Isaiah 55 answers this by saying: the covenant of old sworn to David was not renounced, but transferred. But one must seriously ask whether such an answer, bold or surprising, would ever be a satisfactory answer to the lament of Psalm 89.

By stating the problem in this way, a new context for discussion has emerged, precisely because Isaiah 55 was rightly judged to be properly interpreted with an eye toward certain psalms, as well as the book of Lamentations, to which we have already referred for another purpose. But what has not yet been sufficiently appreciated is not the propriety of relating this or that portion of Isaiah to this or that individual psalm; rather, the question of the proper interpretation of the book of Isaiah *in its entirety* is related to an interpretation likewise of the Psalter *in its entirety*. It would by no means be odd to discover that one of the best controls on unitary reading would be through comparison with some other large-scale work, like the Psalter, which is already conceded to be intimately related to Isaiah.

James Luther Mays once put it this way: "To read Isaiah, one needs to know the psalms. . . . First, the theology assumed in the prophecy of Isaiah is to be found in express form in the psalms. Second, I want to focus on the trajectory of messianic theology in the Bible, and to do that I need to begin in psalmic territory."[11] Mays was referring to First Isaiah and messianism, and to a theology or trajectory of messianism presumed to be common to both Isaiah of Jerusalem and the Psalms. This is fine so far as it goes. But in the brief survey conducted thus far it is clear that some psalms more than others are relevant to a comparison of both works, and that a very similar motif seems to emerge in both Isaiah and the Psalter. That is the question of the persistence of, or disappearance or transfer of, messianic hopes. Has the Psalter as a whole reflected on the question of messianic future in a way that might help us understand the same question in the book of Isaiah?

II. THE PSALTER AS A WHOLE AND ISAIAH

What does it mean to talk about the Psalter as a whole, and why would the shape of the Psalter be any more perspicuous than the shape of Isaiah, such that understanding one might be of help in understanding the other? Are we not just doubling up on problems?

Certain basic observations about the Psalter as a whole seem clear, and in some respects we touch on formal features in the Psalter that are far more obvious than anything comparable in Isaiah. (1) The Psalter is comprised of five books of unequal length and unclearly differentiated content, yet marked by clear doxology refrains, "Blessed be the LORD, the God of Israel, from everlasting to everlasting! Amen and Amen" at the close of Psalm 41 and others like that at the close of Psalms 72, 89, 106, and 150. There is sufficient stereotypicality in these refrains to make the notion of a fivefold collection, similiar to the five-fifths of the Torah or the five-fifths of Lamentations, clearly intended in the final shape of the Psalter. The final psalm is itself nothing but doxology (twelve "praise the LORD" refrains), the obvious culmination of four preceding psalms, themselves each introduced with "Alleluia." This can hardly be accidental and is a good indication that efforts at some structural organization have played a role in the Psalter's final shaping. (2) The crescendo finale of the Psalter has led interpreters to ask whether it is appropriate to seek movement

11. "Isaiah's Royal Theology and the Messiah," in *Reading and Preaching the Book of Isaiah*, ed. C. R. Seitz (Philadelphia: Fortress, 1988) 39.

elsewhere in the Psalter as well. The presence of a clear conclusion would raise the question of the presence of an introduction, and again most acknowledge that Psalms 1 and 2 serve this special purpose, not just for Book 1, but for the Psalter as a whole. Psalm 1 describes the proper posture (Torah obedience) of the reader of the Psalms, and Psalm 2 makes it clear that the Davidic figure will be central to what follows. (3) While each of the five sections may not be uniformly about one theme only, the total then comprising some larger "plot," basic differentiating features do occur that may lend a sense of dramatic movement after all. In this regard, not just loose patterns within a section, but also psalms that lie on the seams of sections, prove to be especially important.

What sort of loose patterns emerge within the separate sections? With rare exceptions, the superscriptions to the psalms of Book 1 wish to indicate that these psalms are about David. Many attach the Psalms not just to David but to events in the life of David. Personal prayers — of entreaty, of confidence, of thanksgiving; for healing, deliverance, and a right attitude for worship — show David at widest reach.

In Book 2 explicit references to David recede somewhat from the psalm superscriptions, as David is joined by the sons of Korah and Asaph. Still, however — and this is particularly clear in Psalms 51 through 63 — events in the life of David are said to lie in the background of the psalms, in confrontation with Nathan after the Bathsheba affair, and especially in relationship to Saul and the Philistines. At the end of Book 2 there are clear signs that David, the man and earthly king, is reaching the end of this life. Psalm 71, with its reference to old age and gray hairs in v. 18, has been described as "an old man's prayer for deliverance from personal enemies" (so the heading in *The New Oxford Annotated* edition of the RSV). Psalm 72's superscription ties the royal blessing of the psalm to the figure of Solomon, David's successor. And following the doxology that closes Book 2, a rubric indicates that "the prayers of David, son of Jesse, are ended" (Ps 72:20). This may not mean that we will hear nothing more about David or the royal promises associated with his rule, but that the focus will shift from his earthly life of prayer to prayers about him and the promises associated with him. Not David the man, but David the paradigmatic ruler, will now be the focus of interest.

In the short Book 3 (Pss 73–89) only one psalm has a reference to David in the superscription, Psalm 86, and the bulk of the psalms (eleven of seventeen) are attached to Asaph, with four for the Korahites. The lone prayer of David in Psalm 86 is a lament and a cry to God for deliverance.

Insolent men have risen up against the king, as Psalm 2 had warned. And the full picture of assault on the royal house is the sole theme of the final psalm of Book 3. Here a recital of God's special work with David is brought to mind, stressing the sworn covenant that would never be broken, that the King of all Creation had once established with David. But the psalm makes clear that the steadfast love of old, sworn to David, seems to have been forgotten by God. God's anointed is mocked by those whom God had sworn in Psalm 2 that David would "dash in pieces like a potter's vessel" (2:9). Neither wise nor warned, the enemies taunt and throw insults. And it is God whom the psalmist addresses so sharply at the close, demanding to see again the faithfulness and steadfast love that God has sworn to uphold to his special servant David.

Before moving to Books 4 and 5, two things are important to note. Book 2 closed with an annotation that the prayers of David were ended, and to an extent Book 3 shows that to be true. At the same time, Book 3 has not forgotten God's promises to the Davidic house, and as the close of the book indicates, these promises are vital to the purposes of God for his people Israel at large, if not also God's purposes with all peoples and nations and the created realm itself. Second, it was the final lament regarding the promises to David in Psalm 89 that Westermann and others rightly linked to Isaiah 55 and the reference there to David as commander to the peoples. But Westermann, reading Psalm 89 not in the flow of the Psalter as a whole but in isolation, saw Isaiah 55 as an effort to answer the objections of the psalmist to forgotten promises to David by saying that God had handed these over to the people as a whole. Psalm 89, even read in isolation, clearly would not have anticipated such a transfer as a legitimate answer to the lament and charges lodged at the conclusion. The whole psalm breathes a clear and unmistakable air of respect and indeed affection for the special role David plays in God's economy, the creator and preserver of the universe and of all nations and peoples within it. In my judgment, the sharp lament perspective at the close of Psalm 89 is not anticipating the sort of transformation of these original promises that Westermann claims Deutero-Isaiah is proposing. Yet what is clear from a comparison of both works in their totality is that they both clearly presuppose the disappearance of the monarchy as a fact in Israel's history, the psalmist by direct and painful reference, Isaiah by failing to bring into prominence Davidic themes clearly at play in Isaiah 1–39.

But the chief question before us, and one that the Psalter may provide help with, is *why* royal themes appear in First Isaiah chapters but drop out in Isaiah 40–66. I am unsatisfied with the full transfer or democratization idea, as well as the notion of a Persian king acting in the capacity and with the authority of the Davidic house. Yet two questions press for resolution. How pregnant is the silence of chapters 40–66 regarding kingship? And how is the matter of Isaiah's unity/disunity affecting the way the problem is presented and then resolved? At stake in this second question is the proper conception of Isaiah's unity to begin with, all the while acknowledging that a lengthy process of growth lies behind the book as it now exists. How is one to understand the relationship between these two main parts of the book? Historical criticism taught us to view them as temporally and even geographically distinct. And the book itself registers a distinction between former and latter or new things, which suggests some change in perspective indigenous to the book of Isaiah itself, not just one imposed by critical theory in search of setting and author.

Still, what is striking is that these two main questions cannot be answered by appeal to Isaiah's unity if one sits too close to the First, Second, Third Isaiah model for reading. For then one will inevitably be stuck with a view that Second Isaiah is somehow responding to or modifying positions articulated earlier in Isaiah. This move requires the reader to recognize this motivation and this distinctive, later point of view as features intended to be recognized and as the indispensable keys to understanding the book as it exists in its final form. But what if chapters 40–66, whatever their point of origin in time and space, were intended to be far more synthetically read — if not as Isaiah's own contribution,[12] then as an organic extension of that original contribution, neither modifying or recalibrating, but filling out an original word with a fuller divine word, so that the word first sent forth would accomplish what God had intended and not return to him empty (so 55:11)? The question in some measure is a redaction-critical one, at the most basic level. Under what constraints and under what sort of pressure from prior traditions do later hands work?

Here is where appeal to the final form of the Psalter is helpful. Here too one can detect movement and change within a larger structure, and here too one sees the problem of the monarchy's final destiny coming into clear play. Psalm 89 brings Book 3 to a close with a lament over the death of the monarchy and a charge that God has abandoned a king to whom he had sworn faithfulness and loving kindness. A deeper charge below even this charge of faithlessness to the Davidic house was also leveled, or

---

12. See my further discussion on the Isaiah "persona" in chapter 13 below.

at least alluded to: that God had himself gone into hiding (89:46). The very same charges lie virtually on the surface in chapters 40–49 of Isaiah, where God must defend himself and his sovereignty before the nations and their gods, and before his own people.

Book 4 of the Psalms, like Book 3, is a brief section of only seventeen psalms. The singularity of a psalm of David in Book 3 (Psalm 86) is matched in the very first psalm of Book 4, with a prayer of none other than Moses himself, the man of God. There is nothing else like this in the entire Psalter. We go straight to the source here, to the man of God, the giver of the law, the law that promised a king (Deut 17:14-20) and in so doing stood in prior relationship to the fulfillment of that promise in David. Moses, the great intercessor, the one with the power to stay God's hand in judgment in the wilderness, by putting him in mind of his great love and his need to preserve his own name, here acknowledges that the wrath Israel experiences has to do with their iniquities and secret sins, and not primarily with the impotence of God or a failure to honor a covenant made with David (Ps 90:8). In fact, that charge is not even referred to, as Moses the man of God makes simple and direct appeal to God's favor, work, and power on behalf of his own people.

The psalm that follows, number 91, has no superscription and in that sense is like Psalm 2. And as with Psalm 2, the explanation for the omission may well be an invitation to read the two psalms together. Perhaps we have a sort of fresh beginning here, in Book 4, on analogy with the beginning of the Psalter, as Moses continues to speak. The content of what is said is clearly relevant to the question at hand. Again no explicit reference is made to God's special anointed one. Instead, God himself is the source of Israel's strength. Not his faithfulness with David, so 89:49, but his faithfulness as such, is shield and buckler before the assaults of the enemy. As in Isa 55:3, what was specially true for David is now specially true for the people themselves, but without a whiff of retraction of the original promises to David, which come under no comment.

In the psalms that follow in Book 4, what is most striking is the frequency of reference to God's *own* kingship instead of the kingship of David as before.

The LORD reigns; he is robed in majesty (93:1).
For the LORD is a great God,
and a great king above all gods (95:3).
Say among the nations, The LORD is king (96:10).

> The LORD reigns; let the earth rejoice (97:1).
> Make a joyful noise before the King, the LORD (98:6).
> Mighty King, Lover of justice,
>> thou hast established equity (99:4).

The exact same emphasis on God's kingship over creation, with Zion at its center, over the nations, and over his own people Israel appears in the opening chapters of Second Isaiah.

> Behold the LORD God comes with might,
>> and his arm rules for him (40:10).
> Bring your proofs, says the King of Jacob (41:21).
> I am the LORD, your Holy One,
>> the Creator of Israel, your King (43:15).
> Thus says the LORD, the King of Israel
>> and his Redeemer, the LORD of Hosts (44:6).

What needs to be avoided here is seeing these two views of kingship, that of God and that of David, as rival or even cleanly separable matters. In Psalm 89 the author asks questions about God's fidelity to David and his covenant with him that strike far deeper than any obvious vindication of the Davidic house might resolve; no, God's own honor before his people and capacity to be God of all creation, king above all gods, to use the language of Psalm 95, was what was at stake. And so that is what is asserted in Book 4. In the same manner, it is misleading with Westermann and others to set up rival views of kingship, one focused on David, but now otiose, and one focused on the people as recipients of promises taken from David and given to them instead. To create a rivalry is to ignore the context in which assertions about kingship — the kingship of David, of God, or even of the people in their relationship to the nations — are being made, toward quite specific ends.

With Book 3 having raised quite specific questions about God's sovereignty with his people and on behalf of creation, Book 4 moves to address these questions, originally under the mantle of Moses, the man of God, but then under the mantle of no one but God himself. Psalms 93, 94, 95, 96, 97, 98, 99, and 100 lack any attribution at all. Can it be any coincidence that these are the psalms in which the kingship of God is proclaimed, extolled, and boldly stated, apparently without need of human agency of the sort familiar elsewhere in the superscriptions of the Psalter?

Then a surprising development takes place, the significance of which is difficult to judge. David reemerges in Psalm 101 to sing of what? Of God's loyalty and justice, the two matters called into question on his behalf in Psalm 89. David having spoken his pledge in this way and having stated what just rule should look like, Psalm 102 lets arise the prayer of one afflicted, an everyman not unlike the voice in Lamentations 3, who here records for a generation not yet born that God did in fact look down from his holy height "to hear the groans of prisoners and set free those doomed to die" (102:19-20). Book 4 then closes with psalms of blessing and praise of God, introduced by David. These long recitals remind one of the recital of Psalm 89 that culminated in charges of God's unfaithfulness. But the culmination here is of another sort, as the memory of God's ways with his people gives rise to one Alleluia upon another.

Does the presence of David psalms here and scattered throughout Book 5 signal concrete plans for the restitution of the monarchy? That is probably saying much more than the shape of the Psalter can tell us. But if nothing else, the presence of these psalms, which mention David fourteen times in the superscriptions (and Solomon once), signals that David has not been forgotten as Israel's king and chief psalmist, the one to be remembered above all others as having sung God's praises almost without ceasing, as Book 5 has it at its close.

The similarity between Isaiah and the Psalter consists most obviously in the transition from earthly to divine kingship, effected in the Psalter in the transition from Book 3 to Book 4. Isaiah 39, the final chapter of the "former things" of Isaiah, also told of the death of King Hezekiah, just prior to our entry into chapters 40ff. with their concern to establish the kingship of God himself. Yet nothing in chapter 39, or in the chapters that immediately precede (36–38), could be taken on analogy with Book 3's bitter conclusion, with its accusation that God had abandoned his covenant with David. Hezekiah is a model king, whose long prayer in Isaiah 38 is clearly meant to show that he is, in the words of 2 Kgs 18:3-5, a second David. What is similar, then, is not a lamenting of the death of kingship, but an apparent need in both Book 4 of the Psalter and Isaiah 40–49, for God to reassert his own kingship — over all gods, over creation, and especially over his own people Israel.

The fact that David does not boldly reemerge in Isaiah 40–66 as in the Psalter, therefore, may not mean at all that hopes associated with the Davidic house have been dropped, transferred, or given over to a Persian ruler in the larger shape of Isaiah. Here the problem involves appreciating just what the final shape of Isaiah means to convey. And here the analogy with the shape of the Psalter is slightly broken.

The fivefold structure of the Psalms assumes a roughly linear movement. We begin with an emphasis on the earthly David. Then David as such begins to play a far less prominent role, and the fate of the nation more broadly considered comes into play — culminating in punishment and exile. Then the special role of David in God's plans is recalled and lamented, leading to God's assertion of his justice as sovereign over all creation. Hopes once associated with David and Zion are then once again brought to the fore as the Psalter concludes with David singing songs of ascent.

Now here we see a sort of crudely linear movement through a fivefold collection. In Isaiah, however, the movement associated with David is handled differently. In chapters 1–39 the main movement is one of contrast: Ahaz the disbelieving and disinherited king, Hezekiah the faithful one whose trust saves Zion. As numerous commentators have pointed out, these two main narrative sections (6–8 and 36–39) are bookends offering a point-by-point contrast regarding God's anointed messiah. Yet a further contrast emerges within these chapters as well. Chapter 11 looks to the birth of a royal shoot of Jesse whose rule will usher in a reign of peace. Does silence regarding this rule in chapters 40–66 mean that such a prophecy is a thing of the past, or at that point are we struggling to understand what it means to read Isaiah as a unity, in both literary and theological terms? Is that simply too linear a way of conceiving the book in its final form, a legacy of the Three Isaiahs model, which thought in terms of a gradually expanding corpus?

We cannot know for sure why royal promises have not been given the same prominence in chapters 40–66 that they have in chapters 1–39. Political and even theological factors have been adduced, by interpreting these chapters — so-called Second and Third Isaiah — against the historical backdrop of exilic and postexilic Israel. That sort of approach is good so far as it goes, and is a clear improvement over efforts to have the historical Isaiah mechanically foreseeing events from an eighth-century vantage point. But the danger is in not really knowing how these chapters were meant to be read in the present Isaiah corpus — as discrete additions treating issues in a new and fresh way, independent of or even critical or transforming, matters spoken of in chapters 1–39? Even if one recognizes their independence and historical distance, does this mean their relationship to chapters 1–39 is one of updating, reactualization, or perhaps even sharper, of rejection?

In an odd sort of way, the question of the relationship between the

Testaments, Old and New, lies not too far afield. That relationship is clearly organic, in that former things serve as the basis for the articulation of new things. And new and bold things are proclaimed that seem to go beyond what has been said before. One can even see in the New a radical critique of features of the Old that might suggest that chapters 40–66 had the same stance toward First Isaiah.

But one fails to find a truly sharp critique in chapters 40–66 of Davidic kingship, even of a very subtle sort. Cyrus is called God's anointed, and the people are seen as bearers of covenant promises of a Davidic sort. But these features fail to live up to the sort of strong modification or rejection necessary to count for a radically new conception regarding Davidic kingship.

There is a still more difficult matter to be addressed, and that involves the theological underpinning of theories of redaction and growth in prophetic books. What would it mean, theologically, to say that chapters 40–66 disregarded or transformed Davidic promises that now exist in the first half of the book? Part of the problem alluded to earlier has been the recognition that royal hopes articulated in Isaiah 11 may well be postexilic — that is, emerging from a similar sort of time frame alleged to form the backdrop of chapters 40–66, when transformations of those promises were afoot. Is there a sort of war going on between two parts of the book, one in favor of kingship, memorializing Hezekiah and then offering a picture of kingship quite effusive and aggrandizing, the other free to transfer over old prophetic language into a kingship of the community or of Persian conqueror? It is one thing to consider enlargement of promises toward a new end, and that even may be the force of 55:11. But to say that the word of God will not return empty but accomplish its true purpose, "the thing for which I sent it," could not mean in the case of royal promises a transfer that left what was first uttered behind in its wake, empty of fulfillment, an overstatement in need of correction.

To read Isaiah as a unity requires more than a simple evolutionary or developmental model. Portions of later chapters clearly utilize language and expression found in earlier chapters. When we are told in 65:25 that

> The wolf and lamb shall feed together,
>> the lion eat straw like the ox;
>> dust shall be the serpent's food.
> They shall not hurt or destroy
>> in all my holy mountain,

we have an obvious citation from 11:6-9. A new thought is introduced: dust will be the serpent's food, which suggests modification or at least creative freedom over against the earlier tradition.[13] But can failure to mention the righteous shoot, in either a positive or a negative sense, mean only that a new conception of kingship has emerged and rendered the old otiose? That is of course not explicitly said. Even making allowance for the powerful way in which God himself has crowded out all forms of earthly rule in these final chapters, can we with confidence know that such forceful expression of divine sovereignty is a rejection, in and of itself, of earlier language in Isaiah regarding the righteous king, equally forceful in tone: "he will smite the earth with the rod of his mouth and with the breath of his lips slay the wicked" (11:4). Qumran interpreters frequently let such distinctions fall to the side, not just because they regarded the book of Isaiah as authored by one individual — if indeed they did — but because they read Isaiah as what many are now straining to imagine, "a unity." Far from being an arbitrary manner of interpretation, this concern with "unity" may well be consistent with those forces and those concerns that have led to the 66-chapter work being preserved in the form we now have it.

In some ways I have come full circle to the concerns of chapter 10 above. Authorship, divine authority, unity — all three are intimately related, giving rise to an expectation of coherence and the possibility of synthesis within a given corpus. In Isaiah this means keeping the royal language and hopes of the first half of the book in coordination with what is said in the second half. This means not seeking to divide and conquer, nor producing artificial harmonization, but instead trying to take seriously Isaiah's own admonition regarding God's word: that it would accomplish — perhaps in some transformed way — that for which it had been first sent.

---

13. Or, more accurately, earlier tradition within the Isaiah book. The combination of earlier Isaiah tradition with Genesis tradition is not a rejection of Isaiah, but inner-biblical exegesis of the sort helpfully analyzed by Michael Fishbane in *Biblical Interpretation in Ancient Israel* (New York: Oxford University, 1985).

13

How Is the Prophet Isaiah Present
in the Latter Half of the Book?

The Logic of Chapters 40–66
within the Book of Isaiah

It is an exciting time in the study of the book of Isaiah. In an effort to comprehend the significance of the book as a whole — if such there be — readers are having to go to school again and ask very fundamental questions.[1] Some older students insist from time to time that a shift of focus is wrongheaded and only indicates a failure to follow through more rigorously with the original methods of form and redaction criticism. Others proceed apace as though the shift toward reading Isaiah as a full collection were not taking place at all, or at most involved a final adjustment or two once work on independent sections had been satisfactorily completed. In this case, one might ask if the reflection that results is still largely determined by the persistence of an approach tied to investigating Isaiah as three discrete, evolving sections — even ones that now might potentially have something to do with one another.[2] In any event, for all readers of Isaiah it is a time of constant course adjustment, as one master

1. Christopher R. Seitz, "The Divine Council: Temporal Transition and New Prophecy in the Book of Isaiah," *JBL* 109 (1990) 229-47.
2. See my remarks in "On the Question of Divisions Internal to the Book of Isaiah," in *SBL 1993 Seminar Papers* (Atlanta: Scholars, 1993) 260-66.

This chapter originally appeared in *Journal of Biblical Literature* 115 (1996) 219-40.

theory is proposed here,[3] while there several alternative and more modest essays are set forth.[4] A shift toward "unified" readings has produced more, not less, in terms of exegetical proposals for comprehending that unity.

Modern hermeneutical theory has reminded us of the commonsense warning that our exegetical findings are likely to be determined by the questions we are asking of the text. One reading the Pentateuch in search of longitudinal sources will be inclined to read the statement in Exod 6:3b not as a circumstantial clause in a larger unit concerned with how God intends to make himself known in the events of the exodus (Exod 6:5-7) but instead as confirmation that one source disagreed with another over how God had theretofore made use of his proper name. To ask how Isaiah is present in chs. 40–66 could be to raise a question extraneous to the book's own presentation, and one that only proceeds from the modern critical preoccupation with what is or is not authentic in this book, so far as Isaianic authorship is concerned. However, two warrants for asking the question can be put forward. First, the question is by no means a modern one only, but formed part of the deliberations of so-called precritical exegesis, even when in a muted or more occasional guise. Second, the question need not involve anything like a concern for what is "authentic" in Isaiah (what did such a term ever really mean?), but instead only seeks to understand how or if the figure of Isaiah is maintained in these twenty-seven chapters.

3. Among others, Edgar W. Conrad, *Reading Isaiah* (OBT; Minneapolis: Fortress, 1991); Christopher R. Seitz, *Zion's Final Destiny* (Minneapolis: Fortress, 1991); Marvin A. Sweeney, *Isaiah 1–4 and the Post-Exilic Understanding of the Isaianic Tradition* (Beihefte zu ZAW 171; Berlin/New York: de Gruyter, 1988); H. G. M. Williamson, *The Book Called Isaiah* (Oxford: Clarendon, 1994).

4. Peter Ackroyd, "An Interpretation of the Babylonian Exile: A Study of 2 Kings 20/Isaiah 38–39," *SJT* 27 (1974) 329-52; idem, "Isaiah 36–39: Structure and Function," in *Von Kanann bis Kerala. Festschrift für Prof Mag. Dr. Dr. J. P. M. van der Ploeg O.P. zur Vollendung des siebrigsten Lebensjahres am 4. Juli 1979,* ed. W. C. Delsman et al. (Neukirchen-Vluyn: Neukirchener, 1982) 3-21; David Carr, "Reaching for Unity in Isaiah," *JSOT* 51 (1993) 61-80; Ronald Clements, "Beyond Tradition-History: Deutero-Isaianic Development of First Isaiah's Themes," *JSOT* 31 (1985) 95-113; Richard J. Clifford, "The Unity of the Book of Isaiah and Its Cosmogonic Language," *CBQ* 55 (1993) 1-17; Rolf Rendtorff, "Zur Komposition des Buches Jesaja," *VT* 34 (1984) 295-320; idem, "Jesaja 6 im Rahmen der Komposition des Jesajabuches," in *The Book of Isaiah,* ed. J. Vermeylen (BETL 81; Leuven: Leuven University, 1989) 73-82; Gerald T. Sheppard, "The Book of Isaiah: Competing Structures according to a Late Modern Description of Its Shape and Scope," in *SBL 1992 Seminar Papers* (Atlanta: Scholars, 1992) 549-82.

For purposes of illustration and to anticipate the discussion that follows, Isaiah could be regarded as a figure of the past, therefore to be treated as such in chs. 40–66 in ways we can identify exegetically; or Isaiah's voice could be regarded as lying behind or above the material that follows chs. 1–39, where he plays a more visible role. In this latter case, the precise *way* the Isaianic voice is resident in chs. 40–66 might well be very nuanced, akin to pseudepigraphic models or with a more general sense of Isaianic "aegis." But what is significant is the degree to which these models can be differentiated, even as they both seek to understand Isaiah as a meaningfully organized sixty-six-chapter totality.

It would be helpful at this point to consider briefly three earlier efforts to deal with this same issue of Isaiah's presence in chs. 40–66. This will give us a sample of the range of premodern attitudes toward this matter, which in turn provides a context in which to assess modern efforts to describe Isaiah's unity as this involves the persona of the prophet Isaiah in the latter chapters of the book associated with him.

I

In Isa 41:25-29 the prophetic voice states that the calling of one from the north was declared "from the beginning . . . and from beforetime" such that now those privy to that declaration can point to it to establish the authority of God. The nations cannot do this. Their gods are not gods but the product of human imagination and highly skilled but vain labor.

Anticipating the objections of C. R. North to an identification of the one called as Abraham,[5] Calvin argues that the one called from the north is Babylon, while the one called from the east is Cyrus (41:25).[6] Calvin knows that the Babylonians were not yet Israel's enemies and that the captivity from which Cyrus would liberate the exiles lay on the distant horizon, so far as Isaiah's own historical context was concerned. One brief section from his remarks will give suitable illustration of the problem he is aware of:

5. C. R. North, "The 'Former Things' and the 'New Things' in Deutero-Isaiah," in *Studies in Old Testament Prophecy,* ed. H. H. Rowley (Edinburgh: Clark, 1950) 111-26.

6. Against most modern interpreters, however, Calvin regarded the figure stirred up earlier in the chapter (41:2) as Abraham (*Calvin's Commentaries* III: *Isaiah* [Grand Rapids: APA, n.d.] 544-64).

> When he says that he calls him "from the north," as I suggested a little before, he predicts the future captivity of which at that time there was no expectation, because the Jews were friends and allies of the Chaldeans. . . . Who would have thought, when matters were in that state, that such things could be believed? . . . [F]or they happened two hundred years after having been predicted by the prophet. . . . This is a remarkable passage for establishing the full and perfect certainty of the oracles of God; for the Jews did not forge these predictions while they were captive in Babylon, but long after the predictions had been delivered to their fathers, they at length recognised the righteous judgment of God, by whom they had been warned in due time.[7]

Calvin concludes by noting that the remarkable character of this sort of declaration is an indication that Isaiah "did not speak at his own suggestion, but that his tongue was moved and guided by the Spirit of God."[8]

Several significant things are to be observed. First, here and elsewhere in Calvin's commentary we are made aware that rival theories concerning the provenance and form ("predictions") of these chapters existed (viz., they came from the period of Babylonian captivity). Second, Calvin fully recognizes the problem of historicality and temporal distance: when Isaiah spoke, the Babylonians were not Israel's enemies and the Persians were not on the scene at all. Third, the speech of Isaiah would not have made any real sense to his contemporaries, and in fact the intended audience is "posterity, who had actual experience of their accomplishment" and who also would understand that they had been warned for some time. This understanding of Isaiah's speech is familiar from the presentation of the latter chapters of Daniel, with the exception that there the element of unrecognizability to contemporaries and Daniel himself is specifically noted in the portrayal (Dan 8:17, 27; also 7:15, 28; 10:14), while for Calvin it need play no role in the case of Isaiah for his own interpretation to gain conviction.

But there is another problem. Although 41:25 might with some effort be understood as a prediction, fully veiled for Isaiah's contemporaries, the force of the passage turns on Israel's future capacity to declare that something spoken beforehand has now come about. To make another loose comparison with Daniel, this is a little like both producing the dream and

7. Ibid., 562.
8. Ibid.

interpreting it (Daniel 2), since not only is the prediction made, but its future force in establishing God's authority vis-à-vis the nations is also foreseen, a force that demands the prophecy's prior utterance. Calvin is prepared to accept such a reading as proof of the extraordinary character of Isaiah as a conduit for the Holy Spirit. But this is stretching the plain sense of the material in a way that has no Daniel-like explanation. Especially the declaration in 41:26 about the long-standing character of the prophecy concerning Babylon and Persia would be difficult to square with Isaianic address to contemporaries, on any reading and on any account of the inspired character of Israel's prophetic witness. For a prediction to be valid, it must have been uttered meaningfully to contemporaries; yet it cannot at the same time carry weight as having been uttered long ago to special witnesses, whose posterity can claim to know something that no one else knows.

One might be prepared to entertain Calvin's proposal under slightly different conditions, but then the gap between Isaiah and Daniel would have to be fully closed. That is, the effort could have been made to depict Isaiah as the authorizer of this passage in Isa 41:25-29, in something of the same sense that Daniel is the authorizer of speech directed to another day in the presentation of that book. But it seems to me that here we have identified the exact difference between these two presentations. The passage in question does not appear to be directed to a future audience, as is the case in Daniel; nor is its incomprehensibility to Isaiah or his contemporaries mentioned, as in Daniel; and finally, its very success at persuasion demands a contemporary audience, for whom the appearance of Cyrus has some probative force as such, but primarily *as having been announced from long ago.* The lack of consistency in Calvin's method and the influence of other factors, especially the plain sense of the MT, can also be detected when at 49:1-7 the first-person voice ceases to be that of Isaiah and becomes that of Christ, again in a passage with no actual "predictive" character.

I would be grossly misunderstood if these remarks were taken as criticisms of Calvin's failure to engage an objective, historical-critical approach, such as would emerge beyond his own day. My concern here is with understanding how Calvin answers the question we have posed: How is the prophet Isaiah present in chs. 40–66? Neither should his lack of consistency be taken as a fatal flaw, for that would beg the question of what is meant by consistency as a good unto itself, or it would imply that every reading can bracket out every other theological context as an equal good unto itself. In answer to the question we are posing here, the prophet Isaiah, for Calvin, remains resident in chs. 40–66 in a fairly direct sense, though he must also share the stage with Christ as well as with audiences beyond his own day. Isaiah does not just hover around in some indistinct sense, nor is Calvin appealing to an Isaianic aegis under which the prophecies of chs. 40–66 circulate or derive their claim to be taken seriously as God's word.

An alternative to this picture of Isaiah's role in chs. 40–66 seems to appear in the Targums, through the effort to explicate the extremely terse opening command to a plural audience (40:1).[9] The question of who is addressed by this double charge to comfort may in fact impinge on the question of Isaianic voice in the chapters that follow. The Targums gloss the verse with "O ye prophets" and therewith supply the object of the charge. While it remains unclear who actually speaks this initial charge on behalf of God, what may be suggested by the supplied object is that the voices that then speak up (vv. 3 and 6) are these same prophets who have been addressed. If this reading of the targumic gloss is correct, we may be witnessing a transition from the voice of Isaiah, strictly speaking, as the voice behind the literature, to other new voices, those of unnamed prophets. Yet this remains unclear.

Interestingly, Calvin, too, speaks of "the Prophet" (Isaiah) commissioning "new prophets" in v. 1, "whom he enjoins to soothe the sorrows of the people by friendly consolation."[10] But that that is the end of it is made clear almost immediately in his interpretation of the first-person voice (so LXX) in 40:6. Here God's voice charges the prophets in general, and Isaiah is the one who responds with "What shall I cry?" And we have seen from Calvin's exegesis at other points that Isaiah's is the voice that continues to speak throughout these chapters, addressing contemporaries, posterity, and pointing ahead to Christ's mission.

Another earlier interpreter, Ibn Ezra, may give us a sense of what the Targums were driving at and how they likely represent a different approach from that of Calvin concerning the Isaianic voice — quite apart from his christological readings.[11] Ibn Ezra is aware of the Babylonian context of the material, yet he cautions the reader against drawing wrong conclusions

9. See my brief discussion in "Divine Council," 230.
10. Calvin, 523.
11. *The Commentary of Ibn Ezra on Isaiah,* ed. M. Friedlander (London, 1873; New York: Philipp Feldheim, n.d.).

from this. He frequently refers to "the prophet," but it is not entirely clear who is meant — that is, an independent and new voice behind the material or someone referred to within the oracles themselves. In neither case is Isaiah the prophet the obvious referent. It would appear that Ibn Ezra is aware of the problem of Isaianic voice in chs. 40–66, because of historical distance and the character of the material in these chapters, but unlike Calvin he does not resolve the problem by an appeal to prediction. Instead he changes the subject. These chapters are also as much about Ibn Ezra's own day as they are about matters in the Babylonian period.

II

Before turning to modern interpreters to inquire how the prophet Isaiah is viewed as present in chs. 40–66, it is important to register that for about a century such a question would have made no sense at all. Bernhard Duhm, for example, was prepared to argue that at one time chs. 40–55 never even circulated in connection with Isaiah at all and that when they were first combined with an extant prophetic collection, Jeremiah and not Isaiah was chosen.[12] Such was the fully artificial and external nature of the connection of this material to Isaiah, when that eventually occurred. The first part of his theory, that chs. 40–55 (and 56–66) once had no connection at all to Isaiah, has dominated the discussion until the recent period, and it remains a very popular conception. It should also be noted that for many interested in comprehending the unity of the book of Isaiah, the place of the prophet Isaiah himself plays only a minor or thematic role.[13] The answer to the question posed would be self-evident: he is not present but belongs to the presentation of chs. 1–39 only. The book does not grow toward "unity" or "disunity" in relation to the figure of the prophet. On this view, it is taken for granted that chs. 40–66 are at too great a temporal distance from chs. 1–39 to be conjoined under a single

---

12. Bernhard Duhm, *Das Buch Jesaia* (Göttingen: Vandenhoeck und Ruprecht, 1892). See my discussion in *Zion's Final Destiny,* 1-29.

13. R. Rendtorff, "The Composition of the Book of Isaiah," in *Canon and Theology* (OBT; Minneapolis: Fortress, 1993) 164; Peter Ackroyd, "Isaiah I–XII: Presentation of a Prophet," in *Congress Volume: Göttingen 1977 (VT* Supplements 29; Leiden: Brill, 1977) 38.

Isaianic perspective, even one fictively constructed (as, for different purposes, such a perspective is achieved in the book of Daniel).

A somewhat related question, however, still remains to be taken up. How, if Isaiah's voice is regarded as a thing of the past, does the material in chs. 40–66 claim prophetic authority? Is such a thing unnecessary? Or was such a concern addressed in the material's original presentation but removed when the material was placed in this larger Isaianic context? Brevard Childs has spoken about historical traces once embedded in this material ("concrete features") that were then erased (by "canonical editors") so the chapters could serve their present function in the book, which he describes as eschatological. If the material once made clear under whose name it was spoken, this has been reduced or eliminated precisely so that the chapters could become "a prophetic word of promise offered to Israel by the eighth-century prophet, Isaiah of Jerusalem."[14]

Older interpreters confident about divisions at chs. 40–55 and 56–66 sought to discover the traditional marker of prophetic authority, the call narrative, within each of these respective sections. It was in this way that the opening unit (40:1-11) took on such prominence in Second Isaiah, while a similar narrative was harder to locate in the case of chs. 56–66. Elsewhere I have questioned whether an interpretation of the opening unit as a call narrative for Second Isaiah could be sustained, either on its own terms or now especially in consideration of the larger shape of the book as a whole, where the prophet Isaiah had already been introduced. But I did not suggest that concrete features had been eliminated. They were never there to begin with.[15]

My view then was that a call narrative for Second Isaiah needed to rely on several factors. First, the MT's reading at 40:6 ("and one said," "and he said") needed to be rejected in favor of the LXX and Qumran's "and I said" (though on its own, I suspect this third-person reading could somehow be tolerated as consistent with a call of Second Isaiah). Still, on text-critical grounds I remain unpersuaded that there is any logical explanation why a shift from an original first person to a third person could have occurred.[16] The obverse is patient of explanation, since it brings our

14. Brevard S. Childs, *Introduction to the Old Testament as Scripture* (Philadelphia: Fortress, 1979) 325.

15. Seitz, "Divine Council," 229-47.

16. Compare Carr, "Reaching for Unity," 67 n. 11.

text into proximity with other call narratives where "but I said" captures the objection in the prophet's first-person reaction.

Following the lead of Peter Ackroyd, my second point was that an interpretation of this key unit had to contend with the existence of a "call narrative" for Isaiah in ch. 6 — for its own sake but especially in the light of the features they have in common.[17] Rolf Rendtorff also made some important observations here. Both accounts involve commissioning voices commingling with the voice of God.[18] Both are concerned with YHWH's glory. Yet at the same time, the period of iniquity and sin has given way to a new era of forgiveness and reconstitution. Isaiah's "How long?" has received an answer in real, and not just in anticipated, terms (6:11-13).

In addition, I was concerned with the question of the role of the prophet Isaiah that this opening unit might well address. This requires some clarification. Ackroyd had spoken suggestively of a "renewal of the Isaianic commission" in 40:1-11.[19] But did he mean that Isaiah's voice was being extended into this material, in an obviously editorial and less direct sense than Calvin had envisioned, or that the first commission was being renewed for another? R. Melugin had also seen the relationship between chs. 40 and 6, but he regarded the first-person voice of 40:6 as intentionally representing Second Isaiah as prophet as well as the people.[20] Finally, David Meade reckoned with a composition of 40:1-11 calibrated to the larger Isaiah tradition and spoke of a "suppression of the prophet's identity" (that is, the voice behind chs. 40–55) because of an awareness of this larger context in which "he" was to be heard, where Isaiah's voice remained in play. He went on to conclude that 40:1-11 served "the dual purpose of authorizing the message while making it clear that it was not independent of the larger whole."[21]

It is clear from these several examples that one can argue for the composition of 40:1-11 as undertaken mindful of a larger context in Isaiah, and still mean slightly different things. Rendtorff does not take up the question of who is speaking in chs. 40–55, Isaiah or another, but instead seeks to understand various theological issues that are raised, addressed,

17. Ackroyd, "Structure and Function."

18. Rendtorff, "Isaiah 6 in the Framework of the Composition of the Book," in *Canon and Theology*, 178.

19. Ackroyd, "Structure and Function," 6.

20. R. Melugin, *The Formation of Isaiah 40–55* (Beihefte zu *ZAW* 141; Berlin: de Gruyter, 1976) 84, 86.

21. David Meade, *Pseudonymity and Canon* (Tübingen: Mohr, 1986) 35.

modified, or redirected in the larger corpus, based on some obscure process of growth and development not entirely open to explanation and rede-scription. Ackroyd's essays are somewhat similar in their concern, though he does not sit so loose to redactional description. Melugin would appear to reckon with a new voice being introduced in chs. 40–55, though one modeled on Isaiah's. Meade is interested in the question of authorization and authority, as a first-order concern, and claims that the text in question authorizes the message to follow. But it remains unclear to me just how it accomplishes that.

In passing it should be noted that Gerald Sheppard has formulated his own view on this matter, attempting to extend what he regards as Childs's pivotal tenet mentioned above — viz., that chs. 40–66 are to be understood as a prophetic word of promise from Isaiah of Jerusalem — by appeal to what he calls Isaiah's "persona."[22] He quotes with sympathy Delitzsch's earlier reflections on how "Isaiah in 40–66 lacks Ezekiel's 'tan-gible reality' and 'is more like a spirit without visible form.'" He cites as suggestive Delitzsch's depiction of Isaiah as one who "floats along through the exile like a being of a higher order, like an angel of God."[23] But equally compelling for Sheppard are Delitzsch's acknowledgments that further prophets have emerged in the book (Delitzsch does refer to a Deutero-Isaiah), and that "these later prophets are really Isaiah's second self." It is not clear to me that Sheppard's citing of Delitzsch is to his best advantage, since Sheppard emphasizes the voice of Isaiah's "persona" throughout.[24]

Several additional questions could be raised at this point, but one thing seems clear. A shift toward understanding Isaiah as a work with its

---

22. Sheppard, "Competing Structures," 561-69. He does not refer to my specific treatment of this subject in "Divine Council."

23. Sheppard, "Competing Structures," 568.

24. Sheppard, "Competing Structures," 569:

The prophetic *persona,* in this sense, is far more related to an internal realism integral to the syntax that parses the human voice(s) of the canonical text itself than it is to any capacity of this representation or lack of it to refer to some unknown person(s) outside the text, available according to ordinary norms of history. The prophetic "voice" in these chapters follows immediately after a description of Isaiah speaking a word from God about Babylon to Hezekiah in chapter 39:5-6. In contrast to Seitz, a canonical approach may regard the "voice" of the *persona* of Isaiah as one of the most significant devices in the presentation of the whole prophetic book as a singular, human witness to God's Word. It offers, among other things, a corrective to the tendency, both left and right, to harmonize literarily and structurally the disparate human traditions in the book . . .

own integrity has not produced a consistent understanding of how the prophetic voice extends throughout, or if it does. Chapter 40 has emerged as important in this regard, not only because it stands on an important temporal and literary boundary but also because it introduces new, anonymous voices who are charged by God to comfort Zion. Moreover, if it is indeed a composition calibrated in some sense to what precedes in the larger Isaiah tradition, then we are confronting not some abstract or external principle of prophetic authority or *persona* but one that the literature has taken up of its own accord, self-consciously, and, we might also conjecture, of theological necessity.

The question to be raised is the degree to which chs. 40–66 take up within their own presentation the matter before us, namely, the voice of Isaiah and the possibility of new voices appearing. It may well be the case that "Isaiah" is a spirit that inhabits all sections of the book and that indeed one might call him its "author" in a very basic sense. But that need not preclude, as Delitzsch himself recognized, other prophets appearing in these latter chapters, who reckoned themselves as "second selves" of Isaiah as well as proclaimers of a new thing, never before heard (42:9; 44:19; 48:6-8). Under such conditions, the "persona" of Isaiah would have to be very differently conceived: not as a "voice" unifying the entire collection but as the one whose original vision was intended for contemporaries, but also for generations beyond his own (so 8:16-22; 29:11-12; 30:8). As we hope to show, these generations include new prophetic voices that appear in the course of the book's own unfolding, so that the former things might at last be attached to their intended referent and that new things might also be proclaimed, filling to fullness and overflowing the legacy of Isaiah.

If this is what is meant by the "persona" of Isaiah extending across all sixty-six chapters, that may indeed capture what the book intends. Yet this should not mislead us into looking for a presentation keyed to a single prophetic voice, since the very character of prophecy in this book demands deafness before hearing, prediction before fulfillment, former things uttered before their latter end transpires. For all of these the passage of time and the emergence of new generations are required. Isaiah, prophet or persona, is not exempt from this passage, even as the word spoken by God through him will not return empty but will accomplish that for which it was purposed (55:11), not in spite of but necessitated by time's inexorable march, which leaves no human voice untouched.

Moreover, if it fails to register a distinction between the prophet Isaiah and a word bequeathed to posterity — a distinction registered at several points in chs. 1–39 — then the term "persona" should be avoided altogether. Isaiah's "persona" is not extended into chs. 40–66 except as his word finds vindication and extension through new voices, perhaps even Isaiah's "second selves," to use Delitzsch's phrase. It is the word of God that stands forever, not Isaiah or his "persona" abstracted from that word.

III

Bind up the testimony, seal the teaching among my disciples.
   I will wait for the LORD, who is hiding his face. . . .
To the teaching and to the testimony!
   Surely for this word . . . there is no dawn (8:16-17, 20, RSV).

And now, go, write it before them on a tablet,
   and inscribe it in a book,
that it may be for the time to come (30:8, RSV).

In an essay published in 1955, D. R. Jones underscored the significance of these two passages for understanding the growth of what he termed "the traditio of the oracles of Isaiah of Jerusalem."[25] More recently, Edgar Conrad has called attention to these two texts (as well as to 29:11-12) as pointing to the process by which the book of Isaiah has developed, not just as "traditio" reworked for a new day but as an actual fixed text opened for a new generation, described in 43:8 as "the people who are blind, yet have eyes, who are deaf, yet have ears." The earlier circumstances of 6:9-11 are annulled. Conrad even suggests that the references to crying aloud in the opening unit (40:1-11) may shade off into the realm of "calling forth," as in reading, in this case, the "vision of Isaiah" bequeathed to posterity. Again the circumstances of 29:11-12 are reversed.[26]

Following the lead of Frank Cross and others, I argued for an interpretation of 40:1-11 as a commissioning from the heavenly council.[27]

---

25. D. R. Jones, "The Traditio of the Oracles of Isaiah of Jerusalem," *ZAW* 67 (1955) 226-46.

26. Conrad, *Reading Isaiah,* 117-68.

27. Frank Moore Cross, "The Council of Yahweh in Second Isaiah," *Journal of Near Eastern Studies* 12 (1953) 274-77.

The various voices were modeled on the entourage familiar from Isaiah 6 (and other such scenes), and in fact the text would prove too obscure if one did not understand that the earlier commissioning scene was being presupposed by the author. Rather than being about the "call" of Deutero-Isaiah, the text served the purpose of moving us from the authorized word of Isaiah into a new dispensation, with prophecy itself in a new mode. As such, the text betrays its "agony of influence," as Isaiah's word of judgment is recalled, by an anonymous voice, in vv. 6-7; but it also moves us forward, as the decree from the divine council is for comfort, forgiveness, an end to a period of service, and the appearance of God's glory. That too is part of what Isaiah has bequeathed to posterity (comfort, 12:1; sin, 1:4; 5:18; 22:14; 30:13, and forgiveness, 27:9; 33:24; YHWH's glory, 6:3).[28]

While the scene utilizes elements from the commissioning of Isaiah in ch. 6 — and Rendtorff, Ackroyd, and Melugin identified their own linkages — it is not clear how we are to interpret this borrowing in terms of the detail in 40:1-11. I argued before that the voices were heavenly and that the third-person voice in v. 6 ("and one said") "belongs to any individual member of the heavenly council."[29] We could infer this on the basis of Isaiah 6, where the seraphs speak to one another, and on the basis of other such scenes in Zechariah, Job, and 1 Kings 22. At the same time, however, I argued that the voice was closely attached to the mundane realm as well, specifically to Isaiah the prophet and his prior prophecy; it served as "a precis of one important dimension of Isaiah's prophecy" viewed from a later perspective.[30] I remain persuaded that the text must be interpreted in the light of other texts now found in chs. 1–39. To bracket out this context in the name of traditional form-critical analysis would be to forfeit the proper interpretive clues without which the text cannot make its intended sense. I am less persuaded that the form of a heavenly council commissioning, such as we find in ch. 6, has been borrowed without modification of its details. Once the linkage has been made, the form begins to go its own way.

It was my thesis that the chief concern of the text involves extending Isaiah's word into a new day, and that also means — at least potentially — raising a question of human agency. Is Isaiah present and speaking, or another? Typically in prophetic books a call narrative answers such ques-

28. See Rendtorff, "Composition."
29. Seitz, "Divine Council," 245.
30. Ibid., 241.

tions by having the prophet autobiographically describe God's address to him, his response, and God's further instruction, cleansing, preparation, and commission. Such was the position of those who held that here Deutero-Isaiah was being called, in his own "prophetic book" (chs. 40–55). Yet in this text virtually all autobiographical perspective is lacking. It is in part for this reason that one could assume, in an earlier day, that the Isaiah already called in ch. 6 remained at work here — such was Calvin's reading, if not also Sheppard's, in a more sophisticated form.[31] Yet, instead of this autobiographical perspective, we have God's voice, anonymous voices, and a final charge involving Zion. Even that remains somewhat unfocused temporally, since it involves a reaction to God's own activity, not yet undertaken (vv. 9b-11).

One striking feature of the unit, again not notable in call narratives, is the way the unit breaks into subsections, with the second two closed by reference to God's speech or word (v. 5, "for the mouth of the LORD has spoken it"; v. 8, "the word of our God will stand forever"). I would argue that this is not rhetorical flourish or a reference to God's present speaking within a heavenly — or earthly — council, with which the voices top off their own proffered speech. The text does not say this as it is presently arranged: divine address appears in vv. 1-2, and then other voices speak up, in seeming response, with no further return to God's address as such. Rather, with these closing refrains reference is being made to *known, previously uttered* words of God, matters already spoken. This is why in the case of the second, seemingly despondent voice, no specific divine rebuttal or correction appears in explicit form. In response to this divine charge, human speech is indeed ephemeral, such that if "one said, what shall I cry?" the answer would have to be, "inadequate — all flesh is grass and its best effort like the flower of the field." And not just the proclaimers but also the recipients of divine speech are like grass of the field, as we know from chs. 1–39. No new speech is inaugurated by God in this unit. The word of our God as already spoken is what will stand forever, as the note in 30:8 had announced in the days of Isaiah.

In the case of the first voice, where no hesitation occurs, the voice proclaiming draws for the content of the proclamation not on inspired utterances from his or her own breast. The command to comfort does not come with a requirement of proper psychological state or creative endowment, but rather the citing of what "the mouth of the LORD has spoken."

31. See n. 24 above.

In this case, search for Deutero-Isaiah's "call" has created a misleading environment, since "call" is concerned with origination, the beginning of a content, from God to freshly authorized prophet. But that is not called for here. The first voice, in responding to the charge to comfort, quotes what the mouth of the LORD has already spoken, in the vision of Isaiah. Chapter 35 contains most of the relevant content, a summation of the prophet's scattered, previously uttered language of hope and restitution (1:26; 6:13; 8:18; 11:16; 12:1-6). Incidentally, this may also explain the placement of this chapter *prior* to the narratives of chs. 36–39, to make it clear that the promise of the LORD's return to Zion, such as that referenced in 40:3, was prophecy from Isaiah, of old, uttered prior to the events of Zion's deliverance and not just in an editorially motivated "bridge" linking discrete and fully independent sections of the book.[32]

The final unit (40:9-11) consists of new charges, now to a herald of good tidings. Reference to God in the third person would suggest that another anonymous voice is again speaking here. But in some respects the effect of the opening exchange has been to relativize such a distinction. In what follows, God will speak directly, with no evidence of human agency. But there is a reason for this, unrelated to whether the "persona" (Sheppard) or concrete person (Calvin) of Isaiah is resident here. Throughout appeal is made by God to what has *already* been revealed to Israel (40:21, 28; 41:27; 43:10; 44:8), and it is on this basis that YHWH, Israel's named God, is God alone, since the capacity to establish providence over history is something God's rivals cannot do. Israel is in a position to state something about her own history as well as extramural affairs, like the calling of Cyrus, while others have no such recourse, and in this consists the demonstration of her own unique status and destiny. Again and again God insists that the "former things" are not just a sufficient but also a particularly compelling testimony to Israel's election. All this turns on there having been "former things" to begin with, and among these is the prophetic word of Isaiah concerning the call of Cyrus (41:25 and 13:17; 21:2).

The reason no new prophet appears, or Isaiah, is that God is here referring Israel to what Isaiah has spoken beforehand and, alongside that, to what Israel's past history was intended to reveal, for its own sake and in conjunction with God's word to Isaiah, at this particular juncture in time and then for all posterity. There could be no better example of

32. Compare Odil H. Steck, *Bereitete Heimkehr* (SBS 121; Stuttgart: Katholisches Bibelwerk, 1985).

emergent "canon consciousness" than what these opening chapters of "Second Isaiah" portray, that is, a sense that the prophetic word, and the word of God, is now constituted and freshly communicated through a past record to which public reference can be made, by Israel, for Israel's own sake and for the sake of God's effective rule over all creation. This is truly prophecy in a new mode, and something like this is suggested in the opening chapter of Zechariah as well:

> And the prophets, do they live forever?
> But my words and my statutes, which I commanded my servants
>   the prophets, did they not overtake your fathers? (1:5-6, RSV).

What is central to the opening unit of Isaiah 40–66 — the appeal to God's word once spoken — is maintained in the same manner in the chapters that follow, especially 40–48. That constitutes their governing force and gives explanation for why no new prophet, or Isaiah, is depicted as speaking. Isaiah the prophet does speak, of course, but not as a "persona." He speaks through the word he spoke in a former time, a word that God reminds Israel it did not then heed. But now, because forgiven, Israel can with opened ears and eyes comprehend matters whose "latter end" even the prophet Isaiah could not previously understand (see especially 21:1-4).[33]

I pointed out in my earlier essay that these opening chapters (40–48) are not entirely devoid of autobiographical reference. There is, of course, the voice that speaks in 40:6; it is not clear if this is a celestial voice or a representative voice more generally.[34] This voice states that no new human word can effect the change God calls for in the opening unit (vv. 1-2). The second voice is, however, equipped to speak a word, by citing God's word spoken through Isaiah (vv. 3-5). As discussed above, the material that follows is essentially divine speech from a trial setting, where God defends himself on the basis of testimony to which Israel alone has recourse. This involves Israel's record in respect of the creation (40:12-31),

---

33. On the significance of this passage, see my treatment in *Isaiah 1–39* (Interpretation; Louisville: Westminster/John Knox, 1993) ad loc.

34. I wish to thank an STM student at Yale Divinity School, Naoto Kamano, for sharing his very insightful paper with me, "New Prophecy Is Not Actually New: Canonical Function of Isaiah 40:1-11 Reconsidered." Kamano makes several good observations in this response to my *JBL* (1990) essay.

the call of Abraham (41:1-13), succor in the wilderness (41:14-20), the prophetic prediction of Cyrus as defeater of Babylon (41:21-29). In ch. 42, reference to the blind and deaf servant (42:18-20) recalls an Israel familiar from chs. 1–39 (especially 6:9-10). Yet this servant has now been punished, as Isaiah had foreseen, burned and burned again by YHWH's wrath (42:25), imagery again reminiscent of ch. 6 (v. 13).

In the midst of this passage (42:18-25) we have a brief first-person reference in the penultimate verse, and it stands out for its singular character amid lengthy divine speech.

> Who gave up Jacob to the spoiler,
>   and Israel to the robbers?
> Was it not the LORD, against whom we have sinned? (42:24, RSV).

This constitutes a corporate confession, similar in form (and possibly function) to Jer 3:24-25. The shift to the third person in the second half of the verse makes it clear that the objects of God's actual historical judgment lie in the past, and the final verse depicts that judgment in succinct terms. This brief glimpse at a confession might explain the shift that occurs in the next chapter, where the people who are blind *yet have eyes,* and who are deaf *yet have ears* (43:8). As many have noted, this amounts to a clear reversal of the circumstances of Isaiah's addressees. A new day is breaking forth on the other side of Isaiah's "How long?"

In the chapters that follow it is the call of Cyrus and the defeat of Babylon that take center stage. Reference is frequently made to Israel's own special counsel in these matters. In these events God is confirming the word of his servants (44:26), declared of old (45:21), accomplishing his counsel in Cyrus (46:11), and performing his purpose on Babylon (47:14). Israel alone can bear witness that they knew about these things long ago, even when they have failed to make proper acknowledgment, then or now.

At the same time, God also mentions new things, which have no history of prediction. "Before they spring forth, I tell you of them" (42:9); "Behold, I am doing a new thing; now it springs forth" (43:19); and "From this time forth I make you hear new things, hidden things which you have not known . . . before today you have never heard of them" (48:6-7). Since this prophecy cannot be related to the authorized word of Isaiah, or any other chapter of Israel's sacred history, already on record, the previous explanation why no prophetic figure is being depicted in these chapters begins to fall to the side. This would present a problem were it not for the fact that at precisely this moment, a first-person voice emerges in 48:16. And then in ch. 49, what could in fact be classified a "call narrative" appears (49:1-6). Could it be that we are seeing a new speaker for new things, "created now, not long ago" (48:7)? That is at least one possible explanation for the convergence of these several factors in the text at this juncture.[35]

The unit in which this initial first-person singular voice speaks runs from v. 14 through v. 16. The opening call to assemble is a familiar one. Also familiar is the way the exact referent is unclear, here and throughout the unit. The references to calling and prospering in v. 15 would be consistent with God's commission of Cyrus, and the references to victory over Babylon in v. 14b likewise commend this interpretation, as does the final unit of the chapter (vv. 20-22), where servant Jacob is liberated from Chaldean exile. That this was announced of old, and not in secret (v. 16), is also consistent with the calling of Cyrus as prophesied by Isaiah — something that cannot be revealed by "them" (v. 14a). In the final line, the introductory וְעַתָּה would appear to distinguish between something that had obtained — the calling of Cyrus by Isaiah — and something now in force: God's sending "me and his spirit." It is also consistent with the sort of transition to "new things" underscored so effectively in 48:6-8. What remains unclear is whether the spirit mentioned here in connection with an individual is related to the spirit with which God endows the servant in 42:1 (נָתַתִּי רוּחִי עָלָיו).

As mentioned, a nearly classic call narrative appears in 49:1-6, even allowing for the curious reference to "Israel" in v. 3. There is no dearth of autobiographical detail here. Certain language is distinctly reminiscent of the call of Jeremiah, for example, being called from the womb. Moreover, the reference to a career involved with "the nations" (49:6) was one that figured prominently in Jeremiah's call, and its peculiarity in light of the book's content has long bothered commentators.

Yet there is one feature that seems inconsistent with a call narrative, whether it be that of Jeremiah, Isaiah, Ezekiel, or another. That is the lack of a serious, *present* encounter with the divine. Instead, the prophet — if we are entitled to call him that — provides as it were a reminiscence. What was said to Jeremiah in direct speech (Jer 1:5) is recollected by this figure using indirect speech (49:1). The objection lodged by the prophet in v. 4

---

35. See "Divine Council," 245-46.

involves not his unfitness for the task, as with Jeremiah or Moses, or his uncleanness, as with Isaiah. It appears to involve a perception that labor already spent has been for nought. The actual charge from God, which again is reported through the prophet's own brokering, comes in v. 6, where we learn that the prophet has an additional, not an initial, vocation, over and above what he has *already been about,* namely, a mission to Jacob/Israel. This is fully consistent with the perspective of v. 4. So the unit is not so much the account of a call as a report of one who had been called, and who is here commissioned for a new task.

We are now beginning to circle a constellation of related issues whose gravity is difficult to escape. Is there to be found in these chapters a series of discrete "servant poems"? Does this series end at ch. 53? Are the poems in meaningful relationship to one another, such that one could speak of movement, development, and culmination? If there is meaningful development across all the poems or a part of them, does this disturb the possibility of organization and development in the chapters as a whole, since their positioning as a cycle is curious? What is the scope of each individual poem and why in all but the last does it appear that further remarks are made *in extenso* (42:5-9; 49:7; 50:10-11)? To raise the question of the servant's identity before these questions are addressed only leads to confusion, as the history of interpretation bears witness.[36]

I am arguing here that yet further consideration needs to come into play that may shed light on these other questions, if not on the servant's identity. This involves the matter under discussion, namely, how Isaiah is present in chs. 40–66. In the opening chapters (40–48) Isaiah is present through his word once spoken, which is cited along with further testimony of old ("former things") to establish God's sovereignty and Israel's election. The prophetic "voice" behind these chapters remains hidden, *of necessity,* so that a word already spoken might bear witness to God's prophetic purpose, a purpose frustrated by deafness and blindness, delayed, but inexorably accomplishing that for which it was sent. The prophet's "persona" is replaced by the testimony of God's word already sent forth.

Nevertheless, the references to "new things" never before spoken increase in frequency once the blind and deaf Israel begins to hear and see the significance of the "former things." In 48:16 we see what may be the

---

36. See most recently R. C. Kratz, *Kyros im Deuterojesaja-Buch* (Forschungen zum Alten Testament 1; Tübingen: Mohr, 1991); and Odil H. Steck, *Gottesknecht und Zion* (Forschungen zum Alten Testament 4; Tübingen: Mohr, 1992).

signature of the voice at work in these chapters. Then in the second and third "servant poems" (49:1-6, 7; 50:4-9, 10-11) we find clear and uninterrupted first-person speech. A similar speech form is attested in 61:1-4, 10-11. It appears that a first-person voice is in fact being identified, and clearly. The first-person poem that lies closest to the signature of 48:16, namely, 49:1-6, 7, also picks up the theme of something new now to be announced. The voice in the poem reflects on a career that has a distinct history (49:4). The fresh charge from God in v. 6 likewise speaks of a career involving Jacob and Israel. Yet in addition to that the servant will have a task vis-à-vis the nations: "it is too light a thing that you should be my servant to raise up the tribes of Jacob. . . . I will give you as a light to the nations, that my salvation may reach to the ends of the earth" (49:6). The final extension (v. 7) also makes this clear.

If this is a correct interpretation of the temporal perspective of 49:1-7, what are we to make of it? References to frustration and futility do not neatly comport with the presentation in chs. 40–48; it is not as though the speaker of that material is reflecting in 49:1-6 on a difficult career, evidence of which can be seen in what precedes. There we have eyes opened where once they were blind. As we have seen, the unit assumes many of the features of a call narrative, but then it goes its own way. The individual announces to the nations ("you coastlands" and "peoples from afar") that he was called by God in the womb (49:1). This claim had a different effect in the opening chapter of the book of Jeremiah. There God himself tells a young Jeremiah, in direct speech, that he has a present task as prophet to the nations for which he had been consecrated at birth (Jer 1:5). The book does not open with Jeremiah announcing that he had been called at birth for a task (that God must reveal to him) and that it had required great fortitude (we learn that only as the book unfolds). Our passage sounds more like an interim report, with a fresh charge being delivered, than the initial call of a prophet.

To the degree that the opening chapters (Isaiah 40–48) bring into prominence God's prior word, the "author" of this material remains hidden. No "I" appears until 48:16. Yet when what looks like a prophetic figure does emerge, there is the same measure of dependence on past testimony, not only in form but also in substance. A record of prophecy as Israel has known it appears to lie behind this unit, in the same way as Isaiah's word and Israel's history in creation, wilderness, and exodus were former things to which the author of chs. 40–48 made reference. This servant understands his own mission in a larger context of prophetic witness, which has been difficult and seemingly futile, though trust in God has not been destroyed (49:4b). In my judgment, this servant comprehends his own vocation in reference to past prophets, such as Jeremiah — but not Jeremiah at the moment of call, with a vocation, a charge, and a career still ahead. This servant's career picks up where Jeremiah left off, at the end of his career. That is, it is a mission based on all prior prophecy at its own potential end point and dissolution. The servant takes his bearings from the history of God's dealings with Israel through his servants the prophets, including a history of seeming unfulfillment, delay, even failure. This servant carries Israel's history with prophecy in him and, in so doing, is "Israel" in a very specific sense. So it is stated in that curious phrase in 49:3: "You are my servant; (you are) Israel in whom I will be glorified."[37]

Moreover, it would be possible for those examining the record, including this servant, to conjecture that Jeremiah's specific vocation as a prophet to the nations (Jer 1:5, 10) was not fully accomplished — even bracketing out a discussion as to what such a mission entailed in the first place. Jeremiah not only pours out lament to God for a seemingly frustrated vocation to Israel (chs. 12–20); he finds himself at the end of his career in a defeated and overrun capital (chs. 37–39), then to be hauled off to Egypt against his will (chs. 42–44) with no final chapter providing resolution, either in respect of Israel or the nations. The mantle of painful witness is simply handed over to another (ch. 45). Prophecy has returned whence it came, to the place God had said Israel could not return without curse (Deut 17:16). Prophecy's future is by no means clear.[38]

Furthermore, to the degree to which the wider history of prophecy had a vocation involving the nations (within this corpus see Isaiah 2:1-5; 11:9; 13–27; 34–35), one could conjecture that that similar vocation still lacked sufficient, obvious fulfillment. Indeed, the content of the vocation may require for clarification Israel's coming into conjunction with the nations in a particularly direct way in the first place. For that the events of 587 represented a painful possibility. At that moment Israel was in a position to contemplate what was meant by God's call of Jeremiah to be a prophet to the nations, or by Isaiah's speech concerning the destinies of kingdoms beyond Israel's compass.

---

37. Peter Wilcox and David Paton-Williams, "The Servant Songs in Second Isaiah," *JSOT* 42 (1988) 79-102.

38. Christopher R. Seitz, "The Prophet Moses and the Canonical Shape of Jeremiah," *ZAW* 101 (1989) 3-27.

The first section of this material (chs. 40–48) is chiefly concerned with how God's word spoken through Isaiah and elsewhere is coming to fulfillment within Israel's circle of comprehension. The period of blindness and deafness is over. God's past word can now be heard to new effect. From ch. 49 on another aspect of past prophecy emerges alongside this always central concern, namely, how that word was to realize its intended effect on the nations of the world. This does not involve a resolution of the problem of chs. 40–48, which is a specifically intramural one (viz., word grounded in past testimony, over against Israel's reception of it). The focus shifts now to the servant, Israel, with a vocation to the nations. In this role the servant is not just one more individual prophet in a long line of prophets stretching back to Moses; the servant is that history of prophecy individualized, especially in respect of that history as still awaiting fulfillment. The fulfillment of the former things has been pointed to, but for the final consummation of these a new thing is required. This servant will bring to fruition God's destiny for Israel and for the nations, about which questions persist (49:4) and press for a resolution different in kind from anything at work in chs. 40–48.

To the question How is the prophet Isaiah present in chs. 40–66? we would respond thus: in word in chs. 40–48 and in person in chs. 49ff. — but not by himself. Isaiah, together with his fellow "servants the prophets" running all the way back to Moses, is represented by the servant who speaks up in ch. 49, reflecting on hard labor, futility, yet trust in the one who called from the womb. Ironically, Delitzsch's suggestion that Isaiah "is more like a spirit without visible form" in chs. 40–66 is not far off the mark, though for reasons he was not contemplating. The servant is here commissioned for a new task involving an old but unfulfilled vocation to the nations. We learn that the fulfillment of this vocation will transform Israel itself and will finally ask that Israel put on the mantle of prophecy as has the servant in these chapters ("this is the heritage of the servants of the LORD," 55:17). We had a foreshadowing of this in the book of Jeremiah, where the transmission to a new generation, in the figure of Baruch, is an integral part of the book's presentation (especially in chs. 36 and 45). Likewise in the book of Isaiah, the reference in the next first-person poem to the servant being given the tongue of a לִמּוּד (50:4) has long been associated with Isaiah's "taught ones" in 8:16.[39] So within this book's presentation there is also a furtherance of the office through a new genera-

39. Jones, "Traditio," 233.

tion, represented by the servant, and, beyond him, "the servants" (54:17; 63:17; 65:8, 9, 13, 14, 15; 66:14).[40] "Canon consciousness" would then involve not just a shift from historical prophet to a written testimony through which he can continue to speak. It would involve as well a transformation of generations newly addressed by that testimony, until they take on the likeness of those who went before and finally in their own person, through God's grace, bring to completion the work begun in others.

The question of this servant's specific identity may also find an answer in our proposal. The obscurity is not an intentional "device" or a function of our historical distance from the first audience or author's circumstances. The reason we cannot identify the servant in these poems is that he has taken on the mantle of prophets who have gone before, and in that role he is no one who could be particularized without reference to that prior history. He is not another individual prophet in a long chain of prophets. He is God's servant, and in that role he sees himself and his vocation as bringing to completion God's word spoken to the prophets of old. He gets out of the way in a manner different from that conjectured for chs. 40–48: he is the culmination of prophetic Israel, whose testimony he takes up and whose suffering he willingly embraces, so that that testimony and that suffering might effect what God wills for Israel and the nations. Alongside the transition from *prophet* (Isaiah) to *prophetic word* in chs. 40–48, one sees in chs. 49ff. a transition from *prophets* to *servant* and then *servants*. We are in a new dispensation, because of the emergence and authoritative force of a written prophetic record, from which God's word still presses for fulfillment.

In my judgment, the servant described in 49:1-7 and 50:4-9 was an actual historical figure as well as the prophetic voice at work in these chapters (40–55). That is, more is at work in these passages than literary representation for the purpose of resolving prophecy's complex legacy. Furthermore, in my view a genetic relationship exists between this voice and the servant who speaks in the first person in 61:1-7, and for this and other reasons a new description of the relationship between chs. 40–55 and 56–66 is called for.[41] In the first-person account in 50:4-9, an in-

---

40. W. A. M. Beuken, "The Main Theme of Trito-Isaiah: The 'Servants of YHWH,'" *JSOT* 47 (1990) 67-87.

41. See my remarks in "On the Question of Divisions," 265-66. I have been persuaded by the work of Beuken on this transition from servant to servants (see preceding note).

dividual describes a vocation of suffering and affliction not unlike that of Jeremiah or of many other figures in Israel's experience. Prophecy is described in a way that comports with what we know from Israel's record of it, including its unclear completion according to God's designs for it. A real figure, who is the speaker of God's word in the sections surrounding these descriptions, here understands his suffering as consistent with and the culmination of prophecy as it has taken form in Israel's past. What is less clear is whether this same figure is being described, now in a lengthy and detailed third-person report, in the dramatic fourth poem (52:13–53:12). My view is that the same figure is being described, now by other servants (54:17) who reflect on the significance of the servant's death. The narrator of 52:13–53:12 is one of the servants who joins in the plural confession found at 53:14.

Failure to identify the stricken servant, whose mission is confessed to have such enormous consequences, gives one pause; it is anonymity of a nature different from what has obtained for the first-person voice we have been focusing on thus far. In constructing the record of past figures, to what is reckoned banal go no names, not to the consequential. Yet within this account the central concern, arguably, is for consequentiality (52:15; 53:4-6) as well as for the posterity who will encounter and acknowledge this servant's accomplishment (53:11).

In the light of these factors, one must ask if the refusal to identify is in this case deliberate[42] and somehow part of the servant's accomplishment as the narrator has interpreted it. That narrator has himself rejected identification, consistent with the servant's own deference to a prophetic record still in force and still pressing for fulfillment. In the case of the stricken servant about whom he is bearing poignant testimony, his ignominy in life (53:2-3) is corroborated by the faceless character of his sacrifice, the effects of his service obliterating his particularity as a named individual, along lines traditionally conceived for Israel's prophets and great figures. Moses' grave is unmarked because his legacy lies elsewhere (the written Torah), and this constitutes his true and most enduring memorial; this servant's identity remains hidden that his chief accomplishment, the removal of sin, might

---

42. For other reasons, several modern interpreters (Clines, Westermann) have also regarded the failure to identify as deliberate, or at least a caution to exegetes not to press for details the text has not chosen to supply. See D. J. A. Clines, *I, He, We, They — A Literary Approach to Isa 53* (*JSOT* Supplement Series 1; Sheffield: JSOT, 1976); Claus Westermann, *Isaiah 40–55* (Philadelphia: Westminster, 1969).

emerge as his fundamental legacy. The anonymous first-person voice here joins with others to testify to an anonymity even more purposeful than his own. As the narrator records it, the sacrifice of the servant is complete. It extends to his very identification for posterity. His exaltation consists of his complete self-surrender, literally, on behalf of the servants and in obedience to God's will. Whatever else the servant's mission accomplishes, it begins with the awareness that this servant's identification is not the key to his activity and its consequences for posterity. Such identification has been deliberately withheld from the record.

This is a retraction of the prophetic persona different in kind and effect from what we have been tracing thus far. But it is similar in that the record of the servant's achievement has been aggrandized precisely through the decision — we are arguing that it was deliberate — not to attach the record to a specific person in history and not to include as part of his legacy his name.[43] Precisely in its commitment to silence, within the fabric of this moving scene of obedience and sacrifice, is constituted the eschatological power of the servant's accomplishment. The rich history of this text's interpretation bears this out, even when pursued for reasons extraneous to the account's own compelling form and content.

IV

Many specific issues of exegesis have been passed over in an effort to reflect on this and other key passages in the book of Isaiah from the standpoint of the prophet's presence in the collection to which his name has been attached. Nowhere is this more true than in the poem now under discussion, whose specific details and presentation have given rise to a variety of reconstructions and further questions for consideration. (Did the servant actually die? To what does a "grave with the wicked" refer? Does the servant "sprinkle" the nations in 52:15, and, if so, is this a cultic notion? What of the references in 53:2 to his growing up like a young plant? What is the servant's accomplishment vis-à-vis the nations?)[44] Furthermore, it has

---

43. Note the resemblance to the depiction of the mysterious voice with which this material begins: "and one said, 'What shall I cry?'" (40:6).

44. For a typical treatment, see either Clines *(I, He)* or R. N. Whybray, *Thanksgiving for a Liberated Prophet (JSOT* Supplement Series 4; Sheffield: JSOT, 1978).

been difficult to identify the servant with Israel because of the peculiar details of the account. So too an eschatological figure would appear to be ruled out because the report is retrospective, not prospective, in character.[45] But this is not the place to pursue these matters in detail; for that a commentary treatment is required.[46] My concern in this essay has been to understand the way chs. 40–66 consciously take up the matter of prophetic agency as central to their presentation and dramatic movement. This involves in the first instance the prophet Isaiah, but also prophecy more broadly conceived, as we have seen in the case of the servant and servants in chs. 40–66. If the contribution of the present essay is to shift the way we have thought about this issue in the book of Isaiah, that will be enough. Greater precision and further clarification will then come in due course.

---

45. The eschatological force we are identifying is of a different nature altogether.
46. See my forthcoming commentary in the *New Interpreters Bible.*

14

Isaiah in Parish Bible Study

The Question of the Place of the Reader
in Biblical Texts

The title of this and the following chapter make it clear that the book of Isaiah will remain the center of attention. The focus will be, first, recent changes in reading stategies that have shifted attention to this book as a unified presentation and then Isaiah as a book of Christian scripture, read in the context of the life of the church and in conjunction with the New Testament witness to Jesus Christ. In many of the previous chapters I have argued that for Christian readers, the future for biblical studies involves a conscious, intentional reconnection of the two testaments, Old and New, from the standpoint of instruction, publication, and theological and devotional reflection.[1]

In the case of Isaiah, this means first reading the book for its own sake — what will be called a *per se* reading — and then moving forward to ask in a critical way just how this book of Hebrew Scripture becomes Old Testament when interpreted in reciprocity with the New. That is, there are two tasks confronting the Christian reader: interpreting the Old Testament *per se* and the Old *in novo receptum,* as received in the New. A

---

1. See the essays in the first section on Biblical Theology above. In his own way, the Jewish scholar Jon Levenson has pressed for precisely this larger context as appropriate and necessary for Christian interpretation ("The Eighth Principle of Judaism and the Literary Simultaneity of Scripture," *The Hebrew Bible, the Old Testament, and Historical Criticism* [Louisville: Westminster/John Knox, 1993] 62-81, here especially 80-81).

key question arises at this point. How is the Old heard and reinterpreted, without obliterating or simply moving beyond the original *per se* witness? As we have seen above, something of this process of reinterpretation can be detected within the literary context of the book of Isaiah itself, wherein earlier perspectives have been recast and focused anew without muting the "former things" in favor of the "latter" or "new things" — to use the terms that Isaiah uses for this process of reinterpretation. In the previous essay an argument was put forward that silence in the latter chapters of Isaiah concerning kingship did not mean that earlier statements were now to be regarded as otiose. The relationship between major sections of Isaiah is more dialectical than that, as is the relationship between the Testaments of Christian Scripture, and as is the relationship between this essay and the one to follow. There is a measure of independence, but there is also an affiliation that cannot be described developmentally.

My remarks in this essay involve Isaiah's own *per se* witness, without consideration of the relationship that this witness has with the New Testament. But it would be wrong to move too quickly past the predicating phrase: Isaiah "in parish Bible study," for that might suggest that we know what parish Bible study is and what it hopes to accomplish. But my suspicion is that there are as many questions about what parish Bible study is as there are questions about what constitutes a unitary or holistic approach to reading Isaiah. Here the question of Isaiah as a unitary witness and the question of the goal of parish Bible study converge around one larger issue: where is the place of the reader in this vast 66-chapter book? The slant on Isaiah in parish Bible study developed here will focus on one question: Does the book have a particular reader orientation that we are meant to identify and then orient ourselves around? One of the first goals of parish Bible study would therefore entail a determination of how consciously we as readers and hearers of this work of scriptural witness are actually anticipated by the literature itself, so that we might align ourselves with the natural expectations the literature has of us. And if this is an important question to ask of the book of Isaiah, then the same should be true for other biblical books, in both testaments of the twofold Christian canon.[2]

The issue can be illustrated in the following way. One of the domain assumptions of older critical approaches to reading the Bible was that

2. From a different point of view, see now *The Gospels for All Christians*, ed. R. Bauckham (Grand Rapids: Eerdmans, 1997). This new work questions the historicizing of audience and readership in vogue in New Testament studies.

we, as readers of the finished products of biblical texts, were only ac-
cidentally, or as latecomers or overhearers, anticipated by the literature
itself. It is as though we had found ourselves "reading someone else's
mail," as one modern interpreter has put it, in a phrase we have referred
to at a number of points above.[3] The point of historical-critical labor
was to recreate the situation in life in which the portion of the text under
discussion was once under original utterance and delivery. This task was
pursued not for its own sake, or because the task was challenging, or
because one could make a career doing it, but because it was never
assumed that the material had been shaped to function as scripture for
just any audience who happened to show up and ask, What does this
material have to say to me? Once the various situations-in-life that
together constituted the book's complete history were imaginatively re-
created, then the task would be to reapply a word once delivered to a
changed but analogous modern context.

Now the strengths of such an approach are immediately apparent,
especially in a book like Isaiah, which Luther probably had in mind when
he said, "(the prophets) have a queer way of talking, like people who,
instead of proceeding in an orderly manner, ramble off from one thing
to the next, so that you cannot make head or tail of them or see what
they are getting at."[4] The notion that biblical books were not shaped in
coherent ways so as to address later readers and hearers is not just a
modern one, and the prophets are particularly challenging, as Luther's
statement implies. Critical method could make sense of a complex and
confused text by assigning the material to its original setting and, as an
added bonus, could show us our proper point of standing as readers and
interpreters. Incidentally, this sort of approach, which might be called
"subject-oriented" (as against one focused on readers as objects of address)
struggled to know if we were to relate to the prophet Isaiah as prophetic
subject, or to the people Israel as subject, and if so, at what particular
point on the very long journey from eighth-century oral speech through
Babylonian exile, to final return and consolidation in the aftermath of
that same exile. But even this sort of concern was relatively minor

---

3. Paul van Buren, "On Reading Someone Else's Mail: The Church and Israel's
Scriptures," *Die Hebräische Bibel und ihre zweifache Nachgeschichte* (FS R. Rendtorff;
Neukirchen-Vluyn: Neukirchener, 1990) 595-606.

4. Quoted in G. von Rad, *The Message of the Prophets* (New York: Harper and Row,
1967) 15.

measured against the strengths of an approach which could both make sense of an apparently randomly organized text and also show us where to stand as readers and hearers of the word of God spoken through Isaiah and those who followed him.

Of course there was a practical question immediately felt in most Bible study. Just how did one go about assigning with confidence portions of text to original situations in life, granting even that such a goal was desirable? Would this not require very specialized skills and training, of a sort either intimidating or overly academic for most parish Bible study groups, threatening to create a false dichotomy between "expert readings" (surely the Bible is not just for experts) and overly personalistic or psychological ones? How was one to know for sure whether a text belonged in a period of Assyrian threat, following Zion's deliverance, anticipating Babylon's defeat, from the bosom of exilic hardship or reflecting debates about temple membership in the Persian period? To say that Isaiah could be divided into thirds with perspicuous social-historical settings was to grossly oversimplify the problem of assigning especially this book to points in time when the readerships confronted were so clear-cut. And of course it was also to insist that the actual key to proper interpretation had to be inferred through critical reconstruction and was not an obvious part of the book's own final literary presentation.

To say that such a task was difficult is not to say that the approach was wrongheaded from the start or that it had ignored quite obvious indices structured into the literature whose express purpose was to help us, here in the late twentieth century, know how to read and interpret this book. The critical theory was itself an effort to respond to the very sorts of problems noted by Luther. But, in addition, the theory maximized the potential latent in a certain understanding of prophecy, namely, the prophets as individual inspired speakers. Early historical-critical work operated under a distinctive set of theological and practical concerns, so that if such work is now to be set aside, new theological and practical parameters will have to be worked out. On the old model, traditional theories of inspiration that had insured a book's claim to faithfully report matters in time and space — even predicting the distant future — had been translated into a more diffuse understanding. But the same basic notion of inspiration applied: Word of God to inspired individuals, to receiving communities. On such a model, what was of utmost importance was not the actual book itself, or its larger shape, since these could no longer with confidence be assigned to the traditional author, but rather a critical reconstruction of a variety of inspired individuals and the communities addressed by them. The focus had shifted from inspired book to inspired individuals.[5]

To shift the focus back to the book itself is not to ignore this significant, substituted theory of inspired individuals, but it is to shift attention to the possibility that the final shaping has itself crafted these various inspired voices into an organic whole, capable of speaking with one voice. But the chief point to be made here is that "capacity to speak with one voice" is not the same thing as either an obliteration of historical depth, nor the production of a static text with only one possible meaning.

The process I am referring to, what Brevard Childs has called "canonical shaping," was not executed in the book of Isaiah in this sort of manner. Efforts to anticipate and speak coherently to a readership explicitly outside the book's own historical frame of reference are not registered in such a way as to oppose participation in the book's coming-to-be. At the same time, however, it is Isaiah's concrete, historical coming-to-be that also points in the direction of greater respect for how the final organization and shaping — far from being random — has its own mysterious logic: a sum greater than the parts. That this logic is, in Isaiah, neither chronological nor thematic, should give one pause. In order to make sense of the book of Isaiah's final form, we are inevitably drawn into a world of real historical reference, where distinctions between the Assyrians and the Babylonians, between Cyrus and Sennacherib, between an intact temple and one destroyed, are cleanly registered. But then the book does a surprising thing. Having made such distinctions, it begins to construct its own analogies and linkages, long before we get there as readers of this ancient witness, concerned with recasting the text chronologically, and then moving from ancient historical context to modern twentieth-century application.

I have been speaking in theoretical terms up to this point. It is now time to read texts and illustrate exegetically what has been described hermeneutically. The concern is to comprehend the final shape of the book of Isaiah, without ignoring the fact of its complex prehistory, with the hope that by understanding this shaping, clues might be given as to how readers are to appropriate the message of the book. This might be a novel way to focus the question of Isaiah in parish Bible study, for it assumes that the book was not just stumbled upon, like someone else's mail that must be decoded. Rather, a basic question is asked: How does the book

5. For further study, see the treatment on inspiration in chapter 10 above.

function as a whole, directed toward potential readers? The answer that is given will involve regular, prayerful, chapter-by-chapter reading and reflection. I will make my own proposal here, and it is nothing more than the consequence of my own regular, prayerful, chapter-by-chapter reading. I am modeling my conclusions, but more important to me is the approach by which I reached them, which is what I wish to commend for parish Bible study.

It is sometimes helpful to work on the basis of contrast and comparison. Before moving to Isaiah, let me illustrate this perspective on reading a book's final form by looking at Jeremiah, whose canonical shape also intrigues me, especially as I find it easier to comprehend.[6] After we have cut our teeth on Jeremiah, what we have learned will be extended, where appropriate, to the more complex shape of Isaiah.

II

The first six chapters of Jeremiah, in addition to speaking judgment over northern and southern kingdoms, also hold out the possibility of repentance and a removal of the sentence of judgment.

> Return, faithless Israel, says the LORD.
> I will not look on you in anger, for I am merciful,
> > says the LORD;
> I will not be angry forever.
> Only acknowledge your guilt, that you have rebelled
> > against the LORD. . . .
> And I will take you, one from a city,
> > two from a family,
> > and I will bring you to Zion (3:12-14).

Whether such calls for repentance were originally addressed only to Israel, the northern kingdom, is not so crucial as noting that such calls are in fact noticeably rare in the book. This is made clear as we leave the first six chapters and enter a new section in chapter 7, where the possibility of

6. See my "The Prophet Moses and the Canonical Shape of the Book of Jeremiah," *ZAW* 101 (1989) 1-15.

intercession on Jeremiah's part on behalf of Israel is withdrawn — "As for you, do not pray for this people . . . and do not intercede with me, for I will not hear you" — leading to awesome pictures of coming doom, with no possibility of repentance, and a Jeremiah wracked with anguish and dark foreboding. Now what could the reader hear here but sad testimony to the iniquity of prior generations, so vast as to demand a sentence of judgment virtually without rider. The lesson would be a chilling one, demanding repentance and a confession of guilt. And, in fact, acknowledgments of just sentencing and personal confessions are woven into the text, both in this part of the book (9:12-16) and in the first section.

> Let us lie down in our shame, and let our dishonor cover us;
> For we have sinned against the LORD our God,
>   we and our ancestors, from our youth even to this day;
> And we have not obeyed the voice of the LORD our God (3:25).

The book has been shaped to allow the reader to participate in the refusal of an earlier generation to heed God's calls to repentance and to experience the judgment they eventually experienced, though now with a clear confession of wrongdoing and an acknowledgment that Jeremiah was a true prophet sent by God — something for which he was persecuted rather than honored and heeded.

To take another brief example from this section of the book, note how in chapter 16 eventual readers are addressed almost explicitly:

> And when you tell this people all these words, and they say to you, "Why has the LORD pronounced all this great evil against us? What is our iniquity? What is the sin that we have committed against the LORD our God?" then you shall say to them: "It is because your ancestors have forsaken me," says the LORD (16:10-11).

The indictment continues for another three verses. A response then appears in the form of a brief psalm toward the chapter's conclusion. The response is not Jeremiah's, but is a model for the reader, who confesses: "our ancestors have inherited nothing but lies, worthless things in which there is no profit" (v. 19). A very similar anticipation of readers who are recipients of the punishment of their ancestors can be seen in the closing chapters of Deuteronomy: "When all of these things have happened to you . . . and you call them to mind among all the nations where I have driven you, and you return and obey, then the LORD God will have compassion . . ." (30:1ff.). Not for nothing have scholars insisted on close links between Jeremiah's editing and the shaping of the Deuteronomic traditions. Both are concerned that lessons from the past continue to address future readers.

In chapters 21–45, the next major section of Jeremiah, the situation of unmitigated judgment changes, at the same time a steady reader orientation is maintained. We still find clear sentences of judgment, though now with special emphasis on those exempted from the first exile of 597, who remain in the land with Jeremiah, as against those already carried off to Babylon (especially 24:1-10). And now a timetable for judgment is also introduced: seventy years, after which time God will do a new thing with his people, all of them, whenever they were exiled from the land. But the reader will also note a change over against chapters 7–20. Where before we had clear sentences of judgment, now we find a subjunctive note: "*perhaps* the LORD will change his mind," we now hear. Two key chapters in this section (26 and 36) register this note right away. "It may be that they will turn and listen, all of them, and will turn from their evil way" (26:3); "It may be that when the house of Judah hears of all the disaster that I intend to do to them, all of them may turn from their evil ways, so that I may forgive their iniquity and their sin" (36:3).

That these are not just rhetorical flourishes meant to underscore the heinous nature of Israel's disobedience when that eventually occurs is made clear by the fact that specific individuals *do* heed God's word spoken through the prophet. Not all heed the word, as God has held out for, but instead only a few, whose names are obscure but whose actions clearly show forth exemplary behavior at a time of great hardship: the elders who step forth to defend Jeremiah when he is brought before the prophet-killer Jehoiakim; the lone Ahikam, son of Shaphan, who rescues Jeremiah from danger in that same trial scene; Jeremiah's loyal assistant Baruch; and the obscure assembly of scribes and officials (Elishama, Delaiah ben Shemaiah, Elnathan ben Achbor, Gemariah ben Shaphan, Zedekiah ben Hananiah, Micaiah ben Gemariah) who, in stark contrast to Jehoiakim and his servants, shudder when the king burns God's word in a brazier used to heat his winter house. Earlier, when they heard the scroll read, they knew that what they heard was the word of God, meant to bring about repentance and divine forgiveness.

Here in this section of Jeremiah, the reader sees the emergence of a small but courageous remnant, who in the midst of hardship and a sentence of divine judgment are still able to trust in God's infinite mercy, at great risk to themselves, but confident in exercising the choice that will give them the right to stand together with Jeremiah against those who refuse God's mercies, as recipients of God's forgiveness. Their potential function as paradigms for a remnant in need of hope and forgiveness — a remnant confronted not by Jeremiah himself, but by the book of Jeremiah as a word of scripture — seems clear. In the final section (chs. 37–45) only two such figures stand out in the chiaroscuro of fear and equivocation on the eve of Judah's collapse. The foreigner Ebed-melek and the loyal Baruch are given their lives as a prize of war, because of the trust they have shown in God.

Now the final shaping of Jeremiah has not forced all the material into a tidy scheme whose chief purpose is to confront readers approaching the material as a scriptural word of address. But it has made allowance for a word once addressed by the prophet to past generations to sound forth beyond its own temporal horizon, to address readers of Jeremiah as scripture, in an intentional and not just a fortuitous manner. Moreover, the search for coherence in the final form, and even a direct reader orientation, has not just been artificially imposed, as though the choice were between the text as Rorschach, capable of an unlimited set of reader-imposed meanings, or a text with only one level of distinct intentionality. Rather, loose guidelines are set up to help the reader move through a very complex presentation, with a variety of past intentions whose force has not been obliterated in the final shaping process.

I have argued in another context for a similar sort of organizing lens focused not so much on readers but on the figure of Jeremiah as second Moses: an intercessor like Moses, but forbidden to intercede; a prophet who like Moses shares in the judgment over a disobedient generation; the prophet who refashions a burned scroll as once broken tablets were reconstituted at the foot of Sinai; one who singles out two special individuals exempt from the judgment on a generation, Ebed-melek and Baruch, as once Joshua and Caleb were given their lives as a prize of war; and one who brings to tragic conclusion a prophetic succession whose origins began with Moses in Egypt, now to be brought to conclusion there as well.[7] Again, this larger organizing lens does not totalize the individual chapters, nor is it the whim of readerships looking for unity and larger shape that are not in fact intended. It is what it is: a larger interpretive lens meant to provide loose organization and structure that will guide in interpreting the individual parts of the whole.

7. Ibid.

It seems to me there are several clear implications for parish Bible study of this sort of approach. First, original authorial intention, difficult to reconstruct on an older historical-critical model, is but one level of intentionality and it may well have been recast and reshaped in the final organization of a biblical book. Therefore, one needs to develop other sorts of instincts when reading biblical texts than ones chiefly concerned with what was early or original. As you can see, in this reading of Jeremiah I have shifted the focus from author as subject to reader as intended object of address. I have not rejected intentionality, but asked about it from the standpoint of readers.

Second, and related to this, it is important to try to find larger structure and coherence beyond the scope of an individual passage. This is especially difficult, since in the church's liturgical use of the Bible very rarely if ever do we read through a book chapter by chapter. But such a possibility is available in parish Bible study, even if it means paraphrasing and skipping over passages from time to time. Even then, nothing prohibits one from at least raising the question as to what the present organization of the material seems to be intending. And finally, it is always important to ask whether the material as it presently confronts us speaks a word to readers rather directly, and not just obliquely or through special critical reconstruction. What I have in mind here is not lifting the plain sense of the text immediately into a higher spiritual or personal realm, but rather asking how and why this text has, within the context of other texts, addressed previous generations of hearers, whose ranks have now swollen to include us, in the late twentieth century, in our particular corner of Christ's church.

III

Now to Isaiah. This is a much more complicated literary witness than the book of Jeremiah. The book does not divide easily into sections. It is no longer clear that even the rough-and-ready divisions First Isaiah, Second Isaiah, and Third Isaiah are particularly apposite, though a distinction between former things as comprising chapters 1–33 or 1–39 and latter and new things, chapters 40–66, does seem reasonable.[8]

8. See my "On the Question of Divisions Internal to the Book of Isaiah," in *SBL 1993 Seminar Papers* (Atlanta: Scholars, 1993) 260-66.

In what follows, I will be focusing on (1) the opening chapter and the final two chapters, which have much in common; (2) the two narrative sections in the book, chapters 7–8 and 36–39, the first section having to do with King Ahaz, and the second with King Hezekiah; (3) particularly chapter 8, which speaks of Immanuel in promise, but joins with the promise images of stumbling and conspiracy — this paradoxical combination is, I believe, important. Promise as blessing and as a stone that causes stumbling is a note sounded very frequently in the NT with reference to Isaiah 8. Again my focus overall will be to attend to the way the material has been shaped to address readers.

In trying to explain an order preserved in rabbinic notices, where Jeremiah is first, Ezekiel second, and Isaiah third, the rabbis said that Jeremiah is all judgment, Ezekiel half judgment and half salvation, and Isaiah all salvation. Now a survey of the contents of the books would not bear this out, except in general terms. But in another sense the order is meaningful: Jeremiah presents a past historical judgment that the reader participates in retrospectively. Isaiah, on the other hand, places the reader in a world where judgment has occurred, but where the final climax of God's plans lies on the horizon, for both the reader as well as reconstructed speakers and audience in the book itself. To illustrate this, I will summarize my own emerging picture of Isaiah's complicated coherence, based on two previous books, *Zion's Final Destiny* and *Isaiah 1–39.*[9]

Precritical readers, Luther, Calvin, and Ibn Ezra among them, saw as do moderns the significance of a major division of Isaiah at chapter 40. Here is where the most hopeful notes — heard as salvation both by the rabbis and by Charles Jennens, librettist for Handel's Messiah — are most clearly sounded, as against the more complicated mixture of judgment and salvation found in chs. 1–39, what would come to be called "First Isaiah." Moreover, the final chapters of this first half of Isaiah, chs. 36–39, represent the culmination of much that precedes, suggesting a fitting conclusion: first by showing Hezekiah to be the promised faithful counterpoint to a disbelieving and therefore disestablished Ahaz in fulfillment of 7:14; 9:1-7; and 32:1-8 (familiar Advent texts) and second by giving a very concrete example of the proper fulfillment of Isaiah's subtle Zion theology. As von Rad and others have noted, Isaiah takes the promises of the Zion psalms

---

9. *Zion's Final Destiny: The Development of the Book of Isaiah* (Minneapolis: Fortress, 1991); *Isaiah 1–39* (Interpretation: A Bible Commentary for Teaching and Preaching; Louisville: Westminster/John Knox, 1993).

— that God would protect king and city against the cosmic and concrete onslaughts of the nations — and turns them on their head, particularly in chs. 28–31.[10] There especially the nations are depicted as coming in judgment: "And the multitude of the nations that fight against Ariel shall be like a dream . . . so shall the nations be that fight against Mount Zion" (29:7-8). Yet this turning on the head is not absolute but partial. God will allow the nations kept at bay in the psalms to come in cleansing judgment, but will then rout these same nations, allowing them to "reach only to the neck, sweeping into Judah like a flood," as the image of 8:8 earlier made clear. "So the LORD of Hosts will come down to fight upon Mount Zion . . . [to] protect it and deliver it, he will spare and rescue it" (31:4-5). Immanuel and Zion will be finally and mysteriously saved. Now this is the image so clearly presented in chapters 36–38, with the blasphemous Assyrians — the quintessence of national hubris — turned back, a remnant preserved, and a king who saves a city from sentence of death through quietness and confidence, which was earlier Isaiah's counsel to Ahaz.

But these same previous chapters (7–8) also made clear that the glorious deliverance would not be universally experienced, any more than Sennacherib would fail to capture all the fortified cities of Judah before turning to Jerusalem. In chapter 8, where the deliverance is foreshadowed in the language of the psalms, following hard upon the vision of future redemption (see vv. 9-10), the text turns to the sort of imagery and paradoxical language of promise for which Isaiah is characteristic. God will be a sanctuary — but one that causes stumbling: a trap and a snare for the inhabitants of Jerusalem (8:14). Next to the promise of Immanuel, reiterated at 8:8 and 8:10, there is the image of conspiracy and stumbling (8:11-15). God's gracious acts of deliverance are ironically connected with conspiracy, fear, and dread, leaving only the possibility that a remnant will respond to Isaiah's instruction and teaching (8:16-22).

It is striking that this is the same collection of images with which the book opens. In chapter 1, instead of a call narrative we have an exhortation to a sinful people, already chastised and curiously unwilling to heed God's call to cleansing and obedience. The image of daughter Zion in v. 26, left as a booth in a vineyard, matches perfectly the picture of delivered Zion in chs. 36–38. But where deliverance should have led to thanksgiving and rejoicing, we find instead the sort of stumbling and conspiracy spoken of in chapter 8.

10. Gerhard von Rad, *Old Testament Theology* II (New York: Harper and Row, 1960) 155-69.

"Offspring of evildoers . . . why do you seek further beatings? . . . your country lies desolate. . . . Hear the word of the LORD, rulers of Sodom . . . cease to do evil, learn to do good." In trying to come to terms with this odd introductory chapter, which drops us down in the middle of things — literally — commentators have suggested that we have an overture, a text that sounds the major notes of the wider First Isaiah collection, composed after the fact and with an explicit eye toward introduction. More recently, it has been argued that the chapter is an overture to the entire book, and the links to chapters 65–66 have been pointed out. It is critical to come to terms with especially this chapter's function since it is the reader's point of entry to the book of Isaiah. Where frequently in the opening chapters of prophetic books attention is paid to the prophets' reception of the word of God, here a divine word, with heaven and earth as witnesses, is addressed directly to sinful Israel.

The question of the chapter's status as an overture, and to what, is important. "Overture" suggests an almost aesthetic effort to bring together the various themes found in what follows, as though without such an external and preliminary depiction of links in the contents that follow, we would be confused as readers — which we may well be anyway! Recently it has been pointed out that the chapter does a poor job of summarizing the contents of Second Isaiah, at least to any obvious extent, and so even granting the links to the final chapters in Third Isaiah, which could be explained as conscious reiteration of chapter 1, the chapter does seem to function best with reference to chapters 1–39. Still, I am skeptical about the terms "overview" or "overture" if by this is meant a secondary effort to summarize key themes in 1–39 or 1–66 from a hand that had the material fully formed before him. Instead, I prefer to see the chapter functioning with reference to the problem of conspiracy in chapters 7–8 and scenes of Zion's deliverance in 36–39, especially given the single concrete image in the chapter: the delivered but recalcitrant Zion of verse 26. Chapter 1, then, is not an overview, but the lens through which to read what follows, with special attention to the sinful people who have not seen in Zion's sparing the hand of God and the cause for repentance.

The chapter does adumbrate important elements of Isaiah's message in the context of exhortation: that a sinful Israel (vv. 2-4), bent on self-destruction (vv. 5-9), must be gleaned by the nations in judgment (vv. 24-25), so that afterward a righteous Zion will emerge (vv. 26-27), with those in rebellion destroyed (vv. 28-31). In First Isaiah the chief nation dispatched for judgment was Assyria. But the original pattern — cleansing

Assyrian judgment, Zion's deliverance, refusal to heed, possibility of righteous remnant — holds the potential for greater amplification beyond the experience of Isaiah and eighth-century Israel. This is accomplished by placing an oracle against Babylon (in chs. 13–14) within a series of "outstretched arm" passages connected with Assyria (five in chs. 5–10 and one in ch. 14). In this way, the two nations — both with key roles to play vis-à-vis Judah, though separated by centuries — are conflated. Assyria's role of judgment and then halting anticipates that of Babylon much later.

Now what effect does this have on our reading of chapter 1? Mention there of God pouring out his wrath on his enemies (v. 24) anticipates nicely the eventual judgment, not just of Assyria and Babylon, but of all the nations enumerated in chapters 13–27. Babylon's final halting is depicted in Second Isaiah, with daughter Zion elevated following the descent of daughter Babylon, which is promised in chapters 13–14 and then brought to fulfillment in chapters 47–48. Edom's promised destruction in chapter 34, meant to usher in a period of peace and rejuvenated creation, is accomplished in chapter 63, where the LORD himself in bloodstained raiment appears to announce victory to his people.

Chapter 1, then, holds the potential for sounding a note quite special to the book of Isaiah as a whole, and this involves the role of the nations. Here the contrast with Jeremiah is again illuminating. In chapter 1 of Jeremiah, the prophet is called a prophet "to nations and kingdoms" (1:5, 10). The passage has struck interpreters as curious given Jeremiah's steady, indigenous concern with Judah and Jerusalem. At the same time, it is clear that the passage seeks to tie the message of plucking up and tearing down, not just to God's own people Israel, but also to the nations at large. These nations are mentioned in an extended section similar to Isaiah 13–27, at the conclusion of the MT (Jeremiah 46–51) and in the middle of the LXX (spliced into chapter 25). Still, for all the potential in Jer 1:10 for treating Israel as just one of the nations, its destiny is quite distinctive. Israel is to be plucked up and then built and planted following a seventy-year term of judgment; the nations are at most built and planted for a mission of judgment, but then they are torn down finally and completely. The culmination of this is to be found in chapters 50–51, where once mighty Babylon is decisively annihilated.

The relationship between the fate of Israel and the fate of the nations is handled differently in Isaiah. Within the nations section itself (chs. 13–23), there are indications that God's dealing with the nations beyond Israel's borders may involve blessing, or to use the language of Jeremiah, building and planting, and not just tearing down and plucking up. Listen to 19:24-25, the conclusion of the oracle concerning Egypt: "On that day Israel will be a third with Egypt and Assyria, a blessing in the midst of the earth, whom the LORD of hosts has blessed, saying, 'Blessed be Egypt my people, and Assyria the work of my hands, and Israel my heritage.' " One should be careful not to hear in Isaiah an orgy of inclusion for its own sake, nor a demotion of Israel vis-à-vis the nations. It is simply that having exposed Israel to the judgment of the nations, having treated Israel in the manner reserved for the nations meriting God's wrath in the Psalms — precisely because Israel has refused to be God's people — God then turns his eye to these peoples and their destinies as nations. Chapter 1 clearly anticipates what will be a major theme of the entire Isaiah collection, setting it off from Jeremiah and Ezekiel, when it begins with an appeal to a sinful nation *(goy),* with the whole creation as witness, addressing Israel as if her rulers were those of another people (Sodom and Gomorrah), and when the scene of judgment as it is portrayed in vv. 24-26 includes Israel in the generic catalogue of God's foes. To state the positive side of this flattening of national distinctions, one needs only turn to the unit following chapter 1, Isaiah's vision concerning Judah and Jerusalem (2:1-4). Here again Israel is addressed in the context of the "many peoples" — who now all come to learn Torah at Zion.

From the very beginning, then, the reader learns that God's dealing with the sinful nation Israel will ultimately involve the nations at large. The judgment of the nations, like the judgment over Israel, unfolds clearly in the presentation of the larger book, especially in chs. 13–23. Zion's dramatic deliverance in 701, reported in the final chapters of "First Isaiah," no longer serves as the culmination of Isaiah's complex judgment-salvation message; chapter 1 encourages us to regard this deliverance as but an occasion for repentance, which if missed, will surely lead to a yet more dramatic cleansing, reaching beyond the neck to overwhelm Zion herself — something that chapter 1 with its odd combination of exhortation and announcement of judgment seems to suggest has in fact occurred.

Moreover, the culminating account of Zion's deliverance in chs. 36–38 no longer forms the dramatic conclusion of a separated First Isaiah book. Framing chapters on front (34–35) and back (37) function to loosen the deliverance from its precise historical setting and place it in the larger context of God's dealings with Zion and the nations.[11] Chapter 39 antic-

---

11. See n. 8 above and the essay cited there.

ipates a time when Assyrian threats will be replaced by those of mighty Babylon, this time reaching beyond Zion's neck to touch even the LORD's anointed. Chapters 34–35, with notes long acknowledged to be similar to those heard in Second Isaiah, asks us to hear the account of Zion's deliverance, not as past record alone, but as a testimony to God's abiding concern for Zion, even given the judgment over her and her king that is yet to come at the hands of the mighty Babylonians. Second Isaiah chapters testify to God's will to bring Zion back to life, to "marry her" and see to her continued bounty and blessing, returning to her children once cut off, defeating those who once threatened to obliterate her in a manner far outstripping the more circumscribed task of judgment envisioned for Assyria in chapters 5–11.

Notice how the horizon of chapter 1 remains the horizon of the book at large and of every reader who enters this highly complex world of historical reference and typological linkage. The opening chapter looks forward to Zion's status as faithful city and the destruction of those who refuse to honor the Holy One of Israel. This final scene of destruction, depicted in vv. 28-31, is not aimed at nations or the collective Israel: it involves individuals and the decisions they chose to make as individuals. "Rebels and sinners shall be destroyed together, and those who have forsaken the LORD shall be consumed." Chapters 40–66 never depict Zion's full recovery and completed status as faithful city, as much as this is promised and reiterated, promised and reiterated. Neither do the nations stream to Zion as chapter 2 envisioned, even as often God announces their eventual visitation, to adorn and do service both with Israel and at Israel's behest. What chapter 1 strains to see, the final chapters simply reiterate, with the same mixed tone of caution and exhortation, promise and expectation.

Attention to the reader has not been secondarily spliced into a past historical record, as in Jeremiah; rather, it belongs to the warp and woof of Isaiah in its emerging and final presentation. Chapter 1 means to provide a lens through which what follows can be properly interpreted. Central to understanding Isaiah is *God's dealing with Israel within the destinies of the nations at large.* This is Isaiah's unique and sustained contribution within the major prophets. The nations will eventually come to worship at Zion, not because of any moral or theological change of heart — on their part or on the part of Israel toward them — but only because God wills it. The nations come to no new understanding of the centrality of Israel's God and of his special relationship to them through his Torah, on their own.

It is that the one God of Israel announces to his people through the vision of Isaiah that he means to have fellowship with all flesh, if even against their will or as a consequence of their submission and sacrificial offering, within and on behalf of Israel and Zion.

The final two chapters of the book appear in many ways to reiterate the message of chapter 1. Where we began is where we leave this book, with the testimony behind us of God's will to deal with Israel and the nations already clearly manifested on the canvas of human time and space. At the conclusion we hear the same concern as earlier, chiefly with right worship and the proper hallowing of God's holy mountain, for only then will wolf lie down with lamb (65:25), exactly as chapter 11 had once seen it. God's creation of new heavens and a new earth in the final two chapters conjures up more than apocalyptic transformation — the mundane giving way to the transhistorical. New heavens and new earth mean that the former things can be forgotten, that the witnesses once called in chapter 1 to hear God's indictment against his people and his enemies at large are now dismissed. Jerusalem is to be created anew, as chapter 1 foresaw. The Zion with evil offspring is replaced by a Zion who delivers children without travail, who nurse and are satisfied at her consoling breast. These are joined by the nations at the farthest extremes of God's creation, reassembling the table of nations of Genesis 10. "All flesh will come to worship before me," the book sonorously concludes. And the same note of warning that concluded chapter 1 sounds again, invoking now the image of the dead Assyrians from chapter 37, who had the day before blasphemed God outside the gates of Zion. Here there is no whiff of punishment for the non-Israelite only, but of any individual who rebels, the same note sounded at the conclusion of chapter 1.

To conclude. The rabbis were right to see a significant distinction between Jeremiah and Isaiah and to regard even the curious, non-chronological order Jeremiah, Ezekiel, Isaiah as requiring explanation. Ironically, from a modern critical standpoint, the order might well be seen as chronological after all, given the presence of so much late material in the book and especially the way coherence has been sought in what are demonstrably the latest stages of the book's development, post-dating Ezekiel and Jeremiah. At the same time, Isaiah is not "all salvation." Past events of both judgment and deliverance, involving Israel and the nations, are used as object lessons for the reader, and in this sense chapter 1 sets the proper tone for the point of entry into Isaiah's sixty-six-chapter presentation. On the other hand, it is clear that the book strains toward a horizon that lies beyond the characters and audiences in the book itself and beyond the reader who waits just as ardently in chapter 66 as in chapter 1 for the fulfillment of God's vision vouchsafed to Isaiah. Isaiah is not so much "all salvation" as a witness to "salvation for all" — or to use the idiom with which the book closes and which plays so central a role in all that precedes: God means that all flesh shall come and worship him, the Holy One of Israel.

As in Jeremiah, so also in Isaiah, parish Bible study should ask how the reader is being addressed by the book as a whole. The answer that is given will not be an exact replication of my own reading, but will come as those participating become familiarized with the contents and structure, the whole shape of this magnificent testimony. Then one might also hope to hear the book in something of the same manner as the New Testament heard it, as a single complex vision of Isaiah. Or listen to the testimony of Sirach, not much more than a century and a half before the coming of Christ:

> In Isaiah's days the sun went backward,
>   and he prolonged the life of the king.
> By his dauntless spirit he saw the future,
>   and comforted the mourners in Zion.
> He revealed what was to occur to the end of time,
>   and the hidden things before they happened (48:23-25).

Former things, new things, latter things: distinct, but related in Isaiah's vision. Not just "someone else's mail" but a divine correspondence in which we who are among the nations learn that Israel's God means to be our God, so that together with Israel and all flesh we might come and offer him right worship, without which we cannot live, hope, or love as God would have us.

But several questions remain. What of the royal themes sounded so prominently in chs. 7, 9, 11, and 32? What place does Israel's messiah play in the vision of Isaiah and the worship of all nations? These questions are the business of the next chapter, where we consider how Isaiah has been heard in the New Testament. Then too we can measure the extent to which this complex vision, as I have set it forth for parish Bible study, is the same vision heard by the New Testament in the proclamation of the gospel of Jesus Christ. So we are not finished, but only halfway through. By my own strictures, it is not enough for the Christian community to hear Isaiah's *per se* voice in isolation. We must press ahead to hear Isaiah as the New Testament has heard this witness, *in novo receptum.* What we need to be prepared to find in the New Testament's *per se* witness, however, is a charge to return to the Old in order to comprehend the final Christian hope: a hope that may link us again to the Israel from whom we first sprung, who taught us to look for the light that would arise and draw all nations to God. It is this reciprocal character of the Old in the New, the New in the Old, that sets the context for confronting the gospel in all its richness and depth, the gospel of Jesus Christ, son of God, the God of Israel and the hope of all the nations.[12] We have looked at Isaiah's *per se* witness. How it is heard in the New Testament and then in turn shapes the New Testament's final hope is the concern of the next chapter.

---

12. Compare the otherwise provocative and helpful remarks of Francis Watson on a late modern christological interpretation of the Old Testament (*Text and Truth: Redefining Biblical Theology* [Grand Rapids: Eerdmans, 1997]).

$\approx$ 15 $\approx$

Isaiah in New Testament, Lectionary, Pulpit

I

In previous chapters I have voiced concern that a major problem facing biblical studies is the divorced character of the disciplines of Old and New Testament study, at a wide variety of levels. To read the Old apart from the New, or even the Hebrew Scriptures apart from the Talmud, threatens to create a misleading *tertium quid:* an "objective" way of reading these scriptures that need not worry about theological or normative issues, that can detach these writings from the concrete, particular claims of two distinct religious bodies and their own respective histories of reading, or that argues that the plain sense of scripture is essentially a historical sense, derived from critical analysis and free from the presuppositions of our modern context. Theological concerns come then as an add-on, supplied by religious communities, based upon appropriate historical analogy to the modern situation.

We have certainly learned over the past two centuries that one needs to attend to the foreignness and the particularity of the word of Old and New, apart from one another and relocated in the proper historical setting. However, if a concern of canonical shaping, understood precisely on historical grounds, is to span the gap between original audience and eventual readership, then it would be wrong to give higher priority to original contexts than to that final creative shaping, as though readers were scientists arriving to inspect an ancient artifact with which they were utterly unfamiliar. The choice is not between objectivity and subjectivity or be-

213

tween perspectives behind the text over against those in front of the text. Rather, the choice is between regarding canonical shaping as a political enterprise (the power of the final hand over a tractable legacy) or as the effort to release an ancient and particular word to a natural readership anticipated by the final shapers of biblical books, who themselves stand under the legacy they strain to hear, interpret, and hand on.

In previous chapters I have referred to the provocative image Paul van Buren has used to illustrate what it means for Christians to read Israel's scriptures — what he calls "reading someone else's mail." When van Buren speaks of "someone else's mail" he means not to relativize the Old on account of the New's hearing of it, but rather to remind the Christian church that the Old, in the first instance, was someone else's *scripture.* Israel's scriptures are a form of correspondence from a particular God to a particular people — the same God Christians confess as having raised Jesus from the dead — and not preamble to be historically recontextualized, even on theological grounds based on a notion of revelation in events *behind* the literature. The church gains beneficial access to the Old on account of Christ's inclusion of the Gentiles in God's eternal plans with his people Israel. Christians are given an invitation, then, to read the Hebrew Scriptures, someone else's mail, as their own, in the form that they were received, an "Old Testament" witness now related to the New Testament.

One concern of these essays has been to argue that the foreignness of the Old — what Barth called "the strange world within the Bible" — consists in something other than its oldness or its historical distance from the church.[1] Rather, the "strangeness" — felt in different ways by modern Jews and Christians — has to do with the special character of God's revelation vouchsafed to Israel. This character, it has been argued, resists both universalization or tranformation into general religious experience and insight. God's revelation to Israel is fully encountered when one respects the particular canonical shape into which Israel has cast its testimony to God, hence the priority given to final or fuller literary form. Christ reveals, opens up, unlocks, displays publicly, that specific shape to those outside the commonwealth of Israel, to the church. He does this not by ignoring its particularity — even down to jot and tittle — but by filling it full in accordance with its own aims and central message.

When the Christian reads Isaiah as *per se* Old Testament witness,

1. Karl Barth, "The Strange World within the Bible."

there is of course a considerable potential for overlap between the way he or she reads it and the way a modern Jew might read it who likewise seeks to hear its *per se* voice. The distance from Sirach to the New Testament is not all that great in terms of how they each approached Isaiah, despite the fact that one represents an avowedly Christian perspective and the other one from within the bosom of Israel. Here a caution is set beside van Buren's central image: one should not press the "someone else's mail" metaphor too hard.[2] The Christian reads the message of Isaiah as promise that God's ways with Israel will eventually have to do with the worship of Israel's God by all flesh; it is this Holy One of Israel that the church confesses raised Jesus from the dead so that those far off might be brought near. Sirach and the New Testament agree that Isaiah is a prophet who speaks about the future, the former emphasizing this for its own sake, the latter drawing specific conclusions based upon the content of Isaiah related to Christ and the life of the church.

As we will see in this essay, it would be wrong to assume that the New read the Old willy-nilly as predictive, as though the hermeneutic reflected in the New was flat-footedly one dimensional in respect of the Old. Hard readings are hard readings, and some are harder than others; but the Old does not become a blank page onto which any New Testament construal can take form. I hope to show that in many respects the New's hearing of Isaiah is very close to the reading set forth in the previous chapter through a simple effort to understand Isaiah's canonical shape. In other words, the concern to describe Isaiah's *per se* witness need not be antithetical to the New's hearing. At times it is fully consistent with it, and clearly based on it — which would have been important if Christian apologetic was to be at all effective in demonstrating that God's act in Jesus Christ was "in accordance with the scriptures" (1 Cor 15:3), since these scriptures were shared by both Israel and the church. Only on these terms can the Old be profitably understood as "someone else's mail," not simply to be subsumed under what the New says about it. Let us see how the New's hearing of Isaiah illustrates this more abstract hermeneutical observation.

2. See also the cautions registered in section one, on Biblical Theology, above.

II

It has been noted that Isaiah is quoted in the New Testament more than any other book of the Old, Psalms falling in second place. Surely this has to do with Isaiah's perspective having been understood, by Sirach among others, as involving the future: a future the church understands as having now arrived, in Christ, en route toward its final *telos*. One might be tempted to say that a book of prophecy having relatively more to say about the Davidic line than other prophets — consider the Immanuel passages, the centrality of Hezekiah, the promise of a shoot sprouting from the stump of Jesse, the promise of a righteous king adorned with a girdle of faithfulness, or on whose shoulders right government rests — that such a prophetic witness to the future, joined with concern for the restored branch of David, might tip the scale cleanly in favor of Isaiah as most-quoted Old Testament witness in the New. But how much is this perspective the effect of lectionary pairings with which the church is now over-familiar, especially those in Advent which link Jesus' birth to Isaiah 7, 9, and 11 and the promise of a coming righteous king — not to mention popular Advent and Christmas hymnody — and how much belongs to the actual witness of the New to Isaiah? Put another way, does the heavy distribution of Isaiah references in the New involve Jesus' claimed messiahship, or does it reflect something else?

There is not time to deal with such a question in detail, surveying every book of the New Testament to see how Isaiah has been heard. On the other hand, a brief survey is possible. Let us begin by looking at Matthew, a book concerned with prophecy and fulfillment, and one that opens with an extended section concerning the birth of Christ replete with Old Testament citation. We will move from Matthew to the other Synoptics, to Paul, to Acts, and finally to the book of Revelation, often overlooked as an important New Testament witness to Isaiah.

There are several explicit Old Testament quotes in the first four chapters of Matthew, at least three from Isaiah. What is striking is that *none of them pick up Isaiah's royal texts for their own sake* to show that Jesus is the messiah promised of old by God's prophets. Even the first one, Matt 1:23, which quotes from the LXX of Isa 7:14, is more concerned to establish Jesus' virgin birth and divinity ("God with us") than to say that he is the messiah promised of old. The second, Matt 3:3, interprets the obscure voice of Isaiah 40:3 — a crux to this day for biblical scholars — as none other than John the Baptist, by understanding, via the LXX, the

216

voice of Isaiah 40 speaking not *about* the wilderness, but *in* the wilderness. The third, Matt 4:15, flirts with the messianic text of Isa 9:1-7 — yet not its chief content, concerning the righteous king, but its capacity to explain Jesus' withdrawal to Galilee, "land of Zebulun, land of Naphtali" (Isa 9:1). Of course it has been argued that partial quotes imply wider Old Testament context for the knowledgeable reader, and that may be true to some extent here, but the larger point is still that Isaiah is quoted by Matthew in ways that pass over or only obliquely draw on seemingly pertinent royal texts. Isaiah is quoted at two other places in Matthew to illustrate Israel's hard-heartedness, as was once experienced by Isaiah the prophet (13:14; 15:8). Another very prominent text from Isaiah quoted by Matthew is the so-called first servant song of Isa 42:1-4, a text not often regarded as royal and probably not utilized by Matthew for that reason anyway. When Matthew cites this text, the point at issue involves Jesus' mission to the Gentiles, as stressed in Isa 42:18 and 42:21 and, as we have seen, a very prominent theme in Isaiah as a whole.

A quick survey of the other Synoptics would show no essential departure from Matthew in respect of use of Isaiah. Luke does have Jesus offering a provocative liturgical reading of Isaiah 61, where he says that the text is about himself! But again the emphasis is not on Jesus' messianic claim but on his spirit-filled mission to the poor, as this is spoken of in Isaiah 61. In a sort of collage citation, Acts 15:16 quotes Amos, Jeremiah, and Isaiah to the effect that God will rebuild the booth of David; but in concluding with a citation from Isaiah, the emphasis shifts back to the same prominent theme: the inclusion of the Gentiles, based for the author of Acts on a loose reading of Isa 45:21.

Near the conclusion of Romans 9 (v. 32) — again having to do with the status of Israel vis-à-vis the church — Paul alludes to Isa 8:14-15, a text treated in our previous chapter. Paul refers to the sanctuary that causes stumbling to explain Israel's failure to fulfill the law through works. He also quotes Isaiah 65 to explain the gospel's rejection by Israel and acceptance by Gentiles (Rom 10:20-21), but then another Third Isaiah text (59:20-21) to demonstrate that all Israel will eventually be saved (Rom 11:26-27). He concludes these three chapters of Romans by directing his hearers to the unsearchable character of God's ways — with Israel and with the Gentiles — by referring to Isa 40:13: "For who has known the mind of the Lord? Or who has been his counselor?" (Rom 11:34). Still, in all this the emphasis remains not on Isaiah showing that Christ fulfills the prophets' royal hopes, but more on Isaiah pointing to the worship of Israel's

God by those brought near in Christ and explaining why Israel has rejected the gospel: they are the same hardhearted nation Isaiah addressed of old. The single reference to Isaiah's "root of Jesse" at Romans 15:12 again serves the primary purpose of establishing Christ's mission to the Gentiles, rather than his simple fulfillment of Isaianic royal hopes as such.

Now what are we to make of the strong overshadowing of Isaiah's royal texts by those concerning God's purposes for the Gentiles? Obviously it is tricky to conjecture and draw conclusions from what is not said. Having said that the New Testament's hearing of the Old ought not totalize the Old's *per se* voice, we can hardly object when it has not done that. Still, the silence is striking, and it extends beyond Isaiah's specific royal passages to others like it elsewhere in the prophets (for example, Jeremiah's righteous branch and new covenant). To note an exception here and there, or to point to more subtle allusions, still establishes the general point as our survey of specific New Testament citations of Isaiah has made clear: the New Testament passes over in silence seemingly pertinent royal passages from the book of Isaiah.

Several possibilities for explaining this silence suggest themselves. First, the character of the argument and the context in which it was made were what determined the Old Testament quotations utilized, and the more important point to be established was Jesus' mission to the Gentiles, not his messiahship per se. While this may be true, it would still explain neither the degree of overshadowing nor the absence of these texts from so wide a range of New Testament witnesses, making different arguments for different contexts.

A second possibility is that the New Testament drew a distinction between Isaiah's word of *past* historical address and a word of address having to do with God's *future* plans. That is, Isaiah's word to the royal house was just that: a word having to do with Ahaz and Hezekiah as past figures, as the superscription to Isaiah made clear, and not to future Davidic figures. Is it the case, then, that Isaiah's complex unity and word to the future was not so much interested in the future of the royal house as such (something modern scholars interested in the unity of Isaiah have argued)? The problem here is, on the one hand, that Isaiah 11 does appear to depict a future royal figure and, on the other, that a sharp distinction between Old Testament word directed to the future and word riveted to the past is doubtless an artificial one for the New Testament.

A third possibility: did Isaiah, and other prophetic witnesses, speak about Israel's coming messiah in ways about which there was some Jewish consensus contemporary with but decidedly not shared by the New Testament, whose authors saw in Jesus radical discontinuity with Old Testament promises? This might explain, for example, why, when royal texts are cited, they are cited somewhat obliquely or with a specific emphasis on Jesus' mission to the Gentiles. So Paul does not cite Isa 11:1-9, the main oracle concerning the root of Jesse, but rather the gloss that follows the oracle and makes the point that this root will "stand as a signal to the peoples; the nations will inquire of him, and his dwelling shall be glorious" (Isa 11:10; Rom 15:12).

There is a more specific form of this third option that we should consider. One way of interpreting the New's silence would be to say that the promises of the Old regarding the coming Davidic king stressed political and civil authority, whereas Christians confessed a crucified Jesus, emptied of political and civil authority, to be the hope of the ages. The notes sounded from Isaiah, then, would more appropriately have to do with God's intentions that all flesh would come to worship him, an unquestionably pervasive theme (see the discussion in the preceding chapter).

There is yet a fourth alternative, but it would ask us to view the New's relationship to the Old rather differently than the first three options, which basically understand the Old in the first instance as a more or less appropriate means by which to make arguments and clarifications regarding the mission and identity of Jesus, the success of which will further the gospel. According to the three views described above the silence of the New in respect of Isaiah's royal promises must be explained as having to do with principles of selection: the promises were incompatible, they had to do with the past, they were in discontinuity with the New's intention in showing Jesus to be the Christ, or they did not belong to the character of the argument or the logic of the narrative as such and were therefore immaterial rather than purposefully avoided. In each case, the New is understood as the proper lens by which to hear the Old.

But what if, and here we have the fourth alternative, the New's use of the Old were differently conceived. As we have seen, Paul was a pretty good reader of Isaiah, sounding precisely the sorts of notes we heard in the previous chapter when examining Isaiah's final canonical shape: notes having to do with Israel's hardheartedness and God's intentions that all flesh worship him, something Paul sees as having been wonderfully fulfilled in the work of God in Christ. And indeed one might assume that Paul's success in making these arguments about Christ turned in no small measure on the actual congruence of his exegesis with the message of Isaiah in its final shape, in the face of those who knew this shape as well as he did.[3] When, then, there is silence in the New concerning Isaiah's royal promises, might this be for reasons not of incompatability, discontinuity, or irrelevance — reasons that assume that the New intends to provide the primary lens for hearing the Old? Instead, what if the New operates with full knowledge that the Old will continue to be heard as its own *per se* witness, including passages that speak of hope for a coming righteous king, and not just on the terms in which the New hears it? Paul's concern to hear Isaiah rightly and on its own terms means that we ought to return to Isaiah and ask what role the royal promises now play in the final shape of the book.

III

It has been noted by scholars interested in the unity of the book of Isaiah that, while Isaiah is regarded as the prophet par excellence of Zion and king, royal language only appears in so-called First Isaiah. The silence we spoke about in the New is also a reality in regard to chapters 40–66. Indeed, chapter 39 concludes with a dire picture of Hezekiah's future offspring serving as "eunuchs" in the palace of the King of Babylon, which if taken literally, would mean the end of the Davidic line.

To explain this problem, scholars argue that royal promises have either (1) shifted to the figure of Cyrus, who is boldly called the Lord's anointed in 45:1, (2) been democratized and transferred to the people as a whole, this based on 55:3, where the eternal covenant to David is allegedly given over to the wider community, or (3) transferred to the priesthood, in view of the frequent concern with priest and cult and covenant in Third Isaiah. All these theories operate with a conception of Isaiah that sees earlier material in the book overtaken by successive interpretive levels, a notion that, while quite modern, probably cannot be transferred to the New's hearing of Isaiah to explain similar reticence to quote royal texts.

What is striking in the final shape of Isaiah is the persistence of the Zion focus, through all levels of the book's development, which can be contrasted with the royal concern. Whatever one might say of the capacity

---

3. I am indebted to Richard Hays for this comment.

of royal promises to continue to sound forth even when they are not explicitly referred to in chapters 40–66, it remains the case that chapters 40–66 are most interested in Zion's restitution, the return of Israel to Zion, and the streaming of the nations to Zion, and these themes are found in both halves of the book.

Now while we are asking about the New's failure to cite royal texts, it might be fair to ask what happened to the specific Zion focus of Isaiah? The answer involves a combination of three factors. In a fashion not often highlighted, to my mind, the New has clearly understood Zion, the special place of God's tabernacling with his people Israel, as now transferred to Christ, in whose flesh God was pleased to dwell. When Isaiah says "Arise, shine, for your light has come" (60:1), he is speaking of Jerusalem's exaltation, the holy mountain where the nations are to stream to learn Torah. Matthew's wise men, representatives of the nations, bring their gifts as Isaiah had foreseen, not to Jerusalem, but to the child himself in the house at Bethlehem. Add to this, secondly, the destruction of the temple not long after the death of Christ — foreshadowed by the tearing of the curtain when Jesus is crucified — and, thirdly, the book of Revelation's concern with the heavenly city, much of the description based upon Isaiah's vision of Zion-Jerusalem, and we can see how the New has in fact heard these Zion notes, but handled them in a fresh way. The streaming of the nations to Zion, as promised by Isaiah, is heard in the New as the promised worship by all flesh of the person of Jesus Christ. Psalm 132 speaks of Zion as God's desired place of habitation; the New Testament speaks of Christ as this same resting place.

Notice here that Isaiah's language concerning Zion went in two directions in the New. On the one hand, the language was translated through a bold reinterpretation: what was true of Zion has been filled with new and fuller content in Christ. But that was not the end of the matter, leaving the New to provide the more exhaustive and complete understanding of the Old's central image. The final book of the Christian canon returns to Isaiah for a yet fuller depiction of the *final* goal of Christian hope, beyond the incarnation, the worship of Christ's person and the inclusion of Gentiles in God's plans for humanity. Revelation 21 depicts (1) a new heaven and a new earth, with (2) the holy city Jerusalem coming down from heaven (3) like a bride — images that could serve as a definitive exegesis of the second half of Isaiah. The text of Isa 25:8 and the refrain of Second Isaiah is then directly quoted by the author: "he will wipe away every tear from their eyes. Death will be no more . . . for the first things have passed away" (Rev 21:4). The "first things" are of course not the Old's witness, which is quoted here to express the Christian final hope; the first things are things that have already passed away within Isaiah's own perspective. Even the final vision of Revelation 21, with no temple to be found, is not a repudiation of Isaiah but an exegesis of it based on Isa 66:1: "what is this temple you would build for me?" The other images used in Revelation — no sun or moon, nations and kings bringing glory to the Lamb, gates never shut, nothing unclean to be found — are all taken straight out of Isaiah, with the Lamb now sharing the stage with Zion.

Using this as an illustration of the way that the New interprets Isaiah and is then in turn interpreted by it in order to express the Christian final hope, what can we say about Isaiah's royal promises? These promises have not been ignored, repudiated, or seen as irrelevant; instead, given the reciprocal character[4] of the relationship between the two testaments just illustrated with the example of Zion, we are urged to return to Isaiah to see in the promises associated with the shoot of Jesse — promises of a fully restored creation, of the streaming of every nation, including Israel, to Zion to learn and do God's law, of a securely dwelling Jerusalem, of wolf and lamb dwelling together — a picture of the *final* Christian hope, of which the risen and ascended Christ is surety and pledge. The Old Testament is not authoritative only where it is *referred* to in the New, but also when it is *deferred* to; when what it has to say forms the final horizon of the church's hope under the present reign of Jesus Christ. While, in the New, Paul's concern and the concern of the Gospels may well be the rejection of Christ by those whose messiah he was, the witness of the Old in Isaiah reminds the church that rejection of the worship of God and the Lamb knows no national borders; where once Israel was hardhearted, the church who claims to be the new vineyard must now herself be on guard against the very rejection of which Isaiah warned Israel and the nations. In this way too the Old illumines the New and points to the common witness of them both to the selfsame divine reality. Not categorically "our mail" or "someone else's," but rather the mail of the one God who was and is and is to be and who, Isaiah reminds us, means to have his ways known by all flesh.

4. Compare here Francis Watson's christological approach in *Text and Truth: Redefining Biblical Theology* (Grand Rapids: Eerdmans, 1997).

IV

These remarks will be drawn together by turning to the practical consequences of the New's hearing of Isaiah for preaching and lectionary.

We have discussed the New Testament's hearing of Isaiah with special attention to the royal promises. What we see modeled in the New's relationship to the Old is a paradigm for both lectionary and preaching. The New does not just interpret the Old and provide its exhaustive and final point of reference. Having heard the New's reading of the Old, the Old also then interprets the New, setting forth its own final horizon. What, then, are the implications of such an understanding of the relationship between the Old and New for lectionary and pulpit?

First, the Christian Bible consists of Old and New Testaments. Dividing the testaments at any level (instructional, devotional, liturgical, homiletical) threatens either Marcionism or Judaizing. At the same time, it is extremely important to be clear about what the character of the relationship between the two actually is. The Christian tendency unfortunately merges almost immediately with the generic modern tendency, which is to understand the relationship as essentially developmental or evolutionary, with an emphasis on what is new over what is old (in line with our consumerist language: "new," "fresh," "just out," and even perhaps, "the New RSV").[5] This is further tempting for Christians because in fact the Old remains scripture for another community of faith in a way untrue of the New; and for the modern, because of an inevitable bias toward developmental frameworks of understanding — a bias now being eroded from the angle of deconstruction. Such a tendency means that how the Old has been heard in the New will *a priori* be the proper way to understand the Old as such, if the Old is to retain any authority at all. Understanding the Old primarily as Israelite religion, even for the best of reasons, will still diminish its present authority for Christian religion or raise the perennial objections of Bultmann or Wellhausen that common religious outlook is certainly *not* the link that binds the Old and New together.

I have attempted to argue, on the basis of the New's own witness, for a different conception, one that returns the church to hear the witness of the Old as illuminating the New, and not just the reverse, precisely

---

5. See my remarks in "On Not Changing 'Old Testament' to 'Hebrew Bible,'" *Pro Ecclesia* 6 (1997) 136-40.

where there is an apparent silence or muting in the New's reception of the Old. Deference, not critical discontinuity, may be a correct interpretation of the New's attitude in respect of certain key themes. On what authority did Paul get the notion that all Israel would be saved if not on the authority of the Old's persistent *per se* voice? Here is an example of explicit deference, not just implied deference. We have argued that Isaiah's witness to Israel's messiah forms the horizon of the book of Revelation and its witness to the second coming, even as that same witness is not prevalent in the gospel's description of the first coming. The problem here is rejection and seeming defeat — humanly speaking — freeing Isaiah's messianic language to describe a final victory and a restored creation only foreshadowed in that first Easter triumph.

This understanding of the Old's relationship to the New extends beyond an assessment of Isaiah's royal language. To choose but one other prominent example from Isaiah, the suffering servant song of chs. 52–53, here is another text that plays surprisingly little role in the Passion narratives of the New, where we might have expected to hear its notes sounded. Yet what text better penetrates to the mystery of the passion and its implications for Christian belief than this one, which originally addressed another time and circumstance? Indeed it is difficult, if not impossible, for the Christian hearing "all we like sheep have gone astray . . . and the LORD has laid on him the iniquity of us all" to bracket out the Passion of Christ altogether in the name of a fair search for Isaiah's real historical referent. Here, for different reasons than those that obtain for the royal promises, the New is illumined by the Old's *per se* voice, a voice once directed to another audience with another burden, but now witnessing to the work of God in Christ.

Let me conclude by looking at two representative selections from the lectionary where the book of Isaiah is the Old Testament reading. By looking at royal texts from Isaiah and the way they have been heard or deferred to in the New, I have set forth a particular way of understanding the reciprocal nature of the relationship between Old and New that I believe is consistent with the form of Christian scripture as this has been bequeathed to us. In an essay to follow (chapter 21) I wish to show in more detail how the present lectionary, with three readings, is open to misinterpretation of the character of Old and New in their dialectical relationship. "Old in light of New, New in light of Old" is most clearly set forth when the reading of one is followed immediately by the other, with no third thing intruding on this relationship.

The two lectionary pairings to be discussed here are (1) Proper 22 from Year A: Isaiah's song of the vineyard (5:1-7) and Matthew's parable of the vineyard (21:33-43), and (2) the set of Advent readings for Year A that pair Isaiah with Matthew. What is the nature of the relationship between these readings, based on our understanding of Isaiah in Old and New? What happens when Isaiah is heard as a word of Christian scripture, and not just as preamble to the New?

One way of hearing Matthew's parable of the vineyard in Proper 22 would be as the central text asserting that the vineyard has been taken from Israel and given to the church: "therefore I tell you, the kingdom of heaven will be taken away from you — the wicked tenants — and given to a people that produces the fruits of the kingdom" (Matt 21:43). Hearing the New apart from the Old — where the New provides the final interpretation of the Old — reinforces such an interpretation. The now classic text of Isa 8:14 — the stone that crushes one who falls on it — is alluded to in the final verse (v. 44) and appears to support an interpretation of Matthew's Jewish opponents — Pharisees and high priest — as those crushed. Even when one hears Isaiah's parable of the vineyard read before this gospel lesson the effect might be to underscore that Israel failed to be good tenants of the vineyard in Isaiah's day, and so too they failed in Jesus' time. That is at least partly Matthew's point.

Acknowledging, then, that the Old can provide an example from the past of the lesson Jesus teaches in his own parable of the vineyard, what happens when one hears Isaiah 5:1-7 — not as a lesson of "Hebrew Scripture," from "someone else's mail," but as an Old Testament lesson from Christian scripture, in reciprocal, not developmental, relationship with the New? The kingdom has been given to the church, Matthew states. But will the church, the vineyard's new tenants, produce the fruits of the kingdom and so prove worthy to be stewards of Christ? Isaiah's song of the vineyard is now not just addressed to Israel as past historical referent, but as a word of Christian scripture, heard in the light of the New, it becomes a word of prophetic address to another "Israel" (Gal 6:6), the new tenants, the church. Matthew's concluding reference to Isa 8:14 is suitably general in its warning: *anyone* who falls on this stone rejected by the builders will be broken to pieces. When one hears that warning in light of Isaiah's song of the vineyard as a word of Christian scripture, then any simple supercessionist reading — with New controlling the meaning of the Old — will be ruled out. Instead, the question will be the same one put to Israel of old by the prophet Isaiah: "What more was there for me to do for my vineyard that I have not already done in it? When I expected it to yield grapes, why did it yield wild grapes?" Can the church say that that word is addressed only to a past people, unless it is prepared with equal confidence to say that it is the people who now produce the fruits of the kingdom in a manner pleasing to God? Hearing the Old in light of the New means also hearing the New in light of the Old. This will mean hearing Isaiah's word of prophetic address as impinging directly on the life of the church, the "Israel of God," and not just on the Israel of old.[6]

The second set of readings — the Advent readings — I have already referred to in some detail: these are Isa 2:1-5 (Zion's exaltation and the streaming of the nations); 11:1-9 (the promise of a shoot from the stump of Jesse); 35:1-10 (the holy way to Zion); 7:10-17 (the promise of Immanuel); and for Christmas day 9:2-7 ("and his name shall be called wonderful counselor"). Of these only the last two are paired with nativity scenes, from Matt 1:18-25 and Luke 2:1-14. This is roughly consistent with the observation that Isaiah's royal promises are not cited to any extent in the New, and instead the inclusion of the Gentiles remains Isaiah's most pervasive contribution.

The first three lessons in Advent from Isaiah are paired, then, not with readings in the New focused on Jesus as incarnate messiah but with passages concerning John the Baptizer as Elijah and with the so-called Matthew apocalypse, which tells of the destruction of the temple and the coming in judgment of the Son of Man. Not exactly what one would call happy or sentimental advance notices of the birth of Christ in Bethlehem.

What we see in the first three Sundays of Advent is Isaiah's voice directed — not so much to the birth of Christ in Bethlehem — but to the second coming, the final consummation of promises uttered by the prophets of Old. Incidentally, it was in precisely this sense that the early church fathers — Cyril of Jerusalem most notably — also heard Isaiah in conjunction with the gospel: as directed toward the second coming of Christ in glory and consummation. This is absolutely clear in Advent 1, where Isaiah 2 and the apocalypse of Matthew, concerning the coming of the Son of Man in judgment, are joined. To be sure, the pairing of the other two

---

6. See Ephraim Radner's essay in *Inhabiting Unity: Theological Perspectives on the Proposed Lutheran-Episcopal Concordat*, ed. E. Radner and R. R. Reno (Grand Rapids: Eerdmans, 1995) 134-52, for a discussion of "Israel" and the problem of supercessionist deployments of the term.

passages with John, Jesus' forerunner, will incline one to see Isaiah's word fulfilled in Jesus of Nazareth, to whom John points — yet not Jesus as the sentimental child of Bethlehem, but the one for whom John's message of repentance is but a shadow. To cleanly distinguish between the earthly Christ and the Christ who is to come is of course no simple matter — and it is liturgy's job to complicate that temporal distinction.

But the larger point is that the horizon of Isaiah in respect of royal promises is not a past fulfillment in Jesus that validates Christian hopes and invalidates those of the Jews. In Advent we do not just look back nostalgically on a perfect fit between the prophet's longings and their absolute fulfillment in Christ: like arrows hitting a bull's-eye. Instead, Isaiah's horizon remains the final horizon for Jew and Christian and Gentile: Christ's coming, Christ's advent in glory and in judgment. This is absolutely consistent with the New's own *per se* witness to Isaiah, as we have seen by tracking how Isaiah is heard *in novo receptum,* where Isaiah's promises are not explicitly referred to as fulfilled, but deferred to as *per se* promises yet to be fulfilled. Not for nothing is Advent both a penitential season and a season whose lessons share much in common with the final readings of the liturgical year associated with Christ the King, at the conclusion — and one might rightly say climax — of the lectionary year (emphasized better by Lutherans than Episcopalians). Advent now is a paradoxical combination of retrospection, in which the birth of Christ is memorialized, and anticipation, as that birth becomes an earnest of promises once articulated by Isaiah and the prophets of the Old Testament, still straining toward their ultimate fulfillment when Christ will come in glory, when wolf lies down with lamb, death is swallowed up, and every tear wiped away for good and forever.

To hear the Old in lectionary pairings with the New means for both preacher and listener an invitation to confront the gospel in all its fullness. As a word of promise, as a word of sure confidence, as a word of judgment and exhortation, and as a word of final hope. Old in New, New in Old: the twofold witness of the Christian canon to the work of God in Christ, illumined in its richness and in its claim by the power of the Holy Spirit, who is at the same time the author of the twofold witness and the guarantor that, as Isaiah puts it, inspired by the same Holy Spirit: the "word will not return to me empty, but will accomplish that for which I sent it."

That word is sent forth and heard most eloquently in the New's final vision, the Revelation of John, which is both a "new thing" and a "former thing," in the sense that Isaiah's former vision remains the church's final vision.

And behold I saw a new heaven and a new earth;
   for the first heaven and the first earth had passed away,
   and the sea was no more.
And I saw the holy city, Jerusalem,
   coming down out of heaven from God,
   prepared as a bride adorned for her husband;
And I heard a loud voice from the throne of heaven saying,
   "Behold, the dwelling of God is with men.
   He will dwell with them and they shall be his people,
   And God himself will be with them [Immanuel];
And he will wipe away every tear from their eyes,
   and death shall be no more,
   neither shall there be mourning nor crying nor pain any more,
   for the former things have passed away (21:1-4).

This is not just vain Christian longing of a generic sort, indistinguishable from that of any poor soul who can imagine reversal of fortune. The author of Revelation reiterates divine promises uttered long ago through Isaiah, which have been fulfilled in Christ, and now strain toward their intended consummation. Old in New, New in Old: the twofold witness to the gospel of Jesus Christ, son of God, God of Israel, and hope of the nations. A witness that cannot be divided without tearing the gospel from both its historic moorings and its final hope, as seen of old by Isaiah the prophet.

16

The Call of Moses and
the "Revelation" of the Divine Name

Source-Critical Logic and Its Legacy

I

No two passages proved more important for emerging source-critical method than Exod 3:1–4:17 and 6:2-9. It is difficult to assign a title to either of these passages without tipping one's hand as to their source-critical significance, but both are frequently referred to as narrating the "call" of Moses. Observations about the phenomenon of doublets elsewhere in the Pentateuch, especially in Genesis, would of necessity come to play a role here as well. Why would Moses be called twice?

But overshadowing this more general problem was the blunt claim in Exod 6:3 that God had not been known by his proper name YHWH until this point in time. Because the name in fact appears in Genesis and in the first five chapters of Exodus, and in the earlier "call" narrative just a few chapters away, a problem was felt for which source criticism had a solution. To a host of compelling literary observations in Genesis could be added a matter of some substance: disagreement as to when the divine name was truly operative in Israel. Now one had some potential purchase on the crazy-quilt alternation of the divine name in Genesis, where YHWH is joined by a host of other appellations (Elohim, El Shaddai, El Elyon, El Olam, etc.).

The results are familiar. The Priestly writer was considered re-

229

sponsible for the second call narrative and those texts that avoid use of the proper name YHWH (at least prior to Exodus 6, if not also problematically after Exodus 6). By contrast, the Yahwist judged the divine name YHWH available and in use in the period of the ancestors and earlier; he gives expression to this belief in Gen 4:26, "At that time people began to invoke the name of YHWH." An Elohist is necessitated to explain non-Priestly texts in Genesis (and beyond) that likewise disagree with the Yahwist about the divine name.

This description of matters should be relatively uncontroversial. There have always been problems with source-critical division at the level of individual texts and in terms of larger conceptuality, and there is a growing literature whose sole purpose is to point out these problems.[1] Nevertheless, one can see from the very terms at work, "Yahwist," "Elohist," "Priestly Writer" (originally called the "later Elohist"), that the criterion of the divine name, based on exegesis of these two texts in Exodus, was central to source-critical logic. This is not to say that other solutions to the plain sense of Exod 6:3 and the problem of the divine name's usage were not available to ancient and modern interpreters — even some who accepted the notion of longitudinal sources. Still, a majority of commentators took the simple existence of these two "call narratives" — and the second's seemingly plain statement regarding the divine name — *as in essential conjunction* with other literary and historical observations. These pointed to the likelihood of continuous sources in the Pentateuch, which saw the matter of the divine name, at least up to Exodus 6, differently. That difference could be interpreted more or less stringently from a theological standpoint, depending on the approach of the individual interpreter.

An extremely thought-provoking alternative to this way of interpreting the two narratives in Exodus and the theological issues surrounding the revelation of the divine name has been put forward by Walter Moberly.[2] Moberly accepts the modern critical judgment that Exod 6:3 does in fact mean to say that the proper name of God, YHWH, was not made known until the time of Moses. He canvasses what he calls "harmonizing efforts," ancient and modern, to correlate divergent perspectives on the divine

---

1. R. Rendtorff, *The Problem of the Process of Transmission in the Pentateuch* (*JSOT* Supplement Series 89; Sheffield: JSOT, 1990); H. H. Schmid, *Der Sogennante Yahwist* (Zurich: Theologischer, 1976); R. N. Whybray, *The Making of the Pentateuch: A Methodological Study* (*JSOT* Supplement Series 53; Sheffield: JSOT, 1987).

2. *The Old Testament of the Old Testament* (OBT; Minneapolis: Fortress, 1992).

name, and he rejects these. He then goes further and trumps modern critical thinking and its rough consensus on the notion of sources itself. He argues that Exod 3:1–4:17, the so-called first call narrative, likewise relates the revelation of the divine name to Moses *for the very first time.* The rug is thus pulled out from under source-critical logic from an unexpected angle. Both call narratives, according to Moberly, are in agreement that the proper name of God was first revealed to Moses and was strictly speaking unknown to the ancestors. Appeal to the divine name as a criterion for source classification in Genesis and elsewhere thus loses its point of departure.

To the obvious question — Then why does the proper name appear in Genesis? — Moberly responds as follows. The narrator of these stories in Genesis — one can no longer call him the Yahwist — operates with full knowledge of the divine name, as does his readers, and therefore is not bothered by what from a historical perspective is the introduction of an anachronism. He merges his perspective with that of the stories and yet assumes that his readers, and also apparently us, will nevertheless catch the full force of the opening chapters of Exodus, which relate as a historical datum God's initial revelation of his name as YHWH. In other words, this would be similar to glossing the Old Testament from the standpoint of the New's plain sense — depicting Abraham as rejoicing at Christ's day — all the while assuming that as a historical reality the birth of Jesus and his significance for Christian faith lie in the future. I choose this illustration with some forethought because Moberly's final purpose is in fact to talk about the relationship between the Christian testaments as analogous to the way Genesis is "the Old Testament of the Old Testament."[3] That is to say, Moberly wishes us to catch the uniform perspective of all biblical narrators that the period of the ancestors is a distinct period, making Genesis an "old testament" prior to Sinai and the revelation of the divine

---

3. I have just, however, shown how this is not altogether true since explicit glossing of the Old did not take place in the manner just mentioned and in the manner Moberly assumes is at subtle work in Genesis, with the divine name YHWH. He recognizes this important distinction (*Old Testament of the Old Testament*, 140):

. . . the text of the Old Testament was stable by the time of the New Testament. So the rereading from the new perspective could not actually influence the text itself. . . . By contrast, at the time of the Yahwistic storytellers and editors the patriarchal traditions were still being retold in such a way that there was not yet one definitive version of them, and so the new perspective could significantly alter the nature of the text itself.

name. Most significantly for source-critical logic, this is not the view of one "Priestly writer" as against one "Yahwistic writer" or of one call narrative of Moses as against another, but of both. Central to his argument, then, is his exegesis of these two Exodus narratives, as was also true for emerging source-critical method.

II

A large percentage of Moberly's exegesis is devoted to a fresh reading of Exod 3:1–4:17. He seeks to establish that the narrative relates a first-time revelation of the divine name and is therefore operating with the same perspective as 6:2-8. In order to do this he focuses on verses 13-15 in a particularly fresh way, due to the thesis he is pursuing. He shows that the logic of the verses is by no means self-evident. As Moberly sees it, these verses introduce a hypothetical situation that is extraneous to a simple divine encounter with the already known YHWH, charging Moses to speak for him on behalf of his people against Pharaoh. They reflect a more mature theological situation.

The scene in which these verses play a role can be easily summarized. Moberly's reading has forced me to reexamine what is being related, by attending to the text in its present form and unfolding logic — rather than assuming from the start a convergence of several sources, which can then be untangled precisely because logical unfolding is absent. This also means setting aside the criterion of the divine name as pointing to sources behind the account.

The narrative relates the following. God makes himself known to Moses as the same One who appeared to the ancestors (v. 6). Though the narrator may use the proper name for the reader (v. 7) it has yet to be revealed to Moses. God then announces his intention to deal with Israel's affliction (vv. 7-9). Moses will be his agent before Pharaoh (v. 10). Moses reacts to this plan of "the God" *(hā 'ĕlōhîm)* who is speaking to him with concern (v. 11). There may be an adumbration of the proper name (YHWH) in verse 12 where God responds to Moses, "I will be with you" *(kî-'ehyeh 'immāk)*, and the status of the sign in the verse has always puzzled interpreters. But as the verse concludes, God still refers to himself in direct speech to Moses as "the God" that Moses is to worship on this mountain.

When the divine name *is* revealed, this happens in the context of a hypothetical situation: Moses is anticipating addressing the people of Israel. Not content with a charge from the God of the ancestors, Moses submits that the Israelites will want to know God's name. In response to these circumstances, not yet unfolded, where the divine name needs to be revealed, Moses asks the God addressing him "what shall I say?" God gives the famous first-person response in the verse that follows, frequently taken as a theologically significant rebuff *('ehyeh 'ăšer 'ehyeh)*. Then he even indicates that a first-person form of the name could serve as an answer to the question of the Israelites: "Say to the Israelites 'I am' sent me to you," even though EHYH does not elsewhere serve as God's proper name (so the third person *ho ōn* in the LXX).

Having begun to introduce the proper name (EHYH/YHWH), the narrator now changes his method of procedure and uses the generic "God" for indirect discourse, "And again God *('ĕlōhîm)* said to Moses. . . ." Now follows the full conjunction, a first-time conjunction as Moberly has it, whereby the God of the ancestors is said by God himself to be YHWH. The solemn ending drives home the gravity of the moment: "this is my name forever and my memorial from generation to generation." Moberly concludes thus:

> [T]he most natural explanation is that the writer is depicting the first revelation of the name to Moses and through him to Israel. Both Moses and Israel start by knowing God as "God of the father(s)" (3:6, 13), and the name YHWH is then given and added to the designation "God of your fathers" in a way that makes clear the identity and continuity of YHWH as Israel's God with the God known to the patriarchs. They still know the same God, but now God is to be known in perpetuity by the new name YHWH.[4]

And as for the account in Exodus 6, it "does not portray the revelation of the name YHWH simply because the name has already been revealed in Exodus 3."[5] The accounts cannot only be coordinated, as others have sought to maintain, they are in absolute agreement on this most essential point. The divine name was first revealed to Moses, and through him, to Israel. "Whatever Israel knows about the name of God, it knows only

4. Ibid., 24.
5. Ibid., 33.

through the mediation of Moses to whom alone a direct self-revelation of God has been given."[6]

One of the most difficult parts of Moberly's argument involves use of the proper name YHWH, especially in direct speech, in the book of Genesis. But I wish to leave that matter to the side for a moment in the interest of pursuing aspects of his stimulating exegesis of Exodus 3 and 6. He has rightly, to my mind, emphasized the signal character of this revelation of the proper name of God to Moses in Exodus 3. And I also believe that the two "calls" are not just coordinatable or compatible, but necessary for the text as a whole to make sense and as such indispensable in the final form of the material. With Moberly I do not think the divine name is a clear arbiter of source division in Genesis. At most it represents an individual narrator's proclivity, and it may have more to do with immediate context than with a consistent theological position maintained throughout longitudinal sources — sources that actually disagree about when the divine name was first known, thus allowing them to be identified in the first place. With him I find the terms "Yahwist" and "Elohist" problematic insofar as they have conflated a question regarding levels of tradition in an aggregate biblical text with a theory about the progressive revelation of the divine name; I would prefer with some recent scholars to speak of early and late traditions or complexes.[7] Even "source" now sounds a bit romantic, and it occasioned an appropriate debate in respect of the priestly level of tradition all along.[8]

Moberly argues that Exodus 3 and 6 both assert that only with Moses is the proper name of God first revealed. Its appearance in Genesis is self-conscious anachronism, which the ancient reader was to recognize as such and to draw neither historical nor theological conclusions from. With Moberly I agree that the reports do not reflect conflicting understandings about when the divine name appeared in Israel. But unlike him I wish to show that both, each in its own distinctive way, presuppose a longstanding use of the proper name for God. The conclusion I will draw from this is

---

6. Ibid., 15.

7. My own rough model would involve a priestly editing and supplementing of various earlier traditions, some of them already formed into independent complexes (ancestors, out of Egypt, wilderness journey, Sinai), as Rendtorff urged (see note 1). The much debated problem of deuteronomistic editing remains a point for further work, though even in Rendtorff's model this contribution consists primarily of ligatures at the latest level of redaction.

8. See among others, K. Koch, "P — Kein Redaktor! Erinnerung an zwei Eckdaten der Quellenschiedung," *VT* 37 (1987) 446-67.

that Old Testament texts never concern themselves with a point in historical time before which the name was hypothetically unknown, such that it might then be dramatically "revealed." The appearance of the tetragrammaton (YHWH Elohim) as early as Gen 2:4 comes with no explanation, and the point of its introduction in conjunction with the *'ĕlōhîm* of Genesis 1 may well be to ease us toward familiarity with God's personal name, as this was extant even in primeval time. In other words, the Old Testament never takes up the question of how the name as such first came to be uttered by humanity. As many have noted, Gen. 4:26 cannot be pressed into service to depict a first-time revelation of a name for God theretofore unknown.[9]

III

Moberly has rightly seen the signal character of the revelation of the divine name to Moses in Exodus 3. But a central contention here will be that he has gone astray by assuming that that signal character holds true for the Israelites as well as for Moses. My simple thesis is that the question posed by Moses in 3:13ff. has stood at the heart of source-critical discussion, and that the issue there turns on the status of Moses and a correct understanding of his role vis-à-vis Israel in the opening chapters of the book of Exodus.

In these chapters we learn straightforwardly several key facts. The three-month-old child of an anonymous man and woman of the Levite line ends up in the care of the daughter of Pharaoh. She infers that he is a Hebrew, has him nursed, names him, and takes him as her son, "for I drew him out of the water" (2:10), just as YHWH will later draw out his own children. The episode that leads to Moses' flight (2:11-15) reveals his ambiguous relationship to his people. He kills an Egyptian who is beating a Hebrew (v. 12). He "goes out" — it is not clear from where — and, seeing two "Hebrews" fighting, seeks to break it up, only to discover his previous avenging is not a secret. Eventually Pharaoh too hears of it and seeks to kill Moses (2:15). The response of his own people is curious — "Do you mean to kill me as you killed the Egyptian?" — and is best explained as an indication of Moses' liminality. Pharaoh treats him not as

9. C. Westermann, *Genesis 1–11* (Minneapolis: Augsburg, 1984) 339-40.

Egyptian, the Israelites not as "Hebrew" — or only confusedly so. Moses flees to Midian and helps some shepherds. When they describe him to their priest, he is "an Egyptian" (2:19). He marries the priest's daughter. The son he sires bears a name more than descriptive of his situation: "I have been a sojourner *(gēr)* in a foreign land" (2:22).

What is clear in these chapters is the separation of Moses from his people: raised by Egyptians, married to a Midianite, with a son whose name more than sums up his status. Now at the risk of putting the question too simply: as the narrative is presenting it, with Moses' estrangement the prominent feature, how might we come to think Moses knows of YHWH at all?

When we move to an interpretation of chapter 3 against this backdrop, several features come into prominence. If one tracks the use of the divine name, alert to the difference between Moses' own perspective, that of the narrator, and that of the reader, then verse-by-half-verse source division — here the Elohist, there the Yahwist — proves unnecessary. In vv. 1-5 the narrator tells us something that Moses does not yet know: it is YHWH who is appearing to him in the burning bush. YHWH begins by telling Moses something that will make sense to him: He is the God of his father (singular, though frequently emended). The meaning of this is usually sought in religio-historical reconstructions of ancestral religion or some other such etic analysis. But might the text mean only what it says: the God addressing Moses is the God of his father, that is, the Levite mentioned in 2:1, who is unknown to Moses? This God is the God of his father and his father's fathers before him, the ancestors Abraham, Isaac, and Jacob. This declaration may itself constitute a revelation of something hitherto unknown; that and the simple presence of *hā 'ĕlōhîm* require Moses to hide his face.

In verse 7, YHWH reveals to Moses and to the reader that he has seen quite clearly the affliction of his people: not *your* cry (Moses and the people) but *their* cry has been heard and *their* anguish God knows. This same perspective is maintained through verse 9, where God speaks to Moses about a people *with whom Moses is himself not explicitly identified.* Moses is addressed directly in verse 10: "Look, I am sending you to Pharaoh to bring forth my people, the children of Israel." Moses responds to "the God" from the same perspective of distinguishability: "Who am I that I should go to Pharaoh, that I should bring out the people of Israel?" Only in verse 12 is the mutuality of the people and Moses and God revealed: "when you bring forth *the people,* you shall serve God on this mountain"; *ta'abdun,* a plural form, meaning Moses and the people, is adopted here for the first time in the narrative. The problem of the mysterious sign might consist in this anticipated union. That is, the sign that "I am with you" is not the worship on the mountain as such, but instead that the Moses being charged by God here is assured that he will eventually worship together with the people he is being sent to address. The sentence might be paraphrased: "I will be *('ehyeh)* is with you *('immāk),* and the sign of this is your eventual worship with the people of Israel on this mountain." Moses will not be rejected; God is with him.

This interpretation finds some support as we read on into verses 13ff., so pivotal in Moberly's discussion. Moses anticipates with "the God" this encounter with God's people. Note how the text does not report Moses saying to them, "the God of *our* fathers has sent me to you" but rather "the God of *your* fathers." Now the full force of their hypothetical question is clear. They inquire of Moses what God's name is not because they do not know it. How would his supplying the name either mean anything or be verifiable before those who do not know it to begin with?[10] They ask the name because they do know it and will not be constrained to listen to a spokesman from God who cannot establish that their named God has indeed sent him. Moses knows this too, which is why he asks to know God's name. Only in this way can he verify before the Israelites that their named God has also revealed himself to him and sent him on this bold mission on their behalf.[11]

---

10. Maimonides' famous treatment was aimed at addressing this conundrum (*The Guide for the Perplexed,* tr. M. Priedlander (London: Routledge, 1951] 93-95).

11. Compare Childs's sophisticated source and form-critical analysis (*The Book of Exodus* [OTL; Philadelphia: Westminster, 1974]). In verse 13 "E" is influenced by the later true-false prophecy discussion and has Moses produce the name to verify his call; "E" also, like "P," thinks the divine name was not revealed until this point. (These two concerns are somewhat at odds since producing the name for verification and producing it for the first time à la "E/P" makes for complication.) Later, when the identification of the proper name with the God of the ancestors was fully assumed, the question made no sense. Verse 14 therefore interprets the request for the name as a request for its significance. Without all the sense of depth and tradition history, Maimonides comes to something of the same conclusion: "God taught Moses how to teach them [the people], and how to establish amongst them the belief in Himself, namely, by saying Ehyeh asher Eyheh. . . . God thus showed Moses the proofs by which His existence would be firmly established among the wise men of His people" (*Guide for the Perplexed,* 94-95). In both of these cases the question is not Moses' capacity to produce a name others know already, but his capacity to explain a name, maybe even one he and others knew already (something that never happens later in the text).

What seems patient of further analysis is the first response God makes to the question of his name, given the mature theological discussion it presupposes. The notion of a careful rebuff or sonorous self-protection, "I am who I am," turns in some measure on the understanding that this is *the* signal revelation of the name.[12] Is Moses being rebuffed, or is the proper name of God, known by the reader and by the Israelites, here being supplied by God with an interpretation of its significance?

That is, this individual revelation of the name to Moses gave the narrator the opportunity to insist that, while Moses was only now coming to knowledge of the name, he was also learning something about it that those who already knew it did not know. This served three purposes: (1) to underscore Moses' special status; even as an outsider he is privy to special knowledge of God, involving attributes to which God's name points; (2) to reveal thereby to the reader something of the meaning of a name with which we are familiar, but only as a proper name as such; (3) to begin to suggest that who God is and has been heretofore is patient of enlargement. God indicates that Moses could just as easily say to the people EHYH as YHWH when speaking of him, even though this never happens and would presumably have had a strange effect. This underscores the significance invested by the narrator in identifying most clearly the known name of God, YHWH, with the verb "to be," whatever the most appropriate translation of *'ehyeh 'ăšer 'ehyeh* might be. The studied adumbration in verse 12 *('ehyeh 'immāk)* points to an interpretation of the divine name as involving most especially God's presence with Moses and the people *in the events of redemption from bondage,* and as such the account in 6:2-9 is anticipated. More on this below.

The sophistication of the narrative is in full evidence in the unit under discussion (3:13-18). To Moses' question about what name he should give for God when he is questioned, there is a simple answer: "my name is YHWH." But God does not give that simple answer. We are eased toward a direct announcement of the name through a series of explanatory glosses. This protraction has led numerous interpreters to conclude that what we have here is a variety of sources being brought into a conjunction sufficiently clumsy that we can posit their existence to begin with.

God does not give his proper name YHWH in response to Moses' question, but instead speaks in the first person in a terse statement: *'ehyeh 'ăšer 'ehyeh.* The *sui generis* "I AM has sent me to you" is only compre-

12. See Childs's brief discussion (*Exodus,* 69).

hensible as an extrapolation, or parsing, of this first response by God. Its point is to show that the potentially circular "I am as I am" is not a rebuttal (cf. *'ănî 'ăšer 'ănî*) but a clue to the meaning of the proper name YHWH. God's name involves something that he will be or become.

But we still have not clarified why this explanation precedes rather than follows the disclosure to Moses of God's name YHWH in verse 15. The answer is that God is truly responding to Moses' request to know his name, but in a way that neither the reader nor Moses is prepared for. God's name is in fact *'ehyeh 'ăšer 'ehyeh*. That is, God's name is the most personal revelation of God's own character, and as such is not a proper name in the strict sense (like Jim or Sally), but a name appropriate to God's character as God. In this case, God's "name" consists of a disclosure of purpose; it "means" something approaching "In the manner that I am, or will be, I am who I am." Yet neither we nor Moses is prepared to understand such a "name" yet, because what God will be, and is most essentially, has not as yet been made manifest. Now are we prepared to understand what is at stake in the second "call narrative" in 6:2-9.

IV

The first thing to note about the second "call narrative" is that it does not immediately follow the first. The second thing to consider is why any such narrative might be necessary at all. Source-critical logic supplied one answer to this question: the sources "P" and "J" disagreed about the revelation of the divine name, thus necessitating a second "call narrative." But the same disagreement over the revelation of the divine name is shared by both "P" and "E." "E" is apparently satisfied to gloss the first account, so why is "P" unsatisfied with this procedure? But there are more serious problems with the "two call accounts" theory that have already been alluded to and that form the starting point for this analysis.

The first consideration, however, regarding the present location of the second divine encounter, is worthy of further attention. Do events transpire that make such an encounter pivotal, especially as this involves the revelation of the divine name and its meaning for Moses and the people of Israel? Our procedure will again be to focus on the unfolding of events in narrative sequence.

At the close of chapter 3 God indicates that the trip into the wilderness to worship (commanded earlier at 3:12) will not take place without resistance (3:18-20). In chapter 4, Moses raises a series of concerns about his own capacities. First, while he can state the name of YHWH, there is nothing preventing the people from asking whether or not YHWH has in fact appeared to him, or at least so Moses reckons (v. 1). To meet this objection God provides two signs: a snake becomes a rod, and woe and weal are created, that is, leprosy is caused and removed (4:2-7). A third sign involves water becoming blood (4:8-9). Aaron is then provided as Moses' spokesman to meet the objection that Moses does not speak well (4:14-16). Again God warns Moses about Pharaoh's recalcitrance and indicates that Moses will have to threaten him with death of the firstborn in exchange for deliverance of God's own firstborn son, Israel (4:22-23). The immediately following Zipporah passage (4:24-26) gives Moses a foreshadowing of what is at stake. The One who can make leprous and then heal, who can turn water to blood, who makes "dumb, deaf, seeing, blind" (4:11) is also the One who will slay the firstborn of the Egyptians, all who are not circumcised like Moses' son (and Moses? cf. 12:43-49). The blood that later spares by marking the lintel and the two doorposts, preventing the destroyer from entering (12:23), here also causes God "to leave him alone" (4:26), due to this obscure circumcision ritual, involving son and father. Whatever else the strange night attack means, it sets the proper life-or-death tone and foreshadows future manifestations of God's designs for Israel and Egypt. A distinction will be made (11:7). Not for nothing does Moses describe "YHWH our God" in his very first meeting with Pharaoh as demanding their worship in the wilderness, "lest he fall upon us with pestilence or with the sword" (5:3). Moses has this on firsthand experience. YHWH's intentions for Israel are life-or-death intentions.

What follows is Moses' encounter with Aaron at the conclusion of the chapter (4:27-31). The words of YHWH are communicated to Aaron, and through him, to the people. The signs work. The people believe and worship. No explanation of the name is requested or given. The significance of the *'ehyeh 'ašer 'ehyeh* and of the name YHWH itself, as this was introduced in 3:13-15, is not referred to here. We will return to this seeming omission in a moment, which might prove very problematic for Moberly's reading, given his theory of the first-time revelation of the name in 3:13ff., whose transmission to the people is here marked by no fanfare whatsoever.

Chapter 5 records the failure of Moses and Aaron's audience with

Pharaoh, as God had predicted. Heavier burdens are the consequence of their entreaty, and the people object that Moses and Aaron "have made us offensive in the sight of Pharaoh and his servants" (5:21). As previous commentators have noted, this chapter introduces a concept that functions as a leitmotif until the deliverance in chapter 14. It begins with Pharaoh's declaration, "Who is the YHWH that I should heed his voice and let Israel go? I do not know YHWH and moreover will not let Israel go" (5:2). It culminates in the solemn pronouncement before the Red Sea life-or-death episode, "And the Egyptians shall know that I am YHWH, when I have gotten glory over Pharaoh, his chariots, and his horsemen" (14:18), a recognition that occurs at 14:25: "Let us flee from before Israel, for YHWH fights for them against the Egyptians." We are prepared for this final recognition at numerous points along the way (7:5, 17; 8:10, 22; 9:14, 29; 10:2; 11:7; 14:4) where the key phrase "that you might know that I am YHWH" or some variation appears. The final statement at 14:31 indicates that full knowledge has come to Israel, "And Israel saw the great work which the LORD did against the Egyptians, and the people feared YHWH; and they believed in YHWH and in his servant Moses."

It is from this specific perspective that the so-called second, Priestly "call narrative" in 6:2-9 is to be understood. Note first of all that *in its present context* this unit is neither a call narrative nor even a "seconding" of a first call. It is a solemn response to Moses' complaint in 5:22 that God has not delivered his people as promised; instead the meeting with Pharaoh has exacerbated matters. God's response to the complaint takes the form of a clarification, by which YHWH explains to Moses privately what will take place in the future. God will honor the oath he swore to the ancestors and give them the land he has promised (6:8). Reference to the covenant made with the ancestors occurs twice, in verses 4 and 5. The author of this important unit clearly has Genesis 17 in mind, which tells of the appearance of YHWH to Abram for the purpose of making a covenant — a text reckoned by most to be from the hand of the Priestly writer. Intriguing in that text is the same collocation of terms as in Exodus 6: the divine name YHWH, the verb "appear" *(wayyērā'; wā'ērā'),* and "El Shaddai." The occurrence of the divine name YHWH in a Priestly text required strict source theorists to speak there of a gloss.

Interpretation of this key unit has foundered, in my view, because of the tendency to read verse 3 in isolation, as pointing to a theory about the origin of the divine name and its usage in Israel. The alternative pursued here will focus on the verse (1) within the larger unit in which it appears, especially verse 7, and (2) within the narrative context in which the verb *yd'* and the so-called recognition formula plays an obvious and central role (chs. 5–14).

There is a slight syntactical problem in verse 3 that is frequently glossed over and which cannot be detected — because it is in some sense impossible to replicate — in translations. The first half of the verse is clear: I appeared to Abraham, Isaac, and Jacob in/as El Shaddai *(bĕʾēl šadday)*. This is consistent with Genesis 17, though at least in theory the narrator *could* have said that YHWH appeared to Abram since that is what a putative glossator, later than and familiar with P's divine name theology, was prepared to assert.[13] The second verse-half does not pick up the preposition *(bĕ)*, though many argue it should be supplied under influence of *bĕʾēl*. The same first-person form of the verb appears, here not *rʾh* (see) but *yd'* (know). Both forms of the verb are *niphal*, which can be construed either as passive or middle ("I appeared," "I was seen," "I was [not] known," "I made [not] myself known"). The problem is combining a nominal form *šĕmî* with a first-person verb, *nôdaʿtî*, without drawing on the preposition in the first half of the verse, producing "my name YHWH I was not known to them." Perhaps for this reason the LXX rendered the verb *edēlōsa*, which matches the *hiphil* of *yd'*, producing "my name YHWH I did not make known (reveal) to them."

The verse is generally understood as involving a contrast, concerning whether the name of God was known or not known in the period of the ancestors, as against that of the Mosaic period. If one pays close attention to the larger unit, this does not appear to be the main burden of the text,

---

13. It could be argued that the alleged glossator working in Gen 17:1 has introduced YHWH not to Abram but to the reader; to Abram, YHWH is El Shaddai. But is even this distinction consistent with a hard and fast position supposedly held by the Priestly writer about the name YHWH only being first revealed to Moses? Are we approaching the sort of subtlety that such a theory has sought to avoid? Moreover, if such a distinction is at play, it could presumably work within the Priestly "source" itself and should find corroboration elsewhere in Genesis.

It may be true that for the author of Exodus 6 and kindred texts in Genesis, "El Shaddai" was a favorite or distinctive appellation, and that is why it is used here in a description of God's appearance to the ancestors. But what the author wishes to assert is not contrast or discontinuity between names for God (El Shaddai then, YHWH hereafter), but continuity — that is, YHWH and El Shaddai are one and the same. The contrast is between *appearance* to the ancestors and *knowledge* of YHWH as YHWH, which comes about in the events of Exodus 14. It is for this reason that the *hiphil* of *yd'* does not appear in Exod 6:3b, while the divine name YHWH does appear in Genesis texts, including 17:1.

nor even a minor theme.[14] The issue is not knowledge of the name *per se* but how God most fully makes himself known as YHWH. "I was not known in respect of my name YHWH" God tells Moses, because this knowledge turns on the events of the exodus, which are as yet unexperienced. The main burden of the unit is revealed in verse 7: "and I will take you for my people, and I will be your God; and you shall know that I am YHWH your God, who has brought you up from the burden of the Egyptians." God has not been truly known as YHWH because this involves the mighty deliverance yet to be accomplished. Such a reading is also consistent with the presentation in chapters 7–14, which center on YHWH making himself known before the Egyptians (7:5), before Pharaoh (7:17), above or beside other gods (8:10), in the midst of the earth (8:22), throughout all the earth (9:16), in all creation (9:29), as distinguisher of Israel (11:7), and before Pharaoh's host (14:4). The recognition formula which appears in 6:7 runs like a red thread through all the subsequent scenes, until the denouement at the sea, when Pharaoh's hosts at last confess, "Let us flee from Israel, for YHWH fights for them" and the Israelites see and fear YHWH and believe in Moses. The author of the unit 6:2-9 knows that YHWH appeared to the ancestors and was sometimes referred to as God Almighty. But God reveals to Moses that he was not known to them as he is about to make himself known.

It is here that the conjunction with the first divine encounter comes into play. Moses was given the divine name in order to appear before the people of Israel as a credible witness. He was also told by God, in response to a request to know God's name, *'ehyeh 'ăšer 'ehyeh,* which we judged to be neither a rebuttal nor a typical proper name, but a statement of God's very self — on the verge of being made manifest. The *hiphil* of *yd'* is not used in the second verse-half of 6:3 precisely to avoid the impression that what is at stake in the contrast between the period of the ancestors and the period at hand is knowledge of the name itself. "I did not make known *(hôda'tî)* my name" might imply that God was known, but simply under another name, like El Shaddai. That is not the contrast the author wishes to make, and therein is a common perspective uniting both accounts. The name YHWH has been known all along, and the first encounter between God and Moses has as one purpose Moses' learning the name so that he might speak in the name of YHWH before those who know the name. What the ancestors failed to know was not the name YHWH, which

14. Here I am indebted to an unpublished paper by J. Janzen.

appears throughout Genesis in direct speech, in indirect narration, on the mouth of foreigner as well as Israelite, or before such distinctions were germane (4:26). Likewise the Israelites in Egypt, Moses, Aaron, Pharaoh, and all his hosts might well know the name of God, but they have yet to know who God wishes to reveal himself as. That will be made manifest in the deliverance of his people and the destruction of those who oppose that deliverance. "He is who he is" in these events and as such makes himself known — fully rather than for the first time — as YHWH.

V

While levels of tradition might prefer to make use of this or that name for God, a comparison of the two calls of Moses in Exodus 3 and 6, and especially verse 3 of the latter, raised to the status of basic criterion a distinction between YHWH and other names for God in pentateuchal texts, at the same time bringing into prominence the notion of a theological disagreement between sources over how and when the personal name of God was revealed to Israel. We have challenged that comparison and its significance for a theory of sources in the Pentateuch. More could be said about the respective functions of Exod 3 and 6. Scolnic's remarks confirm our own, from a different prospective. "Moses, in chapter 6," he notes, "is placed within a genealogy, in the context of his people, which gives a very different impression than the story in Exodus 2–3 of an Egyptian noble who has been disloyal."[15]

We agree and have argued that there is further significance for how and why the personal name of God is used as it is in these two accounts. The first explains how Moses came to privileged knowledge of the name, such that he could state it to the people of Israel. It also indicates that God's "name" involves his freedom to act and be who he most fully is, or *'ehyeh 'ăšer 'ehyeh*. Though God tells Moses to say that this is his name (3:14), we must wait until the second divine encounter to learn just what the name means — or will mean. In this sense, even Exod 6:2-9 does not report the revelation of God as YHWH so much as anticipate it. In the

---

15. B. Scolnic, "Strangers in the PaRDeS: Conservative Judaism and the Torah," *Study Guide to the Discovery,* ed. E. S. Schoenberg (New York: Jewish Theological Seminary, n.d.) 8.

events of the exodus God will be known fully as YHWH. If there is a contrast with the period of the ancestors, so far as God's agency and person is concerned, it would have to involve this full knowledge of God's self. God had appeared, as YHWH and as El Shaddai, to make promises to the ancestors. But in no way did they know him as he would be known in the exodus. A crude distinction may involve not the name under which God is known, but between God's *appearing* — which happens under a variety of names in Genesis — and his *being made known,* which happens in a permanently foundational way in the events of exodus and Sinai. No source, level of tradition, or individual author worked under constraint of a *status confessionis* articulated in Exodus 6 whereby the divine name was not revealed until a second "call narrative" of Moses.[16] What that account seeks to establish is that the God known as YHWH had appeared to the ancestors but was not known as he truly was until Exodus 14 and the victory at the sea. After that the final *'ǎšer 'ehyeh* of "I am who I will be" found its proper content: "I am YHWH your God who brought you out of the land of Egypt" (Exod 20:2).

VI

A final note about method. Source-critical method sought to expose two important realities about biblical narrative: (1) that the events reported were not factual in the strict sense but involved sequent, creative authorial voices and (2) that a single point of view could at most be attributed to a final redactor who, unsuccessfully enough for us to appreciate his efforts, sought to wrest a measure of coherence or control out of what lay before him, for a variety of political, theological, moral, or aesthetic reasons, some too obscure or pedestrian for us to recognize at all. The narratives were thought to be about historical events in the first instance, yet critical theory insisted that this reference to history be understood in a very complex way — both views having to do in the first instance with events behind the

---

16. As has long been recognized, if such a theological position were indeed pivotal for our interpretation of pre–Exodus 6 texts, it would also follow that after this "revelation" of the divine name, the criterion could need to be abandoned. One might even expect the "priestly" level of tradition to begin only using the divine appellation YHWH, in agreement with other "sources" with which it once took issue. But this simple course is not followed.

text to which the text referred and in so doing made its essential point. In this scheme of things, the reader of the material as it existed in its present aggregate form was largely unanticipated, because one audience in history to which one layer of text was directed had been overlaid with new layers and new audiences, the final form proving incapable of completely transcending that complex history of development.

We have returned to the narratives involving the revelation of the divine name and the call of Moses fully aware of this particular history of reading, now several centuries old. How the text is related to the events it reports we acknowledge to be extraordinarily complex, and in no way do we believe that the narrative is simply reporting what happened to Moses or God in a straightforward sense — how in the light of the reality to which the text is referring could this ever be possible? Instead we have sought to determine if the narratives make sense in their present form and within a set intertextual (epic) world of reference. This has entailed being especially alert to the way the narrator might make key distinctions between the reader's frame of reference, that of Moses, and that of the people of Israel. In coming to terms with this set of distinctions we have tried to understand the logic of what is being narrated as this involves Moses and the revelation of the divine name.

Clearly in the books of Exodus and Genesis we are dealing with a variety of authorial voices, whose characteristics involve matters of style, genre, lexical stock, and distinctive theological proclivity. Whether and to what extent the divine name plays a key role in separating these voices is not as clear as has been maintained. At a minimum, we have questioned whether, in distinguishing a hypothetical "J" from a "P" or an "E," one was misled by the notion of some quite crucial theological disagreement over the actual revelation of the name YHWH.

My remarks do not call for a repudiation of levels of tradition, but a different understanding of their character and relationship to one another. In my judgment these are more synthetically related than the old Priestly versus Yahwist theory held. Perhaps the various hands at work deferred to the literary product on which they labored in such a way that it would both bear witness to but also transcend their various, sometimes discrete efforts. To warn of a "disappearing redactor," as has Barton, is potentially misleading.[17] The question is what sort of criteria truly count

17. John Barton, *Reading the Old Testament* (Philadelphia: Westminster, 1984) 56-58.

for distinguishing levels of tradition. Then the harder task is to come to terms with their relationship to one another in the final form of the text. As long as they were depicted as requiring disentanglement, this question never came into serious play. The point of this essay has been to argue that no level of tradition disagreed with any other over so important an issue as the revelation of God's proper name YHWH. That name was known in primeval time and forever thereafter. But God was not known in his name YHWH fully until the events at the sea. All levels of tradition are in essential agreement here.[18]

18. Though we reach different conclusions about when the actual name YHWH was known, I agree with Moberly about a distinction between ancestral and Mosaic period knowledge of God as YHWH.

PRACTICE

17

The Divine Name in Christian Scripture

It will be the larger thesis of this essay that biblical religion always assumes that a *particular* deity is making a claim upon a *particular* people, and that this requires a choice — among several obvious and attractive alternatives — on the part of those claimed. Stated differently, the one God does not reside in essential isolation, only provisionally described by biblical language and statements. "We all worship the same God" is a statement foreign to the Bible's logic.

Seen in this way, the present debates about the "fatherhood" of God or whether God is to be addressed as "he" or "she" are not debates that can issue into meaningful consensus or "truth" if considered unto themselves. Rather, they are subsets of a more problematic (from the modern standpoint) array of claims about and by the God revealed in Christian scripture. It is finally the case that *election* is the pivot on which the question of God's "fatherhood" turns. Only with a recognition of Israel's privileged access to God does a discussion of what Jesus calls God and what we should call God follow. Related to election are questions of the *sufficiency of scripture* to describe God as he really exists, unto himself and toward us.[1] Seen in this way, the modern debate about language for God

1. The traditional practice of using capitals to refer to God as "He" obviously sought to distinguish between male human beings and God. That late modern Christians in the West can now view this as an effort to aggrandize maleness is obviously a deconstruction of this practice, but that does not make its intention any less compelling or helpful. In fact, it might urge its reconsideration, in that it makes makes men and women "lower case" without distinction.

251

is not in the first instance a debate about God's character and self. Instead, it is a debate engendered by the lack of conviction about either election or the sufficiency of scriptural statements to describe God as revealed to his elected people, first to Israel and by adoption to the church. Moreover, it is a debate about whether scripture is God's gift to the church, sufficient to describe God as he truly is, enlivened by God's work as Holy Spirit. Indeed, then, any debate over God's "fatherhood" is absurd if it is detached from a discussion of the Holy Spirit or the nature of the church, as scripture has set these forth and as they are present realities for Christian men and women.

For this reason, what is at stake in modern debates is not whether God is father or can be addressed as "he." *Rather, what is at stake is whether we are entitled to call God anything at all.* The proper question is whether we have any language that God will recognize as his own, such that he will know himself to be called upon, and no other, and within his own counsel then be in a position to respond, or to turn a deaf ear. This description of God is fully consistent with the way God dealt with his people Israel in the Old Testament, long before the question of his relationship with others beyond Israel's circle was ever seriously entertained. To raise for serious discussion whether God is "father" before we have asked whether God is for us or against us, whether God can be known, and by whom, whether we can have any meaningful life with God at all, is to threaten offense against the One who purports to be under discussion and assessment.

I

In theory a distinction can be made between two sorts of arguments for revision of biblical language for God (e.g., Father, Son, Holy Spirit). The first is that all human language, including biblical language (and the language of the Jesus depicted therein), is culturally bound and therefore open to revision by subsequent cultures. That is, human language only imperfectly reflects the reality to which it points. The second sort of argument is more restrictive: God has a "name" that refers directly to him, but "Father, Son, Holy Spirit" is not it. Within this latter arena of reflection, one would be less inclined to think that God's fatherhood, for example, is appropriate because of some essential analogy from the realm of human fathering. Rather, God is "Father in Heaven" because that is what Jesus calls him. If Jesus called him "Mother in Heaven" then that would be the way to call upon God, whatever we thought about human mothering as distinct from human fathering. "Mother in Heaven" would be the name God responds to when it is used of God.

If it is this more restrictive arena in which biblical language for God operates, then that fact is itself worthy of reflection. The notion that God has a name is a prevalent notion in both the Old Testament and in the cultures surrounding it. Here one can distinguish between the terms *elohim* or *baalim,* on the one hand, and YHWH, Marduk, or Asherah, on the other. The former refer to divine beings as a genus, the latter to specific deities. While the former may be used to refer to specific deities, both within the Old Testament and outside it, the latter terms cannot be conjoined. The identity of YHWH, Marduk, or Asherah is tied up with a set of narratives which supply content to the individual deity in question, so that who Marduk is, is by definition different from who YHWH is. The way YHWH is known is by reference to what Israel says about him based upon his prior actions with Israel.

The personal name for God, YHWH, is introduced in Gen 2:4 without any explanation as to how he got that name. I have argued that the initial appearance of the personal name YHWH together with the generic Elohim, used in Genesis 1, was intended to ease us toward familiarity with God's personal name, which was extant even in primeval time.[2] In later narratives (Exodus 3 and 6), we learn that God makes himself definitively known in the events of the exodus (study the recognition formula — "then you will know that I am YHWH" — as this runs from chapters 5 through 14). The named deity whose name existed from time immemorial reveals who he is in the events of liberation from bondage in Egypt. He gets no new name. The old name is filled with fullest content. In the words of God's self revelation at Sinai, in the solemn introduction to the decalogue, "I am YHWH, your Elohim, who brought you up out of the land of Egypt." Here one sees the distinction between a generic and a proper name. Various nations have their various elohim. YHWH is Israel's God, who was made known in bringing Israel out of bondage from Egypt. The narratives tell who this YHWH is; they reflect what this YHWH has done.

The notion that God has a proper name and can be differentiated from other deities with proper names is absolutely clear in the Old Testa-

2. See chapter 16 above.

ment. Other gods (elohim) lay claims on humanity, but Israel is to have no god (elohim) before or beside YHWH (Exod 20:3). Moreover, the character of the name is itself a matter of reverence, since the name really coheres with the God it names (20:7). One cannot therefore malign the name or substitute for the name another name, and somehow leave untouched the deity with whom this name is attached. The very fact that a generic term, elohim, was not deemed satisfactory for describing God or naming Israel's God, is an indication that the proper name YHWH is the name God himself will respond to. There would need to be no concern for God's name, apart from God's self, if in fact such a distinction could be registered in the first place. Concern with revering God's name, such as we find this in the Psalms (8:1), would be a form of idolatry if one could hypothetically detach the name from that to which it refers. In the same Ten Commandments in which all forms of idolatry or image-making are condemned, the name is specifically discussed (20:7). Not taking the name of YHWH in vain implies, at a minimum, understanding that YHWH is not an "accident" detachable from a deeper "substance," that is "God himself."

II

It would seem that the notion that God has a name, a specific set of narratives, and a people whose testimony to him constitutes those narratives, would only make sense against a polytheistic backdrop. To name God YHWH is not to call him something else, and it is also to distinguish him from other deities with other proper names, other peoples, and other narratives. It is a commonplace in handbooks to Old Testament religion to describe a movement from what is called "henotheism" toward what is called "monotheism." The former is reflected in the narratives we have been discussing, and particularly in the Ten Commandments. Other deities exist, but Israel is to cling to their God, YHWH, exclusively. Deuteronomy and the deuteronomistic literature lifts this concern to the level of non-negotiable *status confessionis,* and the determinative force behind all of Israel's successes or failures as God's people.

The shift to what is called "monotheism" is argued to have taken place with Second Isaiah (the prophet of Isaiah 40–55 working in the early Persian period, ca. 550). Theoretically, the elimination of all other gods might render superfluous the proper naming of Israel's YHWH. Yet that never happens in these chapters. While the prophet can be quoted as saying, "I am the first and I am the last; besides me there is no god" (44:6), this remains YHWH's own assertion of his primacy and exclusivity. It is an intramural statement, made by Israel's named deity, that he alone is God. Such a statement is made precisely in the face of a challenge by other peoples and their own religious claims, involving allegiance to Bel and Nebo (46:1), among others. One must carefully distinguish between a claim by YHWH himself to be the only God and the persistence of other named deities and those who believe in them.

To put this in modern terms, nowhere in Second Isaiah would "monotheism" amount to a practical elimination of all gods but one, such that it could be said, "we all worship the same God." Precisely the opposite is true in these chapters: representatives of other nations "shall make supplication to you, saying, 'God is with you only and there is no other, no god besides him'" (45:14). That is, they will make the same sort of claim Israel was commanded to make in the Ten Commandments, that against the rival claims of other gods, YHWH demanded sole allegiance. Now that claim is emboldened with the assertion that other gods are in fact only illusions. This is not a sublime monotheism capable of differentiation from a more concrete henotheism — rather, it is henotheism of a particularly potent stripe. The other elohim that continue to claim allegiance from humanity have detachable names and detachable existences — to the degree that YHWH insists that they do not exist at all and envisions a time when representatives of the nations will make the confession once enjoined of Israel only.

The other obvious fact is that while in Isaiah 40–66 YHWH asserts his own uniqueness and exclusivity, nowhere does this lead to a practical elimination of polytheism. The pressure in the late literature of the Old Testament is therefore not toward a sublime expression of monotheism, but toward an anticipation that soon all nations will come to recognize Israel's named God YHWH as God alone. Ezra-Nehemiah and Daniel focus particularly on the confession of foreign rulers — or the consequences of lack of recognition — of YHWH as God Most High, while other literatures of the period depict in irenic (Zech 8:23) or more stringent terms (Zech 14:16-19) the necessity of seeing Israel's named God as God of all creation, worthy of worship and praise. The same holds true for YHWH's own people, who fight among themselves and against the righteousness of YHWH and his servants (Isaiah 56–66).

III

Before moving into the New Testament to see how this specific naming of God is handled, a brief reflection on the significance of the Old Testament for the modern question of proper language for God is in order.

The notion that there is only one God has ironically led in the modern period to a curious quasi-polytheism. Because this one God is thought to transcend all human expressions, not to mention names, of "him" (scare quotes are required and illustrate the dilemma), and because the many different forms of religious belief and language among Christians are still thought to point to the selfsame reality of "God" (here scare quotes are actually appropriate), we have a theoretical monotheism conjoined to a functionally polymorphous religiosity, summarized nicely by the phrase "We all worship the same God."

As we have seen, in scholarly treatments one is frequently led to believe that faith evolves or develops in respect of "monotheism," theoretically and functionally. That is, Israel's faith, if it is described as monotheistic, is said to have developed toward this, away from something else. If this could actually be demonstrated, it might be the case that the Bible could be used to defend the sort of monotheism with the capacity to relativize all human language about God — that is, a monotheism in which it could be said, "we all worship the same God." This is what has occurred in certain — largely Western, affluent — sections of Christianity. As we have seen, however, there is in fact very little distinction to be made between condemning the worship of other gods — acknowledging their existence within systems of belief and practice — and saying that such gods are in fact no gods at all. These are simply variations of henotheism.

To reject the existence of other gods is not thereby to bring an end to religious beliefs in them or halt their capacity to gain allegiance. This still remains an intramural claim, without any rational basis such as would commend general assent from the disinterested. This claim is made by Second Isaiah only on the basis of an appeal to a history of YHWH's dealings, in time and space, with his own people. One either accepts that evidence or rejects it, especially if it is a history not one's own.

Perhaps the greatest single irony of modern liberal Christianity in the West is that its most self-confident minimal statement (a monotheistic faith) is precisely what has created a functional and widespread polytheism. Because it is claimed that all human language only imprecisely names "the one God who alone is," rival languages, symbol systems, and root metaphors are all tolerated under the umbrella of Christian monotheism, because all of these point beyond themselves to "the One God" who supposedly can never be named. The metaphors can be heaped up, one upon another, in a manner even somewhat more elastic than was true in clearly polytheistic systems. Yet what the Old Testament remains most committed to, at the late period as much as in the early, is the exclusivity of the one named deity, YHWH, who is to be the sole object of worship by his own elected people and, eventually, by all creation. His name is never absorbed, but exalted, preserved, and revered, just as are the narratives that tell who he is and what he intends for his own people and for all creation. It is against this backdrop that the New Testament takes both its bearings and its point of departure.

IV

We have yet to make note of the fact that, as the Old Testament canon began to take final shape, the divine name gradually ceased to be vocalized. How this happened is unclear. Why it happened involved a number of factors, but chief among them was the sense of the name's sanctity. Fear of the name's defilement led to various means of circumlocution ("the name," "the Eternal," "the LORD"). Note that these did not begin as abstractions in search of something definite, but the opposite: glosses on a known and specific name that were intended to serve as the name's more cautious or deferential point of reference. Moreover, they only functioned in a system where the rules were quite clearly known; whenever the circumlocutions were employed, it was to the proper name of Israel's God, YHWH, that they referred. In other words, this was not a move toward abstraction, for its own sake, but a purely functional "shorthand" meant to honor the name, not replace or improve on it.

It is striking that so complete was this convention that nowhere in the New Testament does the proper name appear, except perhaps by allusion, as in "before Abraham was I am" (John 8:58), a clear reference to the *'ehyeh 'ašer 'ehyeh* of Exod 3:15. As this example illustrates, it is the appearance of Jesus as Son of God, and not just the retraction of the divine name, that permitted this sort of highly volatile allusion. That is, on the few occasions where allusions appear, they appear in conjunction with Jesus rather than with the God with whom he claims special relationship.

It requires only a cursory reading of the Gospels to see that Jesus most frequently refers to God as Father ("the Father," "your heavenly Father," "the Father who sent me," "our Father in heaven"). A similarly cursory reading of the Old Testament would show that, in fact, this is a fairly rare way to refer to the named God, YHWH (Isa 63:16). On the other hand, it is quite customary for God to refer to his own people as "son" or "sons," and the title — if that is not too strong a term — plays a specific role in respect of Israel's Anointed One *(mašiah),* as in Psalm 2: "He said of me [David], 'You are my son, today I have begotten you'" (v. 7 in English versions). Even so, from surveying the Old Testament we would gain no special picture of Israel's kings in respect of their own language for God, as involving the term "Father." In the Old Testament the filial relationship is described *from God's perspective,* hence the over-whelming preponderance of "son" over "Father" as descriptive of the divine-human relationship.

This preponderance changes in the New Testament. Two things can be said about this. Most obviously, the term "Father" emerges into greater usage, not because of something in the milieu, suggesting a particularly culture-bound usage that could or should then be open to revision.[3] Rather, the change is perspectival. The filial relationship is the same as in the Old Testament, but in the New it is described *from the standpoint of the Son,* Jesus. Where "son" appeared in the Old Testament, in the New we have "Father." This change, we repeat, has less to do with matters of culture, *or even something more personal or psychological,* and more to do with the appearance of the man Jesus and a change in perspective: from The Son to YHWH, who is referred to from that filial point of standing as "Heavenly Father."

The second point of relevance is that this expression for God in the New Testament emerges in the same climate in which circumlocutions have begun to stand in place of the divine personal name YHWH. Jesus does not refer to God as Father because of the "aptness of the metaphor," at least not in the first instance. In my judgment, this is a particularly

---

3. See the essay of Mary Rose D'Angelo ("*Abba* and 'Father': Imperial Theology and the Jesus Traditions," *JBL* 111 [1992] 611-20), but also the one to which her essay is addressed, by Robert Hamerton-Kelly ("God the Father in the Bible," in *God as Father?* ed. Johannes-Baptist Metz and Edward Schillebeeckx [Edinburgh: Clark, 1981] 101), who refers to "the Abba *experience*" (emphasis added). This experiential emphasis may do more harm than good, and it has detached the discussion from its Old Testament context.

"extramural" view of the matter, which runs the risk of holding the name "Father" hostage to romantic endorsements (Jeremias) or modern revisions, in which human fathering or some other argument from nature is the lens through which the term is refracted and judged satisfactory or lacking.[4] "Father" as a term of usage by Jesus joins other such terms in the period ("the name," "the Eternal One") and as such it is explicitly linked to Israel's specific and personally named deity, YHWH. When Jesus refers to "the Father" he means only YHWH, not a God whose essence is fatherhood or fathering. YHWH, the God of Israel, is addressed by Jesus, the Son, as Father. Obviously there is a fitness to the term, or else some neologism would have been proposed. But that fitness exists within a set universe of meaning, whose compass points are determined by Israel's specific history with her God, the named deity YHWH. To remove the term from its home in Christian scripture, and especially its logic within the Old Testament, inadvertently demonstrates how theology that begins with human existence and human categories only leads to political or psychological debates, and to impasse.

It is necessary to stay longer with the second point, because there is a peculiarly *Christian* perversion of biblical teaching about God as Heavenly Father that must be considered. Jesus refers to God as Father within the context of the Judaism of his day, where the term can only refer to Israel's named deity, YHWH. Modern Christians — with the theoretical exception of Jewish Christians — do not operate from this same perspective. From Jesus' own perspective, to use Paul's blunt language in Ephesians, "we Gentiles" are "strangers to the covenants of promise, having no hope and without God in the world" (Eph 2:12). Jesus' own more bracing image is of our receiving crumbs, like dogs who wait patiently at their master's table (Matt 15:26). It is by Christ's death and resurrection that we are adopted into fellowship with Israel's named LORD. Without this we are estranged, without hope, because "without God in the world." Jesus does not introduce a new deity named Father, to be contrasted with the God of the Old Testament — who in the new guise of Father then becomes a matter for late twentieth-century debate in western Christianity. To call God "our heavenly Father" is to address God as Jesus did, and only from that christological point of standing does the name refer to The God, Israel's named Lord, YHWH. If "we Gentiles" do not regard this language

4. J. Jeremias, *Abba: Studien zur neutestamentlichen Theologies und Zeitgeschichte* (Gottingen: Vandenhoeck und Ruprecht, 1966).

as a gift, privileging us to speak to God, in the first-person plural ("*our* Father") with Jesus, who is our only point of access to YHWH, then no amount of debate or "revision" will expose why this language is proper and good. Rather, it will only expose our forgetfulness about a gift of incorporation upon which our very lives depend.

V

Christian theology does not proceed on the basis of the Old Testament "evolving" into the New, or the New "superceding" the Old, but on the basis of a reflection on God's character as revealed in both, each in its own particular idiom. Here it is significant to note that for Christian theology, what receded in terms of particularity in the divine name YHWH, which is everywhere present in the Old but completely absent in the New, is matched by the emergence of the very specific name Jesus. The same reverence for the name enjoined in the Old attaches to the name Jesus in the New.

In modern debates about "God language" the Christian starting point remains the name of Jesus. It is only through Jesus that we share in the divine life at all, being at one time strangers to the commonwealth of Israel. The specificity of the personal name YHWH, for Israel, naming her God and the only God, is now matched for Christians by the specific name Jesus. We cannot "get at" the divine life by means of general reflection, for the one God of creation revealed himself in a special and providential way with a particular people Israel, who knew his name and his character, and knew that these two aspects cohered perfectly (Exodus 3–14). We are introduced to this special relationship by Israel's own Lord, and in so doing we take our place with those whom the prophets envisioned, who confess that "God is with you only, and there is no other" (Isa 45:14). The God who hides himself (45:15) we outsiders see and know in Jesus. Zechariah speaks of a time when "those from the nations of every tongue take hold of the robe of a Jew saying, 'Let us go with you, for we have heard that God is with you'" (Zech 8:23). That is the confession that we outside the household of Israel make, grasping the robe of Jesus.

To call God "Father" proceeds from Jesus' own language and perspective, and without this we have no access to Israel's life with the named God, YHWH. To call God "Son" is to recognize the nonnegotiable fact of access through Jesus, in the most elevated sense. To call God "Holy Spirit" is to confess that even how we address God is itself a gift from God, not to be debated or probed but received in humility and thanksgiving, with the same sense of reverence that God's people Israel had for the name YHWH, vocalized now for Christians, "Father, Son, and Holy Spirit."

Let me summarize by way of conclusion. Debating whether "father" is an appropriate metaphor for God, given modern sensibilities, is a different matter from asking, With what language can God be addressed, such that he will know himself to be called upon, and not another? Language for God is at the most basic level language of prayer, that is, language used "to call upon God" in direct address. In the Old Testament, where we can witness God's people Israel "calling upon God," God is addressed by his name. As this name becomes unutterable, God does not recede or actually lose contact with those who call upon his name. Rather, his personal name is glossed by terms which mean to protect his transcendent character without sacrificing his specificity and particularity, as he has revealed himself and made himself known within Israel.

Jesus refers to the God of Israel as Father, and in so doing speaks to that specific God and none other, reversing the direction with which Israel was already familiar: rather than from God to his son, from the Son to God "the Father." When the disciples ask Jesus to teach them to pray, the language of address, "Our Father," specifies the God of Israel. The first-person plural "our" means to include us with Jesus, who enables us to address the God of Israel, to call on his name, as had been promised of old for the nations (Isa 56:1-8). It is this gracious act of bestowal that the language "Father, Son, Holy Spirit" recalls and bears witness to, at the same time naming God as he truly is. By invoking the triune name at our baptism, we are ourselves given a name, literally, and a voice to address the one God of Israel, his eternal Son, in the unity of the Holy Spirit.

To call God "mother" or "she" would be to call attention to God as truly gendered, simply by the fact that such language means to serve as a replacement for or improvement on the biblically grounded language. Ironically, the biblically grounded language has the capacity to transcend this framework of discussion, because it emerges as a testimony to God's own name and initiative in revealing it, rather than because it conforms to metaphors whose fitness is determined by human debate or divine defense. To defend God as "father" by appeal to suitability of metaphor would in fact undo the logic with which the language emerged in the first place, which is riveted to Israel's particular experience of God's revelation and, through the work of Christ, its extension at Pentecost to all nations and peoples. "Father, Son, and Holy Spirit" emerges from a particular story. Our use of this language preserves that particular story and the God who brought it and us into being, making us his people and allowing us to be faithful witnesses who call upon his name, for our own sakes and for the sake of his creation.

18

Human Sexuality Viewed from the Bible's Understanding of the Human Condition

Recent approaches to human sexuality from a theological perspective begin by granting fairly broad berth to what we know from human experience and then make an effort to relate this to what the Bible, in its variety and richness, has said. Thus, a somewhat dialectical relationship emerges between the Bible and modern experience, which is advantageous because modern experience is kept fully in view. But what would the issue of human sexuality look like viewed solely from the Bible's perspective of what it means to be male and female creatures? In order to address this question, I want, first, to explore what the Bible says about the human condition. I will take a fresh look at such central biblical themes as the human fall, Israel's election, and the destiny of the church over against the kingdoms of the world. Then, I will turn to the special case regarding human sexuality now confronting the church: homosexuality and homosexual behavior in specifically churchly contexts. In this way, I seek to privilege, as far as possible, an encounter with the word of God in scripture over the more prevalent dialectical approach.

This chapter originally appeared in *Theology Today* 52 (1995) 236-46.

BEING HUMAN, BEING FALLEN, BEING ISRAEL

What does it mean to be human? In the modern world, we pose this question and try to answer it by considering human beings as a unique class over against all other living creatures. A theological or biblical perspective, then, restates the question as, What does it mean that this unique class of human creatures is made in the image of God? This is, of course, a very hard question to approach, requiring the cunning of the serpent and a wisdom devoid of the serpent's guile. Even so, to speak of "being human" from the perspective of divine image is not to answer a question at all but to open a window onto many other questions that the Bible only begins to address.

A simpler question, however, can be posed. Does the Bible really consider all human beings as belonging to the same essential and unique class? The answer is yes, and no, depending upon where one looks in the Bible's connected narrative about being human. Humanity is considered a distinct, unified species in Genesis 1–11, but, in these very same chapters, events transpire that permanently alter what it means to be human and what it means for human beings even to pose questions about their own humanity.

There is a longstanding debate about Genesis 3, revisited in recent days by James Barr, about whether human beings "fell" in such a way as to have permanently altered the human condition, sin and death being the consequences of that "fall."[1] The debate is not a modern one nor even primarily a Christian one. A brief survey of the debate can be found in Terence Fretheim's fine review in *Word and World,* and I agree with him that not only does the New Testament assume such a fall, as traditionally understood, but so, too, does the Old Testament.[2] The possibility I am pursuing is a different one. The traditional view of the fall is a problem because it assumes a unitary view of human individuals as a class and ignores the election of Israel and her status over against the nations at large in God's dealing with humanity.

---

1. James Barr, *The Garden of Eden and the Hope of Immortality* (Minneapolis: Fortress, 1993).

2. Terence E. Fretheim, "Is Genesis 3 a Fall Story?" *Word and World* 14 (1994) 144-53. See also the fine essay of R. W. L. Moberly, "Did the Serpent Get It Right?" *Journal of Theological Studies* 39 (1988) 1-21. Moberly reviews Barr's book in *Journal of Theological Studies* 45 (1994) 172-75.

I want to begin not with the traditional concern, namely the effects of the fall on the individual but, instead, with the impact of the fall upon humanity as a class. As a consequence of the growth of sin among human beings and the limited effectiveness of measures like the flood, humanity loses its status as a unified class of creatures. Efforts to have "one language and the same words" (Gen 11:1), the surest mark of humanity as a whole existing as a single group, collapse by divine will. The nations are scattered, and a special denominating within the national variety emerges, with Israel (or Israel-in-promise, made in pledge through Abraham and Sarah) as its focal point.

To underscore how fundamental a move this creating of Israel was, we need to consider three things. First, Israel is not marked off from other creatures physiologically. The most that can be said in this regard involves the later prescribed circumcision, but even that is a human act, divinely ordered but humanly executed, and extending only to males. That women were full members of Israel, as Israel, is nowhere questioned, making this human setting off through circumcision symbolic of a divine intention (Gen 17:1-14). So what constitutes this new denominating of humanity into Israel and the nations is the divine word alone, made in pledge alone, to Abraham. Israel becomes a reality by divine grace only.

Second, Israel, as over against humanity in general, does not possess a different or distinctive moral capacity. Whatever happened to the divine image in Adam extends in equal measure both to Israel and to the other nations. God's special people do not live longer, jump higher, or fail to disappoint just as profoundly; the opposite may well be true. What marks them out is that God will speak to them in a special and persistent way, or to individuals among them who will pass on what they know even when the tongue sticks or Tarshish seems like a safe place to hide from the potent words of the one God. "Has any people ever heard the voice of God speaking out of fire, as you have heard, and lived? . . . To you it was shown, that you might know that the Lord is God; there is no other besides him" (Deut 4:33, 35). It is important to note that God may on occasion speak to the non-Israelite, but these are exceptions that prove the rule. And when the Assyrian Rabshakeh asks, "Is it without the Lord that I have come out against this land to destroy it?" (Isa 36:10), while we hear in his words the same message of divine judgment spoken to Isaiah (Isa 10:5), we know not how he heard it, and we come to learn that his very speaking of it is blasphemy of an order deserving death.

The third consideration involves the most difficult aspect of Israel's specialness. Even when the Bible makes general statements about humanity in toto — for example, "What are human beings that you are mindful of them?" (Ps. 8:4) — we never know for sure whether or not the special voice that speaks these words regards itself as part of humanity in general, that is, as reflecting on a sort of natural revelation accessible to all. Nor are we sure what the significance of such natural or universal knowing of God might be, measured against Israel's own knowing. Israel can speak about humanity in general, itself included, but would Israel accept this wisdom from the mouth of humanity in general, with itself included as only one unprivileged part among others? It is one thing for Philo to describe the Torah from Sinai as an expression of the divine universal will; it is less clear that Philo would regard as legitimate the claims of the nations to know the one God, Israel's Lord of Hosts, under the cover of their own laws, religious customs, and mores. It is important to remember that statements about humanity in general, such as Genesis 1–11, the wisdom of the Queen of Sheba, King Lemuel, or even Balaam's ass, are modified either by appeals to the fear of the LORD as Israel's named God or by the simple virtue of being found not floating free of context but rooted within Israel's own scriptural testimony. When the Rabshakeh says what is true, that God has sent Assyria on a mission of judgment, it is true not because he says it but only because we know that God has said it on Isaiah's testimony and can, therefore, measure its truthfulness. The flip side of this is that non-Israelites may intuit what Israelites know but are afraid to tell — so the sailors and Jonah — but they never know something that Israel must intuit in respect of the one divine will. Just ask any of Daniel's blowhard adversaries; Daniel may have appeared to be in real danger, but only for a time. Kings come to acknowledge his God's truth, or they die condemned.

In sum, when more universal ways of knowing are registered in the Old Testament, these are still rooted in Israel's own special record of revelation and judged as comprehensible only within that context. This record of revelation is shared by no one else. It is this record that marks off Israel as God's elect, alone in a position to judge the truth claims of others in respect of God. The final note of Psalm 147 is not an isolated one: "He declares his word to Jacob, his statutes and ordinances to Israel. He has not dealt thus with any other nation; they do not know his ordinances, Praise the Lord." The Old Testament should never become so comfortable that we lose the irony implied in reading it, as Christian outsiders who once did not know God. With the Psalmist, we rejoice that we did not know what Israel alone knew and then say "Alleluia" because we have now been invited to share what Israel first experienced.

Thus, the Old Testament considers humanity in two categories: one fallen and outside God's special relationship with Israel, the other fallen but marked with the potential for knowing the will of God, a knowledge that sadly cannot preclude disobedience. So, with the special relationship comes also special judgment: "You only have I known of all the families of the earth; therefore I will punish you for all your iniquities" (Amos 3:2). The nations may even inadvertently do God's will and show Israel's status to be perversely a judgment on her: "You are not sent . . . to many peoples of obscure speech and difficult language, whose words you cannot understand. Surely if I sent you to them," God says to Ezekiel, "they would listen to you" (Ezek 3:5-6). But God retains a special bond with his own judged Israel that weighs more in the scale than the inadvertent doing of the will of God by those outside God's covenant. If it were not for Israel's testimony to her own hardheartedness, we would not even know that God would illustrate that hardheartedness by allowing the other nations potentially to do good.

Israel proves incapable of pleasing God, and those outside her circle do so only by indirection. So, neither acts finally in a manner that can bring about the fellowship and sustained righteousness intended in creation. We are left with redoubled efforts on the part of Israel to be the people of God, fully and completely, and promises from God that signal such efforts will never be enough, even when pursued with a pure heart. For God's designs began and ended with a will that the scattered nations would be blessed through Israel's own witness and that these two great divisions of humanity would be joined, as in Genesis 1, to worship as one people on Mount Zion: "In days to come, the mountain of the Lord's house will become the highest of the mountains . . . all the nations shall stream to it. Many peoples shall come and say, Come, let us go up that . . . he may teach us his ways and that we may walk in his paths" (Isa 2:2, 3).[3]

---

3. Incidentally, when Gentiles are included as full participants in the promises of God, through Jesus Christ, this radical move — which is a sticking point to be sure, as the opening chapters of Acts bear witness — is grounded in promises of old, made to God's own special people Israel. To depict as analogous the inclusion in the modern Christian church of men and women engaged in homosexual conduct is simply wrong (see Jeffrey Siker, "How to Decide? Homosexual Christians, the Bible, and Gentile Inclusion," *Theology Today* 51 [1994] 219-34; see also Luke Timothy Johnson's earlier essay in *Commonweal* [January 1994]). It would be equally wrong to say that unmarried "heterosexuals" ought

Practice

Understood in this way, the "fall" of humanity as depicted in Genesis 1–11 is not simply an interior psychological, spiritual, or moral state of the individual human being, repaired in some manner by God's act in

---

to be free to engage in sexual activity because that is their most compelling natural tendency. That is, though this had once been forbidden in an Israel without the love of Christ, now, in Christ, it is to be permitted. The analogy breaks down by simple virtue of the plain sense of scripture. The New Testament does not break ranks with the teaching of the Old Testament on this matter. If anything, it makes yet more stringent the Old Testament's plain sense, as a text like Mark 10:2-12 makes clear. This is also why in the history of the church, until now, the only proper context for sexual expression has been the union of one man and one woman in the covenant of marriage.

An understanding of the council of Jerusalem as a "fresh reinterpretation" of Israel's ethic points to a deeper problem of how to render properly the Old Testament as Christian scripture. The Old Testament does not function for the Christian church merely as religio-historical background for the New. It retains its own proper voice, not in simple historical, but in complex theological relationship with the witness of the New. Siker seems to sense that his evolutionary understanding might be open to charges of the Jews having a separate, less inclusive, ethic in respect of sexual conduct. Though he tries to cover himself on this front ("not in any way suggesting a supercessionist view of Christianity," p. 230) it is hard to see what his options are, having reduced the plain sense of the Old Testament to an ancient teaching in need of repair by a new word from the spirit-filled community.

Also questionable, and somewhat troubling on the same score, is his depiction of the earliest (Jewish) Christian community: "The earliest post-resurrection vision of Christianity did not conceive that Gentiles would become part of the Christian movement as Gentiles, namely apart from essentially first converting to Judaism" (p. 229). The problem again stems from an historicist approach lacking sufficient subtlety: One freezes a moment in time behind the present witness of the New Testament writings and invests it with the authority of "early" or "original," only then to regard it as impoverished from the standpoint of a modern cause. How can an issue still seeking resolution (an understanding of the church's relationship to emerging Judaism, *guided by a scriptural legacy they both shared and sought illumination from*) be both representational and normative, but also flawed, when the debate had yet to issue into a developed understanding one might call representative of the canonical New Testament in its totality, which does not state that Gentiles must "convert" to Judaism in order to be Christians?

The point is that this totality has everything to do with *proper hearing of the Old*, not correction or spirit-filled illumination *ad extra*. (I leave it to New Testament scholars to debate on historical grounds Siker's depiction of "the earliest post-resurrection vision of Christianity," though we are still left with the same question of the probative character of such reconstructions, detached from their canonical context.) That the early community in Acts 10 had difficulty with Gentile inclusion may testify to human hardheartedness, but not an inadequacy inherited from "Judaism" or the Old Testament, now to be updated by an altogether new word. Paul quite naturally uses Isa 49:6 to defend his turning to the Gentiles, as Gentiles, only several chapters later (Acts 13:44-52). Examples such as this are too numerous to record.

268

Jesus Christ, an act we confess and live by even as sin continues to invade our best daily efforts. It is this and more. The fall of humanity also has a concrete, corporate, external reality: the cleavage between "Israel become Judaism" and the church as the "New Israel," and the cleavage between both of these entities and the vast realm of humanity at large. Of these two great cleavages, the individual spiritual dimension is but a manifestation. Genesis 1–11 speaks not only of a fall through disobedience that leads to perplexed existence and death, but also of a scattering of humanity that gives rise to the promise that through God's special relationship with Israel the nations will be finally blessed. So the "fall" has both an individual and a corporate dimension. The emergence of the church as the visible Body of Christ on earth has not permanently altered the fall as a corporate reality, but sadly, if providentially, exacerbated it (Rom 11:13-36), sharpening a line between Judaism and the church that threatens in the modern period to overshadow the line between the church and the world.[4]

THE HUMAN CONDITION

Before turning to the difficult question now facing the church regarding homosexuality, let me draw together several conclusions about the human condition based upon this overview from Scripture:

(1) We cannot truly know God or ourselves by appeal to our essential nature, our emotions, or our sexual urges.

(2) What we know of God we learn through the witness of others: Israel, the prophets and apostles, and the generations of Christians who have been faithful in passing on to us what they learned from these same privileged witnesses.

(3) The testimony of these witnesses is enshrined in the scriptures of the Old and New Testaments.

(4) In those scriptures, we learn that humanity is fallen and therefore unable to set itself in right relationship to God. In the example of Israel, we see God trying with most special purpose. The plan was good, but the partners failed. As a result, the plan was not thrown out or declared to be

---

4. One would need to think long and hard about what a pink triangle worn by "gay" people, Christian and non-Christian alike, for example, may signify to post-Holocaust Jews.

in error. In accordance with its true intention, it was filled full by the holy sacrifice of Christ and then opened up for all, not just Israel, by the work of the Holy Spirit.

(5) Because humanity has been given only a foretaste of God's righteous fellowship, in the witness of Israel and in the person of Christ, we still participate in the fall of Adam: sinners but treated by God as justified. The ongoing power of sin has an individual but also a corporate attestation: the estrangement of Israel from the church.

(6) Because of our corrupted state, we will err in the way we use scripture and hear its plain sense according to the testimony of the Spirit. Satan did not tempt Jesus willy-nilly, but quoted scripture at him, the same scripture to which Jesus then appealed for rebuttal (Matt 4:5-7). Interpreters who justified slavery by appeal to scripture were found to be condemned by scripture. The fault was not in the Spirit's testimony through scripture but in the corrupt and self-serving human heart. The very fact that interpreters err in their best and worst efforts to hear scripture's word is itself a testimony to the power of sin among those who reckon themselves Christians.

(7) There is no separate avenue by which God makes the divine will known to Israel and to the church other than scripture, which means positively that scripture is sufficient to guide the church, and negatively that nothing taught apart from scripture is to be enforced by the church and made binding on the Christian conscience (for example, the theological assertion, above and beyond a civil rights claim, that homosexual activity is congruent with the will of God).

(8) In the sexuality debate or any other like it, we are taught by scripture that appeals to states of nature or human experience as revelatory of the purposes of God in Christ demonstrate nothing, in spite of their extraordinarily strong hold at present. Paul can even insist that our bodies are not our own but are, instead, temples of the Holy Spirit to be used for one purpose only: the glorification of God in word and deed.

(9) That this may now sound like religious utopianism is only a sign of how much the church has merged its anthropology fully and congenially with that of the kingdoms of this world. Their purpose and destiny were set in distinction first to that of Israel and then to that of the church regarding what it meant to be human in this life in preparation for the life to come. In 1 Corinthians, Paul can even sit loose to the general claims for sexual license he observes beyond the church or Israel, "For what have I to do with judging those outside? . . . God will judge those outside"

(1 Cor 5:12-13). Any discussion of the human condition in the modern sexuality debate must come to terms with the separation of Israel from the nations and the separation of the church from the world. Different standards obtain because God's plan of redemption begun in Israel has been extended to the church. These standards cannot be comprehended by taking soundings on the naked human condition, a condition fraught with ambiguity and selfish distortion, but can be determined only by appeal to scripture through the power of the Holy Spirit in the corporate life of the church.

(10) It is precisely the capacity to distinguish between a person's self and his or her behaviors that marks off the Judeo-Christian heritage. All have sinned and fallen short, and precisely here Christ confronts the individual with the transforming power of the cross. One cannot therefore appeal to an innate condition as positively establishing the moral justification for behavior, especially in the area of human sexuality. Antidiscrimination toward those who have designated themselves "gay" is compelled by Christ, but not because a state of nature tells individuals who they are. Instead, scripture reveals that all have fallen short *by nature*. Only that recognition can clear room for the individual to accept Christ's offering, which in turn frees the individual to love truly, mindful of Christ's sacrifice on our behalf, for the first time.

Note, then, a painful irony confronting the present church. By insisting in the case of homosexuality that states of nature and behavior are inseparable, those most in a position to have compassion in the name of Christ are cut off, namely those who believe that Christ does not love us as we are apart from a surrender of the appeal to our own individual will and human nature in order to conform to Christ's. A teachable spirit in respect of scripture's plain sense has always been a hallmark of such a person, claimed by Christ and yearning to become most fully human precisely as the demands of the Old Adam fall away before the hope of glory prepared for the New.

POSTSCRIPT:
HUMAN SEXUALITY IN THE LATE TWENTIETH CENTURY

When Augustine said God did not hold him responsible for his dreams, he was not willfully repressing what frightened him or choosing to remain ignorant of his essential self. No one was more interested in critical self-examination than was Augustine. But in Christ, Augustine was able to sit as loose to these rumblings of the unconscious self as was the Apostle Paul in confronting sexual license in the kingdoms of the world, "For what have I to do with judging those outside?" (1 Cor 5:12). He had learned what Freud later discovered, that is, that fantasy and reality are not simply determinative one of the other but, instead, reveal the essentially chaotic character, the *tohuwabohu* ("chaos and void") of human desiring left to run its own course. Freud referred to this in many instances with the blunt term "polymorphous perversity." In an effort to maximize heterosexual opportunity (an American obsession), many seek to grant this holdover from infantile sexuality an unhealthy permanence. Yet others in the homosexual community are now ironically attempting to resolve its complex character by an act of "coming out," claiming that erotic attraction to the same sex is the "outed" and essential state but that to the opposite sex "repellent." Bisexuality in its various forms must go its own way here, though common cause with the gay community remains strangely unproblematic.

For any individual, regardless of sexual proclivity, to embrace the vagaries of sexual desiring is to claim a nature God does not intend for us, as scripture has insisted, often as a lone voice. On the other hand, to make sharp distinctions among human beings, implied in the terms "homosexuals" and "heterosexuals," is to underestimate how permanently self-referential and self-absorbed is the nature we do have, dooming efforts to "come out" to our best or essential sexual self (efforts that lead instead to moralism or hedonism or the wretched combination of them both).[5] Both moralism and sexual liberationism represent a failure to come to terms with the essentially untrustworthy character (or one might say, more positively, the essentially penultimate character) of appeal to human urgings as such, whose most tragic consequence is our ongoing enslavement to them. For this and other reasons, Christians have described the life of faith as a journey, not a falling back into our essential self but a leaning ahead into the promises of God for us, requiring discipline and self-control so that the promises of God are not squandered.

In what I have said thus far about the "mixed messages" our erotic

5. Which is why, of course, until very recently no one "came out" to their heterosexuality and why some homosexually active men and women argue passionately against "gay marriage" as a servile imitation of the abuses of "heterosexism."

urges send us, it could be claimed that there is nothing more "natural" or "essential" about homosexual or heterosexual or even bisexual attractions and attachments. But this is a rather disembodied way of viewing the matter. The one ineluctable fact of human nature, of being human — persisting through the "fall," the scattering of the nations, the election of Israel, the destiny of the church — is that we are created male and female. More than this, the opening chapters of Genesis insist that maleness and femaleness is what sexual longing is fundamentally about. It is the predicate that makes sense of and grounds erotic attachment as such: "Therefore a man leaves his father and his mother and clings to his wife, and they become one flesh" (Gen 2:24). "Becoming one flesh" is the typically embodied biblical language for sexual coupling. Nowhere is it used of anything but the coupling of a man and a woman. What happens after the "fall" is that desire of man for woman and woman for man still leads to "one flesh" coupling, but now with complication (see Gen 3:16) instead of the original "and the man and his wife were both naked, and were not ashamed" (Gen 2:25). Perhaps human beings as originally created would naturally have grown old and died; that is what time is all about. But now they grasp the full reality of death because it is announced by God to them, with the consequence that their mortality is fully comprehended as meaning the end of time for themselves as man and as woman.

I rehearse this familiar chain of events because we need to ask, Why does being a man or being a woman not cleanly trump any complex package of human desires, leading naturally and always to the "becoming one flesh" of men and women? Why does embodied sexual differentiation not simply exclude desire for the same sex in the condition of being human? I hesitate to conjecture too deeply here since, as Hans Frei reminded us, the Bible's preferred mode of communication is realistic narrative, not rationalistic explanation of a sort open to direct human consent and intelligibility. Nevertheless, in the narrative line of these important stories about being sexual human creatures, a prominent feature stands out.

Part of the package of the "fall" is the full reality of death that now intrudes on the human condition as a frightening and potentially paralyzing reality (Gen 3:19). To be a man is not to be a woman, and to be a woman is not to be a man.[6] It is, instead, to accept our finite and particular mortality in God's creation, and, with the acceptance of our particular

6. Separate words are spoken to Adam and Eve in the judgment in Gen 3:16-19.

otherness, comes the full consciousness of our individual death as an inevitability. To be a man and to be a woman is to stand before the only possibility the Bible recognizes for becoming one flesh, but the way marking that path is guarded by its own kind of flaming sword: acceptance of our bodily state, that of being a man or being a woman, and with it, the inevitability of the deterioration of that body culminating in death. So the somber marriage declaration "till death do us part." The mixed-message world of infantile sexual longing of course knows nothing of death, but only of self and of desire. That is its ongoing attraction. But to know oneself as a man over against a woman or a woman over against a man is to know who we are bodily, and who we are not, a recognition that is not infantile, but adult precisely in its acknowledgment of death.

To confront the other sexually, and not the same, is to comprehend this bodily otherness in a way for which homosexual acts have absolutely no analogy. Here stands the only possibility of becoming one flesh, which is what the reality of being a man and being a woman was originally about, for its own sake and in order to overcome individual isolation and restlessness and lack of purpose (Gen 2:18-24). For the complex package of human longing, a legacy of the fall, to be trumped, there must be a recognition of our own bodily state as men and as women, and with that comes the acceptance of our mortality.

But let the Christian be of good cheer and prayerful hope. The address of the gospel has confronted our fallen human nature in a way more profound and more permanent than the gracious clothing of the first couple by God as they prepared to enter a brave new world (Gen 3:21). The overcoming of death's claim by Christ does not eradicate the bodily reality of men and women who, knowing each other as different also know themselves as mortal; rather, it gives us boldness to become who we were created to be: men and women, with the potential to become one flesh and, thereby, to create life. What was once commanded of humanity, "Be fruitful and multiply," is now shown in Christ to have the capacity to imitate God's love for creation and Christ's love for the church. Celibacy is not the recognition that "one flesh" coupling is impossible or not preferable, but a renunciation of such coupling in order to dedicate one's life individually to an imitation of the love of Christ for the world, God willing.

In light of this, to speak of being born "gay" or "straight" as an essential state of nature, whatever that means, is misleading and confusing. We are born "male" and "female." Acceptance of our bodily identity is frustrated above all by the power of death. The fact that complex sexual urges crowd in on us is a legacy of the fall, for positive developmental reasons as well as more negative ones involving the fear of death and the acceptance of our individual bodily identity and mortality. But it is this fear that Christ has come to conquer and has conquered, now offering the possibility that the marriage of man and woman, with the potential for creating life and manifesting love and purpose, might even mirror the love of God himself. In the realm of human sexuality, this is what it means for Christians to confess that in Christ God was reconciling the world to himself.

19

The City in Christian Scripture

There is no "doctrine" of the city in Christian scripture. No one biblical book dedicated to the topic. No sustained treatment about how the church should exist in the city, as against the country or suburbs. No chapter or subdivision of a book — even one as programmatic as Deuteronomy — devoted specifically to the city. One can find no studied contrast between the perils of city life over against a more contemplative rural existence. With apologies to Jacques Ellul, the city is no more of a problem for God than the country. Both places have their challenges, their potentials; and if anything the city holds far greater prospect for manifesting the presence of God than the country. "There is a river whose streams make glad the city of God" — not the country — "God is in the midst of her; she shall not be moved" (Ps 46:4, 5).

When we speak of cities today, we may have in mind poverty, the homeless, shelters and soup kitchens and drugs, the problems of isolation and loneliness; or, on the other side, ambition, power, excitement, the thrall of the possible. It's not clear how neatly this picture matches city life in antiquity, for many of these matters are the result of technology, not city dwelling per se. The thrall of the possible is now beamed down by satellite onto every roof top from Tokyo to Timbuktu from a height that leaves that tower in ancient Babel looking like, as we say in the south, a piss-ant by comparison.

From the very first, biblical texts tell of the building of cities: from

---

This essay was prepared for a conference on the city sponsored by the Center for Catholic and Evangelical Theology.

Cain's modest construction of the first city of Enoch in Genesis 4, to Nimrod the Great's Babylon and Akkad in Genesis 10; to the famous city and tower of Babel in Genesis 11; up to and including the heavenly city Jerusalem in the Revelation to John, on the Bible's last horizon. Zion-Jerusalem is the focus of much of the Old Testament's reflection: the city of Israel's messiah, the place where God's glory dwells. "I have set my king on Zion, my holy hill" (Ps 2:6). This does not change in the New Testament, though a transformation takes place. This will make inevitable Jesus' setting his face — not back toward the wilderness — but toward Jerusalem, when all is said and done. Jerusalem's historical destruction in AD 70 is anticipated in the Gospels by the transfer of language about Zion from the Old Testament to Jesus in the New, the place of God's full dwelling, a tabernacle not made with human hands. This convergence is further enhanced by the Evangelists' depiction of the temple curtain being torn in two at the hour of Jesus' death.

This having been said, old hopes associated with Zion and the city Jerusalem are not just shunted off onto Jesus and spiritualized. They retain their own integrity and remain central to Christian hope. In John's final vision there is no new *temple* — the rivers that make glad the city of God flow now from the throne of the Lamb, rather than Zion. But we are back in the heavenly Jerusalem, not Eden, not some bucolic substitute, with cities in the meantime demonized. There in John the entire cast of characters from Israel's scriptures is called back for one final scene: the heavenly Jerusalem and her eternal foe, Babylon; the serpent, the Lamb, the Father, and the saints vindicated, as the deceiver of the whole world is finally and forever destroyed. "Stay in *the city*," the risen Lord said earlier in Luke 24, "until you are clothed with power from on high." This promise is made good on in short order when the Spirit is poured out on "devout men from every nation under heaven dwelling in Jerusalem." In Jerusalem a gift of hearing reverses Babel's confusion of tongues. And all this serves as a foretaste of the final victory in the heavenly Jerusalem, come down to earth at last, as the Spirit poured out in Jerusalem now testifies to John on Patmos. My Old Testament ears are reminded of Ezekiel receiving by the Spirit a vision of Jerusalem's coming glory, her full holiness restored, on the banks of the Chebar. The glory of the LORD departs the Holy City and takes up residence on the mountains to the east (Ezek 11:23). But only in preparation for a glorious return. The interim is a time of testing and cleansing and repentance, "that they might know that I am the LORD." The man with the measuring line who describes the new temple in Ezekiel

(40:3) returns in John's revelation in preparation for the new Jerusalem (Rev 11:1-2).

It should be noted in passing that neither are hopes associated with Jerusalem handed over to some other city: a rival temple at Qumran, the Samaritans' Gerizim. This could well have happened: in Rome, Constantinople, Canterbury, Geneva, Wittenberg. Instead that original hope and language shifts to them all, with Jerusalem the original, the others facsimile. Pentecost witnesses to a transfer of God's spirit from Zion to Jesus, and then from Jerusalem to all cities, leaving Rome a mere staging point on the way even to grand American metropolis New York. The church is under challenge in this and every city post-Pentecost, caught between the lures of Babylon on one side and the promises of the heavenly Jerusalem on the other.

How a reflection on Jerusalem's destiny throughout the Old and New Testaments might help us understand the church's role in the city may not at first glance be obvious. And I am wary of making biblical texts do a turn on a dance floor where they do not belong, squeezing out relevance in an artificial way. Still, persistent interest is shown in Jerusalem as the city of God's purposes, directly and indirectly, from beginning to end in Christian scripture. There is no reneging or spiritualizing or rivalizing. A systematic overview is therefore warranted.

But let me confess. This is a huge and sprawling task, and I have wrestled hard with how to get an angle on the topic while respecting the Bible's own specific portrayal. To say that the Bible is interested in Jerusalem and Babylon, from beginning to end, as well as evil and suffering in relation to both, is not the same thing as producing a blueprint for how the church might take guidance from this for its life today. No one text on the city summarizes them all; yet all together do not produce a neatly unfolding or uniform picture. At the same time, the very general title I have chosen reflects not indecision but a preference for reflecting on the canon's wider sweep rather than on this or that individual text. By the term "Christian scripture" I also mean to avoid an approach that sets the Testaments up developmentally or that treats either the Old or the New as containing interesting information from the past, requiring updating, demythologizing, recalibration, and so forth. By "scripture" I mean: texts that mean to teach me, constrain me, reconstruct my vision of the real, by attention to their plain sense and by illumination of the Spirit, as this was given the prophets and apostles in their own day.

One of the things that will emerge is the persistence and radicality of evil in the biblical depiction. By that I mean that to the degree that holiness manifests itself in Jerusalem, there is threat in equal measure. We get no further than the second Psalm before "the nations conspire, and the peoples of the earth plot in vain" — against the LORD, his anointed, and his holy hill in Jerusalem (Ps 2:1-2). Be prepared for a discussion of the city that will sound apocalyptic at times — for that is what my own reflection on the biblical witness has turned up, to a degree I did not anticipate.

If I were to state a thesis at the outset, it would run something like this. The city Jerusalem is the central place where God's presence is known on earth, and the residence of God's messiah, David, and his offspring. City and messiah sin and are judged through the agency of Babylon. This sets in motion a force of evil that had once been contained, or had remained on the far horizon of God's dealings with his people Israel. At the same time, ironically, God's judgment on Jerusalem through Babylon has the effect of opening up Jerusalem as the earthly goal "to which the nations shall go up" — for all God's people, first the scattered Israel, and then all the nations, who would in time come to bring tribute and worship the one God there. Those exiled are accompanied by their exilers and by others. In the words of Zechariah, "In those days ten men from the nations of every tongue shall take hold of the robe of a Judean, saying, 'Let us go with you, for we have heard that God is with you'" (8:23). Or Isaiah, "They will make supplication saying, 'God is with you only and there is no other. Surely thou art a God who hidest thyself, O God of Israel, the Savior'" (45:14-15). If the sons of Abraham were to be the means by which God's blessing would be experienced by all people, the place of that experience in time becomes the city Jerusalem, where God dwells and is not hidden, but makes himself known. Yet frustrating this is a primordial evil force, larger than individual human sin and disobedience, represented by Babylon in the Old Testament and by Satan in the New, both represented in primordial time by the snake and the tower builders of Babel.

In the New Testament, Jesus becomes the place of God's habitation, as Isaiah's star moves from Jerusalem to stop over the place where the infant Messiah is born (Matt 2:9). Tribute is brought by the nations, Isaiah's gold and frankincense, as once this was to be brought to Zion, by kings drawn "to the brightness of her dawning" (Isa 60:3). Jesus becomes the means by which all nations are blessed, picking up and filling to full the role of the suffering Zion, by death on Calvary; and to overflowing, by routing death and Satan — the primal forces threatening Zion, the floods that lift up their voice, the thundering of many waters (Psalm 93). This is followed by the gift of the Spirit at Pentecost, again poured out from the same place of God's glory, Jerusalem. The temple curtain torn in two foreshadows the temple's destruction and the end of its cultic rounds. Strife emerges between the new people of God and the old, as was foreseen by Isaiah, and both are cast adrift in a hostile world as diaspora people. The New Testament insists that Satan has fallen from heaven (Luke 10:18) as once Babylon descended to Sheol in the Old (Isa 14:9), but the aftershocks of their reign on earth are still felt. In Isaiah there is conflict in Zion after the restoration (Isa 56:9–57:13), and the New Testament testifies to struggles within the church and without, as the church spreads from Jerusalem into every city on earth.

My approach to reading Christian scripture on this topic is explicitly typological. Here I am simply following the lead of the New Testament, which sees in the Old types of God's dealings, filled to full and overflowing in Christ. As such, they retain their capacity to teach, after Pentecost and before the eschaton, and display for our guidance the life of the people of God, who now include us brought near.[1] As such, we can expect to see in Zion's destiny something of the destiny of every city in which the church, where God's Holy Spirit now dwells, finds itself. This involves, as we learn from Zion, obedience and repentance, suffering — sometimes unmerited — assaults from Babylon, and conflicts within and beyond our own struggling number. Yet undiminished are hopes for Zion's full restitution, including now those of us modeled on her, because these hopes are grounded in promises from God, bound and sealed in the Old and retaining their force until the vision of scripture's final book comes to pass. These promises do not rely on unaided human striving, but on disciplined service and waiting, because they derive from God himself and are meant to guide and comfort us until all things are put in subjection to Christ. These statements of hope constitute our own source of life as the church in the city, as we await a time when all peoples will at last come together to worship God, when Satan and Babylon are finally defeated forever and when the Messiah reigns as Lord over all.

1. On a figural approach to reading scripture see George Lindbeck, "The Story-Shaped Church: Critical Exegesis and Theological Interpretation," in *Scriptural Authority and Narrative Communication,* ed. G. Green (Philadelphia: Fortress, 1987) 161-76; Ephraim Radner, "The Cost of Communion: A Meditation on Israel and the Divided Church," in *Inhabiting Unity: Theological Perspectives on the Proposed Lutheran-Episcopal Concordat,* ed. E. Radner and R. R. Reno (Grand Rapids: Eerdmans, 1995) 134-51.

Therefore, we see a foretaste in Zion of what is to take place in every city in the Christian dispensation. Zion is not just God's city of old, but as Revelation reminds us, our own hope and final destiny, as the heavenly city descends and takes up into itself every city on earth.

That, in a nutshell, is my working perspective. Now to its slower evolution, from Old Testament to New, each Testament typologically informing the other, neither coming first or last, both witnessing to Christ and the city Jerusalem, each in its own idiom.

Four aspects to being the church in the city will come to the fore. First, the need to take seriously threats from an evil within us and above us that can only be addressed with repentance and worship and trust in the Victorious One. Second, the necessity of bearing unmerited suffering, because the poor and helpless in the city are representations of ourselves, needful of the savior's victory over evil, as we know ourselves to feel that need. Third, the need for persistence through ongoing conflict *within the church itself*, as the aftereffects of Babylon's power and thrall remain forces to reckon with. And finally, the need for a discipline of trust that our city's destiny is God's concern, because the promises lavished on Zion of old have been transferred to the church *wherever* she finds herself, but especially in the city. Revelation's promise of the heavenly Jerusalem is not pie-in-the-sky dreaming, but the conviction borne of the Spirit that God is coming toward us to bring to fruition his plans for a new creation, just as we work through prayer and repentance and suffering and persistence to greet him.

I now want to look in general terms at how the city is depicted in the Old Testament. The path I will take leads from the ideal city, Jerusalem, to city building in general, as this is described in the primeval history, in Genesis 1–11. Special attention is paid to the Tower of Babel story at its conclusion. Then the line that clearly connects Babel to Babylon is followed, taking us to Isaiah, where we again encounter God's special city Jerusalem, now pitted against the mighty Babylon. Because the war between Zion and Babylon — seen in Isaiah 13–14, 21, 24–27, and 46–47 — is so clearly a type for the battle between Satan and Christ, Isaiah will form the center of our reflection on being the church in the city. Reading Isaiah in this way, one discovers the lesson of the church fathers, who called Isaiah the First Apostle, and the lesson of Ambrose, who told the newly converted Augustine where best to hear the gospel of Jesus Christ: in Isaiah. I hope to hear the gospel there as well, where Zion plays so central a role and offers a glimpse at the city's destiny in our own dispensation post-Pentecost.

In Israel, Jerusalem is the city where God dwells. His presence is described as *kabod,* glory, effulgence, filling the tabernacle in the temple, a holiness before which all is unclean, even the most righteous of prophets. His presence is also known through his chosen agent of justice, his son, the messiah or anointed one, David, and his offspring up to and including the Messiah, Jesus. The relationship between messiah, Lord, and city is not bulletproof, but is open to changes and chances. God can actually absent himself, with the city still intact: so Ezekiel watches God's glory depart from Jerusalem *before* the city is destroyed. Or the messiah can be absent, or meriting judgment, with God's presence in Jerusalem untouched. Or the messiah can be both present and a proper agent of God's *mishpat* ("justice") without specific attachment to a place. So God promises David that his lineage will stand forever (2 Sam 7:12) before he takes up the request to build in Jerusalem "a house for my name."

At the same time, it is clear that God's intention in the fullest sense is for all three — city, messiah, divine presence — to cohere in such a way that blessing is felt through all creation. "Great is the LORD and greatly to be praised, in the city of our God, his holy mountain is the joy of all the earth" (Ps 48:1-2). The promise of an eternal lineage for David is completed with a promise of an actual physical house, in Jerusalem. The choice of Zion as God's dwelling place, the psalmist insists, includes the Davidic messiah: "I have set my king on Zion, my holy hill" (Ps 2:6). As the psalm continues the anointed one is addressed as God's own son: "today I have begotten you." Assaults on the LORD are assaults on his anointed, his messiah. The Ezekiel who watches God's glory depart and whose opinion of anointed shepherds is most cautious also envisions God replanting his messiah, "the topmost cedar sprout," again on Mount Zion, "that it may bring forth boughs and bear fruit, and become a noble cedar; in the shade of its branches birds of every sort shall nest" (Ezek 17:22, 23). However subsequent history conspired against the promises for David, original promises and promises reissued after the destruction of Jerusalem, the promises are not withdrawn. Following Ezekiel's lead, they are often expanded: God's messiah is to be the sign of God's rule and protection for all peoples. The shoot from the stump of Jesse means nothing less than that "the earth will be full of the knowledge of the LORD as the waters cover the sea" (Isa 11:9). To Jerusalem all the nations will stream, "for out of Zion shall go forth the law, and the word of the LORD from Jerusalem" (Isa 2:3). What the psalmist stated in terms of warning at the beginning, "O rulers of the earth, serve the LORD with fear, with trembling kiss his feet" (Ps 2:10-11), at the end the psalmist strains to express in language of praise, extended through all creation. "Let everything that breathes praise the LORD" (Ps 150:6).

The mature history of Israel could in fact be traced by attending to this fragile but critical symbiosis: city, messiah, Lord. Jerusalem is the city where God is present and from which justice is to go forth to benefit all cities in Israel and eventually in all the earth. If Jerusalem did not have that status to begin with, after Zion's Babylonian defeat that increasingly is her role: navel of the universe, destination of all peoples, the health of the entire cosmos dependent on her. The bulk of the psalms, especially those in Books IV and V, have this as their sole theme. "There is a river that makes glad the city of God, the holy habitation of the Most High. God is in the midst of her; she shall not be moved" (Ps 46:4). "The LORD is great in Zion, he is exalted over all the peoples" (Ps 99:2). "That men may declare in Zion the name of the LORD, and in Jerusalem his praise, when peoples gather together, and kingdoms, to worship the LORD" (Ps 103:22). "Those who trust in the LORD are like Mount Zion, which cannot be moved, but abides forever" (Ps 125:1). I could easily devote my energy to nothing but quoting from the psalms on this theme.

So why is this divine intention for the holy city — city of cities — frustrated? It bears repeating that there is nothing inherently flawed about cities in the Bible. Cities are not set in contrast to the country. When did Israel murmur? When it was in the country, where the rule of the road is wild beasts, lack of food, snares, and pits.

Cities are depicted as being built as soon as the flaming sword was in place to guard the way to the tree of life (Gen 3:24). There is no sustained period of country living that then devolves into city life. The first city is built by Cain in Genesis 4 and named after his son. It represents the desire for protection and shelter, for oneself and in the name of one's children. The city has no name, no other purpose, than that. The same Hebrew word, *'ir,* applies to foreign cities and cities in the promised land, cities big and small, cities holding potential for blessing (Jerusalem) or curse (Sodom).

Still, it seems that because city-building can get one a name, can serve as a manifestation of human strength, there is the potential for particular evil of a different sort than what Israel would eventually experience in the wilderness. Cities are mentioned as being built or already in existence shortly after Cain's modest and necessary construction in Genesis 4. Following the flood, the nations emerge from the sons of Noah and begin to spread out. Cities are built for them. Anticipating the tower of

Babel story, Genesis 10 reports the specific building of cities in Assyria and the land of Shinar, that is, Babylonia. Babel, Erech, Akkad, Nineveh, Rehoboth-Ir, Calah, the great city, are all built by Nimrod in Genesis 10. He is the first on earth to be a *gibbor*, a Schwarzenegger whose power is tinged with violence. Nimrod is a mighty hunter, the pithy note at 10:9 reads; to hunt is to be more powerful than animals, to subdue nature. Cities and civilization entail the subjugation of nature. For this Nimrod is renowned. And there is no romantic memory of savage innocence here, an unspoiled time before civilization, Rousseau's lost Eden, just a matter-of-fact description of the movement from one period to the next.

These early Genesis stories, before God calls Abraham, are about the establishment of limits, painful but necessary, and in the end beneficial. Exposed are the limits within which blessing can be experienced: in sexual relationship, in social relationship, in knowledge, in the desires of the heart, in human ambition and in human labor. Round and round these themes the stories in Genesis 1–11 circle.

Cities are monuments to human labor. They provide shelter from one generation to the next. But they can also get tied up with the wrong sort of human ambition. To get a name is not wrong in itself. But in Genesis 11, the final episode in primordial time, city-building is connected by the citizens of Babel with an effort to thwart God's designs. This can be the only explanation for the story's curious placement, *after* scattering has occurred and languages have emerged. Yet the citizens propose: "Come let us build a city, and a tower with its top in the heavens, and let us get a name for ourselves, lest we be scattered abroad upon the face of the earth" (Gen 11:4). The connection between getting a name and not being spread abroad, otherwise unclear, is explicable as wanting to undo what God has previously wrought. That it is God's will, and not a judgment, that humanity scatter is made clear by the preceding chapter, where the nations emerge with different languages and identities after the flood in fulfillment of the command to be fruitful and multiply, fill the earth, and subdue it. That was our only original charge from God in Genesis 1: to fill the earth and subdue it. Babel's citizens wanted to subdue, but on their own terms and not those imposed by the original charge.

The Babel story, the final episode before the call of Abraham, means to take another run at why humanity is scattered and speaks different tongues. Not because this was the logical outcome of dispersion and naturalization over time, as God intended, but because there had been an instinct in the human heart connecting labor with getting a name through unity of purpose, unfrustrated by language barriers. And with this came an unfortunate catalyzing — depicted as a raid on heaven itself. How these various distinct things are logically connected is left unclear by the narrator: getting a name, grand achievement, not wanting to spread abroad, unity of language and purpose. But at some point God is forced to conclude, "this is only the beginning of what they will do; and *nothing* they now devise will be impossible for them" (11:6).

What the story reveals is that an element of devising emerges in the wake of human success, which is in the nature of things set against the will of God. Cities, because they contain populations in compression, have the capacity for mobilizing energies and diversities toward a common goal, and at some point accomplishment itself breeds "devices and desires" in the human heart of which we may remain unconscious, but which constitute an affront to God and a threat to true human thriving as God intends it. The successful project intrudes between God and humanity precisely as it takes on a life of its own in externalization (the magnificent tower), which then serves as a point of reference for humans beyond simple naming. Ironically, as the story leaves it, through their search for a name known abroad, the citizens of Babel remain forever anonymous. This capacity to externalize human labor into something monumental distinguishes humanity from nature, but it also brings with it a false form of name-getting, through identification by human projection rather than by God's address. So God confuses all this, leaving even simple names incomprehensible and strange across language groups.

Why this must be so is as unclear as why there is a tree from which we must not eat, whose very prohibition is the source of its appeal. The problem with city-building is that no one can tell exactly when the appropriate need for protection, justice, and organization slides over into name-getting, human endeavor in love with itself, and a false sense of independence and unity, achieved rather than granted. The story warns about that and lets the example of Babel stand as a signpost.

Yet that is not the end of it. The flaming sword that turns every direction, guarding the tree of life, closes off a period of existence forever. But in Babel we are clearly meant to see Babylon. Here we have an obvious leak into real time and space, and the destiny of a real city. When Babylon the Great then appears in history, there is the distinct possibility that the tower the citizens left off building will be tackled again with fresh mortar and up-to-date plans. A lesson learned could have two outcomes: stop, or try again, wiser and more bent on success than ever.

By contrast consider Sodom and Gomorrah. These cities too are mentioned in Genesis 10, alongside Babylon. For whatever reason, they are not described as having been built, but simply appear. Their ultimate fate is described in history, tied up as this is with the destiny of Abram's nephew Lot and his family, as well as that of the Moabites and Ammonites. Still, after the destruction of Sodom and Gomorrah reported at Genesis 19 their names are only a byword, recalling a fate from the distant past intended to serve as a warning in the present. Babylon, on the other hand, emerges on the canvas of history, intertwined with Israel's fate, at a much later date, as the replacement for the mighty Assyrians (Isa 23:13). No Pharaoh, not even the nameless tyrant who refused to let God's people go, ascends as high as Babylon's height. In all the registers of oracles against foreign nations in the prophets of the Old Testament, Babylon's position remains sure, highest of the high. Above the cedars of Lebanon, according to Isaiah 14, there is Babylon: "You who said in your heart, 'I will ascend to heaven, above the stars of God, and set my throne on high'" (v. 13). And then the kicker: "I will make myself like the Most High" (v. 14). The brief glimpse at Babel's faulty tower prepares us in primordial time for an evil that will wreak havoc on all creation, not just on an about-to-be-scattered few.

Assyria and Babylonia are frequently conflated in the Old Testament, yet their identities are safeguarded and distinct, just as we know the difference between the Nineveh of Jonah and Nahum and the Babylon of Isaiah and Daniel. When they are closely related, as in Isaiah and Habakkuk, this is because the one is viewed as a foreshadow or advance guard of the other. This is a cause for despair in Habakkuk, as the prophet watches God dispatch Babylon, the bitter and hasty nation whose justice proceeds from itself, on an ironic mission of judgment against Assyria (Hab 1:6-7). In Isaiah, it is a simple fact of history, as Assyria, rod of God's fury, sent against a godless nation, is replaced and then upstaged by Babylon. In both cases, there is the clear paradox of a world judgment being executed by the epitome of injustice, pride, and violence.

I mention Jonah in passing and it is worth remembering that a better example of the unforgivable being forgiven, the unrepentant turning from wickedness to live, would have sent the reluctant prophet packing for Babylon, not Nineveh. Yet this is exactly what distinguishes these two superpowers. In Babylon there is a display of evil and violence so rank that it cannot be forgiven, because it feeds on its very status as unforgivable. To come to terms with Babylon outside primordial time is to approach a proud tower of redoubled effort, which God allows to stand and which he must limit in another way than simple scattering. It is important to understand how Babylon is not Nineveh, nor Sodom, whose only vestige is salt pillars and a whiff of sulphur (Gen 19:24-28). Particularly as depicted in Isaiah, Babylon emerges as the inverse of Zion, several stages out beyond Assyria, who began as the *just* rod of God's fury, a role Babylon never had.

Let me reconnect with my opening remarks at this point. I believe we should understand the modern city as thriving under the same conditions set forth for God's own place of habitation, Zion, yet now in the dispensation of the Messiah who has come and who will return to judge the world. In the earlier dispensation of Israel it is crucial to see exactly where the threat to God's city comes from and what it looks like. What we glimpse as threatening human thriving in the Babel story we see in mature and full-blown form in Babylon. To talk about being the church in the city without coming to terms with large-scale forces seeking to undermine that would be foolhardy. There is an irrational, transpersonal force, illustrated by the biblical Babylon, that runs roughshod over unaided goodwill or human projects for self-reform. The church's first job is therefore to preach the gospel, aware that pitted against it are inevitable principalities and powers. To call on the name of Jesus is to address the only one capable of routing those forces, within and outside the church, in ways that transcend our comprehension. The church in the city without a Messiah is as doomed as Zion before Babylon's might.

The prominent Christian ethicist Stanley Hauerwas can urge that the church not just have a social ethic but be a social ethic, yet even this distinction pales if one is thinking only about the church pressing its cause on neutral territory through initiatives of action or simple presence or good works. There is an Enemy pitted against the church, an Enemy that takes up residence in the human heart and that is likely to be more interested, as Luther reminded us, in the godly than the ungodly. No territory is neutral. The church's first activity in therefore repentance; its second, worship and praise. All three the Enemy hates because they do not represent earthly mobilizations on behalf of this or that just cause, where the slings and arrows of ambition and achievement invade and infect. Instead, by primary attention to the unclean human heart we are constantly reminded that we do those things we ought not do and leave undone what we ought to have done, because that is the naked human condition. All social action flows from prayer addressed to God, mindful of the power of sin and the devil. The cleansing of the one and the crushing of the other are wholly God's act in Christ, the only one capable of defeating the Babylon pitted against Zion, the only one capable of turning flawed human endeavor into the means of grace and hope of glory, for ourselves and for those we seek to serve in Christ's name. "Simon, Satan has sought to sift you like wheat, but I have prayed for you" (Luke 22:31-32). The church in the city stands or falls by this prayer.

In short, if one sets out to track the city in Christian scripture, one will in time come upon Babylon — a city that continually presents a threat to all cities, just as Zion and messiah, on the flip side, represent and offer hope and life and victory. The tower of Babylon is nothing but the logical culmination of human pride and ambition, as we see it in primordial time and witness it in all times and places, permitted by God to go its perilous and all-consuming way.

Isaiah depicts Babylon's defeat and at the same time depicts a battle so devastating and horrendous as to frustrate simple connection with any moment in past history. "Behold the LORD will lay waste the earth and make it desolate, and he will twist its surface and scatter its inhabitants; the earth shall be utterly laid waste and utterly despoiled, for the LORD has spoken this word" (Isa 24:1, 3). Here we see the inner nerve of the book of Isaiah: more than any other prophetic book, events are typologically fraught, that is, they mean what they mean for contemporaries but contain within themselves a significance that ramifies into the future. There is dramatic movement within the book: Assyria gives way to Babylon; Babylon is defeated by Cyrus; Israel goes home and Zion is restored. Yet, through contact with this agent of judgment, Babylon, forces are unleashed on the cosmos that turn a defeat by Cyrus, however impressive in its day, into something provisional, a foreshadowing of a yet greater battle among forces that can only be called principalities and powers. Chapters 24–27 describe such a battle. A neat connection between justice and protection, righteousness and blessing, was broken, and into the vacuum created by this came mighty Babylon. The aftermath is then anything but neat. The raw power unleashed creates ripples throughout history, within but also beyond Isaiah's own literary horizon.

So we come to the second aspect of being the city, exemplified by Zion's plight, once Babylon has been permitted to unleash a judgment more awful and more ungodly than Assyria's. Zion must suffer. Chapter 47 tells of Babylon's terror. "You showed them no mercy . . . you made your yoke exceedingly heavy . . . secure in your wickedness you said, 'No one sees me' . . . 'I am, and there is no one besides me.'" Even the LORD's own "I am who I am" is here preempted by Babylon. In God's dealing with Israel's sins through such a vile worker of judgment, there was spillage, and Zion bears the brunt of that.

To be the church in the city is to bear a degree of unmerited suffering. Zion has sinned and for that endures punishment, but in addition she suffers on behalf of her children: "for your transgressions," the prophet tells Zion's citizens, "your mother was put away" (50:1). To be the church in the city is to take up a cross, simply because Babylon's fury persists and catches in its thrall those who misuse power and in so doing injure the helpless. Because cities are locations of amassed resources and raw power, proud towers are built that often fall on the innocent. The church is that place where we acknowledge our capacity to generate evil and inflict pain and extend Babylon's legacy. It takes the Messiah's victory to stop the cycle of sin and guilt, which frees us to attend to innocent suffering and to the hurt we ourselves have caused. This is certainly a chief vocation for the church in the city: as the suffering Zion, to see in the poor and helpless Babylon's victims, and yet the rescued of Christ, in the same way we know that rescue has given us new life and hope.

In the book of Lamentations the author's identification with the suffering Zion reveals a broken and contrite heart — "How lonely sits the city, weeping bitterly in the night: Is it nothing to you, all you who pass by? Look and see if there is any sorrow like my sorrow" — a heart prepared by God to identify with and serve the poor. Not out of general human decency, but because the suffering Zion foreshadows the king who carried his own cross to die in order to break open hearts to imitate and serve him.

It is striking that at this junction of the book of Isaiah, Israel's messiah is missing. Zion bears the suffering for her wayward children and double for all her own sins. Next to Zion is the nameless Man of Sorrows, who works atonement for those who confess his suffering and death to be an expiation for their sins, while for Babylon, chapter 47 concludes, "there is no savior." The remainder of the book speaks of God's intention to save Zion and restore to her her children, to be joined now by the nations. But this intention is frustrated, now as much within as without. Zion's period of intense suffering and humiliation is over, but in its wake comes a different threat: fighting among God's own people. The righteous servants of God buffeted by those in their own midst. All this frustrates and postpones God's return to Zion and her promised exaltation as the place where all nations will worship. Yet the prophet never gives up hope. "Arise, shine;

for your light has come, and the glory of the LORD has risen upon you, nations shall come to your light and kings to the brightness of your dawning, they shall bring gold and frankincense, and shall proclaim the praise of the LORD" (Isa 60:1, 3, 6). What the prophet there strains to see, the gospel proclaims as arrived. Jesus is the missing Messiah, the suffering and the resplendent Zion, the Man of Sorrows, and the Victorious Victim.

The coming of the nations — those of us who are not of the household of Israel — is accomplished through Christ, the New Jerusalem, the embodied place where God's spirit resides and is poured forth. As in Isaiah, this creates tension within Israel, as those outside are brought near. "The shepherds have no understanding; they have all turned to their own way, each to his own gain, one and all" (Isa 56:11). But it is a tension that is not so fundamental as to stand in the way of God's final designs for all creation: that it be restored and renewed, that which divides being overshadowed by and through our common worship. Just as there is conflict between the New and the Old Israel in Isaiah and just as this conflict creates a special tension within the original people of God themselves, so too the church must now experience conflict and tension within its own ranks. This is the third reality facing the church in the city: the presence of conflict within the community. We are not to be caught off guard by this or long for a unity that may mask a tower-building desire or the hope of getting that one single language without any confusion that tells us that we have it all right at last — which could be a raid on heaven rather than a healthy God-given concern. On the other side, the challenge is how to rightly interpret the conflict that emerges when it does, and not simply welcome conflict as the sign of healthy diversity, until Christian believing has no excluding form whatsoever and devolves into sentimentality.

In Isaiah this tension, on the positive side, has to do with the birthpangs caused as Zion gathers to herself, in Christ, children she did not know she had. But Isaiah insists that there will be room. "Enlarge the place of your tent, and let the curtains of your habitation be stretched out; hold not back, lengthen your cords and strengthen your stakes" (Isa 54:2). Yet not as an orgy of inclusion *for its own sake*. Much of the conflict we witness in the last eleven chapters is borne of an assault on God's holiness in Zion, idolatry, and false worship, which leads not to inclusion but to destruction for those within and outside the community of faith. In the synagogue, the forbidding last line of Isaiah — rebels in eternal fire — is rendered less final by rereading the preceding verse: "all flesh shall come to worship before me, says the LORD." But even this practice does not keep the community unaware that conflict and diversity are never goods unto themselves, and when God's holiness is offended against and inclusion leads to syncretism, the judgment of God is absolute. There can be no "celebration" of conflict, even as it may well witness to a bringing about of God's plans in spite of human sin and offense. Diversity is no good unto itself, even as human distinction is not erased, but caught up in the worship of one God, in one place, where the victorious Messiah is now eternally enthroned, because he is that throne in himself.

The last word of Isaiah is not its penultimate verse, but the spirit's gift to John on Patmos, which is more indebted to Isaiah than any other of Israel's scriptures. There Isaiah's unfinished business is finished. The true last line is supplied. Isaiah's war of judgment on earth had its counterpart in heaven, we learn in Revelation 13. As Babylon's descent in Isaiah was foreshadowed in primordial time by the throwing down of Babel's proud tower, the war in heaven shows the Lamb victorious over the foe from all eternity. End time and primordial time turn out to be wound on the same clock. Then in the fourteenth chapter the Lamb appears on Mount Zion, and an angel announces as final what seemed in Isaiah only provisional: "Fallen, fallen is Babylon the great." Chapter 18 is a revel to this defeat, woven from God's word of old to Isaiah, after which the saints who have endured and those who have died in the Lord together witness the great city Jerusalem coming down out of heaven for her long-promised exaltation, with the Messiah himself not just her throne but her temple, the source of living and healing water for all nations.

John knows that we are living between the times and must now endure. But our hope is sure. We see our destiny in that of Zion, and the spirit has testified to God's own purpose at work to reward the saints. It is that hope that we live by in times of evil assault, suffering, and conflict, whose issue is not ours to know, except as that is given to us by the one who has conquered evil before the foundation of the world and who calls us to be faithful in the middle time. Let the risen Lord's word to the disciples be our own, in this middle time: "Behold, I send the promise of my Father upon you; but stay in the city, until you are clothed with power from on high" (Luke 24:49). "So they returned to Jerusalem with great joy, and were continually in the temple blessing God" (24:52-53).

20

Reader Competence and the Offense of Biblical Language

The Limitations of So-Called Inclusive Language

As I write this, the Church of England has approved the ordination of women to the priesthood. This decision will be viewed by many as a sign of hope, the tearing down of barriers that kept women from important leadership roles in the church. Some who share this view will nevertheless worry that in its wake will come redoubled efforts at finally ridding ourselves of the "sexist" language of the Bible, to be replaced by new and more "inclusive" images for liturgy, hymnody, and general talk about God in the community of faith and in the culture at large. Is it possible to regard the ordination of women as a biblically sound decision, long overdue, and at the same time worry about the many ways in which our understanding of God as revealed by these same scriptures is increasingly under fire?

In this brief essay I want to look at the logic of the Bible's language for speaking about God. I then want to ask again, from a different angle than the now traditional one concerning inclusion and exclusion, why biblical language for God is under assault. I will propose that the problem lies not with our texts but with our own fast diminishing "reader competence" as a church and as a culture for comprehending the subtle world of biblical discourse.

This chapter originally appeared in *Pro Ecclesia* 2 (1993) 15-22.

In its use of language for God, the Bible presents us with a paradox. The very book that uses masculine address for God is the same book that insists God is neither male nor female but the wholly other creator God, Lord of all creation — who is not to be constrained by any image, "in heaven or on earth," as the second commandment puts it.

The paradox confronts us on the first page of the Bible. God creates humanity: male and female he creates them. The Bible asserts that God is above human sexuality; yet then it speaks of God with masculine address and masculine metaphors. By contrast, other religious texts from the ancient world never lifted their discourse to the same level of paradox and — may we say — sophistication, choosing instead to speak not of the One Holy God, but of many gods and by having female gods alongside explicitly male ones. (And also usually making the male deity the chief deity, with female deities challenging this domination from time to time — something that sounds fairly modern, given the inclusive language debate.)

But the Old Testament rejects this description of God: God is neither male nor female. At the same time, neither is God addressed as "mother," "she," "her." The rejection of female language is not an insistence that God is male but rather an insistence that as language of address, masculine language is appropriate and fitting. It will be the purpose of this essay to explore how and why this is true. To repeat: the Bible assumes a distinction between *fitness* as appropriate speech about God, as against a claim for the *actual male identity* of God. If you had asked an ancient Israelite, male or female, if the God addressed as "he" were in fact a man, the response would have been puzzlement.

The Old Testament is at such pains to protect the otherness of God, the nonsexual character of God, that it does not frequently employ the metaphor "father," even as it does speak of God with the third person masculine "he." God, addressed as "he," can even be said to care for his children like a mother (see Hos 11:4). But to take another example: God never cares for *her* children like a mother. This language is never used as direct or indirect address in the Old Testament. It is quite appropriate for modern liturgies and hymnody to speak of God acting like a mother. It is a simile that fits, according to the Bible's own frame of reference — though it should be added that even this sort of usage is quite rare in the Bible. And to speak of God comforting children like a mother (Isaiah 66) is not the same thing as addressing God as "she" or referring to God as "our mother." Such language is not employed in the world of biblical reference.

It is the New Testament that makes wider use of the metaphor "father." In so doing it picks up a fit metaphor from the Old Testament, used there for the primary purpose of stressing the close familiarity between God and Israel, God's son; or God and king, called "son" in Psalm 2. But again, to say that Israel is God's son, or God's bride, is not to say that God is a man or a husband in a sexual sense, any more than it means that Israel is only male (son), or only female (bride). In the same way, when we call God "Father," following the example of Jesus, we are not saying anything about God's sexuality. Rather, we are participating in a frame of reference where language functions in a certain specific way. God is not our human sexual father, but "our Father who art in heaven," "our heavenly Father." Jesus does not refer to God as Father to assert the maleness of God but to assert the closest personal relationship between himself and the transcendent God of Israel. What could be closer than the personal language he uses? The language also serves to indicate that God's intention with Israel, firstborn son, is now embodied in Jesus, son of God. "Mother" is further unfit in this instance as a term of address because Jesus' mother is Mary, a woman. But Jesus' father is not a man, on crude analogue with Mary the woman, but the wholly other God of Israel, who, nevertheless, is spoken to on the most intimate terms possible. By speaking of God as Father, Jesus points the way toward a particularly intimate and personal relationship with God, one that he himself knows and then offers to us and the world at large. This is not an act of sexual oppression but an act of sheer grace and mercy.

So the question naturally arises: why stick with *this* system of biblical discourse, and not another, more modern substitute? How negotiable is the biblical world of language reference?

First, let us be clear about the character of such a question. Does it arise in order to reject the maleness of God? If so, we have to remember that it is the Bible itself that asserts that God is no man. In a very real sense the Bible was a unique voice in the ancient world because it rejected imparting sexuality to God or speaking of both female and male gods. Reject this biblical representation, and you reject the paradox it guards and protects, whereby God is wholly other, yet addressed in personal language.

But why not call God "mother," as well as, in addition to, "father"? If God is "he" — even in a system of address that insists that God is not a man — why not also "she"? If father, why not also mother? Again, let us be clear that this sort of question is a thoroughly modern one. It is never raised in the pages of the Bible itself (except when other religions and other rival ways of speaking of God are being rejected). And female language for God would have functioned with great difficulty in the New Testament for reasons already mentioned. Therefore any answer we supply is mere conjecture. Why not call God mother as well as father? Why does the Bible refuse to multiply and complement the language for God?

One possibility is that to do so would be to suggest that God is actually not without sexuality, but is the totality of sexuality: both male and female. Yet this would not adequately protect God's transcendence as *creator* of sexuality and would rather imply that God is the full embodiment of sexuality. Human sexuality would then be a way to comprehend God rather than a gift of God to be used responsibly and sacrificially. The Bible rejects human sexuality as the prime means of comprehending God.

Then why not refuse to call God "Father," "he," "him" and adopt instead "mother," "she," "her" as fit metaphors — remember that we are talking about a system of discourse, not actual descriptions of God as a sexual being. Would this not protect the transcendence of God and the otherness of God from his creation?

It may be that the metaphor of "mother" loses its appropriateness because of the intimate and direct way in which human mothers participate in procreation (so the theologian Robert Jenson: God's creation is not to be confused with procreation, but is something more external, indirect, and mysterious). But this is sheer conjecture and the Bible never raises the topic for discussion in the same way that "inclusive" language proponents are doing today. Female language for God would also run into severe problems given the logic of the New Testament, where Jesus' mother is Mary.

Again it is critical to remind ourselves how specific to our age this sort of inquiry is. Can we really adjust or modify a system of discourse like the one given in the Bible, without doing irreparable harm to the source of all our discourse about God? Can we really penetrate the logic of its discourse in some rationalistic way, why it has chosen masculine language of address as the most appropriate for insisting on God's non-sexual nature? Or does the very fact that questions are now being raised point to another sort of problem that has nothing to do with the fitness of metaphors, the transcendence of God, or the language of address in the Bible? I want now to turn the discussion in a slightly different direction and ask: why is the traditional language seen as inadequate?

The quick answer usually given is that male language for God is a reflection of a male-dominated culture, of patriarchal efforts at projecting male power wishes onto the deity, thereby creating God in man's image (in the phrase of one "inclusive" language proponent, "if God is male, male is God"). A milder version of this objection to male language argues that women are thereby shut out from the life of God in a way that is not true for men. Male language for God includes men but excludes women.

Both the milder and stronger forms of objection, however, work not so much from the side of the biblical presentation as from the side of human experience. That is, because of the sheer passion and concern about male and female equality in the modern age, the paradox of biblical language is forgotten and misunderstood, whereby masculine language of address did not describe God's maleness so that men could feel included, but was simply the fittest language for insisting on God's nonsexual character. In the climate of modern debates about inclusivity, suddenly what is true about God is that he really is a man and that women, not surprisingly, feel shut out. The paradox of biblical language is undone. If biblical language were in fact nonparadoxical and meant rather specifically to identify God as a man, women would be quite right in insisting on changing the language, adding female language, or substituting female images and language for male ones.

Another question must be raised at this juncture. How did masculine language of address once function for other generations in such a way that both women and men felt appropriately addressed and no objections concerning inclusion or exclusion were ever raised? Was it simply that women in previous generations were too oppressed to object? And why are some modern liberated women unwilling to modify the traditional biblical language?

Here, it seems to me, we begin to touch on the deeper reason that objections are presently being raised. The underlying reason has less to do with inclusion or exclusion and more to do with what has been called "the eclipse of biblical narrative" (the phrase is that of the late Hans Frei); that is, the thoroughgoing loss of the biblical world as a key agent in informing our world in the modern age and the loss of confidence in how to read and live into these biblical stories, from Old and New Testament. For none of our forefathers or mothers who lived and breathed the world of the Bible would ever have suggested that God's representation as father was anything like human fathering in a direct and exact sense, allowing men to feel warmly included and women bluntly excluded. A man who read of God's freeing of *his* people from bondage in Egypt did not feel that our efforts at social justice were being imitated by God, warmly embraced by God, or included by God, but challenged, judged, and even sharply excluded. In a prior day both men and women felt the sharp distance between God and humanity and gave thanks that God was God and not man (or woman), because God could save and deliver in ways that we cannot. The man who hears of God's raising *his* only Son from the dead identifies neither with God nor with Jesus, except as a grateful recipient of the same unearned love and justice from this God whom humans address as "he" when they speak of him, "you, thou" when they speak to him. The female child of an alcoholic father is right to object that God is not her father; God is her heavenly Father whose justice condemns the abuse she has suffered and whose mercy extends forgiveness only to the penitent.

The point is: masculine language for God functioned within a specific biblical realm that every reader knew was distinct and set over against the daily best efforts of men and women. The content of a term like "Father" was not determined by what we could say at the best or worst of times about our earthly fathers, but was determined instead by the biblical stories themselves and their descriptions of how God has acted, judged, saved, and delivered from sin and death — actions that neither men nor women identified with inclusively, as imitations of our earthly fathers, but as a sign that God was God and not man. Thank God!

Is it at all surprising that a book is judged inadequate and noninclusive whose basic content is increasingly unknown and whose full narrative world is no longer gratefully inhabited? Instead this book comes to us in the form of isolated bits and pieces (the lectionary is partly responsible for this), forced into our late twentieth-century, allegedly more enlightened, frame of reference, reduced to a disconnected collage of uprooted and transplanted images. Now when we hear of God as Father, what he has done for his children, "Father," "he," and "his" mean only what they mean to us as language about our fathers, our sons, our men. These key biblical images are removed bodily from their contexts. They are lugged into our human frame of reference, where, not surprisingly, fathers, sons, and men seem like inadequate substitutes for the love, justice, and compassion of God — Father, Son, and Holy Spirit. But this is a problem of the eclipse of biblical narrative and the loss of the biblical world as a trustworthy, challenging, cleansing world that all Christians longed to inhabit. That loss came in the first instance not because the Bible was seen as noninclusive, but because the modern secular world no longer struggled to make sense of this strange and difficult, yet life-giving book, from a time and place other than our own. The Bible will not become "inclusive" by our "sanitizing" all references to God as "he." Rather, it will become merely humanized in the worst sense of the word: its authority will no longer reside in the sheer force of its presentation, but rather in the authorization strategies of whatever group — on the left or on the right — is in power. Multiplying possible images for God by reflecting on our human experience rather than the biblical text is the worst sort of consumeristic mentality, whereby more brand names, more channels, more options are better than less — especially when we get to do the choosing.

One should always be suspicious of enlightened efforts to cleanse and modify the Bible's own language — are we to swap the collective wisdom of the ages for the wisdom of some new power group? Where will the swapping end? What if the power group is on the right, and not the left? Nazi Germany also argued that its creative adaptations and selections from the Bible were better than the Bible's own statements (Jesus was not a Jew). What Protestant denominations historically fought for was the freedom of the Bible to serve as a corrective against the abuses of the church. Ironically, it is now from these same Protestant ranks that we find such concerted efforts to make the Bible subservient to more enlightened churchly interpretations. All this seems foreign to the spirit of Protestantism, if not also Catholicism, where the Bible stood as a measuring rod — if not bulwark — against which all preaching, teaching, and general talk about God was to be judged.

The trinitarian language "Father, Son, and Holy Spirit" is to be retained because it belongs to a set story about Jesus that the church did not invent but inherited. To sever our link with that story, including details we may not like, is to begin to sever our link with the person and the events themselves. Revelation will become only a personal individual thing, having to do with our experiences, our inward longings, and even our strongly held convictions, and not with a fuller story, with a corporate claim, a social history, and an ultimate link with real people in real times and places, among them the prophets and apostles and a Jesus who spoke of God as Father in heaven.

The biblical narratives belong to a coherent, integral, and integrated fuller story. Individual details cannot be swapped and exchanged like so many negotiable bits and pieces without final damage being done to the larger organic story itself, its saving purpose, and its faithful representation of the divine life. Terms like Father, Son, and Spirit belong to a broad and rich skein of meaning and significance, stretching across both Testaments, spanning the lives of Israel, Jesus, Paul, and the church through the ages. There is a critical organic character to these language associations that is, to put it bluntly, nonnegotiable, because the organism will simply fail to thrive if these historical, social, and theological connections are severed.

The chief task before the church is not to sanitize and correct the Bible from the outside, but rather to learn again from the inside the connected universe of the Bible's presentation; to learn to become competent readers again of a scripture whose intention is not only to include, but to address and judge and cleanse and save. No project for inclusion is so important, nor will it finally succeed, if it comes at the cost of sacrificing the Bible's own unique and life-giving language for describing the divine life and the way that life intersects with our own, so as to change us into a new creation, fit citizens for a kingdom inaugurated by Christ and still awaiting its final consummation.

For further reading: See especially B. S. Childs, "Is the God of the Old Testament a Male Deity?" in *Old Testament Theology in a Canonical Context* (Philadelphia: Fortress, 1985) 39-40. Childs says: "The point is that the Bible functions in such a way that such terms as 'father' and 'king' gain their theological content from the character of God, who continues to be worshipped in the conventions of a language which believers have always understood as inadequate for rendering the full divine reality. When such biblical terms to designate God become stumbling blocks, the hermeneutical question must be raised whether the problem lies with the imagery, or with a generation which no longer possesses the needed 'reader competence' to render the Bible as Scripture of the church" (p. 40). See also G. Lindbeck's *The Nature of Doctrine* (Philadelphia: Westminster, 1984). Lindbeck states at one point: "To become a Christian involves learning the story of Israel and of Jesus well enough to experience oneself and one's world *in its terms* [emphasis added]. A religion is above all an external word, a *verbum externum,* that molds and shapes the self and its world, rather than an expression or thematization of a persisting self or preconceptual experience" (p. 34). The influence of both Childs and Lindbeck on my formulation should be clear.

21

The Lectionary as Theological Construction

In this essay I want to look at the present lectionary from the standpoint of biblical theology. In the context of Lutheran-Episcopal discussions, my concern is twofold. First, would this not be a good time to reconsider the logic of the lectionary that both of us employ and that both of us have inherited from others? My second concern is more fundamental and is covered in part by my frequent reference to the lectionary *and* biblical theology: How are we to communicate the gospel when this involves making selections from the Bible to be read in public assembly? What is "the gospel"? Is "the gospel" fundamentally related to the literary witness of the four Gospels of the New Testament and, if so, how does this witness relate to the remainder of the Christian canon? Does the present distinction between Epistle and Gospel influence conceptions of "the gospel"? How does the Old Testament proclaim "the gospel" — if in fact it does so at all? In short, how does the shape of the present lectionaries affect the church's proclamation of "the gospel"?

In what follows I will make some preliminary remarks about the lectionary from the standpoint of biblical theology and the practical problem of general biblical illiteracy facing the churches. I will then consider the emphasis of the present lectionary and make an argument in favor of two rather than three readings. Following this I will briefly examine the theological and hermeneutical implications of freeing the Old Testament

This chapter originally appeared in *Inhabiting Unity: Theological Perspectives on the Proposed Lutheran-Episcopal Concordat*, ed. E. Radner and R. Reno (Grand Rapids: Eerdmans, 1995) 173-91.

to be heard in immediate reciprocal relationship with the New Testament. In the final section I will make several suggestions about how a different lectionary might take form, in the light of this essay.

My larger thesis is that the lectionary offers the greatest possibility for rejuvenating serious interest in the Bible as the source of the church's life and identity before God, for the broadest possible constituency. That one can speak of such a possibility at all is due to the astonishingly widespread adoption of some sort of lectionary scheme by a broad assortment of denominations, many of whom would once have denounced any notion of prescribed readings (and along with it, the very concept of a liturgical year). Further, I believe that far more is done in the name of biblical theology by the lectionary and the way it is used than is generally recognized, for good and for ill. But my chief aim will be to propose a different sort of lectionary, one that capitalizes on the present widespread acceptance of the notion of prescribed readings but is more sensitive to the way every selection is itself an act of biblical theology and therefore ought to be made with great care and attention.

BIBLICAL THEOLOGY AND THE LECTIONARY

One of the first tasks of biblical theology is to describe appropriate ways for the two testaments of the Christian canon to be related. Every pairing — and tripling — of readings makes a statement about the relationship between the Testaments, which is in turn a statement about biblical theology. To take an example from Jewish liturgical practice: When a *lectio continua* reading from the first five books of the Bible (Torah) is followed by a selected reading from the prophets or writings (Haftorah), a statement is being made about the relationship between these two sections, their relative authority, and the identity of the God who inspired them both, whose identity governs the destiny and life of Israel. Lectionary is inevitably theological construction. In this simple example, law has taken priority over prophecy, since the first reading is *lectio continua* over the course of the year and selections from the other sections of the Hebrew canon are keyed toward this central cycle of texts.

The theological construction imposed by any lectionary strategy points to the set of concerns that will preoccupy me throughout this essay. First, one of the underlying problems with the modern lectionary system involves a series of tacit assumptions about the character of biblical narrative, reinforced every time the Bible is read and heard through the lens of the lectionary. One assumption is that there is some sort of obvious independent integrity to individual passages read as such, detached from original literary contexts or supplied with new contexts due to the juxtaposition of one discrete reading with several other discrete readings (and in some cases, with a psalm and a collect). The final effect of the present lectionary implies that individual passages have no inherent relatedness to the literary contexts out of which they have been taken. As individual passages they are to find their true context either from some historical reconstruction, supplied by the seminary-trained preacher, or from the mode of consciousness of the hearer, commentator, or preacher. The very logic of the increasingly popular "illuminations" (brief statements read aloud to introduce the lessons) is precisely to jump into this breach and supply a "context" for listening — again, usually personalistic, psychological, or historical-critical (not surprisingly, the latter move is most often used with the Old Testament lesson, which, because it is "old," requires proper historical contextualization). I have frequently wondered if a different sort of "illumination" might be generated that would address the matter of literary or theological context, but this would be to concede the logic of the lectionary to begin with, a logic that may in fact be responsible for the sorts of problems that "illuminations" seek to resolve.

Second, and of more direct theological concern, is whether the Bible has already considered the issue of context on its own terms, within its own canonical presentation. To say that the Bible might wish to be heard in a certain way is to make a very bold claim over against the training of most preachers (and the lectionary framers themselves) in historical-critical logic. The decision to read biblical passages without attention to larger literary contexts conforms nicely to much of the theory of form-critical method, whose starting and ending point is the individual pericope. It may be pure fortuity that an earlier, precritical decision to read biblical passages as individual units based on liturgical and calendrical considerations, not in *lectio continua* formats, has coincided with the pericope mentality of form criticism. It is also clear that other ways of hearing the Bible read aloud and preached on in public worship also existed (see Calvin's commentaries). What we may well have is an accidental convergence of precritical concern for "hearability" and liturgical appropriateness and the modern critical instinct to isolate "original units" out of the larger context of the final canonical form of a biblical book.

In fairness, the lectionary I am referring to was probably never intended to function in this way, at least as I understand it. A second, more comprehensive daily lectionary would have supplied the necessary *lectio continua* context from which the Sunday lections would take their bearings. This daily lectionary was to be a part of the central discipline of the prayer life of the clergy and dedicated laypersons (several popular day-by-day devotional helps are keyed to this lectionary). Yet even here the positive contribution of a "continuous reading" approach for setting in context the Sunday lessons is very indirect, and can of course succeed only if such a daily discipline is followed.

But we are only touching the outskirts of the problem. At this juncture I am not interested in pleading for a continuous reading approach for its own sake as much as I am interested in pointing out that our present lectionary makes too great a demand on the preacher and the congregation. When one considers the larger cultural problem of the loss of biblical literacy — especially among those churches that use the lectionary! — the possibility that the congregation might be in a position to supply the needed literary framework for individual lections is practically nil. In a situation where the content of the Bible is increasingly unknown, the lectionary bears the special and maybe even unwanted burden of being the chief means by which the Bible is communicated to the church at large. Therefore it would seem expedient to reconsider its logic and to ask whether the lectionary, as it is now conceived, is a symptom or a contributing cause of problems besetting the church's competent use of the scriptures.

My own instinct is to argue that three lessons are simply too many to try to listen to or preach on with any real success. I also believe that from the standpoint of biblical theology the wrong sort of message is sent by the order of the readings (Old Testament, Epistle, Gospel), by the linkages that are urged on us, and by the threefold character of the biblical presentation (the Psalm reading further complicates this). Further, I am suggesting that a "continuous reading" approach has always done a better job of emphasizing, implicitly if not explicitly, the key role that literary context plays in understanding individual passages of scripture. And finally I believe that a key challenge facing the church is lack of familiarity with the larger biblical narrative. On the one hand, then, I am arguing for a smaller set of readings for the Sunday lectionary (two rather than three), while at the same time I am concerned about remedying, with the help of the lectionary, widespread biblical illiteracy and reader incompetence. In this regard, then, how could less be better?

Here one quickly recognizes that no lectionary sets out to do every-thing, but at the heart of every lectionary is a system of priority, with one set of considerations given more weight than others. What I will do here is examime the system of priority of the present lectionary. An alternative proposal will not set out to do everything (improve on lectionary pairings, do better biblical theology, increase biblical literacy but also attend to "hearability" and liturgical year considerations, cover the whole Bible in three years, etc.), but will set priorities for what it seeks to do, given the various constraints under which it must operate, mindful of its larger goals.

THE PRESENT LECTIONARY

We need to consider the four questions that deal with various aspects of the lectionary. First, how many lessons should be read? Second, in what order should we read them? Though the order we now follow may seem self-evident, it is instructive to recall the example from Jewish liturgy, where the first, not the last, lesson is intended to have priority; here too the actual number of lessons read will play a role. Third, what sort of selections are made? Here we need to consider the proper length of the passages; should there be elisions, and of what sort; should efforts be made to give a sense of continuous reading through the selections made? Obviously if the answer to the last question is yes, then the significance of literary context for the interpretation of individual passages would be underscored. Apart from the literary aspect of selections to be made is the question of the nature of the selections themselves. On what basis are these to be made? And finally, what principles should govern the pairing or tripling of lessons?

At this last point especially the implications for biblical theology are clearest. Here I touch again on what seems to me to be the real issue at stake. The lectionary we have inherited — and modified denominationally — does biblical theology. It operates with a system of priority, with theo-logical consequences. One of the problems with the lectionary, again probably unintended, is that while the readings themselves have been inherited, relatively consciously, the principles by which they were selected have not been equally consciously inherited. I want to emphasize that this is not a matter of assigning blame for some sort of failure to render the principles of selection immediately evident and accessible. The original constructors of the modern lectionary were Roman Catholic, and it may well be consistent with their ecclesiology and understanding of biblical theology that such principles are better inferred, if considered at all, than set forth liturgically along with the readings themselves. To put it differently, the lectionary assumes that the Bible is the church's book, to be shaped and handled as the church sees fit. It is not necessary that within the liturgy itself principles governing the selection of passages be declared, and in fact this might be a mistake. Nor is it necessary that those who prepare sermons or use the lections for Bible study have consistently before them the logic that originally governed selections made week to week. At the same time, I do wonder if the rise of "illuminations" was fostered in part by a felt need to have context and logic addressed more explicitly than the lectionary as inherited now does.

I can modify this description of things even further. On the whole it is fairly obvious why the Gospel readings have been chosen, and perhaps no further clarification is necessary: they attend to themes that are keyed to and then reinforced by a liturgical calendar, with various familiar and distinct seasons. And with a three-year cycle it seems clear that one Synoptic Gospel should be assigned to each of the three successive years. John gets spliced in at various moments in the liturgical year for reasons that are less obvious, but not all that confusing to the general observer. The other lessons (Old Testament and sometimes Epistle) generally take their cue from the Gospel lesson, which, as noted, is itself keyed to liturgical year considerations (the exceptions prove the general rule). To risk simplifying matters prematurely, it could be said that the Bible's own canonical organization, however one might understand that, has deferred to a larger conceptual statement about what constitutes the essential episodes in the Christian story, primarily brokered in the Gospel lessons through the course of one year, from the promised return of Christ (this theme noticeably more muted than the others) to the birth of Christ to the birth of the church.[1]

Now it is clear that the distinction between "the Bible's own canonical organization" and "the organizing story constituted by the concept of a Christian year" could easily be overdrawn and misleading. It may not be at all clear what "the Bible's own canonically organized statement" really is, or if such a thing even exists. But I think it is fairly clear that in the present lectionary the assumption is that no such statement is being

---

1. Advent readings are prepared to sound these notes, if they are not drowned out by the general anticipation of Christmas.

obviously or practically made and that it is the responsibility of the church, then, to supply one, which it has. My own argument will not be in favor of rejecting the conceptual system undergirding the present lectionary, much less in favor of rejecting the notion that there is a "Christian story" external to the Bible that seeks to state for Christians what the gist of the two-testament story is. Rather, I want the principles governing the present lectionary made quite clear and then enriched from time to time by other principles of selection more attuned to what I have called "the Bible's own canonically organized" patterns and internal relationships. This will result in a slightly different formulation of biblical theology, with much of the mystery and givenness of present lectionary logic brought into fuller consciousness.

The Number of Readings

Let me move from the abstract and conceptual to the concrete and practical by considering the matter of the number of lessons read. The lectionary system I have been referring to, with its roots in Vatican II liturgiology, assigns three lessons for Sunday worship. Why? We could answer this question by investigating the deliberations that went into the lectionary's construction. But I want to bracket out that sort of research project and simply ask what the effect of such a move is from the standpoint of biblical theology. In other words, I want to consider the theological effect produced by the three-lesson presentation of the Bible in a year-long liturgical sequence.

A discussion of number inevitably involves order, so let that be on the table as well. In the confession to which I belong, we sit for the first two lessons and stand for the third, the Gospel reading. Whether or not this practice is adopted elsewhere, it does capture at least one aspect of the threefold, particularly ordered lectionary: its movement, in terms of relative priority, from Old Testament to Epistle to crowning moment in the reading of the Gospel. That other possibilities exist for how a particular order might differently function is made clear by reference to the Torah-Haftorah practice of Jewish synagogue worship. One might want to argue that it is logical and right for the Gospel to be the crowning moment in worship, and that this is best reinforced not by having it read first (place of priority) but last (place of priority), and in my own Anglican tradition, by standing when it is read. This is all well and good and I think uncontroversial.

But if this is in fact the point of the order, why are we reading an Epistle between the Old Testament and the Gospel? At this point I wish to return to the distinction I made earlier between the Bible's own canonical organization and that imposed by the lectionary. Surely it belongs to no recognizable biblical pattern that we read an Old Testament lesson, then an Epistle or some other portion of the non-Gospel New Testament writings, and then the Gospel itself. When one considers the difficulty of listening to or successfully (in my judgment) preaching on three distinct lessons, the problem of order and number takes on a different sort of burden. It is doubtless for this reason that many congregations make the decision to select out the first or second lesson only and then pair it with the Gospel. But if the three truly belong together in some intentionally structured marriage, with a codependency mysterious yet necessary for threefold survival, then can or should one be able to simply subtract a lesson at will? Does this not disturb some subtle balance that was the express goal and hard-won accomplishment of the framers of the lectionary to begin with?

And what is the effect from the standpoint of biblical theology? First, there is no "threefoldness" anywhere structured into the Christian canon. It has been argued that threefold structures belong to the essence of each testament taken on its own (Torah, Prophets, Writings; Gospels, Acts, Epistles) but not with great success or lasting theological significance (especially for the New Testament).[2] And of course we are not interested in structures attested to in either testament individually, but in the larger Christian canon itself, where the basic struture is transparently twofold: Old and New Testaments. Having lived with this lectionary for some time now, it is my judgment that one subtle but long-lasting effect of the threefold model is that the Old Testament lesson has been overshadowed, literally outnumbered. More difficult to state is the effect achieved when the Old Testament lesson is not related directly to the New Testament but is more complicatedly content to sit astride a first non-Gospel New Testament reading, itself oddly situated before the actual Gospel reading. Not only is the twofold character of the Christian canon lost, the way the Old Testament is related to the New Testament has become blurred. Does it

2. See Donn Morgan, *Between Text and Community: The "Writings" in Canonical Interpretation* (Minneapolis: Fortress, 1990).

relate to the Gospel by way of the Epistle? Surely not. That would be an artificial move and one unattested to in any known literary structure of the canon. How then is the Old Testament related to the New?

My own view is that the present lectionary will inevitably reinforce an understanding of the Old Testament as a document from the past, a historical preamble, as it were, because in this sort of arrangement it has become the first in a series of three, outnumbered by two lessons whose organic connection is taken to be more obvious given their common home in the New Testament, both directly speaking of Christ. This is not simply a matter of two against one. The connection between the Old and the New cannot be grasped rightly if an Epistle intrudes in a series of three, with the final lesson being set up as the finale and crowning moment in the series. Here order and number conspire to upset the delicate way in which Old Testament and New Testament are related and together, each in its own individual way, "preach Christ."

Let me be clear. The culprit is not the Epistle itself as against "the Gospel"; rather, it is the existence of a threefold pattern that breaks the Old Testament–New Testament dialectic so essential for hearing the Old Testament as a witness to Christ. The result is that the Old Testament cannot preach Christ, but must be content to provide historical background only, literally the first in a series of three. Even when the framers of the lectionary have clearly sought out passages from the Old Testament whose relationship to one or the other of the New Testament lessons is typological or allegorical, the very fact of the three-in-a-series movement will tend to produce a developmental or generally historical effect, overriding the content of the selections themselves and their very reason for being. In my judgment, this effect would be greatly reduced — if not eliminated — if we heard only two lessons each Sunday: one from the Old Testament, then one from the New. The actual dialectical relationship between Old and New Testaments would remain intact, with the consequence that the fullest possible range of ways of relating the Old and New in witness to Christ might be safeguarded and not preempted by a model whose very threefoldness potentially trumps the content and intention of the selections made.

THEOLOGICAL AND HERMENEUTICAL IMPLICATIONS

In the context of these remarks concerning the biblical theological construal of the scriptures in lectionary presentation, I have drawn a distinction between the Bible's own canonical shape and intention and the churchly decision to set forth on its own terms the character of that shape and intention in a specific lectionary arrangement involving three lessons and a liturgical year whose parameters are set according to some understanding of what is the "gist" of the Christian story. It ought to be clear by now that these two matters cannot be neatly isolated, tradition on one side, Bible on the other, even though one (lectionary) flows from the other (Christian canon), with the success of one (lectionary) dependent on its faithfulness in comprehending the other (Christian canon). But in terms of actual practice, the two working together is an inevitability that is to be neither mourned nor resolved, but refined and rethought and reshaped for each successive generation so that the fullest range of the biblical witness might be heard in its optimal tuning. A lectionary should remind the listener that there is no such thing as reading the Bible, especially the Old Testament, without an obvious point of standing.

Old Testament selections, then, ought to capture the witness of the Old Testament in its historical particularity as the scriptures of Israel while at the same time, by a careful juxtaposition with New Testament proclamation, being free to witness to Christ. How this witnessing goes on will be varied, because it is varied within the biblical witness itself. My concern with the threefoldness of the present lectionary is that certain types of relatedness sought out and presented by the lectionary cannot be heard in their full force because of the stereotypical character of the sequential threefold arrangement (Old Testament, Epistle, Gospel), maintained throughout the year without change or variation (except occasionally on Easter).[3] Because of the historical and developmental preoccupation of the modern critical method and the modern mind itself, it has been very difficult to appreciate how certain unself-conscious New Testament hearings of the Old Testament might also be recaptured in the modern pulpit, as though to do so would be to abandon a point of standing that is

---

3. Another way to put this is that the threefold practice tends toward a "salvation history" model for biblical theology, while a twofold practice allows a more dialectical relationship to emerge. The actual selections from the Old Testament seem clearly at times to be striving for this type of relationship.

unbiased and concerned only to hear the Old Testament on its own terms. But how could this possibly be the only desired point of standing, especially when we are not "Israel" except by adoption and when even modern Jews must strain to hear a direct word, given the intrusion of over two thousand years of commentary and simple historical distance between themselves and "Israel."

It seems at this point that the historical-critical method has an overly romanticized view of historical reconstruction, as though by an act of sheer imagination and critical decipherment we could ourselves participate in biblical events now long past and stand alongside Moses and Joshua without any consideration that our only true access to these figures was through the cross of Christ. The cross allows us who are far off to draw near to God's own people Israel, who might now serve as examples to God's new people in Christ and as such "witness" to him and us (see Eph 2:11-22). Even efforts to reconstruct the mind of an author, the actual preaching content of an Israelite prophet, or the theological additions made by a redactor, and similar sorts of critical endeavor — do these not depend on some prior notion of universal revelation or general accessibility to truth that the biblical texts themselves insist is unavailable in the form in which the critical method seeks to extract it?[4]

Apart from the (eventual) witness of the New Testament, what we know about God, we know secondhand from Israel through the witness of her scriptures, in accordance with which our creeds claim that Christ died and rose again. How we are entitled to know this as God's people involves the work of Christ in incorporating us into God's plan begun with Israel, which at the level of literary witness involves the beneficial retention of what Christians now call the "Old Testament" (compare simply "the scriptures" or "law and prophets"), as part one of a fuller scriptural witness. Can this particular sequence of events, involving a chain of theological cause-and-effect, be simply sidestepped by the "neutral"

4. See the discussion above in Section One (Biblical Theology). Within the logic of the Old Testament and its understanding of revelation and election, the Psalmist concludes (Ps 147:20): "He has not dealt thus with any other nation; they do not know his ordinances. Praise the LORD!" In the New Testament witness, Paul says of the "Israelites": "To them belong the adoption, the glory, the covenants, the giving of the law, the worship, and the promises; to them belong the patriarchs, and from them, according to the flesh, comes the Messiah, who is over all, God be blessed forever. Amen" (Rom 9:4f.; cf. Eph 2:12f.).

critical mind seeking the "truth" of the Old Testament text directly, without need of confessional overlay or point of standing?

Much more could be said about this. My concern in the context of the lectionary is not to have ruled out by the particular threefold structure typological and figural readings of the Old Testament that illustrate clearly our christological — one might better say, trinitarian — point of standing, readings that stand as a corrective to much historical-critical logic and rationale involving objectivity and critical neutrality.[5]

One of the positive characteristics of the lectionary has been its capacity to retain pairings from the Old to the New (whether in the Epistle or the Gospel) with deep roots in the church's history of interpretation. These served as reminders that christological, figural, or allegorical readings of the Old Testament, while not now in vogue in seminaries under the influence of strictly "objective" and historical modes of reading, were nevertheless fully a part of the church's exegetical and homiletical repertoire. To say that the Old Testament can "preach Christ" is regarded by most critical minds as a hopeless anachronism (or possible only in strict historical terms).

But I think we stand on the threshold of a recognition that all reading of the Bible is invariably affected by one's point of standing. While historicality was brought into keen consciousness in modern biblical study, what dropped in inverse proportion was the consciousness of a certain inevitable — religious, theological, or even purely academic — lens through which the scriptures are always viewed. This is changing, however, due in large measure to forces secular and academic (deconstruction), with

---

5. For a fresh reassertion of the historical-critical method, see J. Collins, "Historical Criticism and the State of Biblical Theology," *The Christian Century*, July 28–August 4, 1993, 743-47. Collins is quick to label Brevard Childs's approach "Barthian Protestantism" and Jon Levenson's "orthodox Judaism" in a tone that suggests that they have now been fully comprehended and their "bias" exposed. Also lurking around his analysis is the sense that he has no such obvious theological point of standing and can continue to point to some area in the academy where "reasoned argument," not "confessional character," rules among the "community of scholars." Does this mean that there is such a thing as a real "community of scholars" studying the Bible, where "reasoned argument" can be neatly differentiated from "confessionalism" or theological perspective per se? How is that possible, especially in the late twentieth century? It may be that Collins's milder review of James Barr suggests that the key is "natural theology" of the sort that Barr defends, which would make available, presumably, some sort of universal grid of rational inquiry, biblically rooted and endorsed. Why that should make any difference in the "community of scholars" where "reasoned argument" reigns and is its own reward is not clear to me.

derivative and in a great many cases negative consequences for theological exegesis.[6]

But again the sword has two edges. One consequence of this sort of change is that it renders possible self-consciously christological (or trinitarian) readings of the Old Testament, however we might define these (this was no monolith in the so-called precritical period). In respect to the lectionary, my only point has been that I believe that a twofold (Old and New) model has a better chance of showcasing this than does the present threefold system.[7]

SELECTING PASSAGES

Having made a "two's company, three's a crowd" proposal for lectionary modification, and having tried to defend it with an eye toward biblical theology and modern critical trends, let me move now beyond the question of number and order to a more specific look at the selection process itself. My general point thus far has been that three lessons inevitably set up a progression while two allow for a measure of reciprocity more true to the actual character of the relationship between Old and New Testaments in the two-part Christian canon.

For purposes of eventual illustration, let me digress for a moment into a very brief history of the lectionary in the Episcopal Church. My observations will be basic and crude, restricted to recent changes in the lectionary brought on by the adoption of a new *Book of Common Prayer* in 1979 (with waves of earlier "trial" worship books). The earlier (1928) *Book of Common Prayer* had in fact two separate lectionaries: one for

6. See the exchange between Philip Davies and Francis Watson (Davies, *Whose Bible Is It Anyway?* [Sheffield: Sheffield Academic, 1995]; Watson, "Bible, Theology, and the University: A Response to Philip Davies," *JSOT* 71 [1996] 3-16). Compare as well Walter Brueggemann's *The Bible and Postmodern Imagination: Texts under Negotiation* (London: SCM, 1993).

7. For a sustained and sophisticated discussion of the relationship between the biblical witness and the subject matter to which, for Christian confession, it points (the triune God), and especially on the possibility of returning to that same witness, particularly the Old Testament, with the knowledge of its ultimate subject matter ("the full divine reality"), see now B. S. Childs, *Biblical Theology of the Old and New Testaments: Theological Reflection on the Christian Bible* (Minneapolis: Fortress, 1992), 379-83.

Morning Prayer Sunday services (with weekday Morning Prayer lessons as well), and another for Sundays when Holy Communion was to be the service of the day (or the earlier service prior to, and unrelated to, the main Morning Prayer service). In both instances only two lessons were ever read: in the former, the first was from the Old Testament and the second was from the New Testament (the Gospel-Epistle distinction playing no consistent role); in the latter, the usual practice was the first from an Epistle, the second from a Gospel (readings from the Old Testament being generally rare as first lessons). However, in the Episcopal Church, and other confessions that shortly followed suit in terms at least of the lectionary, eucharistic worship became the norm for Sunday assembly, which created a need to modify the older eucharistic lectionary to include Old Testament readings. This resulted in the three-lesson model presently in place. It is not clear that simply adding an additional first lesson to the two customarily read on eucharistic Sundays has solved the problem created by the move away from Morning Prayer worship and its lectionary.

A perusal of this older lectionary, "Psalms and Lessons for the Christian Year," incidentally reveals one further matter that pertained to the Sunday Morning Prayer (and Evening Prayer) lectionary. Each Sunday, choices were given of two, and sometimes three, Old Testament–New Testament pairings. In addition, one could swap lessons from Evening and Morning Prayer listings, giving one anywhere from four to six choices of Old and New pairings ("the choice thereof is at the discretion of the Minister"). That clergy sat around deliberating which pairings to adopt is unlikely, of course; the first set given was probably chosen. Also little effort was probably expended trying to key one set to one year, the next set to the next, and so forth. Nowhere in the rubrics is any suggestion made that this lectionary was to conform to anything more than a single year cycle.

One of the ironies of prayer book revision in the Episcopal Church is that while choices were introduced for main services at every opportunity (Morning Prayer I; Evening Prayer II; Eucharistic Prayer IV), giving the new book a sort of smorgasbord feel, the same was not true of the lectionary. In a way, for all the diversity of content over a three-year cycle, from Sunday to Sunday it maintains a rather relentless stereotype in form. The reason I stress this point is that any move from a three-lesson to a two-lesson lectionary system is going to have to reckon with subtractions. Until now I have been arguing that especially the Epistle reading, intruding between Old Testament and Gospel, is confusing and disruptive of essential patterns in the two-testament canon. The older prayer book lectionary may have sensed this, but in any event it kept a two-lesson system by ignoring a Gospel-Epistle distinction for noneucharistic Sundays.

In my view, three main options exist for reversion to an Old Testament–New Testament lesson model. The first would be to ignore the Gospel-Epistle distinction in all Sunday worship, whether eucharistic or otherwise. The first lesson would be taken from the Old Testament, the second from the New. Church year considerations would control the reading chosen from the New, and would in turn affect the selection from the Old. A second option would be to isolate one or more parts of the Christian year when different models would obtain. For example, as it now stands the long summer season (Pentecost, Trinity, Ordinary Time) may in fact take up over half the actual year (twenty-nine propers are provided for the Sundays from Pentecost to Advent). This would be a good time to let Epistle readings predominate over Gospel readings. Continuous reading would continue to be a very workable option, now with emphasis on Epistle as the second and only New Testament reading. A final option would be to return to something of the flavor of the older two-lesson lectionary I have been describing by allowing the minister several choices throughout the course of the year. These choices would all involve two lessons, one from Old and one from New, but with the focus either on Epistle or Gospel or some combination of the two. Having had the experience of trying to sort out the relationship between three lessons each Sunday, a return to a two-lesson model would be like removing leg weights for the preacher and congregant.

In addition, rather than let the decisions why certain pairings have been made remain unstated, for the preacher and congregant to puzzle out or to invent, the range of choices provided could be illustrative of different, clearly stated patterns in the two-testament canon. Here the lectionary might hold the potential for becoming a teaching aid for the church, preacher and congregant alike. In this same manner, from pulpit and lectern might come readings and exposition of scripture more exemplary of patterns already at work within the full Christian canon itself.

Using the sort of clearly stated principles of selection that I have been advocating, just what might these pairings from Old and New Testament look like? Unfortunately, I have only enough space to list several possibilities.

I have repeatedly spoken about deferring to pairings that seem to be urged by the texts themselves. This can be stated more clearly and simply. The New Testament obviously can be detached from the Old, but even

Marcion realized that this was not altogether easy, because the New has a material connection to the Old within its own independent literary presentation. One index to follow when making pairings, then, would be to ask whether the New Testament reading — from the Gospels or Epistles — took form with an eye toward some specific Old Testament text. Obviously, on occasion such texts are quoted or are otherwise referred to explicitly. On other occasions, as New Testament scholars have taught us, the relationship is far more subtle. Showcasing this material relationship between Old and New would be simply achieved in the lectionary by allowing the first lesson to be the same lesson referred to in the New.

One could argue that these sorts of pairings would blur the Old's *per se* voice in favor of the Old as heard *in Novo receptum*. But that would not be true in every instance. Matthew uses Isaiah's song of the vineyard to point out that the Israel that rejected proper stewardship in Isaiah's day has done so as well in Jesus' time. The present lectionary rightly pairs Isa 5:1-7 with Matt 21:33-43 and thereby illustrates the Old as heard *in Novo receptum*. But in the context of Christian worship, to hear Isaiah not just as Matthew heard it, but on its own terms as a first scriptural lesson, means a word of prophetic address to Israel of old now also falls on the church, the "Israel of God" (Gal 6:16). In this manner, the lectionary pairing illustrates the Old as heard both *in Novo receptum* and with its persistent *per se* voice. And to return to my other point, to hear a lesson from Philippians — which in Year A is read roughly as *lectio continua* from week to week — between Isaiah and Matthew interferes with the close relationship rightly seen between Old and New. Trying to combine two separate principles (continuous reading and the Old's material use in the New) does not enhance "the gospel" but in fact intrudes on it. In this instance, hearing the Old in light of the New and the New in light of the Old illustrates their essential reciprocity in communicating the gospel.

Of course, how the Old is utilized in the New is quite varied. For example, consider the lessons from Old and New used on Epiphany (Isa 60:1-9; Matt 2:1-12). Isaiah speaks of a light that is to arise, ostensibly that of the resplendent Zion; Matthew speaks of the light over Bethlehem toward which the wise men are drawn. Here the relationship between Old and New would appear to be figural: What is said of Zion, God's special place of tabernacling, is seen as a type of Christ, in whose flesh God was pleased to dwell. This understanding of the relationship between Old and New, while not at odds with Matthew's own plain sense, does not require an assertion that Matthew intentionally heard Isaiah 60 in the same direction as that of the lectionary. Matthew actually quotes an Old Testament text here, but it is Micah's promise of a ruler to come from Judah. One lectionary option would be to read that Micah text as a first lesson on some general understanding of prophecy and fulfillment as the principle relating Old and New. But this might underscore the wrong sort of connection (which may be why the lectionary avoids Micah), since Micah is here quoted by the religious officials being inquired of by the wicked Herod, not so much for its own sake, but to determine where the child can be found so as to be destroyed.

A close reading of the Matthew text shows what a strange set of circumstances it is in fact relating. The appearance of a star signals the birth of "the king of the Jews" (2:2) to wise men from the East. Herod, frightened, wants to know where this king should be born and learns, from Micah, in Bethlehem. Herod then sends the wise men to Bethlehem "to pay tribute," and the star they had originally seen now "stops" over just the right place. They offer tribute, but instead of returning to Herod to tell him where the child is, they are warned in a dream and find their way home "by another road."

An Old Testament text that speaks of a wicked king who seeks to destroy but instead ironically effects blessing and homage; that tells of a wise man from the East who offers right worship, whose eye is properly directed by God, and who sees a "star come out of Jacob" is the story of Balaam the seer in the Book of Numbers (chs. 22–24). Linking all or part of this Old Testament story to Matthew's account of the journey of the Magi might well connect with Matthew's own scriptural frame of reference, texts that in this instance are never cited directly. The relationship between Old and New would here be figural, with less of an actual contrast between Zion and the Christ child as in the present lectionary pairing. Now the continuity would be not just between the wise and obedient Balaam and Matthew's wise men from the East, but also between the wicked Balak, a foreign king and hindrance to God's people Israel, and Herod, Israel's own king.

I mentioned in passing the avoidance of Micah by lectionary framers as a first lesson to be paired with Matthew's birth narratives, a pairing that could potentially illustrate the familiar prophecy-fulfillment conception of how the Old and New are related. Advent lessons are traditionally thought of as illustrating this same conception, by using as first readings passages from Israel's prophets that tell of a righteous king (Messiah). Ironically, very rarely are such passages actually quoted to the same effect in the New

Testament itself. And when one looks more closely at the majority of Advent pairings, Old Testament prophecies regarding a coming Messiah frequently direct the hearer through the witness of the New not to Jesus' past birth and incarnation, but ahead in time to the Second Coming.[8]

This particular perspective might be better reinforced in the lectionary if Old Testament passages such as these were linked to New Testament passages that direct the hearer to Christ's promised return in glory. For the sake of economy, we can return to the text just cited from Isaiah 60, which tells of Zion's exaltation. Instead of seeking a linkage where Zion's special status has been connected through figuration to Christ, one might instead select readings from the final chapters of Revelation. There, texts from Isaiah are cited to depict the Christian's final hope, in such a way that Isaiah's *per se* force has not been figurally translated, but retained and interpreted anew in light of Christ's incarnation, death, and ascension. Likewise, Pauline texts that direct the reader to Christ's return or to the nature of the relationship between Israel and the Gentiles brought near in Christ might also be linked to so-called "messianic texts" from the prophets. Romans 9–11 offer a rich skein of scriptural citation; there Paul takes up Old Testament texts and interprets them in some fresh way or defers to their persistent per se force. Linking such texts directly with the New Testament witness from Paul, without need of a further "Gospel" reading, is not now possible given the present lectionary format. But to what extent would "the gospel" be actually compromised or shortchanged if one only heard the Old and Paul's use of the Old in the context of his epistolary proclamation? Would not the now widespread eucharistic focus of Sunday assembly be sufficient to cover reference to the work and person of Christ as such, without need of some third more explicit "gospel" lesson?

Perhaps these few examples of pairings from Old and New illustrate my larger point regarding the sufficiency and appropriateness of a two-lesson lectionary. One should not defer in every instance to the New's explicit or apparent scriptural frame of reference for determining what passage from the Old should be read. Other principles presently at work in the lectionary, some tried and true, should be retained. But in every instance, these principles should be clearly spelled out to those who use the lectionary readings, if not also forming an explicit part of something akin to the "illuminations" used at present. And even if the New Testament

---

8. See my discussion in *Proclamation 4: Aids for Interpreting the Lessons of the Church Year* (Philadelphia: Fortress, 1988).

is taken as an appropriate guide to selecting lessons from the Old, one need not worry that some form of monolithic or stereotypical conception of the Old's relationship to the New will emerge; much less is it clear that some sort of extreme selectivity in respect of the Old's *per se* voice would result (as the example of Matthew's use of the Balaam narratives should make clear). The New Testament's use of the Old is quite rich and varied. And in the context of Christian liturgy, with two lessons being read, the Old will not just be heard in light of the New; the New will also be heard in light of the Old, where frequently the Old's *per se* voice has not been translated, transformed, or stilled, but continues to sound forth in the proclamation of "the gospel." What makes this possible is the return to a two-lesson format, with far closer attention being paid to instances when the Old already serves to proclaim the gospel through its own witness as brokered in the New.

$$\approx \quad 22 \quad \approx$$

Sexuality and Scripture's Plain Sense

The Christian Community and the Law of God

I

This essay assumes that scripture is the authority that guides the church's reflection on human sexual behavior. It also assumes that the problem with the present debate is that both sides are appealing to scripture, in some measure, in order to ground what are diametrically opposing views. The thesis argued here is that we have lost the ability to hear a *connected* Old and New Testament witness to God in Christ and have substituted for it a model that isolates texts from their specific canonical context in order to place them in earlier, discrete, historically reconstructed ("original") circumstances. A contest then ensues as to what individual texts "really mean," by appeal to the correct historical context, to the specific cultural circumstances out of which the text is said to have emerged, or to learned lexicographical analysis. This is fine so far as it goes, but it has failed to achieve any consensus in the present debate. Book after book is written, with a mixture of scholarly and popular essays, and the stalemate actually stimulates rather than dampens new publishing efforts.

The thesis argued here is that both sides in the debate are in some measure "biblicistic" — that is, there has been a failure on both sides to relate the exegesis and interpretation of individual texts to the church's understanding of how the two-testament canon of scripture is to be heard, interbiblically, according to the rule of faith. This rule constrains the church to bring into relationship distinct portions of scripture, especially

319

across the testaments. The pattern for this is found in the church's reflection on the separatedness, but also the essential unity, of the persons of the trinity.[1] A Christian discussion of human sexual behavior entails a discussion of the law of God as this is revealed to Israel in the Old Testament, radically reconsidered in and by Jesus Christ, and retained with reference to God's work in him, by virtue of the church's decision to hear the word of God through Israel's witness in the Old Testament, in conjunction with the apostolic witness to Jesus Christ in the New.

In the course of the discussion that follows, older understandings of Christian interpretation of Old Testament law are briefly considered. Then texts other than the usual "proof texts" are discussed, with an eye toward understanding the place of the Christian before God's law. These include Rom 3:31; 7:13-25; Matt 5:17-48; Gal 5:16-24; John 8:1-11; 19:30; Deut 22:23-24; Lev 20:13; Heb 10:1-31; and Mark 7:1-23. Older distinctions among "moral," and "ritual," and "ceremonial," law are reconsidered in the light of the present debate over homosexuality. There is no lengthy engagement with recent secondary literature, but only an occasional reference. This literature has put on display much historical-critical heavy lifting, but only here and there does this particular slant on interpretation produce results that can be reconnected with the church's chief task: faithful hearing of the witness to God in Christ from the two-testament Christian scripture.

What the homosexuality debate has exposed is a deep crisis within the church and the academic settings related to its life and mission. Whatever we might think about the appropriateness of homosexual acts, in culture and in the church, yet more widely divergent are our assumptions about how scripture functions normatively. It is no revelation that the assumptions grounding historical-critical endeavor are under massive reappraisal, and so it should come as no surprise that on the fault line separating the older critical consensus and newer postliberal approaches sits a debate tailor-made to expose our differences.

On the one side, there is maintained an insistence on the *pluriformity* of the scriptural witness, both within the Old Testament and the New. Related to this, though not identical with it, are those tendencies within Christian circles to privilege, often in very subtle and sophisticated ways, the New Testament witness(es) over against the Old Testament, even though in this case and in others there may in fact be very little difference

---

1. Compare the discussion above in chs. 1 and 2.

between them. Nevertheless, the homosexuality debate is tailor-made for this because it works, implicitly or explicitly, with a theory of development or progress. That is, there is some general consensus — John Boswell's more recent efforts notwithstanding — that in the modern homosexual phenomenon we are confronting something truly without precedent, within the life of the church if not also within culture. This dovetails nicely with a notion that we move toward gradual enlightenment as we cross from one testament to the other. This sense of movement, then, informs and enhances a similar feeling about the way the church is confronting a new thing, perhaps on analogy with Gentile inclusion, and so must formulate a new position on a topic which may have been on the relative periphery in the biblical witness, but is at the dead center of our concerns today.

Here one sees how historical thinking has the potential to flatten the complex *literary and theological* interrelatedness of scripture — for all the apparent pluriformity that is gained — by simply getting it to conform to a way of thinking in vogue in the West for the past two hundred years, geared to linear development and change.[2] Since it is in the Old Testament where gender differentiation is grounded theologically and homosexual acts proscribed (anal intercourse), one can see how an issue like the modern homosexual phenomenon needs only to highlight the element of development and change that exists within a literary corpus of two parts, one "old" and one "new," and thereby catalyze a sentiment in favor of seeing this issue as truly new and in need of new and enlightened thinking.

Finally, the lasting hallmark of historical-critical endeavor, and the thing that gave it an academic potential in connection with, or divorced from, church life, was its interest in cultural and social contextualization *as truly indispensable for the task of reading and appropriating scripture "correctly."* The appeal of this sort of objectivism has been enormous. It has energized generation after generation of critical readerships, who have expended enormous amounts of effort setting a text's plain literary sense in the proper time and space category. On the matter at hand, however, it looked like those in favor of churchly endorsement of homosexual behavior had run into a firewall even historical-critical endeavor could not remove. This was one of those places where the plain sense of the text did not appear to be materially affected by efforts to recover original authorial

2. See Hans Frei's *The Eclipse of Biblical Narrative* (Hew Haven: Yale University, 1974).

intention or clearer socio-historical circumstances. At a minimum, there is no positive statement backing same-sex physical unions in scripture, occasional or lifelong and committed. And Leviticus and Romans had always been taken as proscribing homosexual behavior, offering one of those instances when Old Testament and New Testament teaching were in basic agreement. Yet over time, greater efforts at critical analysis at last presented a more complex picture, and the older consensus about the plain sense of scripture on this issue began to collapse.

The relevant question to ask historical-critical endeavor at this juncture is whether it is driven, for all practical purposes, by the necessary requirement to uncover the novel, the different, the complex. That is, historical-criticism is *obliged* by its own character to make sure no plain sense consensus, binding Old and New Testament witnesses, emerges, because to do so would be to admit that the plain sense had a certain priority, in a great many cases, over reconstructions of an "original," historical sense argued to be at odds with it. It would also be to suggest that the way scripture actually functions normatively — especially on the matter of homosexual activity — is a good deal less complex and less needful of academic reconstructions than one might have thought, as one views the energy expended in the present debate. Deconstruction has presented historical-critical method with two very different faces: one that outflanks its claims to objective meaning gained through historical reconstruction, and one that contests any notion of authority residing in texts to begin with that is not put there by interpreters — precritical and critical alike.

Given this sea change in attitude toward historical-critical method, the debate over homosexual behavior could not be more significantly timed. At stake is not whether the Bible proscribes or does not proscribe homosexual behavior, but just what *proscription* might in fact mean today? Historical criticism may have cut the rug out from under itself with its appeal to objective truth gained through historical analogizing, for now it has been around long enough to cast its own historical shadow, and suddenly the possibility that it too must be examined as a historical phenomenon of the "modern" age looms large. What if, after all, "Holy Scripture" plainly does proscribe homosexual behavior? The question then to be asked is how or if historical criticism pursues its goals in connection with church life. The old enemy was "dogmaticism," but there is little vestige of that in the form it was first denounced by historical criticism, at least in circles where homosexual behavior is being advocated. So what is historical criticism's mandate in such an instance? It would be curious if where once it stood against the stifling influence of church teaching, now it is its greatest ally, in the name of new church teaching on this old issue. I introduce my fairly traditional reassertion of the church's proscription of homosexual acts in this way in order to candidly confess a misgiving and to point to what I believe is a real hypocrisy in this debate. My misgiving is that it does not seem to me that the church was ever in much real doubt about this issue. If it were not for massive changes in sexual behavior over the past decades, I doubt that we would be considering this issue on the grounds that *it is one contested within scripture itself.* What I judge to be hypocrisy, and probably worth a treatment of its own, is the ongoing appeal to new findings and new learning that will presumably take place if people on opposite sides of this issue, listening hard to the hard work of others, stay "in dialogue" long enough. I may be wrong, but what I see is a hardening of resolve on both sides and greater conviction that one's own side is right after all. This is what is being produced by the appeal to "stay in dialogue." What seems hypocritical, then, at this juncture, is to say that one has wrestled hard to come to some clear conscience on this matter, but that perhaps over time we will all agree. How can that possibly happen?

I think it is better for us to witness to the truth and to clarify how it is we come to it, than to assume that what is confused are our sources of authority and that with just more historical-critical work we will succeed in eliminating the confusion and persuading the other side. Isaiah knew full well that the word of God closed ears as well as opened them, and that for some verdicts to be established it would take the judgment of God in history, and the emergence of a new generation with ears opened by God himself. When Jeremiah confronted Hananiah, he simply appealed to the tradition in which prophets stand, and from which Hananiah departed. God rendered the verdict, in that instance quicker than Jeremiah probably thought. Sometimes, opposing sides are *not* brought closer together, and both Testaments witness to this tragic reality *within* the people of God. I fear that in this instance, where the church is being asked to change a teaching it has held for its entire existence, we must frankly admit that we are in schism and that God will judge the appeal to his word being made by both sides. In the meantime both sides are obliged to testify to the truth and clarify how they have come to it, without any assumption that a consensus will emerge this side of the judgment of God himself.

II

If it could be shown that scripture plainly forbids homosexual acts as an offense to God in Christ, would that be sufficient to constrain the church to proscribe homosexual behavior among its members today?[3]

The question is important because a distinction can be made between (1) recognizing the Bible's plain sense on this issue and saying that it does not matter, over against (2) arguing that no such thing is said in scripture that plainly and directly. Obviously there are modern people engaged in homosexual acts who understand that their behavior is clearly forbidden in the Old Testament and the New, by Moses, Jesus, and Paul, but who do not regard this as relevant. Some may even believe in notions like "holiness" or "offense" or "God" or "Christ" — but they also believe homosexual acts and relationships cannot be wrong if they are said to be "loving" and "caring" or "committed" relationships.

One modern problem is that the "church" now consists of people on both sides of such a distinction, where in the past the church consisted of only one of these groups, namely, those who granted the Bible's authority but who may not have agreed on its plain sense. At the same time, it is increasingly the case that those who favor revision — especially within mainline Protestant or liberal Catholic circles — wish to do so on the basis of an appeal to scripture, if that is possible. This raises a question as to the relationship between scripture and its history of interpretation in church and synagogue, without obvious analogy. For all the issues that divided the church in the past — over which Anabaptists, Lutherans, the Reformed, Anglicans, Methodists, Roman Catholics, Pentecostals, and others might have disagreed — tolerance or blessing of homosexual acts was never one of them.[4] Apparently scripture's plain sense was simply too plain when it came

---

3. That this immediately raises the question of appropriate pastoral care is obvious and reminds one how allergic the church has become to dealing with matters of the flesh in general, as central to the disciplined Christian life. In other words, to answer the question "yes" would oblige the church to think much more seriously about its responsibility in the "cure of souls" than it may at present be doing. The failure to address the difficult pastoral dimensions of appropriate sexual conduct fits hand-in-glove with a sense that the proper answer to the question is no longer self-evident. One gets a sense that the proper pastoral stance is now one of lifting sexual taboos, raising cultural consciousness, encouraging "outed" lifestyles, and so forth.

4. The analogy to slavery does not hold up, on closer scrutiny, in spite of its rhetorical appeal. First, there is a failure to distinguish between forms of debt service in antiquity —

to homosexual behavior. The history of interpretation, Jewish and Christian, bears witness to the "plainness" of scripture on this matter.

One ought not move too quickly past this fact, since scripture's plain sense is contained in a wide range of texts, thus leaving open the possibility of disagreement over which texts are to interpret others and offer the controlling context and perspective. It has long been possible to set the Testaments in opposition or disagreement (is tithing required or the sabbath to be observed?), to distinguish between canonical and deutero-canonical or apocryphal books (purgatory, prayers for the dead), Paul or Moses in tension with Jesus (divorce and remarriage), or even the magisterium or the Spirit or tradition over against scripture itself (on ministry and authority in the church).

An example from an earlier day may serve to illustrate the problem. It is obvious that debates over scripture's plain sense are not new and that especially problematic has been the relationship between the Old Testament and the New. Luther was unhappy with the citing of Old Testament law by "the enthusiasts" as binding on the Christian community, reinforced with the assertion, "God says." He made a distinction between *what* God said and *to whom* he said it (Israel or the church). Yet even Luther understood that at a large number of points there was considerable overlap between what God prescribed as binding on Israel and subsequently, in Christ, on the church. In his zeal to curb "enthusiasm" or "legality," Luther did not reject divine law per se, which might positively constrain the church; rather, he focused instead on the Lawgiver, Christ, in relationship to such constraint. There could well be a great measure of continuity on matters enjoined in the Old and in the New, and certainly sexual behavior between a man and a woman in marriage was one of them. To point out the law's capacity to drive one to despair (Rom 7:13-25) did not mean for even Luther's extraordinarily dialectical mind a rejection of the law, but an acknowledgment of the law as good and holy and tutor to Christ (Rom 3:31; 7:7-12), who is the law's *telos*.

---

some of them arguably a social good and dealt with in unique ways within Israel and the early church — and kidnapping, that is the capture and forced servitude of populations in war or other situations of economic power, harshly displayed. In the American South, the latter form of slavery sought approval from Christian interpreters on the grounds of a scripture at fundamental odds with it and was finally defeated on those very grounds. Homosexual activity, incidentally, was intimately tied up with various forms of slavery in the Greco-Roman world.

A less dialectical way of putting this can be found in the Thirty-Nine Articles of sixteenth-century Anglicanism. After asserting the continuity between Old Testament and New as grounded in Christ, it takes up two areas of possible discontinuity. First, the promises to the Fathers, that is, the old people of Israel: such promises did not involve transitory matters only, but truly anticipated the gospel, as Christians would later confess this. Second, the law: "Although the Law given from God by Moses, as touching Ceremonies and Rites, do not bind Christian men, nor the Civil precepts thereof ought of necessity to be received in any commonwealth" — here is Luther's concern with "enthusiasts" — "yet notwithstanding, no Christian man whatsoever is free from the obedience of the Commandments which are called Moral" (Article VII).

That Luther or Cranmer agreed that "no Christian man whatsoever is free from the obedience of the Commandments which are called moral" did not mean that they simply equated the Christian life with obedience to the law's demands as an end unto itself. Above all, the relationship to God's will for the individual Christian was understood christologically. We relate to God's law *in Christ, through Christ.* To say that Christ has utterly abolished the law revealed in the Old Testament and that Christians have no law but "love" would be to move beyond the plain sense of the New Testament into the realm of "principles" or spiritual abstractions. The New Testament understands the Christian relationship to the Law much more dialectically. In some respects, the New Testament witness suggests that the law of God as revealed in the Old, while holy and good and to be retained, is however insufficient in detailing the extent of God's total claim on the sinful human heart (Matt 5:17-48). To say that Jesus or Paul is "critical" of the Law, or that they see the Law refracted in a certain way, is true — but this may move in precisely the opposite direction from laxity or abolition.

For this reason, the epistle that most stresses the Christian's freedom from the law, *as the means of access to God or the righteousness of God in Christ,* the letter to the Galatians, is also the letter that concludes with a litany on how the Christian under the Spirit — as against the law qua law — is enjoined to behaviors the law once attempted to regulate (5:16-24). The criticism is therefore not directed toward the law's content, but toward the law's incapacity to engender the good and the holy, as God requires. The Christian is free from the law only insofar as she or he is a slave to Christ, "and those who belong to Christ Jesus have crucified the flesh with its passions and desires" (Gal 5:24). In Christ, the content of the law is revealed for what it truly is: God's own holy will, which, without Christ, cannot be obeyed. In sum, to say that Paul or Jesus has "abolished" the Law of God would be to misunderstand the distinction both make between the *content* and the *bestowal* of righteousness, the latter clearing room for obedience to the former.

It is for this reason that the Thirty-Nine Articles are fully representative of Christian thought when, reflecting on the ongoing authority of the Old Testament, they conclude that "no one whatsoever is free from the Commandments which are called moral." This article draws a distinction between matters moral and matters cultic or ceremonial, and in so doing introduces a *discrimens* to be applied to the *content* of the Old Testament law. We will take up this distinction in further detail in a moment. It should be clear, however, that such a distinction attempts to comprehend the Christian relationship to the Law as this is set forth in the New Testament, where the content is not abolished but released through Christ and in Christ toward God's desired righteousness of life. What one sees enjoined of the Christian, crucified in the flesh with Christ, are certain specific virtues and behaviors whose compatibility with Old Testament "moral" law should be clear.

On the basis of this, it seems clear that reflecting on scripture's plain sense in order to describe proper sexual behavior for the Christian community is not a foreign or "legalistic" concept in the church's life in the past. The roots of such reflection lie in the New Testament itself, where Jesus is the *telos* of the Law as this was revealed in Israel's scriptures.

An example of the dialectical and christological character of the law for the Israel of God, the church, is perfectly illustrated in John's narrative of the woman caught in adultery (John 8:1-11).[5] The woman is brought before Jesus. The law of Moses is clear, whether she is married (Lev 20:10) or a "betrothed virgin" (Deut 22:23-24), though one might well ask about the male offender, since in both texts his role is addressed as well. The

---

5. For an insightful discussion of the pericope and of the difficulty surrounding text-critical conclusions in regard to it, see Gail R. O'Day, "John 7:53–8:11: A Study in Misreading," *JBL* 111 (1992) 631-40. The impact of the history of interpretation of the text on its proper text-critical evaluation (that is, "[t]he canonical instability of John 7:53–8:11," 639) is taken up by O'Day at the close of her remarks (638-40). Her conclusion is that text-critical marginality cannot be translated into claims for lack of historicity or similar such dismissals. As is becoming clearer in Old Testament text criticism, so-called "higher" and "lower" critical dimensions of a text turn out to occupy similar terrain for one critical phase of their existence.

Deuteronomy text stipulates stoning as the means by which the death penalty is to be executed. This is the penalty referred to by the scribes and Pharisees (John 8:5).

Jesus' famous response, "Let him who is without sin among you be the first to throw a stone at her," is not in the first instance a rejection of the law's content regarding adulterous behavior. It is a response directed at what the law attempts to regulate: human sin. This extends to the scribes and Pharisees in such measure that they refuse to exact the penalty prescribed by the law. Jesus has successfully linked the execution of the law's demand to human sinfulness, generally speaking. The question, however, remains: how then is the holy demand of the law to be satisfied, since no one is sufficiently free of sin to execute its penalties as prescribed? Is the content of the law now to be dispensed with, along with the penalty? The obvious answer to the first question is: it would require someone without sin to enforce the law. No one has condemned her, and neither does Jesus, who alone is in a position to do so. As the "one among them without sin," he still does not pick up a stone. On the other hand, he reiterates the content of the law: "Go and sin no more." Adultery is sin. Continuity exists over the law's content. Discontinuity exists over how that content is approached and obeyed: through Jesus.

Yet one might ask, what of the due punishment for the crime committed, since adultery offended against God's holiness and against one within the covenant assembly? And what if the woman does not obey the "statute" of Jesus and instead goes and sins again? How can Jesus take on the role of dispensing justice and relaxing the demand of the law, if its content is regarded as good and holy? This concern is in the foreground in Jesus' confrontations with the custodians of the law, because of the arrogation to himself of interpreting and even enforcing the Law, by forgiving sins (John 8:12; 11:57). Yet the fullest answer is not given until John 19:30. Jesus himself bears the curse and penalty of the law of God on behalf of all: "It is finished," the law's penalty "has been paid for," by Jesus himself, in his own flesh. This is the scandal of the cross, that the law's demands are now, in Christian confession, matters pertaining to Jesus. The content of the law is understood as binding, in him, through him. As the narrative concerning the adulterous woman makes clear, adultery remains sin, but Jesus is the means by which forgiveness is possible. That such forgiveness may not lead to obedience is precisely the love of God made manifest in Christ. Christ continues to pay the penalty even if the adultery persists, making forgiveness in his name always possible. But never

328

does adultery stop being a sin and an offense to God. Without Christ's healing and intervention, sin still leads to death, now understood less immediately, if not also more eternally.

It has been objected in recent years that Jesus nowhere pronounces on homosexual behavior in the New Testament and that this silence is probative. It could just as easily be concluded that all we learn from this silence is that adultery was a more prevalent sin in Israel than homosexual behavior among men; this would explain its more frequent discussion in both the Old Testament and the New. That the prohibition against adultery, together with the death penalty, appears in the same context in Leviticus as the prohibition against homosexual behavior (Lev 20:13) might lead one to conclude that Jesus would have reacted in exactly the same way if the scribes had brought to him the unusual case of a man accused of "lying with a male as with a woman." In such an account, Jesus would become the means of the accused man's forgiveness, the sinless one who refuses to cast the first stone. Yet then we would have to expect the same final "statute" of Christ: "Go and sin no more." That Jesus does more than simply pay the penalty in obedience to the Father's will entails his capacity both to forgive and to heal, which is amply described in the New Testament. The relationship to Christ is not only one that satisifies the demands of the Law juridically, but also opens up an entirely new way of living in relationship to God that sets free from sin and death.

The Thirty-Nine Articles distinguished between "ceremonial" or "ritual" commandments in the Old Testament, and "those called Moral," from which no Christian was free. This represented an effort to comprehend the profound distinction introduced in the New Testament, and illustrated in the encounter between the adulterous woman, Jesus, and the law of Moses, or in the theological reflections of Paul, regarding the content and purpose and ongoing validity of the law as "holy and just and good" (Rom 7:12). Sexual behavior is not regarded as a "cultic" or ritual matter, in spite of what some recent interpreters have argued, but as a central existential category of ongoing concern and Godly purpose.

A different sort of relationship exists between the Christian and the law in respect of matters "ritual" or "ceremonial," as these also exist in the Old Testament. The older rites and ceremonies are summed up in Christ, who reveals what those rites and ceremonies were truly about. For those outside Israel, brought near in Christ, those rites and ceremonies are now experienced as completed *in him,* both high priest and sacrificial victim. They are seen to be shadows of a Reality by whose light their true form is recognized and comprehended in the first place, and hence they have no binding character in any independent sense (Heb 10:1-31). We know this because the New Testament has specifically addressed them on these terms. In a similar way, explicit handling of ritual laws in the New Testament has made clear their provisional character and judged them no longer binding on Christian men and women (Mark 7:1-23). In other words, the status of the law for the "Israel of God," the church, is wholly governed by the New Testament's plain sense treatment of the law's content and purpose, and it is here that distinctions of various sorts have been introduced. To point out the flaws in those terms chosen for comprehending these distinctions ("moral," "ritual," "ceremonial") would not be the same thing as saying that no such distinctions exist or that the law is even-handedly dispensed with in the church, with a New Lawgiver, High Priest, and Perfect Offering.

Even in texts in the New Testament that address ritual and ceremonial aspects of the law, there is no suggestion that Jesus' chief concern is with correction or criticism according to some new enlightened standard (e.g., the laws of Leviticus are too "harsh").[6] In Mark 7, where the narrator understands Jesus as "declaring all foods clean" (v. 19), the form of the discussion is not so straightforward as basic revision or updating due to inherent "Jewish parochialism" or "harshness" or some other such criterion, before which the law itself is judged deficient. The opening exchange (vv. 1-13) introduces a distinction between "traditions" and "the tradition of the elders," on the one side, and "the commandment of God," on the other. Jesus even uses the prophet Isaiah (no foe of "harshness") as support against the Pharisees. The charge is not over-zealous or rigid attention to a harsh Law, but exchanging for God's law "the precepts of men." The corban illustration (vv. 9-13) provides further evidence of Jesus' concern: "making void the word of God through your tradition which you hand on" (v. 13).[7]

The problem with the ritual laws is not that they are ungodly. Rather, they can be manipulated or rationalized into a system that diverts from their true purpose. And further: they do not reach into the place where

---

6. See, e.g., John S. Spong, *Living in Sin? A Bishop Rethinks Human Sexuality* (San Francisco: Harper and Row, 1988). The Old Testament, and much of the New, is judged by the episcopal bishop according to standards imported from modern culture. "Harshness" and "ignorance" are at obvious odds with his moral and intellectual horizon.

7. See Markus Bockmuehl, "Halakhah and Ethics in the Jesus Tradition," in *Early Christian Thought in Its Jewish Context,* ed. J. Barclay and J. Sweet (Cambridge: Cambridge University, 1996) 264-78.

clean and unclean originate, "from within" (v. 21). The dietary laws of Leviticus are not "traditions of men" or "clear examples of premodern ignorance."[8] The whole point of the distinctions introduced in Mark 7:1-13 is to make this clear. These laws fall short *because of the nature of the problem they are addressing*, not because they were wrong in and of themselves. They fail to get at the problem; they are not the problem. One might have expected Mark's Jesus, based upon some recent interpretations of the status of the law in the New Testament, to have been chiefly about throwing out distinctions such as clean and unclean altogether. Instead, Jesus begins his ministry with exorcisms! The battle over clean and unclean is more, not less, decisive, even as it is fought on a new front, by the One whom Matthew quotes as saying: "Think not that I have come to abolish the law and the prophets; I have not come to abolish them but to fulfill them. . . . Whoever then relaxes one of the least of these commandments and teaches men so, shall be called the least in the kingdom of heaven" (Matt 5:17, 19). The righteousness of Jesus' disciples is to *exceed* that of the scribes and Pharisees in respect of the Law (5:20). Harshness or premodern ignorance are irrelevant to the issue at hand.

A similar assessment of the law for Christians can be seen in Hebrews, whose concern is more directly with "ceremonial" laws. These are "but a shadow of the good things to come" (10:1). Sacrificial offerings failed to achieve what Jesus' offering of himself achieved. It would have been far simpler to say that these offerings were too harsh or were examples of premodern ignorance. Jesus' response was "Lo, I have come to do thy will" (10:9). Jesus has given Christians access, by his blood, to confident entry into the sanctuary (10:19) — something the continual offering, year after year, of the blood of bulls and goats could not do (10:1-4).

Here the author makes clear the provisional character of the Law of Moses, seen from the perspective of Christ's one-time offering of himself. Christians have no temple in Jerusalem, no Levitical priests, no ark, no mercy seat, and no ceremonial life drawn directly from Leviticus. But the point and purpose of these remains, *in Christ*. At this point, then, the author must contend with a factor the first covenant could regulate, but because now taken up into Christ, cannot in the same way. What of deliberate sin "after receiving the knowledge of the truth"? That is, the

---

8. Spong, *Living in Sin?* 146. Spong's arrogance toward the past could be described as "imperialism of the modern" were it not that he is speaking out of an already postmodern western context.

bold claim by Christians about the status of the law fulfilled in Christ comes with its own provisions, which again exceed in their own way the righteousness enjoined by obedience to the law within the Old Covenant. "It is a fearful thing to fall into the hands of the living God" (Heb 10:31). How much simpler it would be if we were dealing with premodern ignorance or a harshness now tempered by kindly sentiment.[9]

I will bring these various remarks on the Law of God, intertextually considered, to conclusion by examining one phenomenon both Testaments of Christian scripture hold in common.

It has been pointed out that the Bible is not particularly obsessed with the topic of homosexuality — not nearly as obsessed, at any rate, as are church and culture in the late modern West. This may of course point to the relative infrequency of homosexual conduct within Israel, or in the frame of reference of the church's confessed Messiah of Israel, as was earlier suggested. The singular treatments of scripture (Genesis 18, Romans 1) are indeed rare, and now they too are being subjected to revisionist interpretations, over against the time-honored ones in church and synagogue. It does not follow from this, however, that the sin of homosexuality is just one among others, of equal character, in the Old Testament. To range the offense of "lying with another man as with a woman" together with incest, bestiality, and adultery and to stipulate the penalty for infringement as capital punishment (Lev 20:10-16), distinguishes this particular sin from others and suggests a seriousness of concern with which even other "abominations" are not treated. One must take this seriousness into account in any discussion of homosexuality in the modern period, whether from a historical-critical perspective or an interbiblical perspective.

The variety and degree of offenses against God's holiness in the Old Testament is recognized at points in the New, and yet all are caught up within Christ's final sacrifice on behalf of God's creation. At the same time, the "bundling" and "leveling" of offenses and their collective treatment with all other sins is a characteristic of the New Testament that has radicalized and not lessened the force of Old Testament law. Richard Hays has argued convincingly that the rhetorical force of Romans 1 entails linking the specific depravity of homosexual acts (1:24-27) to all manner of human offense against God's holiness (1:28-32).[10] To pass judgment

9. See also the discussion above in ch. 2.
10. Richard B. Hays, "Relations Natural and Unnatural: A Response to John Boswell's Exegesis of Romans 1," *Journal of Religious Ethics* 14 (1986) 184-215.

on others is to condemn oneself (2:1) only if the extent and character of all human sinfulness is of like nature, seen from the aspect of God's work in Christ. One is therefore right to say that homosexual conduct is seen as no worse a sin than greed, drunkenness, robbery, and so forth (1 Cor 6:9).

The conclusion to be drawn from this seems to me the opposite of what is now frequently argued. First, it is clear that members of the body of Christ are enjoined to standards of conduct every bit as stringent as that enjoined on the Old Covenant community, if not more so. The grounding for and facilitation of that enjoining are what have changed. What is truly radical about the love of God in Christ is not that all manner of sinfulness is leveled and dispensed with, but that the distance God is prepared to go to bring creation into fellowship with him *extends even to offenses held by him to demand the death penalty*. That penalty is paid by God's own son. This is the mystery Paul is pondering in Romans 1. But there it is a matter of reflection because of the obligation it places all creation under: the knowledge that the wrath of God is poured out on all offense, and yet our recourse is the love of the same God made manifest in Christ. It is for this reason that offenses of different character and degree from the Old can be bundled in the way they are in the New.

It follows from this, not that homosexual behavior is less offensive than anger or greed and ought therefore to be permitted, but that it partakes of the selfsame character for which the love of God in Christ was and is the only saving force, set in motion by the one who gave the holy law to his people Israel. To join "love" with "lying with a man as with a woman" would be to ask one sensitive to this dynamic in the New Testament to consider as well "blessed greed" or "holy drunkenness." The bundling has gone on in a very different direction and toward a very different purpose: to show the extent to which God obliterated all distinctions of offense in the sacrifice of his Son, so that "those who belong to Christ Jesus have crucified the flesh with its passions and desires" (Gal 5:24). Paul is stating a fact about the Christian life, achieved by the work of Christ, that grounds his appeal to "live by the Spirit and not gratify the desires of the flesh" (5:16). One could no more "bless" homosexual unions than one could bless anger or adultery, for there is no clear warrant for this in the work of Christ as the New Testament understands it. The logic of its bundling has gone in precisely the opposite direction.

It is the conclusion of this essay that the church is constrained on the basis of scripture's plain sense to proscribe homosexual behavior among its members. It must, however, carefully distinguish this from "passing judgment" in the manner Paul warns against in Rom 2:1. The proscription flows from an understanding of the holiness of the law and the work of God in Christ. The church has no authority to "bless" gay unions because there is no warrant for this in scripture. Instead one finds there a specific reminder that along with innumerable other sins, such behavior is inconsistent with the kingdom of God. The proper response of the church remains not condemnation, but the address of the gospel, as this is set forth in the two-testament Christian scripture.

III

I want to make two concluding observations. The first has to do with the topic in question, the plain sense of scripture and homosexual practice in the modern church. The second involves the question of how appropriate New Testament methodology is to be deployed in the exegesis of Romans 1–2.

    1. It seems to me the place where the testaments display their most obvious plain-sense conformity on the matter of human sexuality involves appeal to God's action in creation. Mark 10 makes this clear. When asked about divorce and remarriage, Jesus offers no private opinion, but appeals to scripture. And even though scripture itself witnesses to some obvious tension ("what did Moses command you?" v. 3), this is linked to human sinfulness, not to fresh revelation or shifts in the mind of God. Jesus assembles texts from Genesis 1–2 to establish God's will for sexuality, "From the beginning of creation, 'God made them male and female.' 'For this reason a man shall leave his father and mother and be joined to his wife, and the two shall become one flesh'" (Mark 10:6-8). How could any departure from this teaching, for the purposes of endorsing other forms of human sexual intercourse, be anything less than a similar instance of human hardheartedness? If what God revealed to Moses was an accommodation to human sinfulness and not what God fully intended — and Christ alone speaks with the authority to reveal this, and dies on the basis of that authority — then how could the church depart from this will of God and speak not of hardened hearts, but of actual blessing and positive endorsement? This flies in the face of the logic of Jesus as revealed in its apostolic witness. To say this is not to offer a condemnation of divorce or

same-sex physical relationships but to point to the problem of the human heart the gospel is fundamentally concerned to address.

2. What cries out desperately for resolution is the use by New Testament scholarship of source material from the Greco-Roman milieu in an effort to clarify the thought of Paul. Richard Hays's deployment of a term like "echo" reveals the nature of the problem even as it points to a possible model for hermeneutics and modern interpretation. He of course means by "echo" the resonance, not from the Greco-Roman milieu as such, but from texts of the Old Testament and whatever "milieu" they may come to present to Paul.

An alternative understanding, sometimes working in conjunction with the above, posits the influence of milieu differently. Does the resemblance between certain aspects of Paul's thought in Romans 1 and that of Greek and Roman sources point to a material and substantive comparative base? Or is the resemblance more oblique and essentially adventitious, making appeals to such material for the purposes of clarification insufficiently controlled? How acquainted with his milieu and its reflections on sexuality was Paul, and perhaps more importantly, how probative would such reflections have been for Paul?

These questions prove relevant precisely when one reckons with a clear epistemological distinction that runs throughout the Epistle to the Romans. This distinction is derived from Israel's scriptures, which as a *single,* epistemologically privileged witness nevertheless serves to reveal *two* distinctive categories for knowing God and relating to him, through the law of Moses and prior to and apart from that revelation. Adam and Abraham are examples from Israel's scriptures of life prior to and apart from God's revelation to Moses. Both led "commanded lives," to be sure (Rom 4:1-25; 5:15-20), but because they lived apart from the law as revealed to Moses, and because Paul takes that distinction as meaningful for him and for the present church, they remain typologically or figurally representative of life as it is lived in the world more generally.

This means that when Paul seeks to understand how God is at work in the world more broadly, his version of "natural law" is one fundamentally rooted in Israel's privileged witness. To seek to understand how God relates to the created order apart from his specific relationship to Israel, Paul studies Israel's scripture. This is not to say that he lives in a cave or never picks up a copy of The Athenian Times, with its reflections of the "milieu" morality, but that his categories of knowing and his reflections on knowing are fundamentally stamped by the scriptures of Israel. They "echo" in ways that are not always easy to track down, in strict exegetical terms — much in the same way as MS-DOS is indispensable to my writing this piece, even though it remains invisible. Here the analogy is broken, of course, because scripture is not invisible in Paul but intrudes itself explicitly as well as implicitly, or yet more subtly. The MS-DOS of scripture is fully available for independent study and investigation.

As one who lives exegetically as much or more in the Old Testament than the New, I am struck by the resonances that appear to surface in Romans 1. Many of these are noted by interpreters. Before looking at these, consider the logic of Paul's argument more generally. At verse 18 Paul is most concerned to demonstrate how all humanity — that is, humanity apart from Israel — is without excuse in the same way that Israel is without excuse (2:1). The latter has God's revealed Law and is therefore without excuse before God. The former is likewise without excuse, but for different reasons.

Now where does Paul get this understanding of the natural person? One governing assumption tracks the flow of the argument and sees the eventual appeal to the self-evidently immoral and idolatrous character of same-sex relationships (vv. 24-27) as evidence of widely-held views to this effect in Paul's milieu. Paul's appeal here serves to catch his own religious compatriots in their judgmental conceit (ch. 2). God shows no partiality (2:11). The law does not give one higher moral ground, but ground for God's judgment as "without excuse."

How would Paul's Jewish listeners know for sure that God's judgment had been so manifestly poured out on Gentile idolaters?[11] The argument runs that Greco-Roman literature reveals a sort of natural law logic on the depravity or inappropriateness of same-sex physical relationships as examples of unrestrained sexual desire. Moderation and temperance overthrown in the name of desire brings its own punishment. The self-evidence of these claims is thrown in the face of Paul's Jewish listeners to the rhetorical purpose of exposing their own sinfulness before God's holiness. The scholarly task of collating sources from the Greco-Roman milieu is

11. I adopt the general view here that the force of Paul's argument in Romans 1–2 is ultimately aimed at Christians who have lived under the law as Jews. They constitute the "implied audience" if not the real audience of Paul's initial argument in these opening chapters. The Jew-Greek distinction and its reorientation by God in Christ frames the argument (1:16; 2:9-10). For a provocative effort to see it otherwise, derived from an analysis of the problem of "audience" in the letter, see Stanley K. Stowers, *A Rereading of Romans: Justice, Jews, and Gentiles* (New Haven: Yale University, 1994).

vindicated by demonstrating their utility and the indispensability of their observations, as these now function in the movement from Romans 1 to Romans 2.

But would such an appeal to God's judgment on same-sex relationships, as this is grounded in Greco-Roman sources, have proven probative to Paul's Jewish listeners/readers? Would the *theology* of these sources and their theological account of moral law in creation have been adequate to serve the purpose of persuading Paul's listeners about God's judgment? Could Paul entertain the notion of a general "godly judgment" and a correlative "moral law" displayed in creation, apart from the specific judgment of the God of Israel, whose will against homosexual activity is revealed in the Old Testament? Critical for Paul's argument at this point is the citing of evidence of judgment upon those *outside the covenant community*, thereby establishing them as "without excuse" before God in a manner convincing to his Jewish audience.

It might be objected that Paul is appealing to judgments on same-sex behavior only subsequently described in Greco-Roman sources, and therefore has in mind the behavior itself, as he observes it and its consequences, and not the logic associated with its impropriety in the source material. This may well be true. But it seems to me likely that if Paul were aware of same-sex behavior in his "milieu" and the self-evidence of God's judgment on it, the source for his information in this regard would be the "oracles of God entrusted to the Jews" (Rom 3:2). Their "echo" would override any logic about divine judgment available in the "milieu." Appeal to the wrongfulness of such behavior, as such and as rhetorically useful, given his audience, would best be grounded by appeal to Israel's witness to God's will in the Old Testament.

With this perspective in view, how does the word of the Old Testament about God's judgment in creation make itself felt in Romans 1? The whole discussion is preceded by a quote from Hab 2:4, "the one who is righteous will live by faith" (NRSV), as if to signal Paul's main "source" for commending what God has done and is doing in Jesus Christ, that is, the scriptures entrusted to Israel. The present judgment to which appeal is eventually made (Rom 1:24-27) is grounded in a past record: "ever since the creation of the world" (v. 20). When idolatry is concretely described as the outcome of foolish minds (1:23), the categories into which it is poured are those of Genesis 1: "a mortal human being or birds or four-footed animals or reptiles." The "claiming to be wise" of Rom 1:22 evokes the challenge of the serpent (Gen 3:5) and the description of the narrator in the story of the Garden (Gen 3:6). Striking in this regard is the use of the definite article in Rom 1:25: "they exchanged the truth about God for *the* lie," which has been noted by commentators as traceable to the same Genesis account.[12] Worshiping the creature instead of the Creator has a certain rhetorical generality (1:25), but in the context of Genesis "the creature" who moves human beings away from God by means of "the lie" is none other than the serpent.

When Paul goes on to describe the "degrading passions" that inflame those given up by God to their darkened minds (v. 26), is he speaking about homosexual activity in his milieu, of which he and his audience are aware and whose inappropriateness is confirmed in Greco-Roman sources? The first part of this is of course quite possible. But the past tense description would allow a further dimension to come into play: Paul and his audience share knowledge of God's judgment on homosexual activity on the basis of the Old Testament. He has introduced his argument with reference to "the wrath of God revealed from heaven against all ungodliness and wickedness" (1:18) and has spoken about the obvious way that God has made known his character, "his eternal power and divine nature" (1:19). In my judgment, Paul assumes here a continuity between the judgments visited on natural man in the Old Testament, apart from the law, and those that could be evidenced in the present period.

It is one thing to argue in the modern period that the story about the outcry and grave sin (Gen 18:20) of the citizens of Sodom did not entail homosexuality between consenting adults. It is another thing to ask how Paul himself might have heard the story of God's wrath from heaven being poured out on that city (Gen 19:24) and the blindness with which God struck those whose inhospitality included the demand, "Where are the men who came to you tonight? Bring them out to us, so that we might know them" (19:5). Given the flow of Paul's argument, beginning at Rom 1:18 and running into chapter 2, it would seem reasonable to assume that Paul was searching for an example of God's wrath being made immediately and unequivocally manifest upon natural man, one known to his Jewish audience and testified to in "the oracles of God" (3:2). He chooses an

---

12. In an unpublished paper conveying preliminary commentary on Romans, Robert Jewett speaks of "the fundamental ploy of humans to replace God with themselves, visible from the Fall to the crucifixion of Christ." J. Fitzmyer (*Romans: A New Translation with Introduction and Commentary* [New York: Doubleday, 1993] 284f.) refers to the "big lie . . . the deception that smothers the truth."

example appropriate to his rhetorical context and capable of recognition and correlation in the example of that homosexual activity known to him, in his "milieu."

If this reading is correct, then Paul chooses homosexual behavior not because he regards it as a worse sin than others, but because the judgment of God on it was such a visible manifestation of his wrath against ungodliness, patent and deserving of attention by natural man. If one thought that the ways of God with the natural world were subtle enough to leave the latter "with excuse," Paul reminds his readers of instances from the Old Testament that prove otherwise, and that do so with particular urgency. It could be the case that God's judgment against homosexual behavior opened up in a particularly potent way the possibility for feelings of superiority on the part of Paul's audience, which are then roundly rejected in Romans 2. But in my judgment the example is not chosen for that reason, but rather because it illustrated an instance when the wrath of God was so visibly displayed against natural man, apart from the law or any special revelation from God to his people Israel. Whether Greco-Roman sources confirm or deny Paul's logic from the Old Testament in the case of contemporaneous homosexual activity — including that of women (Rom 1:26) — is an interesting question from the perspective of intellectual history. But such an inquiry could prove distracting in coming to terms with Paul's logic in Romans 1–2.

Conclusion

In my judgment, the question facing the field of biblical studies today is *whose* book is the Old Testament and *why* is it being read in the first place? A similar question holds for the New Testament as well. In one way or another all the preceding essays keep this question in the forefront.[1]

The fact that the question is not being put so forcefully, if at all, within the field is itself worthy of reflection. There are rare exceptions, of course. I have mentioned especially the names of Jon Levenson, Paul van Buren, and Brevard Childs at many points above. The title of Levenson's volume *(The Hebrew Bible, the Old Testament, and Historical Criticism)*, like that of van Buren's essay ("On Reading Someone Else's Mail"), makes clear what is at stake. While these three men have answered the question in different ways, there can be no doubt they are in agreement about its significance for the modern interpretation of Old and New Testaments.

One needs to consider the location of most serious, formal biblical study today in America, as having shifted from proximity to religious communities or serious theological discourse and into departments of Religion, into divinity schools engaged more in the study of religion than the preparation of students for professions of preaching and teaching in the churches, or into seminaries whose connection to the churches is either one of advocacy or revision. This is no tirade. Real changes have taken place on

---

1. See the recent discussion by Philip R. Davies, *Whose Bible Is It Anyway?* (Sheffield: Sheffield Academic, 1995), a treatment from the theological left that seeks to disengage the Bible from religious convictions and indeed from any constructive "God claim."

340

the American front in theological education that have inevitably changed the way biblical study is undertaken, in many cases in places where the old leadership was once quite strong. Not surprisingly, this means that new methods of reading and altogether new understandings of what is being read have emerged. With serious questions about the identity of the church in the late modern period has come a blurring of distinctions that once stressed the particularity of religious communities in the past. An academic approach to reading scripture has taught us to value objectivity and neutrality, and now an opposite emphasis has come into play: the impossibility of meaning residing in a text that was not put there by the interpreter to begin with.

To raise in very basic ways the question, *whose* book are we reading, is at a minimum to remind the modern reader that the Old and New Testaments emerged from religious communities with specific identities. These sacred texts were intended for communities striving to share or at least participate in those same religious convictions, hopes, and practices. The Bible is not a "bestseller" in search of interested readers or readers who wish to have their imaginations stretched or their worldviews broadened, even when this may occur.

Nowhere is this better illustrated than when one revisits a debate not very old. From a somewhat different perspective, one can see how the question of *whose* book the Old Testament was touched on the most basic matters of reading and appropriation, disallowing the possibility of objectivity or neutrality altogether:

> But what are Adam and Eve to us, what are Abraham, Isaac, and Jacob, what are Moses and David to us? They are alien to us; they are of no great concern to us. They are worse *than merely a matter of indifference.*

To lay this extreme view of Paul de Lagarde at the feet of German Nationalist Socialism or unfortunate Lutheran exaggeration would be to miss the deeper issue.[2] Lagarde, like Luther before him,[3] was in fact right to raise

2. Paul de Lagarde, "Zum Unterrichtsgesetz" (1878), quoted in K. H. Miskotte, *When the Gods Are Silent,* tr. J. Doberstein (London: Collins, 1967) 53-54 (emphasis added).

3. "How Christians Should Regard Moses," in *Martin Luther's Basic Theological Writings,* ed. Timothy Lull (Minneapolis: Fortress, 1989) 135-48. In this complicated essay we find Luther invoking natural law as the means by which a *discrimens* will effectively sort out where Moses can command the Christian. That too has lost its power to persuade in the late modern period.

the question because it should never be considered self-evident how the Old Testament or Hebrew Bible is in fact just anyone's book to read. His rejection of the Old Testament was repugnant in the form he went on to state it, and an obvious foreshadowing of the horrors of the Holocaust. One might well ask whether, as with Marcion before him, the New Testament would be the next to fall, leaving de Lagarde with nothing but his own personalized and romanticized Jesus, shorn of all cultural embodiment, a mythological emanation.[4]

My point here is obviously not to endorse the views of de Lagarde but to argue that he saw that the point of access to the Old Testament for non-Jews needed to be clarified. His own answer was simply: it is not our book. And, in addition, he concluded that it would be necessary to dislodge Jesus from the claims made about him in the New Testament too because they were likewise contaminated by a perspective absolutely foreign, hermetically Jewish, of a piece with "their book."

But now the problem arises. It is one thing to sense the extremism of de Lagarde and reject it *tout court*. But we are still left with his otherwise important starting point. How are Moses and Abraham about those who stand outside the circle of Israel? How is the Old Testament a book for and about those who stand outside a circle it assumes as operative by the very logic of its own discourse?[5] One would be tempted in the modern climate of biblical study to say that the Old Testament is a book for anyone who wishes to read it, and as a practical reality that is incontrovertible. The book is accessible; it can be purchased and read, as one book among others to be recommended for purchase, in a staggering variety of translations, at the local bookstore.[6] But does that fact itself confuse us about

4. This he clearly recognizes when he continues: "Original sin, the doctrine of the atonement depend on Adam and Eve, faith on Abraham, the Law on Moses, the Messiah and the system of fulfillment on David. . . . If you do not want the orthodox dogmas and views, you German fathers, then first get rid of the biblical stories of the Old Testament, but do it so thoroughly that your children in the present will never be allowed to mention their names" (quoted in *When the Gods Are Silent,* 54).

5. The Jewish scholar Jon Levenson has also remarked that "the Hebrew Bible is largely foreign to both traditions [Jews and Christians] and precedes them both" (*The Hebrew Bible, the Old Testament, and Historical Criticism* [Louisville: Westminster/John Knox, 1993], 105). I am not suggesting that modern Judaism is equivalent to "Israel," though even here a distinction between Christians and Jews in respect of access to the Old Testament/Hebrew Bible/Tanak is still relevant.

6. Along these lines, it was interesting to watch the editor of *The New Republic* struggle with a request to write a jacket blurb for an edition of the Bible about to be

whose book this is, in a way that the quote from de Lagarde drives home, however repugnant his sentiments?

In discussing de Lagarde's extremism, Heiko Miskotte posed the question: spectator or participant? And he then went on in his own way to answer "participant," from a distinctly Christian perspective, yet fully aware of the issues at stake. Yet even in his own very bold endorsement of the Old Testament for the Christian church — Reventlow and many Lutheran reviewers[7] classified his position under the heading, "the superiority of the Old Testament" — one can still see a dialectic of sorts at work. This dialectic avoids the reductionism of de Lagarde and yet would be offended by the modern, over-hasty accessibility or universalizing tendencies. Notice the subtlety of his own view, difficult as it is to follow:

> We do not wish here to say all that really must be said on this point, namely, that the specific quality "Word of God" (= Christ) does not so much raise the Old Testament to the level of a fully valid voice of proclamation, but rather reveals it *to be such.* . . . Here we wish only to say that even *without existential participation* the mode of our spectatorship vis-à-vis the Old Testament is radically altered through "Christianity."[8]

Speaking then of the problems confronting his own age, he proceeds further to discuss matters of direct importance for our own reflections on what it means to confront the Old Testament instructionally at the end of the twentieth century.

> The presupposition of biblical instruction . . . is therefore that we accept this peculiar character of our spectatorship, this way in which we are drawn into the Bible, and allow it to stand. If need be, one may say that we must act as if the Old Testament does concern us. . . . This is why the critical historical study of the Old Testament has so often contributed, not because of its methods or because of its results, but through its abstract attitude of spectatorship, to a progressive alienation

---

published with some new and exciting packaging. Even he sensed that there was something perverse about the request.

7. See even the cautions of Doberstein in the "Translator's Introduction" to Miskotte's work (ix-xv).

8. Miskotte, *When the Gods Are Silent,* 54, emphasis added.

. . . from the Old Testament. We are therefore not talking about the fact that the Old Testament is the Word of God for the church, but only of the fact that it was through the church that it came to the nations with at least the substance of religion which *concerned* them.[9]

What is important in this quotation is not the answer Miskotte himself supplies — which combines postwar existentialism with a theology of the church and Word of God in respect of the Old Testament's address — but rather that he discusses the issues of access in the first place, as of true importance, and not just because of the claims of those like de Lagarde made in the previous century. Today, however, the problem may not be an "abstract attitude of spectatorship" born of objective critical reconstruction, but rather that and something ironically attending it, namely, the sense of deserved and obvious imaginative participation without any reflection on the sorts of problems of intended readership, revelation, universality, and the like that Miskotte addresses in detail in this stimulating work.

At many points in the chapters that precede I have offered my own reflections on how this book from Israel has become a word to the church, and it would serve no purpose to rehearse them again here. I conclude only with a plea that the field of biblical studies — to the degree that it is a field and not an eclectic, careerist necessity — wrestle seriously with these questions, as did Miskotte and others in their day, rather than simply assume that the answers are self-evident. That, it seems to me, is the task that needs to be taken up at all levels of biblical study at the present period. The task involves questions of accessibility, of the proprietary character of the literature of Old and New Testaments, and of the way in which a reading of both Testaments asks yet further, unavoidable questions about *who* is reading and *to what end* that reading is being undertaken.

9. Ibid., 54-55.

Index of Authors

Index of Scripture References

352

353

Index of Scripture References

NEW TESTAMENT